GENDER DISCRIMINATION LAW OF THE EUROPEAN COMMUNITY

GENDER DISCRIMINATION LAW OF THE EUROPEAN COMMUNITY

SACHA PRECHAL
Legal Secretary
European Court of Justice
Luxembourg

NOREEN BURROWS
Lecturer in Law
University of Glasgow

DARTMOUTH

Published by
Dartmouth Publishing Company Limited
Gower House
Croft Road
Aldershot
Hants GU11 3HR

Gower Publishing Company
Old Post Road
Brookfield
Vermont 05036
USA

British Library Cataloguing in Publication Data

Prechal, Sacha
  Gender discrimination law of the European Community.
  1. European Community countries. Sex discrimination. Law
  I. Title II. Burrows, Noreen
  341.7'6

Library of Congress Cataloging-in-Publication Data

Prechal, Sacha.
  European community law relating to gender discrimination/by
Sacha Prechal and Noreen Burrows.
      p. cm.
  Includes bibliographical references.
  ISBN 1-85521-058-4 : $60.00 (U.S. : est.)
  1. Sex discrimination against women--Law and legislation--European
Economic Community countries. I. Burrows, Noreen, 1951-
II. Title.
KJE5144.W84P74 1990
342.4'0878--dc20
[344.02878]

ISBN 1 85521 058 4

Printed in Great Britain by
Billing & Sons Ltd, Worcester

Contents

Foreword

This book was conceived as part of a project on women and the law at the Faculty of Law of the University of Limburg, Maastricht. The aim of that project was to initiate a series of studies relating to international legal developments which attempt to advance the status of women. The authors met in the context of a seminar at Maastricht and decided to write the book. That was in 1986. At that time Sacha Prechal was Lecturer in Law at the University of Limburg and Noreen Burrows was (and still is) Lecturer in European Law at the University of Glasgow. In 1987 Sacha Prechal was appointed Legal Secretary to the Dutch Judge at the European Court of Justice in Luxembourg, and she still holds this post. At the outset it should be stressed that all the views expressed in this book, except where otherwise indicated, are those of the authors and should not be taken as representing the opinion of the European Court nor of any other institution.

The book itself attempts to explain and describe European Community law relating to gender-based discrimination. As readers will come to realize, this is an area of law which is exceedingly complex, highly technical and very detailed. By their nature as rules which are meant to affect the workings of the legal systems within the Community, and as compromise solutions to the conflicting views of the Member States, the Directives described in this book sometimes raise extraordinarily complex problems of interpretation. So too has the apparently and deceptively simple Article 119 of the Treaty of Rome raised problems which to an outsider must seem either arcane or incomprehensible or both. We do not, therefore, present any apologies for spending time on a detailed examination of the legislation and case-law. For anyone wishing to argue a case relating to Community law in their national courts, such a detailed understanding of the substantive rules is essential. Moreover, as any student of Community law knows, it is not enough to understand the immediate rules of substantive law on any given topic. Such rules must be seen as part of the entire scheme of Community law, a scheme which is governed by general principles of law developed over the years in the jurisprudence of the European Court of Justice. This book analyses the substantive rules relating to gender-based discrimination within the framework of Community law as a whole. This is not a study of the domestic legislation of the individual Member States of the European Community. Judgements of the national courts and national legislation are discussed in so far as they illustrate the impact of the rulings of the European Court of Justice on the national legal systems. Most of the cases discussed in this book originated in the courts of the member States and ultimately were resolved there. We consider it important, therefore, to follow through such cases to examine how the national courts have come to terms with the interpretations given by the European Court. We must also stress that this is a book about law. It is not a study of the politics or sociology of gender based discrimination. Others, better qualified, have explored these issues. Our aim is to explore the law as it stands and to point out its weaknesses and strengths.

The book is written primarily for those individuals and their advisers who believe they have been unfairly prejudiced by the operation of national laws which discriminate against them on the basis of their gender. Such individuals may wish to seek a remedy in European law. It is also written for other persons who are more generally interested in the subject of sex discrimination. Furthermore, the cases which have been brought to the European Court of Justice have been instrumental in developing several important principles of Community law and the book, therefore, contains lessons for all who are interested in the operation of the Community legal order.

There is now a considerable volume of material published relating to Community sex discrimination law and it may be objected that a new work is not required. What we have tried to do in this book, however, is to provide an overall picture and to place all the case-law and legislation within a framework which displays the mutual relationships and interactions between the different legal provisions. In this respect it should be noted that the bibliography which appears at the end of book is not an exhaustive list but refers only to literature quoted in the text.

We have many people to thank for their assistance in preparing the book. Our thanks are extended to our colleagues in the Universities of Limburg and Glasgow and at the European Court of Justice for their support. Particular thanks must go to Margaret Ashman, Ria Caldwell, Isabelle Leick-Bouly and Helen Thomson for their transformation of our rough copy into a presentable manuscript, and to Gower who have waited for it.

The law is as it stands on 31 December 1988, although we have been able to take account of some more recent developments of cases before the European Court of Justice.

Sacha Prechal, Luxembourg
February 1989
Noreen Burrows, Glasgow
February 1989

1 Concepts of Discrimination and Equality in European Community Law

Concepts relating to discrimination and equality, and in particular the principle of non-discrimination, are central to European Community law. This is not to say that sex discrimination and its abolition have a central place in the Treaty of Rome, although it does have a place, but that the main thrust of the Treaty lies in the elimination of discrimination based on nationality. This emphasis is understandable as the aim of the Treaty is to create a common market out of separate national markets and to forge an ever closer union based on dismantling of national barriers. For this reason the principle of non-discrimination on the grounds of nationality is a central tenet of the Treaty and is enshrined in Article 7 thereof.[1] There is no comparable article relating to the elimination of sex-based discrimination; however, the elimination of sex-based discrimination has emerged as one of the more important issues within the Community, in particular within Community social policies. It is, therefore, useful to ask some pertinent questions about the nature, scope and extent of the Community concepts of equality and discrimination.

It is the aim of this chapter to discover what meanings have been attached by the Court of Justice to these terms, specifically in the context of sex discrimination, and also, although in very general terms, in the context of the elimination of other forms of discrimination. In doing so, it is not the aim of the chapter to compare different types of discrimination; nor is it the aim to draw analogies from one type of discrimination to the other. Indeed an advocate general has warned against the dangers of doing precisely that. Advocate General Capotorti made it clear that:

> no prohibition on discrimination in working conditions on the grounds of sex can be drawn, either by deduction or by analogy, from the prohibition of discrimination on grounds of nationality... Nationality is a ground of discrimination quite different from that of sex... It therefore appears to me vain for Miss Defrenne to attempt to draw from the decided cases of the Court of Justice relating to the prohibition on discrimination between workers on grounds of nationality arguments to support the analogous application of the criterion of equality of treatment made no sense between male and female workers.[2]

The Advocate General here pointed to a very important factor which will get explored throughout this book, namely, that not all discrimination based on sex is outlawed by the law of the European Community. In this case Miss Defrenne complained of discrimination in an area which was not, at that time, covered by Community law and in fact many of the cases which have come to the Court have turned on the issue of whether the discrimination complained of fell within the scope of Community provisions. The Advocate General was pointing to the fact that because Community law prohibits discrimination between workers on the ground of nationality that does not mean that it automatically prohibits discrimination on the ground of sex.

However, it is useful to examine the decided cases of the Court of Justice in order to discover what meaning the Court has placed on concepts such as discrimination in whatever context they might arise. There is in fact good precedent for doing so as the Court itself, and even advocates general, have referred back to their past definitions and used them time after time. Moreover, tests which have been developed in areas other than sex-based discrimination may prove useful sources of inspiration.

The principle of equality

The principle of equality has been at issue before the European Court on numerous occasions, as has the concept of discrimination. The Court has declared that the principle of equality is a fundamental principle of Community law and that the prohibition of discrimination in Community provisions is merely a specific enunciation of this general principle. Furthermore, the principle requires that similar situations may not be treated differently[3], nor may dissimilar situations be treated equally[4], unless any such treatment is objectively justified. Flowing from the principle of equality, the Court has distinguished a further principle which it sometimes equates with a particular right: the right to or principle of equal treatment. It is this right or principle which provides the standard of behaviour required to avoid the charge of discrimination.

Two elements of discrimination may be deduced from the judgements of the Court. The first relates to the comparability of the cases under consideration and the second relates to the presence or absence of objectively justified reasons for the difference in treatment. A third element should also, perhaps, be discussed and that is whether the complainer had suffered any harmful effects following the alleged discrimination. This is a difficult area since in all the cases which have come before the Court there has been an element of harm complained of. Indeed it is difficult to see why a case would be brought if no harmful effects had been suffered. Suffice it to say that in the earlier cases the Court had considered that some harm must have been suffered to satisfy a claim of discrimination but that in the more recent cases this aspect is not considered.[5]

To see how the Court applies its concept of discrimination it is important to ask two questions. The first is how the Court examines the issue of comparability, and the second is how the Court determines what may be considered as an objective justification for the behaviour in question.

The issue of comparability was discussed by the Advocate General in *Ruckdeschel*.[6] This particular case concerned refunds for the manufacture of products derived from maize. Manufacturers of quellmehl were, under a council regulation, paid a lesser amount of refund than those manufacturing starch. In this case the advocate general stated:

> in order to determine whether provisions which introduce a difference in treatment are discriminatory, it is first of all necessary that the conditions and situations in which undertakings are placed shall be comparable in the sector to which the rules in question apply. Clearly the concept of comparability of situations does not mean that they should be exactly alike. Comparability must be determined against the background of competition...and in each case in the light of the objectives of the measure at issue; it is principally in the light of those objectives that it is possible to determine whether certain differences existing between undertakings are sufficient to make it impossible to treat them as comparable cases and, in consequence, to subject them to different treatment.[7]

Thus, the comparability test is applied in the light of the objectives of the measure in question. Furthermore, it is not essential that the situation be identical. In this particular case the Court asked itself the question whether quellmehl and starch were in a comparable situation, given the substitutability of the products.

The Court is not always so specific in its approach as this test would seem to imply. In *Uberschar*[8] the Court examined a problem of alleged discrimination against foreign workers residing in the Federal Republic of Germany. Here the Court approached the issue of comparability from a different angle, by examining the advantages and disadvantages of the legal situation of German and foreign workers. The Court seemed to accept without discussion that the situation of both sets of workers could be compared and then went on to examine the differences in treatment. Perhaps here the comparability issue was so obvious as not to warrant a detailed examination. What was important was to view the differences in treatment in the light of the objectives of the measure.

The second question arising from the Court's concept of discrimination is a rather more difficult one. How does the Court determine whether a difference in treatment can be objectively justified? In this respect it should be stressed that there can be no clear definition of what may constitute an objective justification in legal terms since the decision as to objectivity is in itself left to the discretion of a higher authority than the person making the initial decision and, as such, it may change in the light of different circumstances. It is not surprising, therefore, to find that the Court has never given a definition of its own phrase. However, some guidance can be obtained from its decisions.

In the first place there are cases where the Court has decided that the situations in the case before it are not comparable and, therefore, almost by definition that a difference in treatment can be objectively justified. In *Hoffmann's Stärkefabriken*, for example, the Court decided, after having established that the situations of potato-starch producers and maize-starch producers were not comparable because the payment of restitutions in those two sectors was arranged in different ways, that:

> There are thus objective grounds for the difference between the treatment accorded potato-starch producers and that accorded maize-starch producers so that the transitional measures enacted in connection with the production refund for potato starch does not constitute a discrimination against maize-starch producers.[9]

In cases such as this the comparability test coincides with the justification test.

In the second place, the Court has suggested that inequality of treatment may be justified because certain legitimate policy aims are pursued or because differential treatment is required to protect other interests. In the context of free movement of goods, in *Commission* v. *Ireland*[10] (the Irish Souvenirs case), the Court was asked to examine the compatibility of domestic measures, which required all souvenirs and articles of jewellery imported from other Member States to bear an indication of origin or the word 'Foreign', with Community law. The Irish government claimed these measures were necessary in the interest of consumer protection and fairness in commercial transactions. The Court found the measures discriminatory, since they applied to imported products only. However, then the Court continued to examine whether the arguments put forward by the Irish government could justify the differential treatment. It held that:

> it is important to note that the interests of consumers and fair trading would be adequately safeguarded if it were left to domestic manufacturers to take appropriate steps such as affixing, if they so wished, their mark of origin to their own products or packaging.[11]

In *Bela-Muhle*[12], a regulation adopted under the Common Agricultural Policy was successfully challenged on the grounds that it placed a discriminatory burden of costs on a particular agricultural sector. The Court stated:

> Nor...was such an obligation necessary in order to attain the objective in

view, namely the disposal of stocks of skimmed-milk powder. It could not be justified for the purposes of attaining the objectives of the Common Agricultural Policy.[13]

It appears from these two examples that measures may be adopted which are necessary to attain the objective at issue, i.e. consumer protection, fairness in commercial transactions or certain objectives of the Common Agricultural Policy. Such measures may justify differential treatment as may also certain measures which are adopted in pursuance of economic policy objectives which are compatible with the Treaty and Community secondary legislation.[14] However, the measures in *Bela-Muhle* and *Irish Souvenirs* could not be upheld since they were not strictly necessary to attain the aforesaid objectives. This is the third step which the Court may take in order to determine whether the measures at issue should be considered to be discriminatory or not. The Court examines then whether, given that the objectives do in fact justify differential treatment, the means are reasonably proportionate for the attainment of the objective. More specifically, it examines whether the objective could be attained in a way which would not give rise to discrimination. In other words, it applies the principle of proportionality.[15]

There are instances, however, where the Court seems to apply a different test, and in these cases it examines the behaviour of the authority to establish whether it has exceeded its powers. In *Roquette-Frères*, for example, the Court stated:

> In reviewing the exercise of such a power the Court must confine itself to examining whether it contains a manifest error or constitutes a misuse of powers or whether the authority in question did not clearly exceed the bounds of its discretion.[16]

Here the Court equates the principle of non-discrimination more or less to a prohibition of arbitrary treatment[17] although in times of emergency the authorities are given more leeway. In *Merkur* the Court held:

> Regulation No. 974/71 is evidently an emergency measure...Since the assessment which the Commission had to make was perforce an overall one, the possibility that some of the decisions it made might subsequently appear to be debatable on economic grounds or subject to modification would not in itself be sufficient to prove the existence of a violation of the principle of non-discrimination, once it was established that the considerations adopted by it for guidance were not manifestly erroneous.[18]

The test of arbitrariness is, of course, less stringent than the justification test. However, it seems only to have been used in cases where a challenge has been made to the validity of a Community act and, therefore, it is unlikely that the Court would transpose the test to other aspects of discriminatory treatment.

One of the problems with such a test scheme, relying as it does on the Court's own decisions, is that the Court is not always consistent in applying it. As the cases cited show, sometimes it examines both comparability and the objective justification and sometimes only the justification. Moreover, when examining the justification it sometimes applies the proportionality test and sometimes it does not. There is, therefore, a degree of confusion in the Court's own definition of what might be described as discrimination and what may not.

A related problem arises out of the question as to who potential discriminators can be. This issue was raised in *Debauve*, a case concerning cable diffusion of television.[19] In Belgium, commercial advertising is forbidden on both television and radio. It is similarly forbidden in broadcasts from cable television which originate outside the Belgian territory. In a request for a preliminary ruling on the compatibility of these provisions with Community law, the Court was asked to determine whether 'such rules would introduce discrimination based on the geographical locality of the foreign broadcasting station'[20] given that the natural receiving zone of each station might be of different interest from an advertising point of view. Both the Advocate General and the Court rejected the view that this could amount to discrimination.

The Court accepted that technical and natural factors could lead to differences in reception of television signals but firmly denied that this could be seen as discrimination. The Treaty, the Court said, 'regards only differences in treatment arising from human activity, and especially from measures taken by public authorities, as discrimination.'[21] Therefore discrimination cannot arise by mere chance, dictated by the laws of nature; it is a social and political fact arising out of the behaviour of individuals, particularly those in power.

Arising from the Court's broad definition of discrimination, and from its judgements, it is possible to distinguish several different types of discrimination: discrimination in form and discrimination in substance, direct and indirect discrimination and disguised discrimination.

Discrimination in form and discrimination in substance

In the case of *Italy* v. *Commission*, [22] the Court suggested that a distinction should be made between discrimination in form and discrimination in substance. The case related to protective measures authorized by the Commission and imposed by France on Italian refrigerators. In examining the issue of discrimination the Court held:

> The different treatment of non-comparable situations does not lead automatically to the conclusion that there is discrimination. An appearance of discrimination in form may therefore correspond in fact

to an absence of discrimination in substance. Discrimination in substance would consist in treating either similar situations differently or different situations identically.[23]

What the Court was apparently trying to express here is that it is often necessary to go beyond the appearance of discrimination. Where differential treatment is applied in non-comparable situations it might seem, on the face of it, discriminatory but in reality there is no substantial discrimination, since it is to be expected that non-comparable situations would, in fact, be treated in a different way. It is especially this, the equal treatment of different situations, that is known as discrimination in substance or material discrimination.

This concept has been applied in several subsequent cases, although the Court tends not to use the terms discrimination in form and in substance specifically.[24] A good example is the case of *Choquet*[25] where a French national was fined, following an accident in Germany in which he was involved and was found to be driving without a driving licence. He had a valid French driving licence at the time. The Court held that it is not in principle incompatible with Community law for a state to require of a national of another member state, who is permanently established in its territory, to obtain a domestic driving licence, even if he possesses a driving licence issued by his own state:

> Legislative provisions of this kind could be considered contrary to Community law only if their application were to cause persons in one Member State who had obtained a driving licence in another Member State such difficulties that those persons would in fact be hindered in the free exercise of the rights which Articles 48, 52 and 59 of the Treaty guarantee them in connection with the free movement of persons, freedom of establishment and freedom to provide services. Insistence on a driving test which clearly duplicates a test taken in another Member State for the classes of vehicle which the person concerned wishes to drive, or linguistic difficulties arising out of the procedure laid down for the conduct of any checks, or the imposition of exorbitant charges for completing the requisite formalities could all be examples of this.
>
> Such obstacles to the recognition of a driving licence issued by another Member State are not in fact in due proportion to the requirements for the safety of highway traffic.[26]

Here the insistence that all drivers in Germany should have a valid German licence might appear not to be discriminatory. The question arises, however, whether potential drivers are all in the same situation and the suggestion to be taken from the Court's ruling is that it would amount to discrimination to treat foreigners with a valid driving licence obtained after a similar test in their own State in the same way as nationals without a licence at all.

The same basic idea underlying the concept of material discrimination is found in the cases of *Van Wesemael*[27] and *Webb*[28]. The former case relates to the licensing of fee-charging employment agencies and the latter to the licensing of manpower agencies.

In *Van Wesemael*, the Court held that the requirement to obtain a licence by a Member State cannot be objectively justified when, *inter alia*, the person providing the service already holds a licence issued under comparable conditions by his own State. In *Webb*, the Court upheld the right of a State to require of foreigners possession of a licence issued on the same conditions as in the case of its own nationals. However, in the granting of such a licence the Member State may not disregard the evidence and guarantees already furnished by the provider of the service for the pursuit of his or her activities in his or her own Member State. As in *Choquet*, the situations of the nationals and non-nationals is not the same in these cases. Nationals without licences at all should not be treated in the same way as non-nationals holding licences obtained in their own Member States.

Direct and indirect discrimination – covert discrimination

The distinction between direct and indirect discrimination is known to a number of legal systems. Direct discrimination arises where a forbidden ground of discrimination is used in order to apply differential treatment where there is no justifiable use of that criterion. This necessarily presupposes that there are in fact forbidden grounds of discrimination, and as stated earlier, within the context of the European Community the most important forbidden ground is that of nationality. Indirect discrimination arises where a criterion other than the forbidden ground is used to apply differential treatment and the use of this other criterion leads to the same result. Where a legal system does provide forbidden grounds of discrimination, it is likely that indirect discrimination will occur more frequently. It is, therefore, important to look beyond the appearance of a particular legal situation to its reality, as the Court recognized in the Italian refrigerators' case.

Within the terms of its own definition of discrimination, the treating of like cases differently and different cases alike, it is possible to outlaw both direct and indirect discrimination.

The Court has recognized the distinction between direct and indirect discrimination where both nationality and sex have been the forbidden ground although the Court does not use the term indirect discrimination. Sex-based discrimination is discussed later in this chapter. In the case of nationality, the distinction between direct and indirect discrimination was first discussed by the Court in a case relating to the elimination of discrimination based on nationality in the context of the free movement of workers.[29] The facts of the dispute were relatively simple. Mr Sotgiu, an Italian national, was employed in Germany by the German Post Office. He received a separation allowance (his family were resident in Italy) on the same terms as the separation allowance paid to German workers employed away from home. The rate of the allowance was subsequently increased for workers employed away from their place of residence within the Federal Republic, but it remained the same for workers whose residence was outside the Federal Republic at the time of their initial employment. Mr Sotgiu claimed that such differential treatment amounted to discrimination based on nationality and, as such, was prohibited by regulation 1612/68/EEC.

In its observations to the Court, the Commission argued that discrimination based on nationality could result from the application of criteria other than nationality in the assessment of the beneficiaries of a separation allowance. 'Such would be the case', the Commission argued, 'if the application of certain criteria of differentiation were to result, in all cases or in the vast majority of cases, in foreigners alone being affected without any objective justification'.[30]

Both the Advocate General and the Court addressed themselves to the problem outlined by the Commission. The Advocate General pointed out that discrimination may be 'hidden or disguised'. He went on to state that:

> [T]his is the case in particular when a national law or national rules, without referring to nationality, make the grant of payments or advantages linked to employment dependent upon criteria pertaining for example to descent, place of birth or normal residence on the national territory in such a way that enjoyment of these advantages is in fact reserved for nationals and cannot, with certain exceptions, apply to workers who are nationals of other Member states.
>
> Must we not, in such cases, going beyond appearances, condemn a violation of equality of treatment...[31]

The Court took up the view of the Advocate General – that a provision of law must be examined as to its effects on non-nationals as 'the rules regarding equality of treatment, forbid not only overt discrimination by reason of nationality but also all covert forms of discrimination which, by application of other criteria of differentiation, lead in fact to the same result'.[32] However, it is not sufficient to conclude that discrimination arises merely because the particular provision affects adversely one group of persons as against another, as there may be objective differences in the situations of the workers affected by the provision.[33]

In this case the terms indirect, covert, hidden and disguised seem to be used interchangeably. However, the differences in terminology do not seem to be important as the arguments of the Commission, Court and Advocate General point to the same conclusion: a particular provision must be examined in the light of its effects on the members of the group who claim to have been the victims of discrimination. The test to be applied subsequently to such a provision is whether there are objective reasons for the application of the rule.

The distinction drawn in Mr Sotgiu's case between direct and indirect discrimination (whatever the terminology used) has subsequently been upheld by the Court in cases relating to discrimination based on nationality.[34] In all these cases the Court looks beyond the criteria for differentiation which appear to form the rationale of the provision and looks to its effects. However, to determine whether a particular provision is discriminatory the Court suggests that the objectivity of the provision be examined.

Disguised discrimination

In Mr Sotgiu's case the terms indirect, covert, hidden and disguised discrimination were used interchangeably. However, in the jurisprudence of the Court it is possible to distinguish a separate concept of disguised discrimination particularly in relation to sex-based discrimination (although the Court has approached this issue only in the area of equal pay). Disguised discrimination relates to the underlying causes of discrimination, for example in the way that job segregation relates to the overall problem of inequality of incomes. Very often legislation is not aimed at this type of discrimination; indeed it is questionable whether or not the law would be capable of eliminating it. Therefore, one of the major questions faced by the Court is to determine the limits of Community law in matters relating to discrimination. As will be seen below, this is a particularly difficult question in the area of sex-based discrimination.

The principle of equality of the sexes in Community law

As has already been stated in this chapter, there is no general principle of non-discrimination based on sex enunciated in the Treaties establishing the European Community. The quotation from Advocate General Capotorti from the Defrenne case given earlier warns us that it is not possible to derive a general principle of non-discrimination based on sex from Article 7 of the Treaty which outlaws discrimination based on nationality. Nonetheless, the Court of Justice, several advocates-general and numerous parties in disputes which have come before the Court have argued that such a principle does in fact form part of Community law, and it has been the Court which has introduced that principle into the Community legal system.

The existence of the principle of non-discrimination based on sex was not accepted universally in the earlier years of the Community.

In Sabbatini[35] Advocate General Roemer dismissed the arguments of the plaintiffs that such a superior rule of law existed. In a rather angry opinion, which was fortunately not accepted by the Court, the Advocate General stated that:

> the further arguments which the applicants devoted to this matter in their replies are not such as to show that the precept on which they rely exists in the form of a general principle of law which is binding in all circumstances...the legal systems of the Member States do not recognise any general principle imposing in absolute terms equality of treatment as between men and women.[36]

In this case the Court itself did not state that such a principle existed but it was tacitly accepted and the discriminatory behaviour was declared void.

Some two and a half years later another advocate general addressed himself to the same problem. In Airola[37] Advocate General Trabucchi accepted the 'basic principle of equality of the sexes, which is enshrined in the law of the Community'.[38] The principle however was circumscribed both by 'reason and feasibility'.[39]

What then is meant by the general principle of equality of the sexes? A very simple explanation could be that a general principle is, in itself, a guideline which the Court will use to assess the legality of particular practices. A general principle is not of itself a right but it is capable of giving rise to rights. What the general principle does is to indicate to the Court how a particular problem should be settled. The general principle itself cannot be circumscribed by 'reason and feasibility', for it reflects both reason and feasibility, but its application to a concrete situation might be circumscribed by reason and feasibility, for example, if the application of the principle to an individual in a given case might give rise to harm to others.

Furthermore, the Court has declared that the principle of equality of the sexes and the elimination of discrimination based on sex are part of the fundamental personal human rights which form part of the general principles of Community law.[40] The specific right which emerges from Community law is the right to equal treatment.

Having accepted that the principle of non-discrimination based on sex is a general principle of Community law does not imply that it has become a general principle of law in all the Member States of the Community. It does mean that it is a principle which governs the Institutions and the Member States where they act in a Community capacity. The scope of the principle was explained by Advocate General Capotorti in the following way:

> the rule that there should be no discrimination is a general principle of the Community legal order. It is a principle contained in the list of fundamental

human rights recognised within the Member States and within the context of the European Convention on Human Rights and Fundamental Freedoms; consequently it forms part of Community law and must be protected by the Court of Justice...I may add that in the context of positive law and modern legal thinking the exclusion of discrimination on the ground of sex is one of the fundamental features of the principle in question...[t]he respect for fundamental rights is a limitation on all Community acts: any measure whereby the powers of the Community institutions are exercised is subject to that limitation and in that sense the entire structure of the Community is under an obligation to observe that limitation. Secondly where directly applicable Community measures exist...they must be interpreted in a manner which accords with the principle that human rights must be respected.[41]

The fact that the principle of non-discrimination based on sex is applicable across the whole range of Community activity has been stated very clearly by the Court. In *Razzouk and Beydoun* the Court recognized:

the need to ensure equal treatment of men and women employed by the Community itself within the framework of the Staff Regulations. Consequently, in relations between the Community institutions, on the one hand and their employees and the dependants of employees, on the other, the requirements imposed by the principle of equal treatment are in no way limited to those resulting from Article 119 of the EEC Treaty or from the Community directives adopted in this field.[42]

Thus employees of the institutions have far wider rights arising from the principle of non-discrimination based on sex than employees elsewhere in the Community. For the latter they may derive rights only from specific, directly effective Community provisions. Advocate General Caportorti succinctly expressed it thus:

in the Community order there exists no principle having direct effect which confers on individuals within the Community the right to enjoy equal working conditions without discrimination on grounds of sex.[43]

The general principle itself does not give rise to rights except where a specific provision of Community law exists.[44]

Direct and indirect discrimination in the area of gender discrimination

In the preliminary references which have come to the Court relating to sex-based discrimination, the Court has not been asked to decide whether a particular provision amounts to direct discrimination, since in all these cases the discrimination complained of was either obvious or not disputed.[45] The issue in these cases centred on the scope of Community law and the direct effects of specific Community provisions.[46] However in *Commission* v. *Italy* [47] the Court was required to decide whether an Italian provision which permitted adoptive mothers three months' leave following the entry of a child into the family but denied such leave to adoptive fathers was directly discriminatory. The Court decided that it was not but did not use its previous definition of discrimination to justify its decision. It did not make use of the formula that discrimination arises where similar situations are treated differently or dissimilar situations are treated alike. The basis of its decision is more concerned with the social policy underlying the Italian legislation and it made no attempt to examine the issue of whether adoptive parents were in the same situation as natural ones. It is impossible to conclude from one single instance that the Court adopts a different approach to the concept of discrimination where sex-based discrimination is concerned as compared to other types of discrimination. However, in this case, and there have been no other, the Court certainly did adopt a different test.

In a group of cases brought by women employees of the European Institutions, the Court has examined the ways in which apparently sex-neutral criteria have, in fact, led to direct discrimination against women. Monique Bauduin and Luisa Sabbatini both complained to the Court that they suffered from discrimination when their expatriation allowances were withdrawn on the occasion of their respective marriages.[48] The Staff Regulations stated that the expatriation allowance became forfeit unless the official who was getting married became, on marriage, 'the head of the household'. Furthermore, the Regulations automatically considered a male official to be head of the household, whereas a female was so considered only in exceptional circumstances.

Given these factors, and in the light of the purpose of the expatriation allowance, the Court held that the Regulations were illegal as they 'created an arbitrary difference of treatment' whereas 'the staff regulations cannot however treat officials differently according to whether the staff are male or female, since termination of the status of expatriate must be dependent for both male and female officials on uniform criteria, irrespective of sex'.[49]

Following these cases the Commission expunged the offending provision from the Regulations and replaced it with a clause which related the grant of the expatriation allowance to the nationality of the official. This provision caused a difficulty for Jeanne Airola, a Belgian female official married to an Italian non-official.[50] On marriage she declared, as was possible under Belgian law, that she wished to retain her Belgian nationality. However, under Italian law she acquired the Italian nationality of her husband. The Commission decided to follow the Italian definition of nationality and deemed her to be Italian. As she was employed in Ispra at the time, the Commission decided that, as an Italian national working in Italy, she was no longer eligible for the expatriation allowance.

In the case before the Court in which Airola contested the decision, the Commission argued that the provision did indeed give rise to indirect discrimination:

> The Commission nevertheless recognises that as women alone may acquire second nationality through marriage and alone may thereby suffer possible loss in terms of their statutory entitlement to the expatriation allowance, there is a *de facto* discrimination between male and female officials.[51]

The Court recognized that the application of the apparently sex-neutral criterion of nationality amounted to discrimination based on sex 'since under no national legislation does the male official acquire the nationality of his wife'.[52] In the particular instance Airola had had the nationality of her husband forced upon her, although she had declared her intention to retain her former Belgian nationality. The case of Chantal Van den Broeck was similar except that on her marriage to a Belgian national she failed to exercise her right to retain her French nationality.[53] In these circumstances the Court concluded that 'there are no reasons associated with equal treatment why her Belgian nationality should not be taken into account in applying the provision concerned'.[54]

In both cases the Court recognized that a criterion which was apparently unrelated to sex could give rise to discrimination against women. The Court argued, however, that the circumstances of each case and the provision should be examined in the light of a particular factual situation. The use of nationality as the determining factor as to who could or could not receive the expatriation allowance was not thought by the Court to violate the principle of equal treatment. Only when the Commission interpreted the provision in such a way as to contradict the express wish of the official concerned did the Court accept that indirect discrimination could arise.

This pragmatic stance is very far from the argument of the Commission in *Airola*. Here the Commission argued that the principle of equal treatment required that the provision be examined as to its impact on a particular group. Only women, it argued, could be affected by a change of nationality on marriage. Such a change *never* happened in the case of a male official; it *could* in the case of a female. The provision itself, concluded the Commission, violated the principle of equal treatment. The Court did not take this argument on board but argued that the provision itself did not violate the principle of equal treatment but that it might do so in particular circumstances. The Court failed to recognize that the existence of the provision placed women who married in a different situation from men, as it placed an additional obstacle in the way of women officials who wished to retain the expatriation allowance on marriage.

These staff cases show that the Court is willing to draw a distinction between direct and indirect discrimination in matters relating to discrimination based on sex. It is not clear from the cases, however, that the Court has a clearly defined view as to the nature of indirect discrimination. The Court did not apply the same standard as it had developed in the cases quoted above relating to nationality. In the nationality cases the Court was willing to examine the provision in question and to measure it against a standard of equal treatment. The same standard was not applied to the women in the expatriation allowance cases. The Court was willing to accept that equal treatment did not require the same treatment for men and women and was willing to place an additional burden on women.

The picture becomes more confused when some of the preliminary references which raise the question of direct and indirect discrimination are examined. In these cases the Court introduces entirely novel ways of distinguishing direct from indirect discrimination. In *Defrenne*[55] the Court was asked to rule on the question of the direct effects of Article 119 EEC. In its judgement the Court drew a distinction between direct and overt discrimination, and indirect and disguised discrimination. The former, said the Court, could be identified 'solely with the aid of the criteria based on equal work and equal pay referred to by the article in question'.[56] The latter could be identified 'by reference to more explicit implementing provisions of a community or national character'.[57] The Court went on to give an example of the kind of direct discrimination at which Article 119 aims:

> Among the forms of direct discrimination which may be identified solely by reference to the criteria laid down by Article 119 must be included in particular those which have their origin in legislative provisions or in collective labour agreements and which may be detected on the basis of a purely legal analysis of the situation.[58]

This judgement is unhelpful in assessing the meaning which the Court attaches to the concept of direct and indirect discrimination as it does not relate to the use of these terms in either the nationality cases or in the expatriation allowance cases.

The judgement did, however, have an enormous impact on later cases and, in particular, on the way in which they were argued. In the subsequent Defrenne case the confusion of everyone concerned became apparent.[59] In this case Ms Defrenne wanted to know whether Article 119 could be interpreted as including equality in respect of working conditions other than pay and, in particular, if it included the right of female cabin staff to continue to work beyond the age of 40 as male colleagues were entitled so to do.

In pursuing her claims Defrenne used the argument developed by the Court itself. She argued that the Court had recognized the direct applicability of Article 119 especially 'as regards those types of discrimination which derive directly from legislative provision or collective labour agreements'.[60] Her case was governed by a collective labour agreement which fixed a lower age limit for retirement for females. The clause was discriminatory and amounted to discrimination in remuneration because it deprived females of their jobs and, hence, their remuneration. In effect she was arguing that the provision constituted discrimination in the area of pay and it was of the sort envisaged by the Court in its earlier Defrenne judgement.

Her view was supported by Italy. In its written observations Italy stated that:

> The discrimination at issue in the main action appears to be comparable, within the meaning of the Court of Justice, to 'direct' discrimination: it derives from a contractual provision, it may be identified by means of purely legal analysis and it exists in relation to equal work carried out in a single establishment. It may, in addition, be regarded as 'indirect and disguised' discrimination, in as much as it arises out of a provision which does not directly concern the amount of the remuneration, but whose application has repercussions on that remuneration.[61]

In these submissions Italy was drawing the distinction, as accepted by the Court in *Sotgiu*, between direct and indirect discrimination but was also endeavouring to fit its observations into the pattern set by Court in *Defrenne*.

The Court did not, in its judgement, address itself to the issue of indirect discrimination and, therefore, no further guidance on this issue can be gathered from its wording. Neither can much help be drawn from *Macarthys*[62] where the Court relied on its own definition to decide that Article 119 applied to situations where a female worker could compare her pay with that of a previously employed male employee.

Advocate General Warner found the distinction drawn in Defrenne 'puzzling' in *Worringham and Humphreys*.[63] He agreed that Article 119 had direct effects when the domestic Court could apply its provisions by reference to the criteria laid down in that Article, and that it did not have direct effects in areas where further implementing provisions were required. What did puzzle him was 'why the concepts of "direct and overt" discrimination should be relevant in that connection.'[64] He went on to state that the Court had, in the wake of *Sotgiu*, determined that covert discrimination was just as much discrimination as overt discrimination but in none of the cases following *Sotgiu* 'was it suggested, or could it sensibly have been suggested, that the distinction between overt and covert discrimination affected the question whether the relevant provision of Community Law had direct effect or not'.[65]

This opinion by Advocate General Warner is very welcome in helping to sort out the mess created by the unfortunate wording in *Defrenne*. It opened the way for others to be able to argue rationally about the nature of indirect discrimination in *Jenkins*.[66]

The Jenkins case turned on the issue of whether part-time workers should be paid at the same rate as full-time workers. In a very closely argued submission Ms Jenkins claimed that indirect discrimination arises out of the differential in pay rates between part-time and full-time workers since part-time work is mainly done by female workers who are routinely paid lower rates.[67] She argued that the Court should examine not the intention of the employer but the effect of the employer's policy. In her argument she cited Griggs,[68] an American case, which enunciated the principle of 'adverse impact' and claimed that adverse impact was the American version of the British concept of indirect discrimination. Indirect discrimination in this sense is a practice, the effect of which is to discriminate against an individual by virtue of their membership of a particular group and is not 'discrimination which can only be suppressed by national and Community legislative measures more detailed...[than Article 119]'.[69]

These arguments were taken up by Advocate General Warner who agreed that the 'adverse impact' approach was the correct approach to indirect discrimination:

> The requirement that an employee should work 40 hours a week to earn the full hourly rate must obviously hit, in a disproportionate way, at women, compared with men. That did not necessarily mean that there was discrimination, but it did mean that there was *prima facie* discrimination in effect, which required 'some special justification from the employer'.[70]

The Advocate General went on to compare the approach of the European Court of Justice with the United States Supreme Court and drew comfort from the fact that he reached the same conclusions as the latter. He further argued that this approach was also in line with the European Court's own finding in cases such as *Sotgiu* that a provision must be examined to discover whether its effect is to lead to a difference in treatment and, if so, to see if there are objective reasons for such treatment. Again Advocate General Warner referred to the difficulties arising out of the Defrenne judgement and invited the Court to clarify the difficulties which had arisen subsequently. He argued that dicta in *Defrenne*:

> Could be interpreted as meaning that the test for determining whether there is 'covert' discrimination, in the sense meant in the *Sotgiu, Commission* v. *Ireland* and *Toia* cases, is the same as the test for identifying the kind of discrimination as regards which article 119 has no direct effect. In my opinion the two tests are not the same and I doubt if the Court can ever have intended to say that they were.[71]

The Court did little to clarify the question in the way the Advocate

General might have wished. Indeed it created further confusion by the very vague formulation of its decision. The Court held:

> If there is no such distinction, (i.e. a distinction based on sex) therefore, the fact that work paid at time rates is remunerated at an hourly rate which varies according to the number of hours worked per week does not offend against the principle of equal pay laid down in Article 119 of the Treaty in so far as the difference in pay between part-time work and full-time work is attributable to factors which are objectively justified and are in no way related to any discrimination based on sex.
>
> Such may be the case, in particular, when by giving hourly rates of pay which are lower for part-time work the employer is endeavouring, on economic grounds which may be objectively justified, to encourage full-time work irrespective of the sex of the worker.
>
> By contrast, if it is established that a considerably smaller percentage of women than of men perform the minimum number of weekly working hours required in order to be able to claim the full-time hourly rate of pay, the inequality in pay will be contrary to Article 119 of the Treaty where, regard being had to the difficulties encountered by women in arranging to work that minimum number of hours per week, the pay policy of the undertaking in question cannot be explained by factors other than discrimination based on sex.
>
> Where the hourly rate of pay differs according to whether the work is part-time or full-time it is for the national court to decide in each individual case whether, regard being had to the facts of the case, its history and the employer's intention, a pay policy such as that which is at issue in the main proceedings although represented as a difference based on weekly working hours is or is not in reality discrimination based on the sex of the worker.[72]

If the Court had accepted the 'adverse impact' approach suggested by the Advocate General it would have examined whether women as a group suffered greater harm than men as a group from the existences of different rates of pay for full-time and part-time work. If women did suffer such an adverse impact then an employer would have to show a special justification, other than sex, for paying differential rates. In its own jurisprudence in other contexts the Court developed a system for determining whether differential treatment might be objectively justified but it does not seem to have applied to previous tests in the Jenkins case. What it did was to reverse the normal pattern for determining the existence of discrimination by examining whether there existed a justification for the distinction made and then to ask, if there was no justification, whether the differential treatment may be discriminatory. Furthermore, the Court gave no clear indication as to what the objectively justified factors could be except to suggest that the employer's intention should be taken into account. The would appear to be contrary to the requirements of any objective justification since the intention of the employer is inherently subjective. If the employer intended to discriminate there would be no problem.

However, discrimination might arise unintentionally; the rationale for paying full-time workers less might be that they work harder – this would have to be tested by objective inquiry. Furthermore, in order to satisfy the principle of equality the interests of the employer must be weighed against the interest of women being equally paid. None of these issues, however, emerge clearly from the decision of the Court.

More recently the Court has addressed this particular problem in *Bilka*[73] and seems to have returned to the formulation of indirect discrimination as it was laid down in *Sotgiu*. *Bilka* concerned the question as to whether an occupational pension scheme could be considered as pay within the meaning of Article 119. If it could be so considered, did the fact that such a pension scheme was only available to full-time workers constitute discrimination, given the fact that the vast majority of part-time workers were female? The Court decided that occupational pension schemes of the type described in *Bilka* did amount to pay within the meaning of Article 119. Ms Weber argued that 'the requirement for receiving an occupational pension of a minimum period of full-time employment is to the detriment of female workers who, in order to be able to take care of their families and children, are more likely to be induced to choose part-time work than their male colleagues'.[74] Bilka argued that the decision to exclude part-time employees 'was based on objectively justified economic grounds'[75] namely, their desire to recruit a predominantly full-time work force.

The Court examined both these arguments and concluded that:

> Article 119 of the EEC Treaty is infringed by a department store company which excludes part-time employees from its occupational pension scheme where that exclusion affects a much greater number of women than men, unless the enterprise shows that the exclusion is based on objectively justified factors which are unrelated to any discrimination based on sex.[76]

What the Court did in *Bilka* was to revert to its own classical definition of indirect discrimination which it had developed in the nationality cases following *Sotgiu*. The Court examined the criterion which was the basis for the treatment, the length of hours worked. If, it said, a considerably smaller number of women worked full-time, and therefore the majority of women were excluded from the benefit in question then there was discrimination. It would be up to the employer to prove that there were objectively justifiable factors unrelated to discrimination based on sex if the employer wished to avoid the charge of discrimination. Unlike in *Jenkins*, however, in *Bilka* the Court qualified this test by demanding that the means chosen for that objective (i.e. to employ as few part-time workers as possible) correspond to a real need on the part of the undertaking, are approximate with a view to achieving the objective in question and are necessary to that end.[77] In other words, the Court applied the proportionality test.

Conclusions

From the foregoing discussion it is apparent that the Court of Justice has had to confront issues relating to discrimination on numerous occasions and that it has had, over time, the opportunity to develop a very rich jurisprudence of its own in this area. From the decisions of the Court it is possible to distinguish several important ideas relating to gender-based discrimination and the concept of discrimination itself. Most importantly the Court has acknowledged that the principle of equality of the sexes and the elimination of discrimination based on sex are part of the fundamental human rights which, in turn, form part of the general principles of Community law. It may be questioned whether, without such a statement, the political institutions would have made the progress which they have in the adoption of new legislation in the area of equal treatment of men and women. Nor, perhaps, would individuals within the Community have come alive to the legal possibilities of the new legal order to the extent which they have. However, the Court must recognize its own limits. It has recognized that it, on its own motion, cannot eliminate discrimination and has thus had to confront questions relating to the extent to which Community law can create individual rights.

Within its own boundaries, however, the Court has been innovative and encouraging. It has shown a willingness to develop concepts in order to give real meaning to the vaguer principles of equality. It has recognized that discrimination may arise both where the same treatment is applied to persons who are not in a comparable situation and where different treatment is applied to them where they are in a comparable situation. Furthermore, the Court has suggested the rigorous tests of objective justification and proportionality to determine if either of these two approaches do amount to discrimination. The Court may be criticized as being not always consistent in its own approach but this may be hardly surprising given that the cases which come before it do so based on a large variety of circumstances and from varied legal backgrounds.

It has recognized the distinction between direct and indirect discrimination, although its own terminology relates to direct or covert discrimination, and it appears that it has now reached a clear view as to what these forms of discrimination are. Direct discrimination arises where sex (or any other forbidden ground of discrimination) is used as a means to deny equality of treatment. Covert (indirect) discrimination arises where a criterion other than sex is used but it can be shown that it adversely affects more women than men (or vice versa). However, the use of the criterion may be objectively justified. The justification test is narrowed considerably by the requirement of proportionality.[78] This chapter has not analysed all the cases relating to sex discrimination which have come before the Court – the remaining chapters of this book will do that. What it has shown are the difficulties which have sometimes arisen where individuals have sought a remedy for their belief that they have suffered an injustice. In the area of sex discrimination the law demands to be shown not only that an injustice has occurred but also that proof be led that illegal discrimination has occurred. Thus courts must develop a conceptual framework within which cases must be argued. Sometimes, confusion has arisen out of the judgements of the European Court of Justice. However, it is working in a difficult framework and such confusions are not unique to it.

Notes

1   Article 7 reads: 'Within the scope of application of this Treaty, and without prejudice to any special provisions contained therein, any discrimination on grounds of nationality shall be prohibited...'
The treaty also provides for the prohibition of discrimination between producers and consumers in agriculture (Article 40); and outlaws the application of dissimilar conditions to equivalent transactions with trading partners in competition law (Articles 85 1 (d) and 86 (c)).

2   Case 149/77 *Defrenne* v. *Sabena* (1978) E.C.R. 1365, p. 1384.

3   See, for example, joined cases 117/76 and 16/77 *Ruckdeschel* (1977) E.C.R. 1753; joined cases 124/76 and 20/77 *Moulins et Huileries de Pont-à-Mousson* (1977) E.C.R. 1795; case 125/77 *Koninklijke Scholten-Honig* (1978) E.C.R. 1991; joined cases 103 and 145/77 *Royal Scholten-Honig (Holdings) Ltd* (1978) E.C.R. 2037; 166/78 *Italy* v. *Commission* 1979 E.C.R. 2575; 810/79 *Uberschar* 1980 E.C.R. 2764; 32/80 *Kortmann* (1981) E.C.R. 251; joined cases 198 to 202/81 *Micheli* (1982) E.C.R. 2885; 15/83 *Denkavit* (1984) E.C.R. 2171.

4   Cases 130/75 *Prais* v. *Council of the European Communities* (1976) E.C.R. 1589; 8/82 *Hans-Otto Wagner GmbH* [1982] E.C.R. 371; 281/82 *Unifrex* [1984] E.C.R. 1969; 106/83 *Sermide* [1984] E.C.R. 4209; 283/83 *Racke* (1984) E.C.R. 3791.

5   In a case relating to a scrap metal levy imposed by a decision of the High Authority under the European Coal and Steel Community Treaty, the Court stated that 'For the High Authority to be accused of discrimination it must be shown to have treated like cases differently, thereby subjecting some to disadvantages as opposed to others, without such differentiation being justified by the existence of substantial objective differences.' Joined cases 17 and 20/61 *Klockner* v. *High Authority* (1962) E.C.R. 325, p. 345.

6   Joined cases 117/76 and 16/77 *loc. cit.* note 3.

7   p. 1779. For a further discussion of comparability see case 6/71 *Rheinmuhlen* (1971) E.C.R. 823.

8   Case 810/79 *loc. cit.* note 3.

9   Case 2/77 *Hoffmann's Stärkefabriken* v. *Hauptzollampt Bielfeld* (1977) E.C.R. 1375 p. 1396. See also cases 136/77 *Racke* (1978) E.C.R. 1245; 21/74 *Jeanne Airola* v. *Commission of the E. C.* (1975) E.C.R. 221.

10   Case 113/80 *Commission* v. *Ireland* (1981) E.C.R. 1625.

11   *Ibid.* p. 1641.

12   Case 114/76 *Bela-Muhle* v. *Grows-Farm* (1977) E.C.R. 1211.

13   *Ibid.* p. 1221.

14   Cases 140/79 *Chemical Farmaceutici SpA* v. *Dar SpA* (1981) E.C.R. 1; 46/80 *SpA Vinal* v. *SpA Orbat* (1981) E.C.R. 77.

15   See cases 114/76 and 113/80 *loc. cit.* notes 12 and 10.

16   Case 138/79 *Roquette-Frères* v. *Council* (1980) E.C.R. 3333 p. 3358. See also case 139/79 *Maizena GmbH* v. *Council* (1980) E.C.R. 3393.

17   See also case 20/71 *Sabbatini* v. *Commission* (1972) E.C.R. 345.
18   Case 43/72 *Merkur* v. *Commission* (1973) E.C.R. 1055 p. 1074.
19   Case 52/79 *Procureur du Roi* v. *Marc J.V.C. Debauve and Others* (1980) E.C.R. 833.
20   *Ibid.* p. 854.
21   *Ibid.* p. 858. And see the Advocate General, 'the provisions of the Treaty forbidding discrimination are concerned with the discrimination artificially brought about by measures taken by Government or other persons in positions of power', p. 869.
22   Case 13/63 *Italy* v. *Commission* (1963) E.C.R. 165.
23   *Ibid* p. 177.
24   See cases 1/78 *Kenny* v. *Insurance Officer* (1978) E.C.R. 1489; 15/78 *Société Générale Alsacienne de Banque S. A.* v. *Koestler* (1978) E.C.R. 1971.
25   Case 16/78 *Criminal Proceedings* v. *Michel Choquet* (1978) E.C.R. 2293.
26   p. 2302.
27   Case 111/78 *Ministère Public and Chambre Syndicale des Agents Artistiques et Impresarii de Belgique* v. *Willy Van Wesemael* (1979) E.C.R. 35.
28   Case 279/80 *Criminal Proceedings Against Alfred John Webb* (1981) E.C.R. 3305.
29   Case 152/73 *Sotgiu* v. *Deutsche Bundespost* (1974) E.C.R. 153.
30   p. 161.
31   p. 173.
32   p. 164.
33   p. 165.
34   See cases 61/77 *Commission* v. *Ireland* (1978) E.C.R. 417; 237/78 *Cram* v. *Toia* (1979) E.C.R. 2645; 22/80 *Boussac Saint-Frères* v. *Gerstenmeier* (1980) E.C.R. 3427; joined cases 142 and 143/80 *Administrazione delle Finanze Dello Stato* v. *Essevi SpA and Salengo* (1981) E.C.R. 1413; joined cases 62 and 63/81 *Seco SA and Desquenne and Giral SA* v. *EVI* (1982) E.C.R. 223; case 20/85 *Roviello* v. *Landesversicherungsanstalt Schwaben* (not yet reported). However see case 155/80 *Sergius Oebel* (1981) E.C.R. 1993 where the Court held that the principle of non-discrimination is not infringed by rules which are applied not on the basis of the nationality of the trader but on the basis of their location.
35   Case 20/71 *loc. cit.* note 17.
36   *Ibid.* p. 355.
37   Case 21/74 *loc. cit.* note 9.
38   *Ibid.* p. 233.
39   *Ibid.* p. 231.
40   Case 149/77 *Defrenne* v. *Sabena loc. cit.* note 2, p. 1385. The Court had declared the importance of the protection of human rights in a series of cases beginning with case 25/69 *Stauder* v. *City of Ulm* (1969) E.C.R. 419.
41   Joined cases 75 and 117/82 *C. Razzouk and A. Beydoun* v. *Commission* (1984) E.C.R. 1509.
42   *Ibid.* p. 1530.
43   Case 149/77 p. 1387 *loc. cit.* note 40.
44   In the chapters below all these provisions are discussed extensively.
45   See, for example, cases 12/81 *Garland* v. *British Rail Engineering Ltd* (1982) E.C.R. 359 (travel facilities given to men and not to women); 19/81 *Burton* v. *British Railways Board* (1982) E.C.R. 555 (retirement age five years earlier for women); 152/84 *Marshall* v. *Southampton and South West Hampshire Area Health Authority (Teaching)* (1986) 1 C. M.L.R. 688 (compulsory dismissal for women at 60 rather than 65); 150/85 *Drake* v. *Chief Adjudication Officer* (1986) 3 C. M.L.R. 43 (denial of invalidity care allowance to women); 286/85 *McDermott and Cotter* v. *Minister for Social Welfare and the Attorney General* (1987) 2 C.M.L.R. 607 (lower unemployment benefit rates for women).
46   These issues are discussed extensively in the following chapters of this book.
47   Case 163/82 *Commission* v. *Italy* (1983) E.C.R. 3273. This case is discussed extensively in Chapter 4 below.
48   Cases 32/71 *Bauduin* v. *Commission* (1972) E.C.R. 363 and 20/71 *loc. cit.* note 17.

49   *Ibid.* p. 351.
50   Case 21/74 *loc. cit.* note 9.
51   p. 225.
52   p. 228.
53   Case 37/74 *Chantal Van den Broeck* v. *Commission* (1975) E.C.R. 235.
54   p. 245.
55   Case 43/75 *Defrenne* v. *Sabena* (1976) E.C.R. 455.
56   *Ibid.* p. 473.
57   *Ibid.*
58   *Ibid.*
59   Case 149/77 *Defrenne* v. *Sabena* (1978) E.C.R. 1365.
60   *Ibid.* p. 1368
61   *Ibid.* p. 1369.
62   Case 129/79 *Macarthys Ltd.* v. *Wendy Smith* (1980) E.C.R. 1275.
63   Case 69/80 *Worringham and Humphreys* v. *Lloyds Bank Limited* (1981) E.C.R. 767, p. 803.
64   *Ibid.*
65   *Ibid.*
66   Case 96/80 *Jenkins* v. *Kingsgate (Clothing Productions) Ltd* (1981) E.C.R. 911.
67   *Ibid.* p. 915 ff. Her submissions on these matters are well worth reading in full.
68   *Griggs* v. *Duke Power Co.* 301 U. S. 424 (1971).
69   96/80 *loc. cit.* p. 918.
70   96/80 *Ibid.* p. 936.
71   *Ibid.* p. 937.
72   *Ibid.* p. 925.
73   Case 170/84 *Bilka Kaufhaus GmbH* v. *Karin Weber Von Hartz* (1986) 2 C. M.L.R. 701.
74   *Ibid.* p. 716.
75   *Ibid.*
76   *Ibid.* p. 720.
77   *Ibid.* p. 721.
78   Indirect discrimination is discussed in Chapters 3, 4, 5, 6, pp. 71-7, 106-10, 173-77, 194, 206, 244.

2 The New Legal Order – Its Consequences for Individuals

Early in the 1960s it appeared from the case-law of the Court of Justice that the Community constitutes a new, autonomous legal system. In the *Van Gend en Loos* case the Court held:

> that the Community constitutes a new legal order of international law for the benefit of which the states have limited their sovereign rights, albeit within limited fields, and the subjects of which comprise not only Member States but also their nationals. Independently of the legislation of Member States, Community law therefore not only imposes obligations on individuals but is also intended to confer upon them rights which become part of their legal heritage. These rights arise not only where they are expressly granted by the Treaty, but also by reason of obligations which the Treaty imposes in a clearly defined way upon individuals as well as upon the Member States and upon the institutions of the Community.[1]

The Court reached this conclusion on the ground that the EEC Treaty is more than an agreement merely creating mutual obligations between the contracting states. Its objective is to establish a Common Market, the functioning of which concerns all interested parties in the Community. This view is confirmed in the preamble of the Treaty which refers not only to governments but also to people. Moreover, the Treaty establishes institutions endowed with sovereign rights, the exercise of which affects the Member States and their citizens. Furthermore, the nationals of the Member States are called upon to cooperate in the functioning of the Community through the European Parliament and the Economic and Social Committee. Finally, it appears from the task assigned to the Court itself under Article 177 that the states have acknowledged that Community law has an authority which can be invoked by their nationals before the domestic courts and tribunals.

The concept of the new legal order has had an important impact on the relationship between national and Community law. Under traditional international law a state is free to decide on the way it will realize its international obligations within its own national legal order. There is no rule of international law requiring that treaty obligations, or obligations arising out of decisions of international organizations be applied directly within the national order or to prevail over a provision of national law. It depends on *national constitutional* provisions how international law will be incorporated within the national legal order. Within the different constitutional provisions dealing with this problem two main approaches can be distinguished.[2]

The first is the so-called monist doctrine. According to this doctrine international law and national law are part of the same legal system. No national transformation measures are required. International law is considered to be a part of the legal system which national courts must apply. If the national provisions conflict with international law the latter usually will prevail. The constitutions of Belgium, France, Luxembourg, Greece and The Netherlands follow, generally speaking, the monist conception of international law.

According to the second approach, the dualist doctrine, the national and international legal orders are two separate systems having very little communication *inter se*. According to this view, rules of international law can be applied within the domestic legal order only *after* their transformation into national rules. Consequently, national courts cannot apply international rules directly. From the international point of view the dualist approach has two serious disadvantages:

- if the version of the national incorporation measures is different from the international version, the former will be applied, even if there is an evident conflict between them;
- any future national law will take priority over the law incorporating the international rule into the national legal order on the basis of the adage *'lex posterior derogat legi priori'*.

Naturally, in both situations, or if the state has not transformed the international rule at all, the state concerned can be called to account for infringement of its international obligations before an international forum, but this possibility will be of little help to an individual involved in legal proceedings.

The dualist approach is the basis of the constitutional provisions and practice of the Federal Republic of Germany, Italy, United Kingdom, Denmark and Ireland.[3]

Using the concept of the *new legal order* as the main argument, the Court of Justice took a position of its own on the relationship between national and community law. It did so in very clear language in *Costa* v. *ENEL*.[4] First, the Court recalled that the Treaty of Rome created its own legal system which became an integral part of the legal systems of the Member States and which the national courts are bound to apply. Then the Court pointed out, in particular, that the Community has real powers stemming from a limitation of sovereignty or a transfer of powers from the Member States to the Community. Consequently, the Member States have limited their sovereign rights, albeit within limited fields, and have thus created a body of law which binds both their nationals and themselves. In these circumstances, the Court found that it was impossible for the Member States to accord precedence to unilateral and subsequen⁴ measure over a legal system accepted by them. The Court continued by stressing the need to ensure a uniform validity and efficacy of Community law, by recalling the basic principles of the Treaty embodied in Articles 5 and 7 of the Treaty, and by referring to the fact that the obligations of the Member States are unconditional. The right to act unilaterally under the Treaty is covered by clear and precise conditions which would lose their purpose if the Member States could renounce their obligations by means of an ordinary law. Finally, the Court invoked Article 189 of the Treaty which provides for a direct and immediate effect of regulations in all Member States. This provision would be quite meaningless if a subsequent national measure could unilaterally deprive regulations of their effect. On this basis the Court held that:

> It follows from all these observations that the law stemming from the Treaty, an independent source of law, could not, because of its special and original nature, be overridden by domestic legal provisions, however framed, without being deprived of its character as Community law and without the legal basis of the Community itself being called into question.
>
> The transfer by the States from their domestic legal system to the Community legal system of the rights and obligations arising under the Treaty carries with it a permanent limitation of their sovereign rights, against which a subsequent unilateral act incompatible with the concept of the Community cannot prevail.[5]

Stressing the necessity for uniform effect of EEC law in all the Member States, the Court clearly rejected the dualist concept of international law. Community law is, as such, incorporated within the national legal systems. Transformation is not only superfluous but unacceptable as it would jeopardize the legal basis of the Community itself. Moreover, it appears from the *Costa* v. *ENEL* judgement that, because the Member States have limited their sovereign rights in favour of the Community legal order, Community rules have internal effect within the national legal order without reference to national constitutional law: constitutional provisions relating to the internal effect of international law do not apply when rules of Community law are at stake. If the national rules conflict with provisions of Community law, national courts must refrain from applying them because the national legislator has acted *ultra vires*.[6]

In its case-law, with *Van Gend en Loos* and *Costa* v. *ENEL* as starting points, the Court of Justice gave concrete form to its ideas on the effect of Community law within the national legal systems by using and further developing two intimately linked doctrines of 'direct effect' and 'supremacy' of Community law. But even in situations where Community provisions at issue have no direct effect, they have considerable impact on the national legal systems.

The 'new character' of the Community also finds expression in a specific system of maintenance of community law. For the purpose of this book only two provisions concerning judicial proceedings will be discussed. First, the preliminary proceedings of Article 177 EEC will be dealt with. These proceedings establish a direct link between the Court of Justice and national courts and play a prominent part in the judicial protection of individuals. Second, the enforcement action of Article 169 EEC will be discussed. This article enables the Commission of the EC to bring proceedings in the Court of Justice where a Member State fails to fulfil its obligations under EEC law.

Direct effect

The doctrine of direct effect has been the subject of extensive legal debate, but the concept is not so difficult as is often thought. It could generally be described as the capacity of a provision of Community law to create individual rights enforceable by all persons concerned in the national courts.[7]

The development of the concept started with the *Van Gend en Loos* case. The basis of direct effect lies in the idea of the new legal order. Community law has as its subjects not only the Member States but also their nationals. The Community legal order confers directly on interested parties individual rights which they can invoke on their own behalf. The difficulty is that many legal rules are of general nature and need further legislation to make them suitable for application to the legal position of parties before the courts. It follows logically from the description of direct effect given by the Court of Justice, which is, as stated above, that the individuals derive rights from a provision of Community law which are enforceable by them in their domestic courts, that a directly effective provision should be applied as a rule of law by a court; it must be 'complete, legally perfect'.[8]

The question whether or not a provision of Community law has direct effect is a matter of interpretation. In *Van Gend en Loos* the Court had already taken a liberal view on this matter: individual rights for private parties are created not only when they are explicitly stated by the Treaty, but also on account of obligations which the Treaty lays down in a very definite manner for individuals as well as for the Member States and the Community institutions. In other words, individuals can derive rights from obligations imposed upon others. In the early case-law of the Court several requirements were laid down which had to be satisfied by a legal provision if they were to be deemed to have direct effect.[9] Nowadays the Court requires the provision to be *unconditional and sufficiently precise*. A provision is unconditional when it is not dependent on the judgement or discretion of an independent body, such as a Community institution or the legislator or administration of a Member State. A provision is not sufficiently precise when it is so vague that the national court is not able to apply it without dealing with questions beyond its competence, such as the economic policy to be pursued. The very basic condition seems to be that no real discretionary power is left in the hands of the implementing authority.[10]

When an authority has a real option or faculty to choose between various solutions, the provision cannot be deemed unconditional in the above-mentioned sense. Vague terms may also imply discretionary powers. However, vagueness as such is not an obstacle for direct effect.[11] Once again, the question whether a (vague) provision grants discretion is a question of interpretation.

Thus, for example, Article 5, paragraph 2, stating that the Member States shall abstain from any measure which could jeopardize the attainment of the objectives of the Treaty of Rome, does not really seem to be a rule suitable for application by a court. Article 12, on the other hand, forbidding the Member States to introduce new custom duties on imports or any charges having equivalent effect, is sufficiently precise to have direct effect. It may be that a national court wonders what is a 'charge having an equivalent effect'. However, it may question on this issue the Court of Justice and, after having obtained interpretation, the national court can apply Article 12 to the facts before it.

A good illustration of the problems raised in connection with the concept of direct effect is Article 119 EEC, which reads:

> Each Member State shall during the first stage ensure and subsequently maintain the application of the principle that men and women should receive equal pay for equal work...

With respect to the direct effect of this provision the Court makes a distinction between two situations.[12] In the first one, sex-based pay discrimination can be identified solely by virtue of the criteria laid down in Article 119: equal pay for equal work. In particular when such discrimination results from provisions of national legislation or collective labour agreements, or in cases where the men and women concerned do the same work in the same establishment or service, the national judge may establish the discrimination by a purely legal analysis. Complex judgements are not necessary. In such a case Article 119 has direct effect. So, for example, in *Garland*,[13] after having established that special travel facilities constitute pay within the meaning of Article 119, the Court held:

Where a national Court is able, using the criteria of equal work and equal pay, without the operation of Community or national measures, to establish that the grant of special transport facilities solely to retired male employees represents discrimination based on difference of sex, the provisions of Article 119 of the Treaty apply directly to such situation.[14]

On the other hand, there are apparently situations in which the criteria of Article 119 are insufficient. Where, in order to implement Article 119, comparative studies of entire branches of industry are necessary and therefore, as a prerequisite, the elaboration by the Community and national authorities of criteria of assessment are required, Article 119 has no direct effect.[15]

The Court in 1974 addressed itself to the problem of whether directives were capable of having direct effect. According to Article 189 EEC a directive is binding only 'as to the result to be achieved' but leaves 'the choice of form and method' to the national authorities. This article has often been used as an argument against direct effect of directives, partly because of this definition and partly because this article states only with respect to regulations that they are directly applicable. However, in *Van Duyn*[16] the Court accepted the direct effect of directives on the following grounds:

If, (...), by virtue of the provisions of Article 189 regulations are directly applicable and, consequently, may by their very nature have direct effects, it does not follow from this that other categories of acts mentioned in that Article can never have similar effects. It would be incompatible with the binding effect attributed to a directive by Article 189 to exclude, in principle, the possibility that the obligation which it imposes may be invoked by those concerned. In particular, where the Community authorities have, by directive, imposed on Member States the obligation to pursue a particular course of conduct, the useful effect of such an act would be weakened if individuals were prevented from relying on it before their national courts and if the latter were prevented from taking it into consideration as an element of Community law. Article 177, which empowers national courts to refer to the Court questions concerning the validity and interpretation of all acts of the Community institutions, without distinction, implies furthermore that these acts may be invoked by individuals in the national courts. It is necessary to examine, in every case, whether the nature, general scheme and wording of the provision in question are capable of having direct effects on the relations between Member States and individuals.[17]

The conditions to be satisfied by a provision of a directive in order to have direct effect are, that it be 'unconditional and sufficiently precise'. Although the wording of the Court sometimes differs, it requires in substance that the same conditions be met irrespective of the nature of the instrument of Community law in which the provision is embodied.[18] The fact that Member States are free to choose the form and method for implementation of a directive does not prevent a 'direct effect'. What is decisive in the Court's test of direct effects is whether real discretion is left as to the result to be achieved in pursuance of the provision of a directive.[19]

It is established case-law today that where a provision of a directive appears to be unconditional and sufficiently precise it may be relied upon by an individual as against the State if the State has failed to implement the directive within the prescribed period or if it has failed to implement it correctly. According to the Court a Member State which has not taken measures to implement the directive within the period prescribed, or has not taken sufficient measures, may not, as against individuals, plead its own failure to perform the obligations which the directive entails.[20]

This possibility to rely on Community law provisions as *against the Member State* is often called vertical direct effect. However, Treaty provisions are able not only to confer rights on private individuals, but also to impose obligations on them, even when a provision is not addressed directly to individuals.[21] This is the basis for the so-called *horizontal direct effect* of Treaty provisions: a private individual may invoke a Treaty provision against another private individual. The case-law of the Court of Justice affirms the horizontal direct effect of Treaty provisions, such as Article 119 and Article 48 EEC.[22]

In 1986, after years of discussion and speculation in legal writing,[23] the problem of horizontal direct effect of directives was settled by the Court. The Court denied the horizontal direct effect to a provision of the Equal Treatment Directive in *Marshall*[24] with the following reasoning:

> according to Article 189 of the EEC Treaty the binding nature of a directive, which constitutes the basis for the possibility of relying on the directive before a national court, exists only in relation to 'each Member State to which it is addressed'. It follows that a directive may not of itself impose obligations on an individual and that a provision of a directive may not be relied upon as against such a person.[25]

The main argument against this decision is that it creates an anomaly. It results in an unfair distinction between state employees and private employees. When (alleged) discrimination occurs, the former can rely on a directive as against their employer, whereas the latter cannot. In *Marshall* it was exactly this argument that was put forward by the British government (not to advocate horizontal direct effect but to argue that provisions of the Equal Treatment Directive have no direct effect at all). The Court dealt with this argument very briefly: such an unfair distinction may easily be avoided if the Member State concerned has correctly implemented the directive in national law.

It may be clear that under these circumstances the question whether the opposite party in legal proceedings, for instance the employer, is to be considered as 'the State', becomes extremely important. In *Marshall* the Court took a quite liberal view when it dismissed the UK argument that a directive can only have direct effect against a Member State *qua* public authority. The Court held that a person may rely on a directive as against the State regardless of the capacity in which the latter is acting, whether employer or public authority. However, it is up the national court to find out how to characterize the party which is said to act in breach of a directive.[26] It is to be expected that this issue will give rise to difficulties. While the position of central and local public authorities may be clear, considerable uncertainty exists with respect to semi-public bodies, public authorities acting through a private artificial person, nationalized industries and so on.

Illustrative in this respect is *Turpie* v. *University of Glasgow*.[27] Mrs Turpie had been dismissed at the age of 60. She submitted that as long as men are allowed to work until 65, her dismissal was in breach of the Equal Treatment Directive as became clear from the judgement of the Court of Justice in *Marshall*. It was not disputed before the Industrial Tribunal that in these circumstances the dismissal was unfair. The whole discussion was focused on the question whether or not the University of Glasgow was an emanation or organ of the State. The Tribunal found that the University was an independent body which could in no sense be regarded as an organ or emanation of the State. The University was governed by legislation which laid down how it must operate, but within those limits the University was 'a free agent, devoted to teaching and research and able to carry out its multiple activities without reference to the State'. Consequently the Tribunal held that the University was a private employer and Mrs Turpie could not rely on the directive against it. The University could thus rely on the Sex Discrimination Act 1975, which provided in Section 6(4) that the prohibition of discrimination does not apply to provisions in relation to death and retirement. It is perhaps interesting to note that if such a problem had arisen in the Netherlands, the person concerned could, as a rule, rely on the directive, since the majority of the universities are *state*, or municipal, universities and the employees are often appointed as civil servants.[28]

Supremacy

The postulate of supremacy of Community law over national law is based on the idea of the necessary unity and effective operation of Community law. Since *Costa* v. *ENEL*[29] it has been confirmed in constant case-law that Community law cannot be overridden by domestic legal provisions.[30] From *Internationale Handelsgesellschaft*[31] it appeared that Community law overrides even constitutional provisions. The Court considered that:

the validity of a Community measure or its effect within a Member State cannot be affected by allegations that it runs counter to either fundamental rights as formulated by the constitution of that State or the principle of a national constitutional structure.[32]

According to the Court, to judge the validity of Community law in the light of national rules would have an adverse effect on its uniformity and efficacy, depriving it of its character as Community law.

Regarding directly effective provisions, the principle of supremacy has as a consequence that these provisions always prevail over a provision of national law, irrespective of whether the Community provision is of an earlier or later date. Conflicting national provisions are 'inapplicable' and the national court must apply directly effective Community rules to the facts of the case. The consequences of the supremacy of Community law in combination with direct effect were stated in very clear terms in *Simmenthal*.[33] The background of this case was a decision of the Italian Constitutional Court of 30 October 1970 in which it ruled that a decision on a conflict between a Community provision and an Italian law is within its exclusive competence. Consequently, Italian courts were held to apply a national law even when it was contrary to Community law as long as that law was not repealed or declared unconstitutional.[34] In *Simmenthal* the pretore was confronted with a national law contrary to Community law. According to the decision of the Constitutional Court, the pretore had to submit the law at issue to the Constitutional Court for constitutional review. Under Community law he was held to apply the Community provision excluding the contrary national law. The pretore sent this problem to the Court of Justice, requesting a preliminary ruling as to the supremacy of Community law over a subsequent national law and as to the consequences of directly effective provisions in the national legal order. First, the Court emphasized that Community rules having direct effect must be fully and uniformly applied in all Member States. They are a direct source of rights and duties for all affected thereby, whether Member States or individuals. In a case within its jurisdiction the national court has the task, as an organ of a Member State, to protect these rights. It continued by explaining that the entry into force of Community directly effective provisions does not only render any conflicting provision of national law automatically inapplicable, but it also precludes the valid adoption of new legislation to the extent to which the latter would be incompatible with Community provisions. Further, the Court considered that the effectiveness of Article 177 would be impaired if the national courts were prevented from applying Community law in accordance with the decisions or the case-law of the Court of Justice. According to the Court it followed from these considerations:

that every national court must, in a case within its jurisdiction, apply Community law in its entirety and protect rights which the latter confers on individuals and must accordingly set aside any provision of national law which may conflict with it, whether prior or subsequent to the Community rule.[35]

The Court added that neither national rules, nor legislative, administrative or judicial practices may deprive the national court of such a power since that would impair the effectiveness of Community law.

The supremacy of Community law is not only confined to provisions with direct effect. It will become evident in the next two sections that even where a provision is not directly effective, national law must be compatible with provisions of Community law and may not impede its effectiveness.

Review of national law regardless of the direct effect of the directive provision

If a provision of a directive leaves discretion to the national authorities, the provision cannot have direct effect and cannot be applied by a court to the case before it. Will then national law have to be applied even if there are doubts about the compatibility of national rules with Community law? In three cases late in the 1970s the Court of Justice seems to place the national courts under a legal duty to review the lawfulness of national law with respect to a directive regardless of whether the relevant provision of the directive can be deemed to have direct effect.

In the *VNO* and *ENKA* judgements,[36] despite preliminary questions on the possible direct effect of certain provisions, the Court did not examine whether the requirements for a provision having direct effect were satisfied. After giving an interpretation of the provision concerned, the Court stated that it is the duty of the national court to take the directive into consideration in order to determine whether the national measures in question are compatible with the provision of the directive as interpreted by the Court. According to the Court, individuals can invoke a provision of a directive before a national court:

in order that the latter shall rule whether the competent national authorities, in exercising the choice which is left to them as to the form and the methods for implementing the directive, have kept within the limits as to their discretion set out in the directive.[37]

Further, the Court held that it is the duty of the national court concerned to determine whether the disputed national measure falls within the margin of the discretion of the Member State. If it does, the measure must be considered as legitimate.

In *Delkvist*[38] the Court considered that if a national provision cannot be regarded as exceeding the margin of discretion left to the Member state, such a provision must be regarded as a provision validly enacted by the State within the limits of the directive.

From this case-law the conclusion can be drawn that the limits set to the discretion of a Member State by Community law can be invoked in a national court and that if national law exceeds these limits, the national rules are not valid and cannot be applied by the national court. This approach increases the possibility for individuals to invoke Community law in national courts. But it may also create a serious problem. If the national court may not apply a national rule because this rule exceeds the limits set by Community law, a legal vacuum may occur when there is no national or Community provision left to be applied.[39] Direct effect, on the other hand, will result in a 'substitution' of the national rule by a Community provision and may thus be much more satisfactory.

Interpretation of national law in conformity with Community law

So far as traditional international law is concerned, as a rule national courts will by means of interpretation try to evade an outright option for one of the two conflicting rules. Similarly, as concerns Community law, a national court confronted with doubt on the compatibility of national law with Community law will try to interpret the national provision in such a way as to avoid conflict between the two rules. Moreover, if a provision of national law implementing a directive needs further interpretation, the national court may be inclined to fall back on the directive. National law will then be interpreted in accordance with the provisions of the directive, often following upon a preliminary ruling given by the Court of Justice at the request of the court concerned. This 'concurring' interpretation is quite common with the Dutch Supreme Court. A good example in this respect is *Beets-Proper*.[40] In the UK examples of concurring interpretation can also be found, for instance *Garland* v. *British Railway Engineering*.[41] In this case, special travel facilities after retirement were at issue, which were more favourable for former male employees than for former female employees. This practice was held contrary to the Sex Discrimination Act 1975 concerning 'provisions in relation to death and retirement'. The House of Lords sent the case to the Court of Justice which held that travel facilities were 'pay' within the meaning of Article 119 and consequently men and women must be treated equally in this respect. Following this judgement, the House of Lords interpreted Section 6(4) of the 1975 Act in a manner to make it consistent with Article 119, restoring effectively the E.A.T. view that Section 6(4) exempted only provisions which were 'part and parcel of an employer's system of catering retirement'. The result was that the discriminatory practice of British Rail was held contrary to UK legislation. Lord Diplock said in this respect that:

it is a principle of construction of United Kingdom statutes, now too well established to call for citation of authority, that the words of the statute passed after the treaty has been signed and dealing with the subject matter of the international obligation of the United Kingdom, are to be construed, if they are reasonably capable of bearing such a meaning, as intended to carry out the obligation, and not to be inconsistent with it. A fortiori is this the case where the Treaty obligation arises under one of the Community treaties to which § 2 of the European Communities Act 1972 applies.[42]

Another, very surprising, example is *Pickstone* v. *Freemans plc*.[43] In this case, the House of Lords was prepared to depart from the common rules of interpretation and it used the intention of the Parliament as an aid to construction in order to arrive at an interpretation in conformity with community law provisions.

In two relatively recent cases, *Von Colson and Kamann* and *Harz*,[44] the Court of Justice availed itself of this method of 'concurring' interpretation in an extensive way with considerable consequences for the protection of individual rights emanating from the Community law. In these two cases the Court considered that although the Member States are free to choose, they are obliged to adopt all the measures necessary to ensure that the directive concerned is fully effective in accordance with the objectives which it pursues. In particular, the Court held that:

> the Member States' obligation arising from a directive to achieve the result envisaged by the directive and their duty under Article 5 of the Treaty to take all appropriate measures, whether general or particular, to ensure the fulfilment of that obligation, is binding on all the authorities of Member States including, for matters within their jurisdiction, the courts.
>
> It follows that, in applying the national law and in particular the provisions of a national law specifically introduced in order to implement Directive n° 76/207, national courts are required to interpret their national law in the light of the wording and the purpose of the directive in order to achieve the result referred to in the third paragraph of Article 189.[45]

It appears from this judgement that the national court is under a legal duty to interpret and apply the legislation adopted for the implementation of the directive in conformity with the requirements of Community law, in so far as it is given discretion to do so under national law. The results to be achieved play a prominent part within this interpretation. Problems with direct effect do not occur and the difficulty of a 'legal vacuum' noticed above may be obviated. Moreover, this 'result-oriented concurring interpretation' applies to other national law, not specifically enacted to implement a directive, as well.

This approach was reaffirmed by the Court in *Johnston*.[46] In this case the Court of Justice established that Article 2 paragraph 2 of the Equal Treatment Directive, an exception to the equal treatment principle, leaves an option to the Member States. It is for the national court to review the national rules enacted in order to implement the exception. The court is under the duty to interpret these rules in the light of the wording and the purpose of the directive in order to give the directive full effectiveness.

However, if the national court concludes that the national exception exceeds the limits set by Article 2, paragraph 2, the question of direct effect of *another* provision by the directive arises 'in order to have a derogation laid down by national legislation set aside'. In the case of Ms Johnston the Court decided that an individual indeed can invoke other provisions of the directive to have set aside the national legislation.

The obligation on the national Court to interpret national provisions in the light of the directive was confirmed again in *Kolpinghuis*.[47] However, this case also adds some new elements. First, the Court reiterated that the national court must take the Directive into consideration in interpreting both national rules enacted in order to implement the Directive at issue, and any other national legal provision. It is noteworthy that both Advocate General Slynn[48] and Advocate General Mischo[49] were of the opinion that this obligation on the national court arose only in the interpretation of provisions adopted to implement the directive. Second, *Kolpinghuis* suggests that the obligation on the national court to find a concurring interpretation exists as soon as the directive comes into force, even before the period of its implementation comes to an end.[50] Finally, the Court stated that the duty of the national court is limited by the general principles of law which are a part of Community law, in particular, by the principle of legal certainty and the prohibition of retroactivity. The announcement of the limits in this case may be explained by the fact that the proceedings which gave rise to the preliminary question were criminal ones. It is a general principle of law embodied in Article 7 of the European Convention on Human Rights and articulated in the Court's former case law,[51] that criminal legislation may not have retroactive effect. If a concurring interpretation of national law would effectively 'create' a new criminal offence, or would increase criminal liability, it would be incompatible with the above-mentioned principle.

At this point, the conclusion must be that the 'concurring' interpretation depends on three factors: the flexibility of the national provision concerned, the discretion left to the court under national law and Community general principles of law. It should be noted the two first factors are to be decided by the national judge, whereas the third concerns a matter of Community law subject, where necessary, to the interpretation of the Court of Justice. Thus if a national court has doubts as to the compatibility of a possible interpretation with, for instance, the principle of legal certainty, they should ask for a preliminary ruling. By using the method of concurring interpretation, the national court may ultimately reach an effect equivalent to horizontal direct effect by creating a new obligation for individuals. To what extent such an interpretation should be accepted is not clear as there exists a continuum between an old rule on the one hand and a new one on the other. It will often depend on the particular case how far the court will go along this continuum. However, it must be considered that interpretation by the courts giving a new and different meaning to legal provisions is certainly nothing new. It may even amount to a derogation from former case-law. In this respect it must be reiterated, that the limit in such cases is to be found in *Community* general principles of law, and in particular in the *Community* principle of legal certainty.[52]

In the light of the foregoing, the position of the English Court of Appeal expressed in two relatively recent cases may be questioned. In *Haughton* v. *Olau Line*[53] Donaldson M. R., with Neill L. J. and Gibson L. J. concurring, found that the Equal Treatment Directive cannot be used to interpret or influence the provisions of the Sex Discrimination Act where the latter is unambiguous in terms of the national rules of interpretation. Further, it appears that the Court of Appeal accepts only that an unambiguous national provision may be overruled by a directly effective directive provision. If this judgement is to be understood as being that only where a national provision is ambiguous the judge is willing to look at the terms of the directive, it may be argued that such an attitude does not comply with the Community obligation of concurring interpretation. This obligation presupposes that as soon as there is *any* possibility of concurring interpretation this opportunity should be seized with both hands. After all, is there not some difference between flexibility of a provision and ambiguity?

Another, maybe even better, example of the rigidity of the Court of Appeal is the problem of different retirement ages for men and women. The Sex Discrimination Act 1975 excluded from its protection in Section 6(4) 'provisions in relation to death or retirement'. It has been suggested that this exclusion should be construed in a restrictive manner as meaning 'a provision consequent upon death and retirement'. However, in *Roberts* v. *Cleveland Area Health Authority*[54] the Court of Appeal decided that this provision means 'about death and retirement'. So it happened that the fixing of different retirement ages was not covered by the Sex Discrimination Act. In *Marshall*,[55] referred to the Court of Justice by this same Court of Appeal, the Court of Justice held, to put it shortly, that the fixing of retirement ages was covered by the Equal Treatment Directive and consequently, different retirement ages for men and women were held discriminatory. In *Marshall* the provisions of the Directive could have been relied upon as against the Health Authority and in this way Section 6(4) of the Sex Discrimination Act was inapplicable.

A year after *Marshall* the Court of Appeal gave judgement in *Duke* v. *Reliance Systems Ltd.*[56] Ms Duke had been dismissed soon after she reached the age of 60, while the retirement age for men was 65. According to *Marshall*, it was clearly a discriminatory dismissal contrary to the Equal Treatment Directive. However, as Reliance Systems Ltd was a private employer, Ms Duke could not rely on the Directive. Thus the only possibility to protect her rights was to interpret Section 6(4) of the Sex Discrimination Act in conformity with the decision of the Court of Justice in *Marshall*, which would obviously require a new interpretation which would derogate from previous cases. The Court of Appeal held, however, that where a statute implementing a directive is capable of two meanings, one conflicting with the directive, the other conforming to it, and an English superior court has previously construed the statute in the conflicting manner, nevertheless this conflicting interpretation must be followed. The doctrine of *stare decisis* should require this. Only a higher court may overrule this 'erroneous' interpretation.

This judgement merits some remarks. Apparently, an interpretation in conformity with *Marshall* was possible. For instance, the construction suggested in the past, stating that 'in relation to retirement' should mean 'consequent upon retirement' would probably suffice to achieve that retirement ages would be covered by the Sex Discrimination Act. Nevertheless, the Court of Appeal was not willing to depart from its former case-law because of the doctrine of *stare decisis*. It may be argued that the application of this doctrine in this case is compatible with Community law. When the national judge has the possibility to construe national provision in conformity with the directive, he or she is, in principle, held to do so, the more when another interpretation results in a violation of the directive at issue. The doctrine of *stare decisis* is in the present case impairing the effectiveness of Community provisions which is the opposite of what should be done following the *Von Colson and Kamann* case. Furthermore, in *Rheinmühlen*[57], the Court of Justice held:

> that a rule of national law whereby a court is bound on points of law by the rulings of a superior court cannot deprive the inferior courts of their power to refer to the Court questions of interpretation of Community law involving such rulings.[58]

This decision may be understood in more general terms, as prohibiting rules which would force an inferior court to apply a decision of a higher court concerning Community law, when the inferior court has doubts as to the content of the decision concerned. Indeed, *Rheinmühlen* concerned in particular the power to refer, but it is obviously of no use to have the power to request a preliminary ruling when a court would be obliged to conform to the decision of a higher court. Seen in this light, the application of *stare decisis* by the Court of Appeal cannot be upheld. It may be admitted that the new interpretation of Section 6(4) may turn the world upside down and a question as to the legal certainty may arise. Nevertheless this is, as previously stated, a matter of interpretation of Community law within the competence of the Court of Justice.

The House of Lords, dealing with Duke in appeal, also refused to construe Section 6(4) of the Sex Discrimination Act 1975 in conformity with the judgement of the Court of Justice in *Marshall* but the Lords did so on different grounds. Basically they held that the construction of a British Act of Parliament was a matter of judgement to be determined by the British courts and to be derived from the language of the legislation considered in the light of circumstances prevailing at the date of enactment. Since the 1975 Act was not passed to give effect to the Equal Treatment Directive but was intended to preserve discriminatory retirement ages, a Community law concurring interpretation was not possible.[59]

Preliminary rulings

Both the concept of direct effect and that of supremacy of Community law were developed within the framework of preliminary rulings provided for by Article 177 EEC. This Article sets up direct cooperation between the Court of Justice and national courts with a view to ensuring uniform interpretation and application of Community law in all the Member States.

The system of preliminary rulings is based on the idea that it is for the national courts to apply Community law to the facts of the case before it. When the national judge is confronted with Community law, the lower court has a discretion, and the highest court is obliged, to request the Court of Justice for a preliminary ruling concerning the interpretation or validity of Community law. The only condition is that the court must consider a decision on the question raised necessary to enable it to give judgement. The decision whether or not to order a reference lies with the national court and not with the parties.

The Court of Justice has accepted two exceptions to the obligation of the highest courts to refer: the 'acte éclairé' and the 'acte clair'. The first exception applies when the interpretation of Community law is clear from a previous preliminary ruling. Or, to put it in the Court's more limited terms:

> when the question raised is materially identical with a question which has already been the subject of a preliminary ruling in a similar case.[60]

The second exception of 'acte clair' means that the national courts are not obliged to refer when they consider the question clear enough to answer it themselves.[61] However, both exceptions must be handled with care. In particular, the courts should not readily consider a matter of Community law to be clear. Community legal concepts may differ from their apparent national counterparts; they may even differ in the respective languages of the Communities. Moreover, the Community legal order as such is a different one, often relatively unknown to the national court, which requires specific Community interpretation of its law, now and then based on comparative studies of the legal notions of the Member States.

Both the exceptions, as with the condition of necessity as well, may possibly be abused by a national court unwilling to ask for a preliminary ruling.[62] A possible but not realistic sanction, due to political susceptibilities, is that an action be instituted by the Commission under Article 169 EEC against a State whose highest court failed to request a preliminary ruling in a case where it was obliged to do so. The same sanction is possible also if a national court does not apply Community law in a case where it should be applied or if the Court applies it incorrectly.

Once the preliminary question has been referred, the Court of Justice itself informs the parties to the national main proceedings, the Member States, the Commission and if Council legislation or another act is at issue, the Council. Within a period of two months they may submit observations. The Commission playing to a certain extent the role of an 'amicus curiae', submits observations in each preliminary proceedings. As a rule, the Member States submit observations in cases referred by its courts. Often in preliminary proceedings they have in fact to defend their legislation or administrative practices.

Under Article 177 the separation between the functions of the Court of Justice and national courts is as follows: the Court interprets Community law and the national court applies the Community provision *as interpreted by the Court of Justice* to the facts of the case. If the Court in a preliminary ruling declares a Community rule invalid, the national court will not apply the Community rule or will consider a national measure based on the invalid Community rule illegal.[63]

To make the interpretation as helpful as possible to the national court, the Court of Justice interprets Community law in the light of the specific context of the case. The Court will never apply Community law to the facts of the case and will, for instance, never rule on the compatibility of national provisions with Community law. However, the preliminary ruling may sometimes go into so much detail that the interpretation is tantamount to application.

Although preliminary rulings have no status as binding precedents, and a national court is always entitled to make a new reference, even if it concerns a question already answered by the Court, in practice preliminary rulings have considerable effect on later cases.

The judgements of the Court given in preliminary proceedings have in principle retroactive effect. Thus an interpretation by the Court in 1990 of a provision of a directive which had to be implemented in 1984 is not only valid from 1990 onwards but also applies to situations between 1984 and 1990. Only in exceptional cases may the Court be willing to restrict the interpretation *ratione temporis* in pursuance of the principle of legal certainty.[64] It must be stressed that it is only the Court of Justice which may limit in this way the effects of its interpretation of Community law. Moreover, the Court will do so only in the ruling as to the interpretation itself and not in a subsequent judgement.[65] So, for instance, a Belgian law of 21 June 1985 restricting the repayment of certain enrolment fees charged to foreign students between 1 September 1976 and 31 December 1984 could not be upheld. On 13 February 1985 the Court held in *Gravier*[66] that the fees concerned were contrary to Article 7 of the Treaty. This interpretation was valid, as in any other case, for the period previous to the judgement. However the Belgian law restricted the repayment *ratione temporis* by providing that the fees will be refunded in accordance with judicial decisions delivered on actions for repayment commenced before Belgian courts before 13 February 1985. Thus, this law made it impossible for the majority of foreign students to rely on Article 7 as interpreted by the Court in *Gravier* so as to challenge the fees paid in the past and to have them refunded. This situation was contrary to Community law because when the Court has not restricted the scope of its judgement *ratione temporis*, the national authorities – legislature, administration, judges – are not allowed to do so on their own.[67]

An apparently comparable problem was at issue in *Deville*[68] which however did not concern a restriction *ratione temporis*, but a procedural limitation imposed, subsequent to a judgement of the Court, on the possibilities of bringing proceedings for recovery. In its judgement of 9 May 1985 the Court held as contrary to Article 95 of the Treaty a certain type of tax on cars. A subsequent French law imposed a time-limit for lodging proceedings for recovery which was shorter than the time-limit which would otherwise apply under French law as it stood at the time of the Court's judgement. The Court held that the national legislature may not adopt any procedural rule which reduces the possibilities of bringing proceedings for recovery of taxes which were wrongly levied. However, it is the national court which must consider whether the national rule reduces the possibilities of recovery which would otherwise have been available, since the Court has no jurisdiction to interpret national law.

Enforcement actions

In the case where a preliminary ruling is involved, it will ultimately be the national judge who will review the compatibility of national law with Community law in a concrete dispute between an individual and national authorities or between two or more individuals. According to Article 169 EEC, it is the Commission of the European Communities which starts the proceedings against a Member State and it is the Court of Justice which passes the final judgement. Under the EEC Treaty, Article 155, the Commission is entrusted with the task of ensuring the application of the Treaties and the measures, for example directives, taken by the Community institutions. If the Commission considers that a Member State has failed to fulfil an obligation under Community law, it will start informal consultations with the Member State concerned. If those consultations do not lead to satisfactory results, the Commission will deliver a formal notice describing the points of dispute and formally requiring the State to submit its observations. In practice this request is the beginning of formal discussions, which are often detailed. If possible, the Commission will try to reach an amicable settlement during these discussions. If the Member State is not prepared to accept the Commission's position, the Commission will deliver a reasoned opinion on the matter, granting the Member State a reasonable time-limit to comply with the opinion. If this administrative stage does not culminate in the desired result, the Commission puts the matter before the Court of Justice for a final ruling. The so-called judicial stage starts.

The judgement of the Court is declaratory in nature. If it establishes a failure of the Member State to fulfil an obligation under Community law, the State is, according to Article 171 EEC, obliged to terminate the violation established by the Court. Although the Court may not prescribe specific measures, it may indicate what kind of measures would be needed.

The Commission may start an enforcement action irrespective of the identity of the defaulter. The Member State as such is responsible for breaches of Community law by its organs.[69] Furthermore, the Commission has the discretion to decide whether to act or not. A private individual or an organization may always lodge a complaint with the Commission about an alleged non-fulfilment of Community law obligations by his or her State. However, there is no guarantee that the Commission will act; nor can it be forced to do so.[70] On the other hand, the Commission has the right to continue the case even if implementation is effected in the meantime by the Member State concerned. The argument often put forward by the Member States that once the obligation is fulfilled the Commission has no further interest in the action, has not been accepted by the Court. The Court considers that its judgement:

> may be of substantive interest as establishing the basis of a responsibility that a Member State can incur as a result of its default, as regards other Member States, the Community or private parties.[71]

Anyhow, in many cases the breach by a Member State is terminated during or after the informal consultation or administrative stage or even during the judicial stage. The Commission's action under Article 169 EEC seems to be a useful means to enforce compliance by the Member States with their obligation under Community law.

In the field of sex discrimination the enforcement actions focus on the non-compliance by the Member States with Community directives because, apart from Article 119 of the Treaty, a directive is binding as to the result to be achieved upon the State to which it is addressed, but it leaves to the national authorities the choice of form and methods. In other words a directive requires national implementation, unless existing national legislation already achieves the objective of the directive.[72] Directives usually intend to approximate or harmonize national legislation instead of replacing it by new Community legislation like regulations often do.[73] The basic general provision on approximation of laws is contained in Article 100 of the Treaty which empowers the Council to adopt directives in order to harmonize national laws in so far as the latter directly affect the establishment or functioning of the common market. A considerable number of directives have this provision as basis. Another, quite common, basis is Article 235 of the Treaty.[74] This provision empowers the Council to adopt 'appropriate measures' to attain the objectives of the Community where the Treaty has not provided the necessary powers. In both situations the Council acts on a proposal from the Commission and after having heard the opinion of the European Parliament and eventually the Economic and Social Committee.[75]

The, by now extensive, case-law of the Court on proper implementation of Community law by the Member States contains some general indications with respect to the implementation of directives. First, the sole expiry of the period for implementation is sufficient to declare that the Member State did not comply with its obligations when, at that very moment, the Member State has not enacted the necessary measures.[76] Constitutional, administrative, legislative or political problems are not accepted as valid excuses.[77]

Second, the directive must be implemented by means of national provisions of a binding nature which ensure effective application of the directive within the national legal order. If the implementation of a directive requires an amendment of existing legislation, the measures implementing it must have the same legal force as the legislation at issue.[78] A mere administrative practice does not amount to implementation.

Third, the implementing measures must be sufficiently precise, clear and transparent; the persons concerned must be made fully aware of their rights and, where appropriate, afforded the possibility of relying on these measures before the national courts.[80] The right of individuals to rely on directly effective Community provision is not sufficient to ensure full and complete implementation. In other words, direct effect is no excuse for the Member State which did not implement the directive properly. Moreover, when a provision of national law is incompatible with a directly effective provision of Community law, and is retained unchanged or not abolished, this creates an ambiguous situation, by keeping the persons concerned in a state of uncertainty and amounts to a failure by the Member State to comply with its Community obligations.[81]

Conclusions

As concerns the protection of an individual considering him or herself to be discriminated on grounds of sex contrary to Community law, the following conclusions may be reached.

The person concerned may bring the case before the competent national court invoking one or more provisions of Community law. If the provision has direct effect, the national court is bound to apply this provision to the case before it, leaving a contrary national rule, if there is any, out of consideration. Treaty provisions may be invoked against the public authorities and against private parties. On the other hand, provisions of directives have no horizontal direct effect. Then the only possibility is to sue the State because of wrongful legislation where this is possible according to the constitutional provisions of the State concerned. A provision has direct effect if it leaves no real discretion to the Member State as to the result to be achieved or, in other words, if it is unconditional and sufficiently precise. But, even if the provision leaves discretion to the implementing authorities, an individual may invoke it. The national court then is under the legal duty to interpret national law – irrespective of whether or not the national rule is enacted in pursuance of Community law – in such a way as to give full effect to the objective of the Community law provision. Such concurring interpretation may apply to a relationship between two individuals and consequently it remedies to a certain extent the lack of horizontal direct effect of directives.

Finally, the national court is under the duty to review national law to establish whether or not the national authorities exceeded the margin of appreciation left by the directive. If this is the case, and a concurring interpretation is not possible, the national court should not apply the national provision as the national authorities acted *ultra vires*. Sometimes the plain non-application of a discriminatory rule will be just what the individual wanted to reach. But if he or she wants something positive, this approach will not always be helpful. Then it depends on the formulation of the disputed rule and the competence of the national court whether the action will lead to the desired result.

The Court of Justice plays a prominent part within the national proceedings dealing with matters of Community law. In its preliminary rulings the Court often gives unexpected solutions to problems and its interpretation of Community law is much more far-reaching than it probably would be if left to national courts. Therefore it is important to the parties concerned to stimulate the national court in referring preliminary questions to the Court.

Another important instrument to enforce community equality law is the power of the Commission to start proceedings under Article 169. The judgement and interpretation given by the Court in an enforcement action may have considerable impact on national legislation and may be very useful in other national or even preliminary proceedings.

Notes

1   Case 26/62 *Van Gend en Loos* v. *Nederlandse administratie der belastingen* (1963) E.C.R. 1, p. 12.
2   Compare Schermers and Waelbroeck (1987) pp. 105–110.
3   See for an outline of the relevant constitutional provisions of the nine Member States Bebr (1981) pp. 616–633.
4   Case 6/64 (1964) E.C.R. p. 585.
5   *Ibid.* p. 594.
6   Kapteyn, VerLoren van Themaat (1989) p. 45 (respectively (1973) p. 30).
7   See for instance case 57/65 *Lütticke* v. *Hauptzollamt Saarlouis* (1966) E.C.R. 205 and case 41/74 *Van Duyn* v. *Home Office* (1974) E.C.R. 1337. In cases concerning directives, the Court uses a different formula, i.e. 'that the provisions may be relied upon by an individual as against any national provision...' See case 8/81 *Becker* v. *Finanzamt Münster-Innenstadt* (1982) E.C.R. 53.
8   Compare case 57/65, *loc. cit.* note 7. See also Timmermans (1979) p. 540.
9   See on these requirements Bebr (1981) pp. 566–581 and Hartley (1988), pp. 186–195.
10 Compare Timmermans (1979) p. 540.
11 See case 27/67 *Fink-Frucht* v. *Hauptzollamt München-Landbergstrasse* (1968) E.C.R. 223.
12 See also Chapter 1, p. 15 and Chapter 3, p. 49. The Janus-faced Article 119 is, however, exceptional since it can be both directly effective or not. Its direct effect seems to depend on the particular case before the courts. With respect to other Treaty provision the Court chose a more straightforward approach.
13 Case 12/81 *Garland* v. *British Rail Engineering* (1982) E.C.R. p. 359, discussed in Chapter 3, p. 70.
14 *Ibid.* p. 370.
15 Compare case 43/75 *Defrenne* v. *Sabena* (1976) E.C.R. 455 and case 129/79 *Macarthys* v. *Smith* (1979) E.C.R. 1275, both discussed in Chapter 3, p. 49 and p. 77 respectively.
16 Case 41/74, *loc. cit.* note 7.
17 *Ibid.* p. 1348.
18 Compare Timmermans (1979) p. 539.
19 In very clear terms case 71/85 *State of the Netherlands* v. *Federatie Nederlandse Vakbeweging*, (1986) E.C.R. 3855, discussed in Chapter 5, p. 185.
20 See in particular case 8/81, *loc. cit.* note 7.
21 Treaty provisions which are directly addressed to private parties, i.e. enterprises, are for instance Articles 85 and 86.
22 See case 43/75 (Defrenne II), *loc. cit.* note 15, case 36/74 *Walrave* v. *Union Cycliste Internationale* (1974) E.C.R. 1405 and case 13/76 *Dona* v. *Mantero* (1976) E.C.R. 1333.
23 See for instance Easson (1979), Wyatt (1983), Timmermans (1979), Nicolaysen (1984).
24 Case 152/84 *Marshall* v. *Southampton and South West Hampshire Area Health Authority* (1986) E.C.R. 723, discussed in Chapter 4, p. 122.
25 *Ibid.* p. 749.
26 *Ibid.* See also case 224/84 *Johnston* v. *Royal Ulster Constabulary* (1986) E.C.R. 1651, discussed in Chapter 4, p. 130.

27   Decision of the Industrial Tribunal in Glasgow, of 23 September 1986 (unreported). See also *Rolls Royce plc* v. *Doughty* (1988) 1 CMLRep 569 and *Foster* v. *British Gas* (1988) 2 CMLRep 697, discussed in Chapter 6, p. 224. Foster has now been referred to the European Court for a preliminary ruling. See case 188/89 *Foster et al.* v. *British Gas* (not yet decided) O.J.C160/11, 27 June 1989.

28   The activities of Dutch universities do, however, not differ considerably from those in the UK. It may be asked whether the activities performed are an appropriate criterion for deciding the issue of direct effect.

29   Case 6/64, *loc. cit.* note 4.

30   See for instance case 14/68 *Walt Wilhelm* v. *Bundeskartellamt* (1969) E.C.R. 1.

31   Case 11/70 *Internationale Handelsgesellschaft* v. *Einfuhr- und Vorratsstelle für Getreide und Futtermittel* (1970) E.C.R. 1125.

32   *Ibid.* p. 1134.

33   Case 106/77 *Amministrazione delle Finanze dello Stato* v. *Simmenthal* (1978) E.C.R. 629.

34   Judgement of 22 October 1975, reported in RTDE (1976) p. 396.

35   Case 106/77, *loc. cit.* note 33, p. 644.

36   Case 51/76 *Verbond van Nederlandse Ondernemingen* v. *Inspecteur der Invoerrechten en Accijnzen* (1977) E.C.R. 113 and case 38/77 *Enka* v. *Inspecteur der Invoerrechten en Accijnzen* (1977) E.C.R. 2203.

37   *Ibid.* p. 127 and p. 2211 respectively.

38   Case 21/78 *Delkvist* v. *Anklagemijndigheden* (1978) E.C.R. 2327.

39   Compare Timmermans (1979) p. 550.

40   Case 262/84 *Beets-Proper* v. *van Lanschot Bankiers* (1986) E.C.R. 773, discussed in Chapter 4, p. 123. See for 'concurring' interpretation by the Hoge Raad Chapter 6, p. 242. As other examples can be mentioned case 110/84 *Gemeente Hillegom* v. *Hillenius* (1985) E.C.R. 3947 and case 24/85 *Spijkers* v. *Benedik* (1986) E.C.R. 1119. The concept of 'concurring interpretation' is sometimes referred to as 'the indirect effect of directives' in the UK; see Fitzpatrick (1987) and Chapter 6 below p. 221.

41   (1982) 2 All ER 402, discussed in Chapter 6, p. 212.

42   *Ibid.* p. 415.

43   (1988) 2 All ER 803, discussed in Chapter 6, p. 218.

44   Case 14/83 *Von Colson and Kamann* v. *Land Nordrhein-Westfalen* (1984) E.C.R. 1891 and case 79/83 *Harz* v. *Deutsche Tradax* (1984) E.C.R. 1921, discussed in Chapter 4, p.135–38.

45   *Ibid.* p. 1909 and p. 1942.

46   Case 224/84, *loc. cit.* note 26.

47   Case 80/86 *Officier van Justitie* v. *Kolpinghuis* [1989] 2 *CMLR* 18.

48   Conclusion in case 152/84 (Marshall), *loc. cit.* note 24, p. 733.

49   Case 80/86, *loc. cit.* Note 47.

50   *Loc. cit.* note 47, consideration 15.

51   Case 63/83 *Kent Kirk* v. *Regina* (1984) E.C.R 2689.

52   On the contents of this Community principle see, for instance, report of Pescatore for the 12th FIDE Congress (1986), p. 26 *et seq.*

53   (1986) CMLRep 730.

54   (1979) ICR 558.

55   Case 152/84, *loc. cit.* note 24.

56   (1987) CMLRep 24.

57   Case 166/73 *Rheinmühlen* v. *Einfuhr- und Vorratsstelle für Getreide und Futtermittel* (1974) E.C.R. 33.

58   *Ibid.* p. 38.

59   *Duke* v. *GEC Reliance Ltd.* (1988) 1 All ER 626. See for a more detailed discussion Chapter 6, p. 227.

60   Joined cases 28–30/62 *Da Costa en Schaake* v. *Nederlandse administratie der belastingen* (1963) E.C.R. 31, p. 38.

61   See case 283/81 *CILFIT* v. *Ministero della Sanita* (1982) E.C.R. 3415, in which

the Court accepted 'acte clair', but only under specific and rather restricted conditions.

62   The most notorious example is probably the decision of the French Conseil d'Etat of 22 December 1978 in case *Cohn-Bendit* (1980) 1 CMLRep 543.

63   In a recent judgement, the Court made clear that it is within its exclusive competence to declare Community Acts invalid. See case 314/85 *Foto-Frost* v. *Hauptzollampt Lübeck-Ost* (1988) 3 CMLR 57.

64   See case 43/75, *loc. cit.* note 15, and more recently case 24/86 *Blaizot* v. *Université de Liège et al.*, (1989) 1 CMLR 57.

65   See case 309/85 *Barra* v. *Belgium and City of Liège* (1988) 2 CMLR 409.

66   Case 293/83, *Gravier* v. *Ville de Liège et al.* (1985) E.C.R. 593.

67   See for an illicit limitation the judgement of the President of the Irish High Court of 10 June 1988 in case McCotter (unreported), discussed in Chapter 6, p. 231.

68   Case 240/87 *Deville* v. *Administration des Impôts*, judgement of 29 June 1988 (not yet reported).

69   See Case 77/69 *Commission* v. *Belgium* (1970) E.C.R. 237. The court held that '... the liability of a Member State under Article 169 arises whatever the agency of the State whose action or inaction is the cause of the failure to fulfil its obligations, even in the case of a constitutionally independent institution.'

70   See case 48/65 *Lütticke* v. *Commission* (1966) E.C.R. 19.

71   See case 39/72 *Commission* v. *Italy* (1973) E.C.R. 101, p. 112.

72   See for example case 248/83 *Commission* v. *FRG* (1985) E.C.R. 1459, discussed in Chapter 4, p. 145.

73   Directives are often associated with harmonization of laws. They are however not the only instrument. Approximation may sometimes be envisaged in, for instance, a regulation or a treaty.

74   Or a directive may be based on two or more provisions, depending on the subject matter concerned.

75   The opinion of the Parliament is always obligatory under Article 235; under Article 100 it is obligatory when the directive implies that the national legislation of one or more Member States must be amended. The opinion of the Committee is obligatory only in the latter situation.

76   See case 10/76 *Commission* v. *Italy* (1976) E.C.R. 1359.

77   See case 163/78 *Commission* v. *Italy* (1979) E.C.R. 771.

78   See case 168/85 *Commission* v. *Italy* (1986) E.C.R. 2945.

79   *Ibid.*

80   See case 29/84 *Commission* v. *FRG* (1985) E.C.R. 1661.

81   See case 167/73 *Commission* v. *France* (1974) E.C.R. 359.

3 Equal Pay

Any discussion of equal pay in European Community law must start with Article 119 of the Treaty of Rome. Article 119 relates to the principle of equal pay and provides:

> Each Member State shall during the first stage ensure and subsequently maintain the application of the principle that men and women should receive equal pay for equal work.
>
> For the purpose of this Article 'pay' means the ordinary basic or minimum wage or salary and any other consideration, whether in cash or in kind, which the worker receives, directly or indirectly, in respect of his employment from his employer.
>
> Equal pay without discrimination based on sex means:
> (a) that pay for the same work at piece rates shall be calculated on the basis of the same unit of measurement;
> (b) that pay for work at time rates shall be the same for the same job.

However, this is not the only legal provision dealing with equal pay in Community law. Directive 75/117/EEC on the approximation of laws of the Member States relating to the application of the principle of equal pay for men and women was adopted by the Council in 1975.[1]

This chapter will examine both these provisions and the case-law to which they have given rise.

Article 119

Article 119 appears in Title III of the Treaty of Rome which relates to social policy. Chapter 1 of that title provides for a Community programme of action in the social field, in particular as regards working conditions and employees' rights. Article 119 stands out from the other articles in this particular part of the Treaty for its explicitness. Other articles provide for action to be taken to determine particular standards, whereas Article 119 itself provides both the standard and the timetable by which the standard is to be achieved.

This distinction is not accidental and the reason for it is explained by the origin of the provisions in the Treaty.[2] Article 119 is based on ILO Convention No. 100 concerning equal remuneration for men and women workers for work of equal value.[3] The two provisions share many common features and are drafted in almost the same terms. Three of the original Member States of the Community had ratified this Convention and three had not on the grounds that it would create difficulties for them in their legal systems. France had ratified the ILO Convention and was instrumental in inserting Article 119 into the Treaty of Rome.

It may not be readily apparent what equal pay has to do with a common market but its relevance is explained by its double objective. Equal pay is a social issue but it is also an economic one, and the States who were engaged in setting up the European Economic Community were particularly interested in ensuring that no member could enhance its competitiveness by relying on a pool of cheap labour – women. Thus, equal pay is a different issue than is the approximation of general working conditions and, for this reason, Article 119 is more explicit in the obligations which it imposes on Member States.

It is this explicitness which has made Article 119 into a very lively source of action within the Community legal system and within several of the Member States since its terms first led the pioneering Gabrielle Defrenne to seek to rely on it in her actions against Belgium and her employer, Sabena, in the Belgian courts. To do this she had of course, to demonstrate the direct effects of Article 119 and to elucidate its scope. She attempted to do this in three successive cases, and she has been joined by several others.

The direct effects of Article 119

The doctrine of direct effects in European Community law has already been examined.[4] It is worthwhile, however, reiterating the importance of the principle to the individual. The doctrine of direct effects allows individuals to rely on Community law as a source of rights which are then applied in the domestic courts. It was crucial, therefore, to determine whether Article 119 gave rise to direct effects so that women could argue for equal pay in the courts and tribunals of the Member States relying on their 'enforceable Community rights' and not be dependent on any implementing legislation adopted by the state concerned.

The question of the direct effects of Article 119 was not faced head on until the second *Defrenne* case,[5] although the Advocate General in the first *Defrenne* case had come to the conclusion that Article 119 was capable of creating rights for individuals.[6] The Defrenne cases concerned differences in the conditions of service for male cabin stewards and female air hostesses working for the Belgian state airline, Sabena. Ms Defrenne unsuccessfully argued in her first case before the Belgian Conseil d'Etat that a Belgian Royal Decree concerning pensions and survivors' pensions for cabin staff infringed Article 119.[7] The Conseil d'Etat requested a preliminary ruling on the matter but did not raise the question of direct effects. Accordingly the Court did not address itself to the issue, although the Advocate General did broach the subject and, after comparing the precise wording of Article 119 with the more generalized provisions of Articles 117 and 118, concluded that Article 119 was capable of giving rise to individual rights. He argued, referring to the conference of Member States which had extended the date by which equal pay was to be achieved, that from 31 December 1964, at least, Article 119 was directly effective.[8]

A few years after this judgement Ms Defrenne again raised an action in the Belgian courts. This time her action was before the Tribunal du Travail in Brussels and she demanded compensation for losses in salary, allowance on termination of service and arrears of pension arising out of the fact that men and women cabin staff did not receive equal pay. This Tribunal dismissed her claim and she appealed to the Cour du Travail. This latter court discussed two heads of her claim but on the claim for arrears of salary the court requested a preliminary ruling on the following questions:

1.   Does Article 119 give rise to direct effects; if so, from what date?
2.   How has Article 119 become applicable in the Member States, by virtue of EEC measures or by national legislation?

The observations submitted to the Court are extremely detailed and show an absolute divergence of views as to the direct effects of Article 119. Ms Defrenne argued for the recognition of direct effects as Article 119 imposes a duty to bring about a specific result during the first phase of the transitional period. Article 119 neither requires nor rules out specific implementing measures by either the Community or the Member States. Furthermore, she argued, the terms of the article are precise so that employees do not have to wait for implementing measures to be adopted and the fact that States *may* adopt provisions of legal, economic or administrative nature is irrelevant. Ms Defrenne then pointed out that the fact that Article 119 was addressed to States did not mean that individuals could not benefit from it, and that the article could only be effective if individuals could rely on it in their national courts. Thus Article 119 'must be regarded as having effect. It must therefore be complied with by the national courts in the actions before them and it gives to nationals individual rights which they may invoke before the competent courts or tribunals'.[9] As to the date on which these rights came into existence, Ms Defrenne argued that this was from the date of ratification of the Treaty and that a conference of Member States which introduced a new timetable was incompetent to amend the Treaty.

The government of the UK intervened in the case to argue that Article 119 did not meet the requirements of precision and clarity which were necessary to determine if a provision of Community law did have direct effects. The UK pointed to the lack of definition of the principle of equal pay for equal work and argued that the very fact that Directive 75/117 had been adopted to explain this concept underscored the lack of clarity and precision in the article itself. Neither, argued the UK was the concept of pay clear and again the Directive was adopted to explain the concept and to allow Member States a discretion in working out the practical details of implementation. Further, problems arose as to fixing the comparators to be used in determining equal value claims, and in deciding which aspects of pay were to be included. Thus, the requirement of precision was not satisfied. The UK did, however, concede the unconditional nature of the obligation imposed by Article 119. The need for further legislation in the form of Directive 75/117 and subsequent national legislation led the UK to argue that Article 119 was incomplete. In view of these matters Article 119 could not have direct effects. Furthermore the UK argued that a finding of direct effects would lead to uncertainty in existing legal relations between employers and employees and place intolerable economic burdens on employers. The UK then argued against the horizontal direct effects of Article 119 on the ground that it imposed an obligation merely on the State concerned and not on individuals.

The government of Ireland agreed that the Court should not attribute direct effects to Article 119. Some of the Irish arguments were similar to those put forward by the UK, in particular as regards the imprecise nature of the provision, and the dire economic consequences which would arise following a finding of direct effects. However, the Irish government put forward other, more interesting, arguments. Analysing previous decisions of the Court, the Irish found that direct effect had only been attributed to provisions in the Treaty whose aim was to attain one of the fundamental freedoms of the Treaty whose object was to benefit the Community rather than a particular class of persons, and 'in no instance do they involve direct intervention in contractual relationships between individual persons'.[10] In other words direct effects is a matter of public, not private, law.[11]

In its arguments, the Commission drew a distinction between what it termed the immediate effect of Article 119 and its direct application. It argued that the Article could not have immediate effect due to the time limitations imposed in the Article which were subsequently extended by the conference of Member States. Once these time limits had expired Article 119 was capable of creating rights between an individual and the state but it was not capable of creating direct effects in relations between individuals, since Article 119 imposes an obligation on States alone to ensure implementation of the principle of equal pay.

On the second question raised, as to the finding of which provision of Community law introduced the principle of equal pay, Ms Defrenne was in no doubt. 'As regards the principle of equal pay' she argued, 'that law is entirely contained in Article 119'.[12] Directive 75/117 merely elaborated details. Both the UK and Ireland argued that the Community principle of equal pay could only be implemented by national measures. The Commission agreed with this view in so far as relations between individual persons were concerned although the national legislatures were bound by the provisions both of Article 119 and the Directive.

Addressing himself to both questions posed by the Cour du Travail, Advocate General Trabucchi, in a closely reasoned opinion, argued for the direct effects of Article 119. He first pointed to the unconditional nature of the provision whose purpose is clear. He agreed that certain aspects of Article 119 required clarification by the national courts but reminded the Court that this in itself was not a bar to a finding of direct effects since the national court, if faced with difficulties in interpretation, could use the Article 177 procedure to request interpretation by the European Court. As to the test of precision, he pointed out that in any particular case whether work is the same is a question of fact but the principle, that of equal pay for equal work, was sufficiently precise to cover all such possible cases. At that stage the Advocate General concluded that Article 119 met the requirements of unconditionality, clarity and precision. The fact that the obligation lay on Member States did not prevent a provision from having direct effects when 'the obligation is expressed clearly and unconditionally, its tenor is precise and no real discretion is left with the Member States with respect to the application of the principle'.[13] Addressing himself to the date on which the principle of equal pay was to take effect he categorized the resolution of the conference of Member States as a political act which was incapable of amending the Treaty rules. Therefore Article 119 imposed an obligation on the Member States to implement the principle within the time limits laid down in the Treaty.

Taking on board the arguments of the intervening States as regards the effects of the provision in relationships between individuals, the Advocate General contended that these arguments misconceived the very basic principles of Community law. It was immaterial to examine the person to whom the obligation was addressed as the determining factor was the spirit, wording and scheme of the provision itself. In this context it only makes sense to attribute direct effects to Article 119 in every employment relationship since that was the clear meaning. Advocate General Trabucchi then underlined the importance of Article 119 in the context of the Treaty, stressing that the principle of equal treatment forms part of the core of fundamental rights which the Court must protect. He then dismissed the argument based on cost as having no relevance in law.

The judgement of the Court was as unequivocal as the opinion of the Advocate General. It first stated that the direct effect of Article 119 could only be considered in the light of the nature of the principle of equal pay and in the context of its place in the Treaty. The Court explained that Article 119 pursued both an economic aim, the aim of avoiding the existence of a pool of cheap labour in the Community, and a social aim and thus showed that the principle of equal pay forms a foundation of the Community. The Court then drew a distinction:

> within the whole area of application of Article 119 between, first, direct and overt discrimination which may be identified solely with the aid of the criteria based on equal work and equal pay referred to by the article in question and, secondly indirect and disguised discrimination which can only be identified by reference to more explicit implementing provisions of a Community or national character. It is impossible not to recognise that the complete implementation of the aim pursued by Article 119, by means of the elimination of all discrimination, direct or indirect, between men and women workers, not only as regards individual undertakings but also entire branches of industry and even of the economic system as a whole, may in certain cases involve the elaboration of criteria whose implementation necessitates the taking of appropriate measures at Community and national level.[14]

This crucial passage subsequently created a great deal of confusion in cases relating to direct and indirect discrimination but it could be interpreted as saying that Article 119 had its limitations and could not of itself solve the whole problem of inequality of pay for men and women for, as the Advocate General had pointed out:

> Discrimination against women is, in fact, often disguised by the pay structure, the classification or description of work, the special characteristics of labour in certain spheres, not to mention inequalities due to job training or promotion systems and general working conditions.[15]

If this interpretation is correct then the Court was merely saying that Article 119 was not in itself sufficient to achieve the principle of equal pay and that other measures may have to be adopted both by the Community institutions and the Member States to realize the principle.[16] However, this did not mean that in the situations covered by the article the national courts were unable to apply a Community principle of equal pay. The Court dismissed the view that the term 'principle' as contained in Article 119 indicated a weakness in the article. A 'principle' for the Court did not mean a vague declaration but rather a fundamental provision. As to the argument that a provision addressed to a Member State could not give rise to direct effects, the Court, following its own previous decisions, stated that the fact that an obligation is formally addressed to a Member State does not 'prevent rights from being conferred at the same time on any individual who has an interest in the performance of the duties thus laid down'.[17] Thus, the Court argued, the courts of the Member States were free to apply the principle of equal pay and this was so whether in cases involving public authorities or in cases relating to 'all agreements which are intended to regulate paid labour collectively, as well as to contracts between individuals'.[18] In the light of all these considerations the Court declared Article 119 to have (horizontal) direct effects.

In the second part of its judgement the Court addressed itself to the relationship between Article 119 and subsequent Community acts. It declared Article 119 to have been directly effective at the end of the transitional period, 1 January 1962 for the old Member States, and since 1 January 1973 for the new Member States. The resolution of the Member States purporting to extend this timetable was ineffective to make any such modifications. Neither could the adoption of Directive 75/117 modify either the timetable set out in Article 119 or its direct effects.

The Court did take on board the arguments advanced by the intervening governments as to the financial consequences of its decision. However, it did not consider that financial considerations alone were sufficient to alter the temporal effects of its judgement. It also took into account the fact that employers had been led to believe, both by the actions of certain States and by the failure of the Commission to institute proceedings against such States, that Article 119 did not create rights for individuals. It therefore decided, in the interest of legal certainty affecting both public and private interests, not to reopen the question as regards the past but to declare that:

> the direct effect of Article 119 cannot be relied on in order to support claims concerning pay periods prior to the date of this judgement,[19] except as regards those workers who have already brought legal proceedings or made an equivalent claim.[20]

In many respects this *Defrenne* judgement has been the most crucial of all the judgements given by the Court in the area of equal pay. Without it employees would have been unable to plead Article 119 as a source of law before their national courts and tribunals, and Member States would not have been given an incentive to put their houses in order and bring their legislation into line with Community standards.[21] Given the reluctance evidenced by the Member States to realize the principle of equal pay, this latter point is important. A finding of direct effects gave employees an immediate right whereas the Member States had in the past delayed affording that right to them. The Court therefore provided a by-pass mechanism for those employees willing to use it.

As soon as employees began to plead Article 119 in their cases before their courts and tribunals it was inevitable that problems of interpretation would arise. As had been indicated in the second *Defrenne* case, there was much in Article 119 which needed clarification. The Advocate General had predicted these difficulties but had pointed to the solution – where a problem of interpretation arises the national court should stay the proceedings and request the European Court for a preliminary ruling on a specific point. In this way the scope of Article 119 could be accurately defined and Community law could be uniformly applied. Subsequently there have been a number of such requests and they fall broadly into three separate issues: the definition of pay, the definition of equal work, and indirect discrimination.

What is pay?

Article 119 defines pay as 'the ordinary basic or minimum wage or salary and any other consideration, whether in cash or in kind, which the worker receives, directly or indirectly, in respect of his employment from his employer'. This definition follows very closely ILO Convention No. 100 which defines remuneration in the following way:

> the term 'remuneration' includes the ordinary, basic or minimum wage or salary and any additional emoluments whatsoever payable directly or indirectly, whether in cash or in kind, by the employer to the worker and arising out of the worker's employment.

Both these definitions appear to be quite precise and, indeed, are intended to cover all eventualities. However, one of the most frequently raised problems before the European Court has been on the question of the scope of the concept of pay.

This issue was raised in the first *Defrenne* case,[22] that is, before the European Court had declared Article 119 to be capable of giving rise to direct effects and the question put to the European Court was whether:

> the retirement pension granted under the terms of the social security financed by contributions from workers, employers and by State subsidy, constitute a consideration which the worker receives indirectly in respect of his employment from his employer?[23]

Ms Defrenne pursued two arguments. She first stated that the concept of 'salary' had come, in modern law, to encompass both the direct salary and the indirect or social salary. The former includes payment for the work performed, whereas the latter includes such benefits as family allowances, paid holidays and retirement pensions. Retirement pensions arise out of the employment relationship, and in her particular situation the pension was funded by contributions from employers and employees but not from the Belgian state. Her pension was, therefore, deferred pay. She then argued that the principle of equality enshrined in Article 119 applied to all conditions of employment.

Belgium argued for a narrower interpretation on the grounds that

Article 119 pursued merely an economic objective and not a social one and, therefore, related only to pay – defined as 'the certain and periodical contractual counterpart paid by the employer to the worker by reason of the work done'.[24] Retirement pensions did not fall within this definition as they relate more to the social security system which requires employers to adopt pension schemes.

The Commission agreed with the Belgian State arguing that there is a legal distinction between the direct salary and the 'salary for non-active status'.[25] The former only is covered by Article 119. The Commission based its arguments on ILO Convention No. 100, as well as on its own previous statements addressed to the Member States and the European Parliament. The Commission argued that Article 119 related only to pay and not to all matters relating to employment.

In his opinion Advocate General Dutheillet de Lamothe pointed out that Article 119 adopted a middle way between the definitions of either the salary as 'price of a service' and 'social salary'.[26] He pointed out that Article 119 refers to the salary properly so called and in addition to any other consideration which the worker receives if it is paid directly or indirectly by his or her employer and it is in respect of his or her employment. He therefore suggested the Court should examine a particular pension scheme to see if it fell within this definition. He excluded, by definition, general pension schemes which are paid to all workers under a national social security system; these pensions are not pay in the sense of Article 119. However, he then defined certain schemes which could be said to fall within Article 119. First, he identified those pensions which the person receives direct from his or her employer. Such a pension is deferred salary which the person receives as a result of occupying a certain post. Second, he identified 'supplemental' pensions which a person receives in addition to that which he or she receives from the general social security scheme. These are paid for by the employer and the employee, but this does not detract from the fact that the employer's contribution is pay since the necessary link between the employer, the pension fund and the employee is established. The Advocate General therefore identified two criteria which can be used to determine whether a pension scheme falls within the scope of Article 119. First, there must be a relationship between the employer's contribution and the benefit received. This relationship might sometimes be clear, but not always. This criterion follows from the wording of Article 119 which reads 'any consideration which the worker receives, directly or indirectly'. The second criterion also arises from the wording of Article 119 and relates to the fact that the worker receives the remuneration 'in respect of his employment from his employer'. Thus the pension must arise out of the employment relationship between an employee and a particular employer in respect of a job performed.

A more difficult question is raised in special schemes of social security where private pension funds are closely tied to those of the general state scheme but which provide particular advantages for certain employees on their retirement. The scheme operated by Sabena which was the subject of the present dispute fell into this category. The crucial difference between such a scheme and the two previously mentioned related to the fact that the employer plays no part in determining the right to or amount of the pension, and they do not fall within the scope of Article 119 since not even an indirect link exists between the employer's contribution and the benefit. These factors are determined by the social security system of which the special scheme is part. Moreover, the Advocate General argued that the special schemes are closely and intimately linked with the general scheme; they may be part of the general system, but not necessarily. In these cases payment of the pension is made by the same funds as the general scheme or, when payment is made by special funds, these funds are financially and administratively linked with the institutions of the general scheme and often depend on them.[27] Such pensions are not covered by Article 119 but fall to be coordinated under the rules laid down in Article 118.

In its judgement the Court gave no general definition of what constitutes pay although it allowed that consideration in the nature of social security benefits is not alien to the concept of pay. However, the Court did not accept that:

> social security schemes or benefits, in particular retirement pensions, directly governed by legislation without any element of agreement within the undertaking or the occupational branch concerned, which are obligatorily applicable to general categories of workers...[28]

could fall within the concept of pay as defined in Article 119. The Court argued that these schemes are governed not by the employment relationship but by considerations of social policy and as such could not be considered as pay. The Court then went on to equate the scheme under consideration, that is a special scheme, with the type of general pension scheme which it had declared to be outside the scope of Article 119. The Court held, therefore, that the special scheme fell outside the scope of Article 119.

This decision of the Court was unfortunate in that it places those employees whose employers operate a special scheme in a less advantageous position than employees in other spheres. In this instance Ms Defrenne received certain benefits because of her employment as an air hostess with Sabena. The Court held, however, that the link between the employer's contribution and the benefit received was insufficient to bring the scheme within the ambit of Article 119. Why the Court decided that this was the case is unclear, since no reasons were given for excluding special schemes, other than the equation of them with general schemes.

The consequences of the decision fall heavily on those employees who happen to be employed by employers who have such a scheme; very often these are people employed in the public sector or in semi-public institutions such as Sabena. People in this situation may not rely on Article 119 whereas others may do so. The fact that such schemes are governed by legislation is irrelevant; this is insufficient in itself to transform a special scheme into a general scheme. It is also irrelevant that it is the government or a government agency who is the employer. Where a person is employed under these circumstances the government agency is an employer and not part of the social security system.

The decision can also be criticized from another point of view since it makes the applicability of Article 119 dependent on the national organization of pension schemes, or even on the choice of the employer, as to the kind of scheme which is adopted. Such an approach lessens the impact of Article 119 considerably.[29]

The issue of pensions was not solved by this case for, as the Advocate General had pointed out, certain types of pension schemes may constitute pay whereas others do not. This particular matter was raised again before the European Court in a preliminary reference from the English Court of Appeal (Civil Division). *Worringham*[30] concerned a contracted-out retirement scheme, membership of which was compulsory for all employees of Lloyds Bank. Advocate General Warner explained to the Court the basic characteristics of such a scheme:

> The legislation governing the British social security system (principally the Social Security Act 1975 and the Social Security Pensions Act 1975) provides for retirement pensions to consist of two elements, a basic component, which is the same for everyone, and a variable earnings related component.
>
> Such pensions are payable out of the National Insurance Fund, which is fed by contributions from earners, employers and the Treasury. The principle of the earnings related component is that the more a person earns, the more he and his employer contribute and the more he receives by way of pension on retirement. Part III of the Social Security Pensions Act 1975 provides for what has been described as a 'partnership' between the State social security scheme and independent occupational pension schemes such as those here in question. Where an occupational pension scheme fulfils requirements laid down in the Act, its members may be 'contracted out' of the earnings related part of the State scheme.[31]

Lloyds Bank provided two separate contracted-out schemes, one for men and one for women which were essentially the same. However, there were two differences between the schemes. The men's scheme, but not the women's, provided for the payment of pensions to a surviving spouse and children. The second, more complicated, difference was explained in the case in the following way:

Male and female employees who leave Lloyd's service before completion of five years' service or attaining the age of 26 are entitled:
–either to the transfer of the accrued rights to another approved retirement benefits scheme, or
–to the payment by Lloyds to the State of the 'contributions equivalent premium' which places the employee in the same position that he or she would have been in in the State scheme had he or she been a member of the State scheme instead of a member of the particular retirement benefits scheme.

In the latter case, where the employer pays the contribution equivalent premium, the employee is entitled to a refund of his or her past contributions to the particular scheme with interest. However, precisely on this point differences arise between the two schemes in question.

By the terms of the men's retirement benefits scheme all male staff are required to contribute 5% of their salary to the fund from the commencement of their employment and regardless of their age: the amount of that contribution is considered as part of the employee's 'salary'. By the terms of the women's retirement benefits scheme all female staff are required to contribute 5% of their salary to the fund but only upon attaining the age of 25.

Moreover since the amount of the 5% increment is incorporated in the total amount of 'a week's pay', a man receives indirect advantages which are not enjoyed by a woman. In fact, in so far as collateral benefits are calculated on the basis of 'a week's pay' (unemployment benefits, redundancy payments, credit facilities, etc.) the fact that the 5% contribution is incorporated in that pay gives a man under 25 higher benefits than those to which a woman under 25 is entitled.[32]

One of the most crucial issues here was the fact that the employer added the 5 per cent contribution to the man's wage and then immediately deducted it to be paid into the men's retirement benefits scheme.

Worringham and Humphreys, two female employees of Lloyds Bank, complained to an Industrial Tribunal that this scheme violated the Equal Pay Act 1970 but their appeal was rejected. The Employment Appeal Tribunal upheld their claim as being a violation of the 1970 Act and the Bank thereafter appealed to the Court of Appeal. That Court referred several questions to the European Court relating to Article 119, Directive 75/117 and the equal treatment Directive, 76/207. Essentially the Appeal Court asked whether the contributions paid by the employer and the benefits received were 'pay' within the meaning of Article 119 or were 'remuneration' within the meaning of Article 1 of Directive 75/117/EEC and, if so, whether either provision created enforceable Community rights for the individuals in this particular case. The Appeal Court then asked the European Court to rule whether, if the answers to its previous questions were negative, these same contributions and benefits fell within the scope of equal working conditions contained in Articles 1 and 5 of Directive 76/207.

Lloyds submitted evidence to show that actuarial statistics pointed to the need to have different schemes for men and women, given their different behaviour patterns and life expectancy. Lloyds then went on to argue that since the contributions paid by the employer are received by the trust fund and not the employee then such contributions could not be included in the concept of pay. Furthermore, the benefits which a particular worker receives under the scheme vary depending on the individual circumstances of that worker and therefore 'any attempt to treat the benefits actually received by the worker or his dependants as "pay" or "consideration" with a resultant requirement of equality is an attempt to achieve the impossible'.[33]

Advocate General Warner felt that the contracted-out scheme operated by Lloyds fell outside the scope of Article 119. He based his view on the fact that in the UK contracted-out schemes were closely linked to the general State scheme and, in particular, that they were intended 'not as a supplement to the State social security scheme...but as a substitute for it or for part of it'.[34] To allow that contracted-out schemes did fall within the scope of Article 119 would lead to the anomalous situation of allowing the State scheme to continue to discriminate but to prevent the substitute scheme from discriminating. The Advocate General pointed to the confusion that would arise if the UK were forced to ensure that all contracted-out schemes were consistent with Article 119. This argument, perhaps sound on a practical level, lacks legal credibility.

In its judgement the Court simplified the issue by looking at the essentials of the questions referred to it and ignored all the irrelevant arguments pleaded before it by both Lloyds and the UK government. The Court formulated the question thus:

whether sums of the kind in question paid by the employer in the name of the employee to a retirement benefits scheme by way of an addition to the gross salary come within the concept of 'pay' within the meaning of Article 119 of the Treaty.[35]

Reiterating the definition of pay given in that Article the Court answered that question in the affirmative. It stated:

Sums such as those in question which are included in the calculation of other advantages linked to the salary, such as redundancy payments, unemployment benefits, family allowances and credit facilities form part of the workers' pay within the meaning of the second paragraph of Article 119 of the Treaty even if they are immediately deducted by the employer and paid to a pension fund on behalf of the employee. This applies a fortiori where these sums are refunded in certain circumstances and subject to certain deductions to the employee as being repayable to him if he ceases to belong to the contractual retirements benefits scheme under which they were deducted.[36]

The Court then examined Article 1 of Directive 75/117 and concluded that that Directive in no way affected the concept of 'pay' as defined in Article 1.

On the question of direct effects the Court reaffirmed its previous statements that 'Article 119 of the Treaty applies directly to all forms of discrimination which may be identified solely with the aid of the criteria of equal work and equal pay referred to by the article in question' and, in this particular case:

> the fact that contributions are paid by the employer solely in the name of men and not in the name of women engaged in the same work or work of equal value leads to unequal pay for men and women which the national court may directly establish with the aid of the pay components in question and the criteria laid down in Article 119 of that Treaty.[37]

In coming to this decision the Court could have followed two routes in its arguments. It could have been decided that since there was a difference in the gross pay of men and women the Lloyds scheme was contrary to Article 119. It could have come to this decision on the basis of the economic objective of Article 119 which seeks to eliminate the possibility of using females as a source of cheap labour. Since what matters to the employer is the gross pay; women, under the Lloyds scheme, were cheaper to employ. However, an examination of the Court's judgement reveals that the Court went beyond the gross pay issue to examine wider issues of discrimination. The Court held:

> Although, where women are not required to pay contributions, the salary of men after deduction of the contributions, is comparable to that of women who do not pay contributions, the inequality between the gross salaries of men is nevertheless *a source of discrimination* contrary to Article 119 of the Treaty *since because of that inequality men receive benefits* from which women engaged in the same work or work of equal value are excluded, or receive on that account greater benefits or social advantages than those to which women are entitled.[38] (Emphasis added.)

Thus, the Court pointed to the fact that there were wider issues of discrimination arising out of the difference in gross pay. It seems, therefore, that the Court based its reasons on the social objective by pointing to the fact that it is what the worker gets, or fails to get, that is important, rather than the issue of competitive advantage.

The Court then turned its attention to the temporal effects of its judgement since Lloyds had asked the Court to limit the effects of its judgement as from the date on which the judgement was given as to do otherwise 'would lead, in a case such as the present, to claims for the retrospective adjustment of pay scales covering a period of years'.[39] The

Court, however, refused to restrict the temporal effects of its judgement and distinguished this case from the second *Defrenne* case stating that the special circumstances of that case no longer appertained, particularly as to the knowledge of the direct effects of Article 119 and as to the number of persons affected by the judgement.

The Court, in this judgement, clearly refrained from giving a wide definition of the types of pension schemes which are to be included under the definition of pay, perhaps because of the existence of a wide variety of types of pension schemes in the Member States. Its reluctance may also be due to the fact that, as the UK pointed out in its intervention, the Commission was at the date of judgement in the process of drafting a new directive dealing with discrimination in occupational pension schemes. However, the lack of precise definition gave rise to subsequent problems.

One such problem arose in the case of *Liefting*,[40] a case which brought to light one of the most complicated pension schemes ever to be devised by a government on behalf of its citizens. The case concerns pension rules which apply to public servants in the Netherlands and was brought initially by a number of female civil servants who were married to other civil servants. Under the Dutch rules, public servants receive two pensions. The first, the general old age pension, is deemed to form part of the civil service pension. The second, the civil service pension itself, tops up the basic pension. However, since the civil service pension itself is very high, the retired civil servant receives only a proportion of the basic old age pension. To compensate civil servants for this loss they were not obliged to make any contributions to the scheme while in employment, contributions being paid by the employing authority.

Married couples were treated as one person for the purposes of benefits from and contributions to the basic old age pension. Contributions both for a single person and for a married couple never exceeded a certain limit. In the case of married civil servants both the employer of the husband and the employer of the wife independently paid the contributions. The amount to be contributed depended on the salary so that on some occasions an employer would pay an amount equal to the stated limit. Since a couple was treated as a single entity, the sum of both contributions would often exceed the limit. Therefore the surplus was paid back, to the civil servant concerned by the tax authorities who collected and administered the contributions.[41] To eliminate such 'over-compensation' (as the surplus was called) the Dutch government introduced an administrative system under which employers (state institutions) informed each other about the transfer of contributions for the employee (or the couple). Married couples were required to declare their incomes and the employing authority of the husband paid his contributions up to the stated level and the wife only contributed if the level of the husband's salary was insufficient to require him to pay the maximum contribution. The consequence of this system was that a female civil servant married to a male civil servant had a lower gross salary than her male colleagues since the pension contributions were (and still are) part of the gross salary both in the public and in the private sector. In the private sector, employees paid the contributions themselves whereas, in the public sector, the contributions were paid by the employer, that is, the state.[42]

Nine wives in this position claimed that this system violated the principle of equal pay. They argued that although their take-home pay was the same as that of men, their gross pay, which formerly included contributions made by their employer to the old age pension fund but now did not, was less than that of married men. Relying on *Worringham* they stated that the employer's contribution to the scheme was pay within the meaning of Article 119 since such contributions were in reality contributions of the employee which just happened to be paid by the employer for historical reasons. The Court accepted their reasoning, and relied on *Worringham* to declare that:

> although the portion which employers are liable to contribute to the financing of statutory social security schemes to which both employees and employers contribute does not constitute pay within the meaning of Article 119 of the Treaty, the same is not true of sums which are included in the calculation of the gross salary payable to the employee and which directly determine the calculation of other advantages linked to the salary such as redundancy payments, unemployment benefits, family allowances and credit facilities. That is also the case if the amounts in question are immediately deducted.

Therefore, the court went on to say that those amounts which public authorities pay to the social security scheme for their employees and which are included in the calculation of their gross pay must be regarded as pay within the meaning of Article 119 in so far as they directly determine the calculation of other advantages linked to the salary.[43]

The Court concluded that, since female civil servants married to husbands who are also civil servants received less advantages than male civil servants, the Dutch provisions were incompatible with the principle of equal pay laid down in Article 119 of the Treaty.

Again the Court, in its judgement, went beyond the issue of discrimination in gross pay to examine the effects of the scheme and its implications on wider issues. The Court held:

> The principle that men and women should receive equal pay for equal work as laid down in Article 119, has not therefore been complied with *in so far as those other advantages* linked to the salary and determined by the gross salary *are not the same for male civil servants and for female civil servants* whose husbands are also civil servants.[44] (Emphasis added.)

The Court took the view that the social objective of Article 119 was an important factor in deciding whether discrimination which is contrary to Article 119 exists.

Perhaps more remarkable than this is that the Court did not apply the criteria which it had adopted in the first Defrenne case to the scheme under consideration in *Liefting*. In this it followed the approach it had adopted in *Worringham*, despite the fact that the intervening governments, the Commission and the Advocate General argued in favour of the *Defrenne* approach. In both *Worringham* and *Liefting* the Court examined the effects of the scheme on the employee. It did not consider the legal nature of the schemes in question. Had it done so, then the outcome of *Liefting* would have been different since the AOW/AWW contributions are contributions to a statutory social security scheme and, according to *Defrenne*, cannot fall within the scope of Article 119. Thus, *Liefting* shows that under certain, albeit limited, circumstances Article 119 applies to certain matters which fall within the scope of the Social Security Directive. In *Liefting* the decisive point was the fact that the contributions were considered as part of the salary of the employee and they were paid by the employer as was the case in *Worringham*. In both *Liefting* and *Worringham*, therefore, the link to 'any other consideration...which the worker receives from his employer' (the wording of Article 119) was established.[45]

A different form of occupational pension scheme was discussed in *Bilka*.[46] This case will be discussed more extensively below in the discussion of the applicability of Article 119 to part-time work but, for the moment, it is important to note that here the Court found that an occupational pension scheme fell within the ambit of Article 119. The pension scheme at issue was a company scheme under which the company was required to pay supplementary retirement benefits to its former employees. In its judgement the Court reiterated its view that pension schemes governed by legislation and without any element of agreement within the industry concerned which were obligatorily applicable to all categories of workers did not fall within the scope of Article 119. However in *Bilka* these conclusions did not apply since what was at issue was a scheme which:

> although adopted in accordance with German legislation for schemes of this type, originates from an agreement made between Bilka and the works council representing its employees with the effect of supplementing, by benefits financed solely by the employer, the social security benefits payable under national legislation which applies generally.[47]

Furthermore, the Court argued, the scheme was contractual rather than statutory and therefore was not a social security scheme so that 'benefits paid to employees under the disputed scheme constitute consideration paid by the employer to the employee in respect of his employment, within the meaning of Article 119'.[48]

In *Bilka* the Court reverted to its position in *Defrenne* and applied the criteria developed in that case. It would seem, therefore, that the Defrenne test is not dead and the Court is willing to apply it to certain situations. The most recent case to have come to the Court relating to retirement benefits is the case of *Newstead*.[49] This case presented difficulties for the Court in deciding how to reconcile various aspects of Community legislation with Article 119 of the Treaty and with its own previous jurisprudence. These difficulties are evidence in the way *Newstead* was handled. In this case the European Court heard the proceedings twice, including the Opinion of the Advocate General, before proceeding to judgement.

Newstead concerned the compulsory deduction of 1.5 per cent of the gross salary of male civil servants which was paid by the employer into a fund to provide for a widows' pension. Mr Newstead, who is unmarried, and has no intention of marrying, objected to this deduction, despite the fact that if he left the civil service still unmarried he would be refunded the sums in full, plus interest. His reason for objecting was based on the fact that he was denied immediate access to the full use of his salary. His case went to the Employment Appeal Tribunal in England which referred to the Court of Justice the question of whether such a deduction was a breach of Article 119 and/or Directives 75/117 and 76/207 (equal treatment in working conditions).[50]

Mr Newstead argued that the scheme in question was discriminatory since his net pay, that is the actual salary he receives, is lower than that received by female employees. He compared his case with that of *Liefting* where a contribution to an occupational pension scheme was paid by the employer in the name of the employee and such a contribution was deemed to fall under Article 119. He argued that it was the contribution that was at issue, not the benefits received under the scheme.

The UK argued that the true meaning to be attached to *Worringham* was that pay, for the purposes of Article 119, related to the gross pay received by the worker, and not his or her pay after deductions of contributions. Relying on *Burton*,[51] the UK distinguished between benefits received under a pension scheme and conditions of access to the scheme. The latter are covered by the equal treatment directive (Directive 76/207). If this assertion is incorrect, argued the British government, then the Court should examine the issue of occupational pension schemes and decide that pension schemes, such as the one in question, fell outside the scope of Article 119 since it was designed to replace the statutory security scheme.

The Commission argued that the issue in question was not one 'of inequality with regard to a financial benefit provided by the employer but in a difference of a condition of employment which has financial consequences'.[52] It would fall to be decided, therefore, under the equal treatment directive which excludes equal treatment in relation to social security.

The Advocate General centred his opinion of the dispute on the question of the obligation to contribute to an occupational pension scheme and not to the effect of the obligation on the net pay of Mr Newstead. The Advocate General found an answer to the question in Directive 79/7 which prohibits discrimination in social security matters.[53] This directive, however, specifically excludes both provisions concerning survivors' benefits and occupational pension schemes. Therefore the Advocate General was forced to conclude that:

> Under Community law as it now stands, there is thus no obligation on a Member-State to apply the principle of equal treatment for men and women to an obligation to make contributions for the purpose of creating survivors' pensions.[54]

Having thus concluded, the Advocate General then had to square this view with the decisions of the Court in *Worringham* and *Liefting*. He did this by pointing out that in the latter cases the issue was not the obligation to contribute which he had qualified as a working condition:

> but sums pursuant thereto...included in the gross salary and used to determine the calculation of other advantages linked to the salary. In plain language – the obligation itself should not be confused with the contribution which is merely the financial consequence thereof.[55]

It is difficult to understand this distinction, however plain the language. From the context of the opinion, however, it seems that the Advocate General was drawing a distinction between gross and net pay, and indicating that compulsory deductions from the gross pay of the worker constituted working conditions rather than pay. It is not clear why this should be the case unless Article 119 is only seen in its economic context. By paying the same gross pay to men and women the economic aim of Article 119 is fulfilled. Allowing the employer to make deductions to finance other benefits for other workers does not, however, meet the social aim of Article 119. What is important to the worker is the take-home pay. The argument put forward by the UK that the take-home pay of workers is rarely identical is disingenuous since it is clearly permissible under European Community law for the state to deduct taxation and social security contributions. What is at issue in *Newstead* is a deduction made by an employer to finance a contracted-out pension scheme; it is the employer's scheme which determines whether deductions from salary will be made.

In his second opinion, the Advocate General saw no reason to change his view although he emphasized in this later opinion the statement by the Court that differences in gross pay may lead to differences in other pay-related benefits.

The Court was not convinced by Mr Newstead's case and examined the reason for the disparity between the cases of male and female civil servants. This was not an issue of a benefit paid to a worker, nor a contribution paid by an employer to a pension scheme, both of which could fall under Article 119. The issue was rather one of a deduction of a contribution to an occupational pension scheme which is a substitute for a general social security scheme. The issue falls to be regulated by Article 118 of the Treaty and not Article 119. The Court distinguished this case from *Worringham* and *Liefting* since in these cases the gross pay of men was higher and this gave them an advantage in the calculation of other salary-related benefits.

It is not clear which tests the Court applied to the civil service contracted-out scheme in order to equate it with a general social security scheme[56] but in doing so the Court is subject to some of the same criticisms levelled at it for its judgement in the first Defrenne case. Those criticisms relate to the adverse effects of the decision on employees whose employers operate one form of pension scheme rather than another and the fact that the Court has allowed that the operation of Article 119 may be dependent on the national organization of pension schemes.

Newstead may be criticized further since there are several discrepancies between it and the previous case-law of the Court. In *Worringham* and *Liefting*, for example, differences in the gross pay of the employees caused inequalities in other gross pay-related advantages and this was enough for the Court to apply Article 119, relying on its social objective. It is paradoxical that the same approach was not taken when net pay was at issue. It is not clear why the Court did not follow the same 'effects' approach and why the fact that the pension scheme was a substitute for the statutory scheme was important in this case whilst the Court did not take that factor into consideration in *Worringham*, and in *Liefting* it even applied Article 119 to contributions made directly to a statutory scheme. It is, of course, true that the facts in *Worringham* and *Liefting* differed from those in Newstead but this is not a sufficiently convincing argument to distinguish the cases (yet the Court gives no further explanation). Moreover the principle of the two earlier cases, that is, that the Court will examine the effects of the different treatments along with the social objective of Article 119, would seem to apply fully in *Newstead*. The only way that some sense can be made of this judgement is to say that the employer did not pay anything to the employee, but the employee was obliged to pay something. However, in the end this argument fails too, on the basis that the employer may achieve the same results by either paying males a higher gross pay and immediately deducting a certain amount from it, or by paying men and women the same gross pay, but obliging men to pay a contribution.

The *Newstead* decision is regrettable in a further sense in that in the UK the government is encouraging privatization of pensions which will be substitutes for the social security schemes. If such schemes were to be covered by the third Directive and not by Article 119, this would raise the question of the direct effects of Community law. Article 119 has horizontal direct effect, whereas the Directive does not, and it contains several important exceptions as the discussion of it in Chapter 5 shows. The new privatized pension schemes are in some ways similar to existing contracted-out schemes and it is not entirely clear from Community law whether such schemes do or do not fall within the scope of Article 119.

An examination of the Court's judgement in *Worringham* does seem to indicate that contributions paid by the employer to a contracted-out scheme do fall within the scope of Article 119, whereas *Newstead* suggests the opposite. It would seem that in the latter case the Court is retreating in the face of the intransigence of the Member States who are determined to subject the review of national pension schemes to their own timetable and to delay implementation of the equal treatment standard in this area. *Newstead* appears to give the go-ahead to such an approach.

Closely related to the issue of pensions is, of course, the issue of pensionable and retirement ages. These issues have been raised by litigants in proceedings relating to Article 119. The third *Defrenne* case raised the question of the date of retirement for air hostesses.[57] Ms Defrenne's contract of employment, which had been the subject of the two previous rulings, provided that the contract terminated when she reached the age of 40. No such age limit was written into the contract of cabin stewards. Ms Defrenne had challenged the legality of such a clause before the Belgian Cour de Cassation and accordingly that Court requested a preliminary ruling from the Court of Justice to discover whether Article 119 prescribed equal working conditions as well as equal pay and, in particular, whether a clause such as the one described above was contrary to Article 119 given that such a clause led inevitably to pecuniary losses on the part of the employee.

Ms Defrenne argued that the principle of equal pay could only be achieved if there were equality of conditions of employment and therefore the Court should give Article 119 its widest possible meaning. Furthermore, she argued, Article 119 was only a specific application of the general principle that there shall be no discrimination based on sex which is a fundamental right recognized by Community law. Her arguments were strongly supported by the government of Italy in its intervention.

The UK, however, found this interpretation of Article 119 to be 'strained and untenable'.[58] The Commission agreed that Article 119 did not lay down a general principle of equality but was restricted to the limited issue of equal pay. It then pointed out that the question of working conditions as such was covered by Articles 117 and 118 of the Treaty which provided for a programme of action to be adopted in the area of working conditions. This theme was taken up by the Advocate General and was upheld by the Court in its judgement. The Court decided that Article 119 could not be 'interpreted as prescribing, in addition to equal pay, equality in respect of the other working conditions applicable to men and women'.[59] The Court then examined Community law as a whole to determine whether it contained any general principle governing working conditions. The Court argued that the elimination of discrimination based on sex forms part of the fundamental human rights, respect for which it is the duty of the Court to ensure. However, at the date of the events before the Belgian Court the Community had not assumed responsibility for determining the relationships of employer and employee in matters of working conditions[60] and, therefore, there was no rule of Community law forbidding discrimination of the type suffered by Ms Defrenne.[61]

In *Burton*,[62] age was the key factor which made Mr Burton challenge a scheme for redundancy payments established by British Rail. The scheme allowed employees to receive additional redundancy payments if they volunteered to retire early – men at 60, women at 55. Mr Burton, who was 58, applied for voluntary redundancy but was turned down. He therefore complained to an Industrial Tribunal that he had been treated less favourably than female employees but his claim under the Equal Pay Act, as amended by the Sex Discrimination Act, was rejected. On appeal to the Employment Appeal Tribunal he conceded that voluntary redundancy benefits paid on early retirement fell outside the scope of the British Acts[63] but argued that those Acts must be construed as subject to the enforceable Community rights conferred by Article 119 of the Treaty. He then argued that voluntary redundancy benefits fell within the scope of the principle of equal pay.

The Employment Appeal Tribunal referred the case to the European Court for a preliminary ruling. Burton argued before the Court that its judgement in *Worringham* took the concept of pay to be a wide one, and that since redundancy payments were paid directly to an employee by an employer then they did fall within the meaning of Article 119. On the question of the age differential Mr Burton argued that the Court had recognized in *Worringham* that inequalities arising from different age requirements are covered by Article 119 and went on to distinguish his case from the third *Defrenne* case in which the Court had rejected the view that the imposition of different retirement ages for men and women was contrary to Article 119. In that case, he argued, no money payment was involved. In his case the age requirement directly governed his pay, if pay were given an extended meaning.

The British Railways Board deemed that voluntary redundancy payments were not 'pay', and they were joined in their argument by the government of the UK. Their argument rested on the premise that the benefit in question could not be related to work performed since it is 'non-contractual, gratuitous and discretionary...conferred in return for a promise to give up work'.[64]

The Advocate General turned his attention to the definition of pay. On the facts of the dispute before him he demonstrated that the redundancy payments in question were indeed payments received by the employee directly or indirectly from the employer. It was more difficult to decide, however, whether the benefits received were paid in respect of his employment. To show that they were paid in respect of his employment the Advocate General suggested that what was required was 'an unseverable causal link between the payment and a worker's employment',[65] and argued that voluntary redundancy benefits fell within this definition since the worker would not receive them if he or she were not employed. Therefore men and women were entitled to the same benefits. However, the Advocate General then argued that Article 119 did not cover *access* to the scheme; the age limit stipulation could, at most, be covered by Directive 76/207 which provides for equality of working conditions.

When it came to give judgement the Court restricted its interpretation to the question of whether the conditions of access to the voluntary redundancy scheme were discriminatory, stating that the question as to whether voluntary redundancy benefits were pay was not at issue in the present case. The Court decided that conditions of access to voluntary redundancy schemes were covered by Directive 76/207 but that since such access was available to all employees within the five years preceeding the minimum pensionable age, and that age is not the same for men and women (which is, as such, permitted under Community law), then the system in question was not discriminatory.[66]

Although the Court did not address itself to the question of whether voluntary redundancy payments came within the definition of pay in Article 119 this case is nonetheless important, since it shows how arguments can be formulated to extend the definition of pay into very wide areas and, once it is accepted that the definition of pay is eminently flexible, the way is open for a wide variety of claims which could fall easily into the definition given by the Advocate General. It is also interesting for the approach adopted by the plaintiff who was prepared to argue his case before the Court on all fronts using whatever weapons European law could provide. What is depressing about the case is that it shows how the impact of Community measures can be blunted by the failure of states to agree on legislative provisions which cover all aspects of sex-based discrimination. In effect Mr Burton won all the arguments but lost on the day.

One further case has come before the Court to determine the scope of pay within the meaning of Article 119. In *Garland*[67] the Court was asked to determine whether British Rail had contravened Article 119 in providing special travel facilities for retired male workers and their families which were not made available to retired female employees. As has been stated previously, provisions relating to death or retirement are excluded from the UK Sex Discrimination Act and, therefore, Ms Garland had lost her claim in the Employment Tribunal, a decision which was subsequently upheld by the Court of Appeal. When the case reached the House of Lords, issues relating to Article 119 were raised for the first time.

Accordingly, the House of Lords requested a preliminary ruling from the European Court to discover whether such discriminatory provisions offended against Article 119, Article 1 of Council Directive 75/117/EEC or Article 1 of Council Directive 76/207/EEC.

Ms Garland argued that the Court had adopted a very wide concept of 'pay' to include benefits which were received after retirement (Defrenne) and which were received not only by the employee but also by his or her family. She was supported in her arguments by the Commission.

British Rail argued that travel concessions did not constitute pay since they were not provided pursuant to any agreement between employer and employee and were, furthermore, incapable of assessment in financial terms.

The UK, not surprisingly, argued for a restrictive interpretation of Article 119 claiming that that Article made the test of whether a particular benefit was pay dependent on the relationship between the benefit and the work performed. Furthermore, benefits granted gratuitously to workers after retirement did not constitute pay. The UK then argued against the direct effects of Article 119 in this situation since the provisions could not be applied without the aid of a national measure which would reconcile the differing retirement ages of men and women, and hence access to the benefit in question.

The Court answered this question very briefly. It examined the nature of the benefit and found that it was granted to male employees and their families on the retirement of the male worker and was thus granted 'directly or indirectly in respect of his employment'. Benefits given on retirement were an extension of those granted during the course of the worker's employment and therefore 'fulfil the criteria enabling them to be treated as pay within the meaning of Article 119 of the EEC Treaty'.[68] The Court then dismissed the argument that benefits must arise from a contractual relationship in order to be considered as pay. Benefits need only be granted in respect of employment for them to fall within the ambit of Article 119.

Indirect discrimination

Pensions and pensionable ages have not been the only issues to come before the Court. Another problem has been the question of discrimination suffered by part-time workers. This issue first arose in *Jenkins*,[69] another reference for a preliminary ruling from the British Employment Appeal Tribunal. In this case Ms Jenkins argued that Article 119 of the Treaty and Directive 75/117 require equal pay for work of equal value irrespective of the number of hours worked. In her case she was paid at a lower rate than a man doing the same job full-time. She had lost her claim under the British Equal Pay Act since the fact that she worked fewer hours than her male colleague was taken by the Industrial Tribunal to constitute a material difference according to Section 1 (3) of the Act.[70] Accordingly, Ms Jenkins appealed to the Employment Appeal Tribunal who asked the Court for a reference on several points, but notably on the issue of whether the principle of equal pay applied irrespective of the hours worked and irrespective of the commercial advantages gained by the employer who pays lower rates to part-time employees. The Tribunal then asked whether the answer to these questions would be different if it were proved that a smaller proportion of women can fulfil the hours required for full-time work.

Ms Jenkins put forward extremely broad-based arguments in support of her view that Article 119 applies both to full-time and part-time workers, pointing out that in the UK the majority of part-time workers were female and, therefore, if Article 119 did not apply to part-time workers women as a whole would suffer from serious disadvantages. In analysing Article 119 she pointed out that that Article focuses on the nature of the work performed and not on the number of hours worked each week. On the question of the commercial advantages gained by the employer Ms Jenkins quite rightly pointed out that this is an 'extrinsic and irrelevant consideration as regards the principle of equal pay'.[71] If this were not the case:

> the employer would be able to pay women less than men for equal work, not on the ground that they were women but because they could be recruited for less pay than men and that this was to the employers commercial advantage.[72]

She then went on to argue that only objectively justifiable differences other than sex could justify discriminatory treatment.

The UK argued that the difference in pay between full-time and part-time workers in this case was unconnected with sex-based discrimination, and that it was for the national court to decide whether there were grounds for retention of the differential rates of pay. Belgium too argued that differential rates of pay might exist between full-time and part-time workers and that there was not necessarily a breach of the principle of equal pay where this was the case.

The Commission took the view that Article 119 requires a comparison between types of work and not the number of hours worked to determine whether a comparison may be made. Any difference in the amount paid to part-time workers 'must depend on factors totally unconnected with the sex of the employees'.[73]

The Advocate General opened his opinion with statistics relating to the employment of women in the Community, stating that 90 per cent of part-time workers are women. He then went on to examine Ms Jenkins's argument that she was employed in the same work as her male comparator. He rejected this argument with an assertion that 'a part-time worker and a full-time worker do not have "the same job", even though they may do "equal work"[74] (although his assertion is not supported by evidence or argument). The Advocate General then rejected the argument put forward by the plaintiff that the Court should find that 'commercial advantages' gained by the employer should be seen as irrelevant considerations in determining the scope of the principle of equal pay. He argued that there may be factors other than those arising out of sex discrimination which led employers to pay part-time workers at lower rates.

Ms Jenkins had also put forward an argument based on the so-called 'Griggs approach' adopted in the United States. This approach was based on the concept of 'adverse impact' and was used where it could be proved that a particular condition imposed by an employer hit disproportionately more women than men. In this case the imposition of a particular criterion, like the minimum number of hours worked, would require special justification. The Advocate General clearly supported this approach as it was the only one capable of rooting out discrimination disguised as differentiation between full- and part-time workers at the same time protecting an employer who has good reason for differentiating between them.

The Court was therefore faced with an extremely difficult set of problems. It is undoubtedly true, in the UK at least, that the vast majority of part-time workers are female and that these workers earn less wages for the same work performed per hour than their full-time colleagues. It is also true that part-time work is more common in certain sectors of the economy than in others and that these tend to be female ghettoes in employment terms. Lower pay, fewer hours and specific jobs are linked by the fact of a predominantly female labour force. However, this is not necessarily a problem relating to the quite narrow concept of unequal pay of men and women; it is a problem which relates to the wider issue of low pay for women workers as a whole. In the UK, women as a group receive less pay then men as a group, but individually few real comparisons can be made since men and women rarely share an employment context. Thus, *Jenkins* highlighted the inherent limitations of both the UK Equal Pay Act and Article 119 since both can operate only where men and women can be genuinely compared and since neither is designed to confront every inequity in the pay structures.

The judgement of the Court reflected this dilemma. The Court decided that a variation in pay for full-time and part-time workers does not offend against Article 119 provided 'that the hourly rates are applied to workers belonging to either category without distinction based on sex', and that such differences are 'objectively justified'.[75] Such would be the case where the employer was endeavouring to encourage full-time work but it would not be the case if the pay policy in question 'cannot be explained by factors other than discrimination based on sex'.[76] Of course the question arises as to why the Court accepted the view that the encouragement of full-time, as opposed to part-time, work was an objectively justified reason which justified otherwise discriminatory behaviour. The Court made no attempt to weigh the business objectives of the firm against the fundamental human rights of women, but merely implied that business objectives had priority over the principle of non-discrimination. The Court went on to say that in every case it is for the national court to decide whether:

> regard being had to the facts of the case, its history and the employer's intention, a pay policy such as that which is at issue in the main proceedings although represented as a difference based on weekly working hours is or is not in reality a discrimination based on the sex of the worker...
>
> ...a difference in pay between full-time and part-time workers does not amount to discrimination prohibited by Article 119 of the Treaty unless it is in reality merely an indirect way of reducing the level of pay of part-time workers on the ground that that group of workers is composed exclusively or predominately of women.[77]

It is not difficult to see the problems which this decision raises. The Court imported the concept of intention into the area of indirect discrimination and, thereby, undermined the whole notion of adverse impact (to use the American phrase) or indirect discrimination (to use the British phrase). Following Jenkins, it would be possible for an employer to use any criterion which in fact resulted in women as a group being discriminated against provided that the employer could show that the intention behind the policy was an aim other than discrimination. The Court in effect is saying that any justification, other than sex, is objective. In fact the judgement in Jenkins created a great number of problems for the Employment Appeal Tribunal and a considerable degree of confusion in British law.[78] It might also have put paid to the possibility of developing a vigorous approach to indirect discrimination since proof of intention is difficult.

Presumably most employers take the employment market as they find it and use the cheapest and most available supply of qualified workers. They do not intend to discriminate but they may continue to benefit from a more systematic devaluation of women which is practised by society as a whole.

The issue of part-time employment arose again in *Bilka*.[79] This case related to the refusal of an employer to pay certain retirement pensions to its part-time employees, the majority of whom were females. As stated above, the Court found that the pension in question did fall within the ambit of Article 119 since the type of pension scheme constituted pay within the meaning of that Article. However, the question of whether or not discrimination in the pay structure existed was a rather trickier one.

Ms Weber argued in this case that the pension scheme was discriminatory in that the requirement that a pension be paid only to staff who have worked a minimum of 15 years full-time is a detriment to females who, due to their family responsibilities, are less likely to be able to work full-time. Bilka argued, however, that there was no intention to discriminate on their part in the operation of the scheme. Their aim was not to discriminate against women but to encourage full-time employment in their department stores. They argued, therefore, that their scheme was based on objectively justified economic grounds.

Faced with these arguments the German Bundesarbeitsgericht referred several questions to the European Court, all of which raise interesting questions as to the scope of Article 119. The German Court wanted to know:

1. May there be an infringement of Article 119 of the EEC Treaty in the form of 'indirect discrimination' where a department store which employs predominantly women excludes part-time employees from benefits under its occupational pension scheme although such exclusion affects disproportionately more women than men?

2. If so:
   (a) Can the undertaking justify that disadvantage on the ground that its objective is to employ as few part-time workers as possible even though in the department store sector reasons of commercial expediency do not necessitate such a staff policy?
   (b) Is the undertaking under a duty to structure its pension scheme in such a way that appropriate account is taken of the special difficulties experienced by employees with family commitments in fulfilling the requirements for an occupational pension?[80]

Relying on its own judgement in *Jenkins* the Court replied to the first question by stating that Article 119 was infringed by a policy which excluded part-time employees from an occupational pension scheme where the exclusion affected a much greater number of women than men, unless it can be shown 'that the exclusion is based on objectively justified factors which are unrelated to any discrimination based on sex'.[81]

The Court then rightly stated that the second question referred to it centred on whether Bilka's pay policy could be considered to be grounded in 'objectively justified economic reasons'. It was for the national court to make this decision but the European Court went on to provide guidelines, based on the principle of proportionality, for the national courts. The Court stated that it was for the employer to prove that the policy in question was chosen to meet a genuine need of the enterprise, was suitable for attaining the objective set and was necessary for the purpose. Thus the European Court set out the limits which the national court may find that the employer is justified in operating an otherwise discriminatory policy. These guidelines adopt the argument proposed by Ms Jenkins in her submissions before the Court and approved by Advocate General Warner in that case. The burden of proof falls on the employer to show some special justification for adopting a policy which is otherwise contrary to Article 119. In the absence of such proof the national court must find for the employee. The effects of *Jenkins* were, therefore, mitigated by *Bilka*.

However the Court did not go on to impose any further obligations on the employer. Article 119 did not require employers to amend their pension schemes in such a way as to take into account periods when women were not working for them but were working in the home. Article 119 did not require such action.

Problems arising out of part-time work provide the issues arising in the case of Ingrid Rinner-Kuhn who is a part-time cleaner working two hours per day from Monday to Friday.[82] In December 1987, she was unable to work due to illness and she asked her employer for a continuation of her wages for the period during which she was absent from work. Her employer refused payment, relying on German legislation which provides that persons employed for less than 10 hours per week may not continue to receive their wages in the event of sickness. Ms Rinner-Kuhn brought her complaint to the Oldenberg Labour Court claiming that this legislative provision was both unconstitutional, being an infringement of the general principle of equality set out in the Grundgesetz, and constituted discrimination against women since a disproportionately large number of women are employed in part-time work. Such discrimination, she argued, is prohibited by Article 119 EEC.

The Labour Court referred the latter issue to the Court asking whether such provisions which derogate from the principle that an employer must continue to pay an employee during illness in the case of employees who work less than 10 hours per week are incompatible with Article 119 and Directive 75/117.

As was rightly pointed out by the German judge, this case turns on the issue of whether such a statutory derogation constitutes indirect discrimination against women. Citing German authorities, he defined indirect discrimination as occurring when:

> the proportion of members of one sex who are or could be adversely affected by the measure is considerably larger than the proportion of members of the other sex... The decisive factor is not the absolute numbers involved but the fact that women are strongly over-represented amongst those adversely affected.[83]

The judge then went on to produce statistical evidence to show that the proportion of women in part-time employment in Germany greatly exceeds that of men, and amongst women the proportion of married women or women with domestic responsibilities greatly exceeds that of single women. From these statistics the judge concluded that there was a link between part-time work (and, by definition, its disadvantages) and women. He then examined whether there was any objective justification for the derogation at issue and found no apparent objective grounds. He pointed out that the Court of Justice had already been asked similar questions relating to individual infringements by employers of Article 119. Now he was asking whether a statutory provision is contrary to Article 119 and Directive 75/117.

The Court of Justice examined the statutory derogation and held first of all that the sick pay scheme fell within the terms of Article 119. Having examined the facts and the statistical evidence, the Court then went on to say that, because less women than men work the minimum number of hours, the legislation in fact introduces discrimination between men and women workers. It is, therefore, contrary to Article 119 unless it can be shown that the difference of treatment introduced by the legislation is justified by objective factors unrelated to sex. In the course of proceedings, the Court had asked Germany to explain why such a derogation was necessary but it has not satisfied with the vague generalizations offered. However, the Court went on to say that measures introduced by a state which respond to a necessary goal of its social policy, which were likely to achieve that goal and were necessary to it, would not be contrary to Article 119 despite the fact that such measures hit a disproportionate number of women. It is for the national court to decide whether the legislation met these criteria. Thus, the Rinner-Kuhn approach is similar to that adopted in *Bilka*.

What is equal work?

Although several cases have come to the European Court relating to the scope of the concept of pay only two have been referred to it on the issue of what is work within the meaning of Article 119. *Macarthys*[84] came to the Court on a reference from the English Court of Appeal and concerned the question of whether the principle of equal pay enshrined in Article 119 and Directive 75/117 is confined to situations where men and women are contemporaneously doing equal work for their employer. Ms Smith was employed as a manager of a warehouse and was paid £50 per week. Her predecessor on the job, who was male, had been paid £60 per week. Accordingly she applied to an industrial tribunal complaining that, by virtue of the Equal Pay Act, she was entitled to the same wage as the man employed previously in the same job. She won her case before the tribunal on the grounds that her job was 'broadly similar' to that of the previous occupant of the post. That decision, in which the issue of contemporaneity was not discussed, was upheld by the Employment Appeal Tribunal, although in doing so it went beyond the provisions of the British Act which provides that the woman must compare herself to a man contemporaneously employed in the same or broadly similar work. The Employment Appeal Tribunal said that their approach would avoid any infringement of the principle of equal pay laid down in Article 119.

Macarthys appealed to the Court of Appeal on the basis of the UK statute, whereas Ms Smith rested her argument on the need to interpret national law in accordance with Community law. Before the European Court Ms Smith argued that there was nothing in Article 119 which confined her to comparing herself with a male currently employed. Furthermore, she argued, Directive 75/117 had extended the scope of equal work to include work of equal value and nothing in the Directive indicated that work must be contemporaneous work. She then argued that the principle of equality is violated when 'a given difference in treatment has no objective and reasonable justification',[85] and went on to introduce the concept of the hypothetical male:

> It is appropriate to compare the treatment of the alleged victim of sex discrimination by the employer and the treatment of an actual or hypothetical worker of the other sex. The relevance of selecting a worker, whether contemporaneously or previously employed on equal work, as a basis of comparison, permits one to ascertain whether there has been a difference of treatment between men and women on grounds of sex in any aspect or condition of a remuneration. Such a comparison is not confined to contemporaneous employment, nor to successive employment; it may include a comparison between the manner in which the employer has treated the alleged victim of sex discrimination and the manner in which the employer has treated or would treat a worker of the other sex.[86]

Ms Smith then claimed support for her arguments for use of the hypothetical male from a report of the Council and from other UK legislation. She was supported in her arguments by the Commission and by the Advocate General. He raised the interesting point that the economic aim of Article 119 would be thwarted if employers could replace their expensive, male workers with cheap, female ones. The whole basis for inclusion of Article 119 in the Treaty would then be lost.

The judges upheld some of Ms Smith's arguments. The concept of equal work, the Court said, is qualitative, and 'is exclusively concerned with the nature of the services in question (and) may not be restricted by the introduction of a requirement of contemporaneity'.[87] However, the Court acknowledged that there may be reasons, unconnected with discrimination based on sex, why an employer pays different rates for the same post at different times.

The Court rejected, however, Ms Smith's arguments for the adoption of the 'hypothetical male' on the basis that Article 119 is confined to situations where parallels may be drawn 'on the basis of concrete appraisals of the work actually performed by employees of different sex within the same establishment or service'.[88] Furthermore, since the dispute could be settled within the framework of Article 119, the Court did not need to address itself to an interpretation of Directive 75/117.

The second case to be referred on the definition of work came from the Irish High Court. *Murphy*[89] concerns the situation of a group of women whose jobs had been evaluated as superior to that of a male employee but who, nonetheless, received less pay. The question put to the Court of Justice was whether, under the terms of Article 119, a worker could compare his or her wages to those of another worker who was paid more for performing work evaluated as being of lesser value than the complainants. On the face of it this seems like a ridiculous question but it throws into light many of the limitations of any equal pay legislation and of the particular difficulties surrounding the concept of value.

In this case the appellants were women whose job was to dismantle, clean, oil and reassemble telephones. They wished to compare themselves to a male stores labourer under section 3 (c) of the Irish Anti-Discrimination (Pay) Act 1974. That Act provides that men and women shall receive equal pay where they are employed on like work. Like work is defined, *inter alia*, as being

> where the work performed by one is equal in value to that performed by the other in terms of the demands it makes in relation to such matters as skill, physical or mental effort, responsibility and working conditions.

The equality officer, whose duty it is to examine in the first instance a claim made under the Act when the claim is not accepted by the employer, rejected the appellants' claim on the grounds that the women's jobs were superior in value to the stores labourer with whom they wished to compare themselves.

Before the Irish High Court, counsel for the appellants argued that the words 'at least' should be read into section 3 (c) so that the work performed should be 'at least equal in value to that performed by the other'. The respondents rejected this view, arguing that the explanation behind the difference in rates of pay 'was the product of grading systems in operation in the industry and not of discrimination on the ground of sex'.[90] They also argued, quite logically, that the solution sought by the appellants would not solve the problem of unequal pay, since the appellants were not arguing, nor could they under the Act, that their pay be increased to a level which would reflect the superior value of their work, but merely that the level be increased to that of the male employees, whose work was of lesser value.

The Irish Judge agreed with the interpretation of the Irish legislation proposed by the respondents but was unable to determine the scope of European Community legislation. He, therefore, requested the Court to determine:

1.   Does the Community law principle of equal pay for equal work extend to a claim for equal pay on the basis of work of equal value in circumstances where the work of the claimant has been assessed to be of higher value than that of the person with whom the claimant sought comparison?
2.   If the answer to Question 1 is in the affirmative, is that answer dependent on the provisions of Article 1 of Council Directive 75/117/EEC of 10 February 1975 on the approximation of the laws of the member-States relating to the application of the principle of equal pay for men and women?
3.   If so, is Article 1 of the said Directive directly applicable in member-States?[91]

The central issue here is that of disguised discrimination, which had first been raised in the second *Defrenne* case. In *Defrenne* the Advocate General had accepted that inequalities of pay arose from many factors. Only rarely does an employer offer differential rates of pay to men and women doing the same work. Discrimination arises out of the operation of pay structures, of job classification schemes, the allocation of types of labour between men and women, or differences in the training and promotion of women. In *Defrenne* he used the term disguised discrimination to cover this type of discrimination but, whilst recognizing its existence, he did not feel, nor did the Court accept, that Article 119 could be used as a means of eliminating discrimination of this kind. Article 119 is insufficient to achieve the complete aim of equal pay for work of equal value and the Court pointed to the need for further measures at Community and national level to eliminate discrimination throughout entire branches of industry. One such measure is the Equal Pay Directive, which is discussed below, or the Equal Treatment Directive which is discussed in the next chapter.

The nearest the Court came to accepting that Article 119 could cover disguised discrimination, in the *Defrenne* sense, came in *Macarthys*. Ms Smith argued for the adoption of the hypothetical male, that is, she asked the Court to decide on the basis of what a man would have got had he been employed in the same job. The Court did not accept such a broad formulation but did agree that a decision as to whether an act of discrimination has occurred might include a comparison of the way in which the employer has in the past treated a worker of the other sex.

The Court's approach in *Murphy*, given this earlier approach, is surprising since it held in this case that the concept of equal pay for work of equal value prohibits differences in pay 'where the lower-paid category of workers is engaged in work of higher value'.[92] The Court's arguments for adopting this stance are based on the fact that to decide otherwise would render the principle of Article 119 ineffective since employers would be able to assign additional duties to females and then pay them lower wages.

The Court's judgement in *Murphy*, which is supported by the Advocate General and the Irish government, strains the wording of Article 119. Article 119 does not, unfortunately, demand that a worker be paid what his or her work is worth. It does not make significant inroads into established pay structures, relying as it does on some notion of comparability. Allowing the Murphy claim could, in fact, lead to the result which the Court was seeking to avoid. Employers are now able to grade women's jobs as being superior in value but to have their wages classified at the level of the lower-paid men. Bord Telecom Eireann put this argument to the Court:

> the interpretation suggested by the appellants in the main proceedings would lead to a result which was both unjust and illogical because the aggrieved female worker would still be in respect of a level of remuneration which was depressed on grounds of sex alone.[93]

The true solution in this case would be for the union and management to renegotiate pay structures reflecting the worth of the jobs concerned and for the Irish government to ensure that Article 119 and the Directive are fully implemented.

The cases which have come before the Court to determine the scope of Article 119 are extremely interesting for more than one reason. They show a desire on the part of the Court to be as flexible as possible in the interpretation of Article 119. This is increasingly obvious if the cases are followed through chronologically. In the first *Defrenne* case the Court seemed hesitant to open what was quite obviously going to be a bed of worms for the Community, but the Court subsequently grew in self-confidence on questions of equal pay and assumed a pioneering role in developing and extending concepts although *Newstead* may indicate a reversal of this trend. In this particular area the Court must be applauded for its willingness not only to make difficult decisions and confront contentious issues but also for its ability to see through the morass of arguments put to it and resolve the problem in a simple and effective way.

The equal pay Directive

Despite the inclusion of Article 119 in the Treaty, equal pay was not fully achieved either formally or practically within the Community. The Commission, the guardian of the Treaty, monitored implementation of Article 119 and drew up regular reports to be discussed by the Council of Ministers. It became obvious that the Member States were unable or unwilling to implement Article 119 by the end of the first stage, 1 January 1962, the date prescribed within the Treaty, despite a recommendation from the Commission of 20 July 1960 which reminded Member States of the obligations which they had assumed. The Member States, therefore, took it upon themselves to adopt a fresh timetable. A resolution of a conference of Member States stipulated that equal pay between men and women must be achieved by 31 December 1964. Both the recommendations and the resolution noted the need for Member States to establish machinery to provide a means of redress for women who believed that an infringement of Article 119 had occurred. As has already been seen, the Court of Justice subsequently pronounced that the resolution of the Member States did not affect Article 119 in any way since that Article could only be amended following the procedures laid down for amendments in the Treaty itself.[94]

Both the recommendation and the resolution do indicate, however, the thinking of both the Commission and the Member States as to the scope of Article 119. In 1960 the doctrine of direct effects itself had not been expounded by the Court, and the nature of the obligation assumed under Article 119 was unclear. Since it was not until 8 April 1976 that the Court declared Article 119 to be capable of creating rights which individuals could claim in their national courts, Member States might be forgiven for believing that the obligation to implement the principle of equal pay was theirs alone.

In addition to the uncertainty as to the legal status of Article 119, it is also important to note the shift in emphasis within the Community towards the development of social policy in the late 1960s and early 1970s. Implementation of the principle of equal pay and the development of other initiatives enhancing the position of women were part of the social policy objectives set out in 1974 by the Community, and thus the full implementation of Article 119 became a priority within the Community.[95]

It is against this background that two actions by the Commission become explicable. The first was to initiate infringement proceedings against those states who had not complied fully with Article 119, and the second was to propose the adoption of a directive whose purpose would be to hasten implementation of Article 119. Only one infringement proceeding eventually reached the Court of Justice, that against Luxembourg. This case will be discussed later in the context of infringement proceedings brought by the Commission for failure to implement the equal pay Directive. At this point it is perhaps worth asking why the Commission delayed so long in bringing enforcement actions against recalcitrant states. It may be that the Commission did not see the development of Community social policy in quite the same light as it does today, or that the Community was so much engaged in developing the rules relating to the customs union and the Common Agricultural Policy that all else paled into insignificance. Human rights too did not assume, juridically, a great deal of importance until the German constitutional cases propelled the European Court into action.[96]

Whatever the reason for the delay in implementation of Article 119, 1972 was the turning point which marked the determination of the Commission to bring equal pay into the Community's agenda in a positive way. In November 1973, the Commission proposed the adoption of a directive which would indicate to the Member States the way in which they could realize the aims contained in Article 119. The Directive was adopted in

1975 and, as its title demonstrates, its aim was to 'approximate' the laws of the Member States relating to the application of the principle of equal pay.[97]

Students of Community law will be familiar with the phrase 'approximation of laws'. Article 100 of the Treaty of Rome authorizes the adoption of directives to approximate such 'provisions laid down by law, regulation or administrative action in Member States as directly affect the establishment or functioning of the common market'. It was by virtue of this provision that Directive 75/117/EEC was adopted. Approximation is not defined in the Treaty but essentially what is asked of States is that they bring domestic provisions into line with a Community rule which is defined in any particular directive. The definition of the directive itself leaves 'the choice of form and methods' to the national authorities but reminds them that it is 'binding, as to the result to be achieved'.[98]

Council Directive 75/117, in its preamble, lays down the basis for its adoption. It recognizes that implementation of Article 119 is an integral part of the establishment and functioning of the Treaty and, thereby, establishes the juridical basis of the Directive. The Directive places the primary responsibility for ensuring the application of the principle on the Member States by the adoption of laws, regulations and administrative provisions and indicates one way in which this may be done – through the provision of a legal means of redress to persons who have been denied the right of equal pay.

The Directive is addressed to the Member States (Article 10) who are given one year from the date of its notification to comply with it (Article 8). This means that the Directive should have been fully transposed into the national laws of the then nine Member States by 12 February 1976.

Article 1 of the Directive defines the principle of equal pay as being 'for the same work or for work to which equal value is attributed, the elimination of all discrimination on grounds of sex with regard to all aspects and conditions of remuneration'. Thus the Directive introduces the concept of equal value as part of the definition of the principle of equal pay. In so doing it does not affect the legal scope of Article 119, but it explains the full extent of the principle itself, bringing the European Community law definition fully into line with the definition of equal pay contained in Convention No. 100 of the International Labour Organization. Like the latter Convention, the Directive provides that where job classification schemes are used to determine pay such schemes 'must be based on the same criteria for both men and women and so drawn up as to exclude any discrimination on grounds of sex'.

The remaining articles of the Directive point to the actions which must be taken by Member States. Article 2 provides that Member States must establish the machinery whereby persons who consider themselves wronged may bring a legal action 'after possible recourse to other competent authorities'. Thus a legal remedy and legal procedures must be adopted. Furthermore, Member States are obliged by Article 3 to abolish existing laws, regulations or administrative provisions which offend against the principle of equal pay and, in particular, according to Article 4 they must ensure that provisions in 'collective agreements, wage scales, wage agreements or individual contracts of employment shall be or may be declared null and void or may be amended'. Article 5 demands protection from dismissal for the employee who initiates action against inequalities of pay, either within the undertaking or before the courts. Article 6 enjoins Member States to take the measures necessary to ensure that the principle of equal pay is applied and to see that effective measures are made available to take care that the principle is observed. Finally, Article 7 obliges Member States to bring to the attention of all employees the provision relating to equal pay already in force, together with the measures they have taken to bring Directive 75/117 into force.

Several questions immediately spring to mind in relation to the Directive. The most obvious is that of the exact relationship between it and Article 119. It was not immediately apparent whether the Directive altered the scope of Article 119 in any way, and if it did whether the Directive created any new rights for individuals which they could claim in their national courts. Pursuers in the national courts, and the national courts themselves, often put forward alternative arguments based on both the Article of the Treaty and on the Directive, but in the main the Court has tended to rely on interpretation of Article 119 rather than on the Directive and has been able to avoid some of the questions which have come to it from the domestic courts. One point of principle should, however, be noted. Article 119, being a Treaty provision, has precedence over any secondary legislation. The Directive is, of course, secondary legislation and, as such, may facilitate, implement or explain Article 119. However, it cannot alter the scope of Article 119 to limit any previously existing rights. This relationship has not always appeared so clear-out to parties to cases before the Court as the discussion below demonstrates.

One of the first cases in which the relationship between the Article and the Directive became an issue was the third *Defrenne* case.[99] In this case the UK argued against the direct effects of Article 119 on the ground that that article failed to satisfy the requirements of clarity and precision. In support of its argument the UK pointed to the reason behind the adoption of Directive 75/117 which was, according to the UK, to give a precise definition of the principle of equal pay, since such a definition was lacking in the Article itself. The Irish government also argued against the direct effects of Article 119, using the Directive in support of its argument that Article 119 requires special implementing measures and, therefore, is legally incomplete.

The Commission, on the other hand, stated that the Directive introduced no new rule of positive law and it was merely a warning light addressed to those states who had failed to implement their obligations under Article

119. Its purpose was to set out details of existing rights which were fully ensured by Article 119. However, the Commission also stated that the Directive was wider in some respects than Article 119:

> The directive covers not only equal pay for equal work but also the provisions of Convention No. 100 of the International Labour Organisation. In the Commission's view, the concept of 'work of equal value', is wider than the actual wording of Article 119. The directive also deals with the problem of job classification, by specifying that where such a system is used, it must be based on the same criteria for both men and women. Finally, it imposes obligations on the Member States of informing and protecting workers which are not expressly set out in Article 119.[100]

The Advocate General turned his attention to the relationship between the two legal instruments, noting that the purpose of the Directive 'was to ensure smooth and effective application of the principle of equal pay and indicated in general terms certain measures which would provide minimum protection'.[101] He stressed, however, that the Directive did not amend Article 119.

The Court, finding that Article 119 did produce direct effects, discussed two aspects of the relationship between the Article and the Directive. The first is in relation to the material scope of Article 119. The Court contented itself in saying that the Directive provided further details regarding the material scope of Article 119 but added that it further demanded that legal procedures be adopted to secure the principle. The second aspect discussed by the Court regarded the possible modification of the time limits laid down in Article 119. Here the Court stressed that the Directive could not affect the time limits set out in the Treaty. The judgement states that the Directive 'was unable to reduce the effectiveness of that article or modify its temporal effect'.[102]

In *Worringham*, the relationship between Article 119 and Article 1 of the Directive was discussed.[103] The plaintiffs had argued that the pension scheme in question in that case constituted pay within the meaning of Article 119. However, if this argument failed they argued in the alternative that it offended against Article 1(1) of the Directive which requires elimination of all discrimination on the grounds of sex 'with regard to all aspects and conditions of remuneration'.

In this case the Court stated that the concept of pay in the Directive is the same as that in Article 119, and that the latter concept is in no way affected by the former. However, the Court pointed out, the definition of 'same work' in Article 119 was clarified by Article 1 of the Directive and this definition included cases of 'work to which equal value is attributed'.[104]

The insistence by the Court that the concept of pay is the same in both Article 119 and the Directive is explained by the fact that, as the Advocate General points out:

> Nothing turns on the change from the use of the word "pay" in Article 119 to the use of the word 'remuneration' in the Directive. That is a feature of the English texts only. In all the other texts the same word is used...[105]

The Court's judgement on the scope of the concept of equal pay as between the Article of the Treaty and the Directive was reiterated in *Jenkins*.[106] The Court stated that Article 1 of the Directive 'is principally designed to facilitate the practical application of the principle of equal pay outlined in Article 119 of the Treaty [and] in no way alters the content or scope of that principle as defined in the Treaty'.[107]

Preliminary rulings relating to the Directive

Two cases have, to date, been referred to the Court for an interpretation of the provisions of the Directive. The case of *Gisela Rummler* was referred to the Court by the Arbeitsgericht (Labour Court) Oldenburg, Germany, and relates to the problem of developing job classification schemes which are entirely sex-neutral.[108] Ms Rummler was employed in the printing industry and her terms and conditions were governed by a nationwide framework agreement for the whole printing industry in West Germany. This framework agreement provided for a job classification scheme based on the following criteria: degree of knowledge, concentration, muscular demand or effort and responsibility. The plaintiff argued that her job was wrongly classified and she wished to be upgraded from Category III to Category IV.

The Arbeitsgericht was concerned with the possible incompatibility of the framework agreement with Article 1 of Directive 75/117 which provides that 'where a job classification system is used for determining pay, it must be based on the same criteria for both men and women and so drawn up as to exclude any discrimination on grounds of sex'. In particular the German Court was worried that the inclusion of criteria based on muscular demand or effort was discriminatory against women since, the Court claimed, women were less able to meet these criteria as they were in general weaker than men.

The difficulties surrounding job classification schemes had been explored by the European Commission in its 'Report to the Council on the Application of the Principle of Equal Pay For Men and Women'. In this report the Commission examined the various types of job classification schemes in existence in the Member States and concluded that:

> It is here that there is most scope for *indirect or disguised* discrimination...in the form of an under-classification of women within job categories which either form a single unit or are insufficiently differentiated, the result being the creation of job categories practically reserved for women.[109]

In the present case Ms Rummler argued that the Directive outlawed any distinction in job evaluation systems made on the basis of muscular effort or on whether the work was heavy or not. Her employer argued that the inclusion of these criteria was not discriminatory since these were only some of the criteria which were applied in the job evaluation scheme. The UK intervened to argue that the inclusion of strength as a criterion would only be discriminatory if the scheme ignored other characteristics such as manual dexterity. The Commission argued that for the purpose of Article 1 of the Directive the whole scheme must be considered.

The Advocate General agreed with the views presented by the Commission and the UK that the scheme must be examined in its entirety. If some of the criteria applied were weighted more in favour of one sex than another then other criteria must be included which balanced the system as a whole so that 'in the aggregate men and women will have the same opportunities under the agreement'.[110]

The Court, in a somewhat obscure judgement, stated that the principle of equal pay requires that it is the nature of the work to be carried out and not the person who carries it out that must be considered, and that any job classification scheme must use the same criteria regardless of whether the work is carried out by a man or a woman. Perhaps the crucial point made by the Court is, however, that the scheme must not be organized *as a whole* in such a way that in practice it discriminates against one sex. Therefore, the Court said, criteria corresponding to the duties performed are permissible where those duties require physical effort or are physically heavy. These criteria must be objective, based on a measurable expenditure of effort or on a measurable assessment of the heaviness of the work. The Court, however, added a corollary to the effect that each criterion must be considered in the context of the whole job classification system, having regard to other criteria which influence rates of pay. The Court stated:

> In order for a job classification system as a whole to be non-discriminatory and thus to comply with the principles of the Directive, it must, however, be established in such a manner that it includes, if the nature of the tasks in question so permit, jobs to which equal value is attributed and for which regard is had to other criteria in relation to which women may have a particular aptitude.[111]

Here the Court seemed to be accepting the balancing approach advocated by the UK. It then placed the responsibility for evaluating a job classification scheme on the national courts who must determine these issues on a case-by-case basis.

The Arbeitsgericht had addressed a further question to the Court which followed from its first. The Court was asked to determine whether, if a job classification scheme used the criterion of strength, it was the average man's strength to be used in assessing the degree of difficulty of the work in question or the average woman's. The Court decided that the principle of equal pay for work of equal value requires that:

> the work actually carried out must be remunerated in accordance with its nature. Any criterion based on values appropriate only to workers of one sex carries with it the risk of discrimination...The failure to take into consideration values corresponding to the average performance of female workers in establishing a progressive pay scale based on the degree of muscle demand and muscular effort may indeed have the effect of placing women workers, who cannot take jobs which are beyond their physical strength, at a disadvantage. That difference in treatment may, however, be objectively justified by the nature of the job when such a difference is necessary in order to ensure a level of pay appropriate to the effort required by the work and thus corresponds to a real need on the part of the undertaking (see the judgement of 13 May 1986 in Case 170/84 *Bilka-Kaufhaus* v. *Weber von Hartz*.[112]

This case, because of its particular factors and the rather obscurely worded judgement, is not very helpful in laying down general guidelines for the national courts in assessing job classification schemes. However, some general points could be made. The first is that Directive 75/117 does not provide for any particular method of job classification scheme, but it does provide that such a scheme, taken as a whole, should not discriminate against one particular sex. Second, individual factors are not automatically outlawed; each factor must be taken in the context of the whole scheme which must balance out factors which relate more closely to the assumed or real capabilities of men and women. Furthermore, the job classification scheme must relate to the demands of the job and should not be based on the sex of the worker performing it. Finally methods of evaluating criteria must not particularly disadvantage a group of workers of a given sex otherwise the use of such methods is indirect discrimination and it is then up to the employer to justify the scheme using the objectivity and proportionality tests developed by the Court in *Bilka*.[113]

The second case relating to Directive 75/117 which has come to the European Court is, at the time of writing, only in the early stages.[114] A Danish Industrial Arbitration Board, when faced with a dispute between a union and an employers' association relating to the terms of a collective agreement, has referred a host of questions to the European Court. These questions are stated in the abstract but are very detailed and it is unclear what answers the European Court will give or, indeed, how it will approach the preliminary ruling. The questions raised by the Danish Board relate to several issues. The first is on the burden of proof and asks the Court to determine on whom the burden of proof lies of proving that a differentiation in pay between two employees is or is not attributable to a circumstance determined by sex. This is, of course, a crucial question and is one to which the Court has not yet directly addressed itself. The

Commission has proposed that a Directive be adopted on the issue of the burden of proof and this proposal is currently being discussed.[115] The second question from the Danish Board relates to the problem of what may constitute an objective justification for differentials in pay. Are subjective criteria – for example staff mobility – compatible with the Directive? The Board then asks the Court whether the Directive permits supplements to be paid for seniority and special training and, if it does, how can an undertaking make a differentiation in pay between members of staff? The Board's next question asks whether it is compatible with the Directive to pay different rates by reference to different vocational training. Another major issue raised by the Board relates to the question of whether there is a presumption of an infringement of the Directive where it can be shown that an undertaking with a large number of employees pays, on average, the women less than the men. If so, the Board asks, must it follow that the two groups of employees (men and women) must receive the same pay? Finally, the Board asks two questions about collective agreements, the first of which is whether the Directive applies to a situation where a difference in pay is attributable to the fact that employees are covered by different collective agreements. The second question is whether it is important in considering that question whether the two agreements concurrently cover, exclusively or to an overwhelming degree, male and female employees respectively.

It is obvious from these questions that national courts and tribunals will find difficulties in interpreting the Directive and may show up many problems of interpretation as they seek to apply the Directive in the cases before them. It is unlikely, therefore, that the Danish case will be the last to be referred to the Court for a ruling.

Infringement proceedings

The adoption of the Directive and its subsequent implementation, together with the more vigorous approach by the Commission to the problem of equal pay, led the Commission to initiate infringement actions against several Member States, on the basis of Article 169 of the Treaty of Rome.

To date, four infringement proceedings have reached the Court of Justice relating to the failure of Luxembourg, the UK, Denmark and Germany to implement fully the principles of equal pay provided for under Community law.[116] It should be stressed that cases reach the Court only after lengthy and detailed discussions between the Commission and the state concerned have taken place and where there has been a failure to reach agreement on a particular aspect of Community law. Such cases are therefore important in that they reflect the divergence of attitudes between the Commission and a Member State and sometimes indicate the reluctance of states to fulfil to the letter their Community obligations. In other cases what becomes apparent is the genuine differences in interpretation which might be given to a complex piece of Community legislation and recourse to the Court provides an opportunity to explore the meaning of particular provisions as well as the extent of the obligations assumed by the Member States.

In *Commission* v. *Luxembourg* the Court was asked to rule that Luxembourg had failed to fulfil its obligations under Article 119 EEC by not adopting within the period prescribed in Article 8(1) of Directive 75/117/EEC the measures necessary to eliminate discrimination in the conditions for the grant of head of household allowances to civil servants.[117] The Commission had informed Luxembourg of its intention to initiate proceedings by letter dated 3 April 1979. Luxembourg was given 60 days in which to reply and did so by letter dated 6 June 1979. In its reply the government did not reject the view of the Commission that the legislation in question violated Community law and indicated that a draft amendment was being prepared. The particular provision in question was the Law of 22 June 1963 relating to the remuneration of civil servants. This Law provided, *inter alia*:

1. A civil servant having the status of head of household shall be granted a head of household allowance.
2. The following shall be regarded as heads of household:
    (a) a male married civil servant and also a female married civil servant whose husband is subject to an infirmity or serious illness rendering him incapable of providing for the household expenses or whose husband receives an income lower than the minimum social wage.[118]

The Luxembourg government acknowledged the discriminatory nature of this provision and any similar provisions which formed part of collective agreements, and informed the Commission that in future it would refuse to assign the force of law to collective agreements which contained such provisions. Progress on this matter was slow and therefore on 8 May 1980 the Commission issued a reasoned opinion, according to the terms of Article 169 EEC, which noted progress made but which pointed to the fact that amending legislation had not been adopted. In its reply the government underlined the progress made and in particular pointed to the fact that 'both sides of industry had formally undertaken to eliminate the discrimination referred to above on renewal of these agreements'.[119] The Commission, therefore, lodged an application to the Court on 16 March 1981 claiming that Luxembourg had failed to implement Community law.

The Luxembourg government informed the Court that it intended to implement the provisions of the Directive but cited legislative difficulties in obtaining amendments to the offending provisions.

In its judgement the Court stated that Article 8 of the Directive required Member States to bring it into force by 12 February 1976. In view of this fact and the fact that Luxembourg had not disputed its failure so to do the Court declared that:

by not adopting within the period prescribed in Article 8(I) of Directive 75/117/EEC of 10 February 1975 the measures necessary in order to eliminate discrimination in the conditions for the grant of head of household allowances to civil servants, the Grand Duchy of Luxembourg has failed to fulfil its obligations under the EEC Treaty.[120]

It may be objected that the Commission's action in bringing this case was pointless, given the stated objective of Luxembourg to implement the Directive in the future. However, such arguments were refuted by the Advocate General in his opinion. He went further than the Court and the Commission in castigating Luxembourg for its delay in implementing its Community obligations and cited the decision of the Court in *Defrenne*[121] which laid down that the six original Member States of the Community were to have secured application of Article 119 as from 1 January 1962, and that this time limit was not affected by the adoption of the Directive. This interesting argument was not taken up by the Court which remained content to base its judgement on the time limit laid down in the Directive. The argument does show, however, that the Commission was fully justified in pursuing Luxembourg in this matter. It is a basic tenet of Community law that states abide by their Community obligations and do so timeously. Whatever difficulties faced the Luxembourg government in 1979 and 1980 could clearly have been avoided if the government had tackled the problem from the date when the Community obligation arose which, as the Advocate General pointed out, was 1 January 1962. Viewed from this perspective the arguments of the Luxembourg government seem very tame indeed. As a postscript it should be noted that following the procedure in the European Court of Justice, the Law of 20 May 1983 was adopted in Luxembourg which amended the legislation in question.[122]

The case of *Commission* v. *United Kingdom*[123] is rather more complex. Directive 75/117 was adopted to clarify more precisely the meaning of the phrase 'equal pay for equal work' found in Article 119. The Directive provides in Article 1 that the principle of equal pay means 'for the same work or for *work to which equal value is attributed*, the elimination of all discrimination on grounds of sex, with regard to all aspects and conditions of remuneration' (emphasis added).

The UK argued that the Equal Pay Act of 1970, as amended by the Sex Discrimination Act 1975, was in complete conformity with Directive 75/117. That Act provided that a woman may claim equal pay where she is employed on 'like work' with a man. Like work in this context is the same work or broadly similar work. She may also claim equal pay if her job and that of a man has been rated as equivalent by a job evaluation scheme. The Act does not make such schemes compulsory and one cannot be introduced without the consent of the employer. In other words the employee has no right to an evaluation.

The Commission claimed that the Equal Pay Act failed to protect the right of an employee to compare her work to that of a male counterpart who performs a job which is not the same but is nonetheless of equal value to hers except in those cases where job evaluation schemes had been introduced. The Commission claimed support from the UK Equal Opportunities Commission which had already proposed amendments to the Act.

The UK rested its defence on several grounds. It pointed to the fact that at the time of the adoption of the Directive in the Council of Ministers the UK had stated that in its view the right of equal pay for work of equal value was protected in the UK by the inclusion of provisions covering situations similar or where pay had been based on a job evaluation scheme. Since the Commission was aware of that view from the deliberations of the Council it was not now in a position to object to the British interpretation. Furthermore, the UK argued, the Directive and Article 119 should be read together and neither requires the right to a job evaluation, and there is no other way of comparing jobs. Finally, it argued that practical considerations, and in particular the expense of job evaluation schemes, militate against the interpretation advocated by the Commission.

In reply the Commission rejected these arguments pointing to the fact that a state could not evade its legal obligations by making explanatory statements within the Council before the adoption of a legal instrument. Furthermore, the Commission pointed to the fact that there were other methods of introducing the concept of equal value into a legislative framework other than by the adoption of compulsory job evaluation schemes and that other Member States had had no difficulty in doing so. Lastly the Commission did not accept that the practical difficulties referred to by the UK would outweigh the advantages of properly implementing the Directive.

Before giving its judgement on this issue the Court asked the Commission to clarify the situation as it existed in the laws of other Member States and also to explain other methods which might be used, if not compulsory evaluation, to ensure the principle of equal pay for work of equal value. The Commission reported that in eight Member States the Directive had been correctly applied and only in the cases of the UK and Denmark was there any problem. It then presented alternative possible ways of implementing this provision as devised by the other states:

> In Belgium, France, Italy and Luxembourg, as also in the Federal Republic of Germany, many problems are resolved by works inspectorates, and where a question falls to be resolved by the courts, the latter are not necessarily bound by the results of job evaluation schemes. In the Netherlands the question whether work is of equal value is assessed on the basis of a reliable system of job evaluation. Under the Irish legislation any dispute on the subject of equal pay may be referred to one of the three Equality Officers who, after investigating the matter, will issue a recommendation.

Since such recommendations are not legally binding, it is ultimately for the Court to decide the matters referred to them.[124]

This enumeration of the possible ways in which the UK could have adopted its legislation certainly belies its argument that a job evaluation scheme is essential if the concept of equal pay for work of equal value is to be realized. However, it does point to genuine difficulties for states in adapting their legal systems to that of the Community. The UK legal system in this respect is problematic because of its inflexibility. Courts and tribunals are expected to apply detailed legislation to cases before them and are unaccustomed to an approach which openly demands a degree of judicial policy making. Giving to British courts or tribunals the power to adjudge on particular equal value claims, given the difficulties which they seem to have had in coming to terms with British sex discrimination legislation, is not necessarily the best way to help British women in their fight for equal pay. There is thus some strength in the argument proposed by the UK in its rejoinder to the Commission that 'where directives are concerned, Member States are free to adapt their legislation by whatever means are most appropriate to their own legal systems'.[125] Furthermore, the UK had argued, 'in response to the Commission's point that other Member States have reproduced the objective of directive facility, the United Kingdom refers to the extract from the European Industrial Relations Review No. 90 of July 1981 which speaks of the "modest impact" of the Netherlands Law on equal pay'.[126] In short, the British argued that in order to ensure the effective implementation of the principle contained in the Directive it was more important to adapt the Community rule to suit the domestic situation rather than to enforce the principle formally yet ineffectively. Such arguments would perhaps be more seductive if the situation in the UK were markedly better than elsewhere in the Community but this does not seem to be the case.

The arguments advanced by the UK were rejected by the Court as being 'a denial of the very existence of a right to equal pay for work of equal value where no classification has been made'.[127] Arising from this right, the Court stated:

It follows that where there is disagreement as to the application of that concept a worker must be entitled to claim before an appropriate authority that his work has the same value as other work and, if that is found to be the case, to have his rights under the Treaty and the Directive acknowledged by a binding decision. Any method which excludes that option prevents the aims of the Directive from being achieved.

The United Kingdom has emphasised the practical difficulties which would stand in the way of implementing the concept of work to which equal value has been attributed if the use of a system laid down by consensus were abandoned. The United Kingdom believes that the criterion of work of equal value is too abstract to be applied by the courts.

The implementation of the Directive implies that the assessment of the 'equal value' to be 'attributed' to particular work, may be effected notwithstanding the employer's wishes, if necessary in the context of adversary proceedings. The Member States must endow an authority with the requisite jurisdiction to decide whether work has the same value as other work, after obtaining such information as may be required.

Thus the Court explicitly stated that an authority was capable of making the assessment of equal value and that this authority might well be a judge. The judgement might also indicate that the authority making the assessment might also be subject to judicial review.

Accordingly the Court declared:

By failing to introduce into its national legal system in implementation of the provisions of Council Directive 75/117/EEC of 10 February 1975 such measures as are necessary to enable all employees who consider themselves wronged by failure to apply the principle of equal pay for men and women for work to which equal value is attributed and for which no system of job classification exists to obtain recognition of such equivalence, the United Kingdom has failed to fulfil its obligations under the Treaty.[128]

Following this decision the UK adopted the Equal Pay (Amendment) Regulations 1983 which introduced an extremely cumbersome procedure under which women were able to make an equal value claim.[129] Subsequently, according to the UK Equal Opportunity Commission, 'the operation of the Equal Pay Act as amended has become significantly more complicated and protracted'.[130] It might seem therefore that in achieving Directive facility the Commission has been unable to persuade the UK government to do more than comply with the letter of the Court's ruling, if that.[131] The 1983 Regulations are far from helpful in practice in giving women an opportunity to make an equal value claim and may well, in the long term, hamper attempts to rectify the acute imbalances in pay which exist in the UK. No doubt this effect was far from the mind of the Commission when bringing the case but, in this particular instance, an intransigent government has shown how easily it may avoid its obligation of ensuring the rights of its citizens arising from Community law where it is determined to do so.

The case brought against Denmark also concerned an alleged failure to incorporate the principle of equal pay for work of equal value into domestic legislation.[132] In this instance Denmark had adopted Act 32 of 4 February 1976 which provided that:

Every person who employs men and women to work must pay them the same salary for the same work [samme arbejde] under this Act if he is not already required to do so pursuant to a collective agreement.

The Danish government argued that the phrase *samme arbejde* covered both equal pay for the same work and for work to which equal value is attributed. It supported this view by arguing that the Act of 4 February 1976 is:

> only a subsidiary guarantee of the principle of equal pay, in cases where observance of that principle is not already ensured under collective agreements: Collective agreements, which govern most employment relationships in Denmark, clearly uphold the idea that the principle of equal pay also applies to work of equal value. That interpretation is based in particular on the 1971 agreement concluded by the main organisations on the labour market, which provides expressly that '' 'equal pay'' means that the same salary is to be paid for work of the same value regardless of sex'. That practice is confirmed by a decision of the Chairman of the Statens Forligsinstitution i Arbejdstridigheder (National Industrial Conciliation Board), acting as arbitrator, of 8 December 1977, in which he applied the principle of equal pay to work 'of the same value to and in production at the place of work'.[133]

The Court accepted that Member States were free to implement directives by means appropriate to their domestic situations and that in this particular case Denmark could *in the first instance* leave the implementation of Directive 75/117 to representatives of management and labour. However, the Court did not find this method sufficient protection for the rights of all workers, especially if they were not members of a union or where the particular industrial sector was not covered by a collective agreement or where such a collective agreement did not guarantee the principle of equal pay. The Court demanded that the state must lay down the principle of equal pay 'in unequivocal wording', so that individuals were clear as to the extent of their rights and so that courts could faithfully ensure that those rights were safeguarded. In this respect the Court declared that the Danish legislation had failed and the fact that Denmark had indicated to the Council of Ministers that the expression *samme arbejde* could continue to be used was irrelevant. It could not. The Court concluded, therefore, that Denmark had failed to fulfil its obligations.

The Court did not address itself to a question discussed extensively in the opinion of the Advocate General as to the permissibility of the inclusion of an additional provision, that of *samme arbejdsplads*, in the Danish legislation. The Advocate General argued that this provision, which limited a worker to comparing her wages to that of another in the same place of work, was an infringement of the Treaty, given that it imposes an additional condition which is not imposed by either Article 119 or the Directive. Unfortunately the Court did not reach any conclusions as to this issue as the Commission had not formally raised the objection. It may be that in the future cases may be brought to clarify this point.[134]

The case of *Commission* v. *Germany*[135] concerns the implementation both of Directive 75/117 and of Directive 76/207 relating to equal treatment. The latter aspects of the case are dealt with elsewhere in this book and only the aspects relating to equal pay are dealt with here.[136]

In this case the Commission argued that Germany had not fully implemented Directive 75/117 with regard to equal pay for employees in the public sector. The German government argued that Article 3 of the German Constitution which provides that 'No one may be prejudiced or favoured because of his sex'. together with Section 612(3) of the Civil Code which lays down that 'a contract of employment may not provide, in the case of the same work or work of equal value, for the payment to an employee of remuneration that is lower, on grounds of sex, than that paid to an employee of the opposite sex...', provided a sufficient guarantee of the right to equal pay as defined under Community law. The Advocate General summed up the dilemma of the Commission in deciding whether these articles were sufficient to implement the Directive in full. He pointed to the nature of the German constitutional provisions which bind 'the legislature, influence the approach by the courts, and are directly binding on the public authorities'.[137] He pointed out that they do not confer obligations on private citizens which may be asserted in the German courts. In order to ensure that individuals could assert their rights, Section 612(3) was inserted into the civil code. However, for certain public sector employees, those recruited by a public service contract and who are not covered by Section 612(3), no action was taken since the public authorities are governed by constitutional rules. The Advocate General pointed out that such employees are not effectively guaranteed the right of equal pay, and thus the Commission had instigated the present action. He summarized the position thus:

> Article 3 makes no mention of 'equal pay...for the same work or for work to which equal value is attributed' (see Article 1 of the Directive and Section 612(3) of the German Civil Code). The same holds true for the legislation on salaries which merely lays down rules for calculating the amount to be paid but does not prohibit the payment of different amounts on grounds of sex. In other words, German law lacks a rule of general validity which clearly imposes an obligation not to discriminate between men and women with regard to remuneration.[138]

The Court, perhaps surprisingly, rejected the opinion of the Advocate General and accepted the argument put forward by Germany that remuneration of public servants was based exclusively on post and grade. It found that the Commission had produced no evidence of sex discrimination in the levels of remuneration paid to public servants and, therefore, that the object of Directive 75/117 'had already been achieved in the Federal Republic of Germany at the time when that directive entered into force, with the result that no specific measure was required for its implementation'.[139] The Court therefore dismissed the complaint.

The Court here was taking a practical rather than a theoretical approach to the situation. Its argument is that, at the time of its decision, no evidence was available to suggest that the system adopted by Germany failed to give effect to the principle of equal pay when constitutional principles and administrative practices were taken together. Presumably should evidence come to light that these administrative practices are changed then the Commission would be free to re-open the proceedings. If the Court had adopted the views of the Advocate General that Germany was required to provide for specific legal remedies, such a future development would not be possible.

In the arguments placed before the Court there did arise a very crucial one about the choice of form and methods open to any state in the implementation of EEC directives. In his closely argued opinion Advocate General Mancini reminded the Court of its previous decisions as to the nature of the obligation imposed on a state by a directive. The Court itself had stated that the method chosen by a state to implement a directive must fully meet 'the requirements of clarity and certainty in legal situations',[140] and, furthermore, that the measures adopted be fully effective. He reminded the Court that it had laid down, as regards Article 6 of Directive 75/117, that each state must provide a guarantee of the principle of equal pay which 'must cover all cases where effective protection is not ensured'[141] (his emphasis). Taken together this meant that constitutional provisions were not in themselves sufficient guarantee of the principles laid down in the Directive unless these constitutional provisions were as clear and as certain as it. In this case the German constitutional provision in question (Article 3) did not meet these requirements.

The logic of this argument is compelling. It is a pity that the Court did not take it on board and remained content to accept the arguments put forward that in practice the system appeared to work. Such a loose approach contrasts quite sharply to its much firmer approach in the cases previously brought.

The four cases brought by the Commission illustrate the difficulties facing it in ensuring that Member States abide by their obligations. The cases brought against the UK and Denmark highlight the reluctance of Member States to accept a Community definition of specific principles and illustrate the national jealousies which prevent the development of Community law in several areas. The insistence of Member States, for example the UK, provides a fine example of the way a state insists on its own view of a particular Community act and shows that the question is not necessarily only one of equal pay, but is one of national pride and national feeling. It seemed self-evident to the British experts on the matter, the Equal Opportunities Commission, that the legislation at issue did not meet the European standard and the arguments put forward in the case show the petulance of the government on the issue rather than the genuine differences in interpretation. To some extent these arguments may too be laid at the door of the Danes. The case of

Luxembourg illustrates another perennial problem of Community law, that of getting states to implement directives on time. In the instant matter the Commission tried repeatedly to prod Luxembourg into activity but it was only judicial proceedings which brought any action.

The Commission had had greater success with other Member States. As stated above, proceedings reach the Court only after quite extensive discussions between the Commission and the state. Informal proceedings can quite often lead to the desired result and here the Commission can be seen to be acting as a friendly expert, guiding the Member States to reach a correct solution.[142] Unfortunately proceedings under Article 169 are confidential until a case is brought to the European Court of Justice and it is, therefore, difficult to assess the impact of the administrative stage. However, Boudard points out that seven infringement procedures were opened and:

> the measures required by the Commission were taken after the delivery of a formal warning letter (1st stage) in two Member States (France and the Federal Republic of Germany), after the issuance of a reasoned opinion (2nd stage) in two further States (the Netherlands and Belgium) and after a judgement of the Court of Justice in two other States (Luxembourg and the United Kingdom). Denmark, condemned by the Court, had just drawn up a modifying Bill.[143]

He analyses these proceedings as to their content:

> – certain supplementary wage advantages connected with the concept of 'head of household' (Belgium, Luxembourg, France);
> – the fact that judicial review was based only on a very general Article of the constitution (the Federal Republic of Germany);
> – the limitation of the law on wage equality to the private sector only (the Netherlands);
> – the incomplete character of the law on wage equality with regard to work 'of equal value' (the United Kingdom and Denmark).

In the absence of more specific information it is impossible to draw firm conclusions from this information except to note the success of the Commission in reaching agreement on the proper implementation of the Directive with the state concerned.

Conclusions

It is difficult to draw definite conclusions from the somewhat conflicting judgements of the Court of Justice in the area of equal pay. However, some propositions are clear. Article 119 is directly effective, that is, individuals may derive rights from it and go to their own courts and tribunals to have this law applied to their cases. Article 119 is, moreover, supreme over any conflicting national legislation. There are limits to Article 119 in the sense that it speaks only of pay, albeit with a wide definition of what constitutes pay. Other aspects of working conditions are not covered by this Treaty Article and, therefore, the Community has adopted subsequent legislation, in the form of Directives, to cover other aspects of discrimination. In the case of Directive 75/117, the Court has made it clear that this Directive adds no new concepts to those already existing under Article 119.

Some other propositions must be stated rather more tentatively. In particular, in the area of pensions, there is a degree of confusion about some aspects of pension schemes.[144] These difficulties have, to a certain extent, been created by the Court itself, but they arise out of a more serious problem which is the lack of will on the part of the Member States to ensure the eradication of discrimination against women in the pension area. The Court has done as much as it could to 'stretch' the concept of pay to include those aspects of pensions which might legitimately be described as pay. It has not been consistent always in the tests to be applied but it might fairly be argued that it is not the function of judges to have to strain the wording of a treaty article to encompass the myriad ways invented to treat one group of workers differently from another. Adequate legislative action early on would have prevented any such problems arising. As is demonstrated in Chapters 5 and 7, where the relationship between Article 119 and subsequent legislation is discussed, the Member States themselves have failed to reach agreements in the area of pensions which will remain a difficult one for some time to come.

Notes

1   O.J. L 45/19, 19 February 1975.
2   These reasons were discussed by Advocate General Dutheillet de Lamothe in his opinion in case 80/70 *Defrenne* v. *Belgium* (Defrenne I) (1971) E.C.R. 445, p. 455.
3   UNTS vol. 165, p. 303.
4   See Chapter 2 above.
5   Case 43/75 *Defrenne* v. *Sabena* (Defrenne II) (1976) E.C.R. 455.
6   Case 80/70 *loc. cit.* note 2.
7   This case is discussed extensively below.
8   Case 80/70 *loc. cit.* note 2, p. 456.
9   Case 43/75 *loc. cit.* note 5, p. 459.
10 *Ibid.* p. 461.
11 The Irish argument is not convincing. In its judgement in case 36/74 *Walrave and Koch* v. *Union Cycliste Internationale* (1974) E.C.R. 1405, delivered on 12 December 1974, the Court had recognized the horizontal direct effects of Treaty provisions.
12 Case 43/75 *loc. cit.* note 5, p. 463.
13 *Ibid.* p. 487.
14 *Ibid.* p. 473.

15   *Ibid.* p. 491.
16   Although this was not how the decision of the Court was subsequently interpreted in succeeding cases. See Chapter 1 above for a discussion of the confusion of concepts arising from this decision.
17   Case 43/75 *loc. cit.* note 5. p. 475.
18   *Ibid.*
19   23 April 1975.
20   *Ibid.* p. 481
21   Member States might have been tempted to introduce equal pay by levelling down pay rates. The Court, aware of this, perhaps, emphasized that Article 119, like Articles 117 and 118, aimed at the improvement of living standards and stated (at p. 472) that 'the obligation that the terms of this article may be observed in other ways than by raising the lowest salaries may be set aside'.
22   Case 80/70 *loc. cit.* note 2.
23   *Ibid.* p. 447.
24   *Ibid.* p. 449.
25   *Ibid.* p. 449.
26   *Ibid.* p. 456.
27   The Advocate General can be criticized for failing to understand the nature of the pension scheme. See the comments on this case in Chapter 5, pp. 170-72.
28   Case 80/70 *loc. cit.* note 2, p. 451.
29   See Chapter 5, p. 171, for a discussion of British contracted-out schemes in the context of social security.
30   Case 69/80 *Worringham and Humphreys* v. *Lloyds Bank Limited* (1981) E.C.R. 767.
31   *Ibid.* p. 798. British legislation on pensions has been substantially altered since then.
32   *Ibid.* p. 769.
33   *Ibid.* p. 779.
34   *Ibid.* p. 806.
35   *Ibid.* p. 790.
36   *Ibid.* p. 790.
37   *Ibid.* p. 793.
38   *Ibid.* p. 792.
39   *Ibid.* p. 794.
40   Case 23/83 *Liefting* v. *Academisch Ziekenhuis bij de Universiteit van Amsterdam* (1984) E.C.R. 3225.
41   Similar problems were met if one person worked for several public authorities since all employers paid the contributions. At the end of the year, when the sum of the contributions exceeded the limits, the surplus was paid back to the person concerned.
42   For a full discussion see Curtin (1987).
43   Case 23/83 *loc. cit.* note 40 p. 3239. The English version reads: 'Consequently the amounts which the public authorities are obliged to pay in respect of contributions owed to the social security scheme by persons working for the State and which are included in the calculation of the gross salary payable to civil servants must be regarded as pay within the meaning of Article 119 *since* they directly determine the calculation of other advantages linked to the salary' (emphasis added). This is a mistranslation of the Dutch which reads *voor zover* (so far as). This point is important. See Chapter 6, p. 241, for further discussion.
44   *Ibid.* p. 3240.
45   Compare this situation with that in *Newstead* (discussed below) where the fact that the employer was not paying something seemed to be the decisive point for the Court. For a further discussion of the relationship between Article 119 and pension-related benefits see Chapters 5 and 7 below, p. 171 and p. 285 respectively.
46   Case 170/84 *Bilka-Kaufhaus GmbH* v. *Karin Weber Von Hartz* (1986) 2 C.M.L.R. 701.

47   *Ibid.* p. 719.
48   *Ibid.* p. 719.
49   Case 192/85 *Newstead* v. *Department of Transport and H.M. Treasury* (1988) 1 C.M.L.R. 219.
50   See Chapter 4 below , p. 126, for a full discussion of the latter aspect.
51   Case 19/81 *Burton* v. *British Railways Board* (1982) E.C.R. 555.
52   Case 192/85 p. 226.
53   See Chapter 5 below.
54   Case 192/85 *loc. cit.* note 49 p. 231.
55   *Ibid.* p. 233.
56   Although Advocate General Warner had equated contracted-out schemes in this way in *Worringham.*
57   Case 149/77 *Defrenne* v. *Sabena* (Defrenne III) (1978) E.C.R. 1365.
58   *Ibid.* p. 1371.
59   *Ibid.* p. 1377.
60   Although it has now. See Chapter 4 below.
61   But compare case 152/84 *Marshall* v. *Southampton and South West Hampshire Area Health Authority (Training)* (1986) E.C.R. 723, discussed in Chapter 4, p. 122.
62   Case 19/81 *loc. cit.* note 51.
63   The Equal Pay Act does not cover non-contractual matters. The Sex Discrimination Act makes it unlawful for an employer to discriminate against a worker in access to voluntary redundancy benefits. However, the Act does not apply to provisions in relation to death or retirement. The Sex Discrimination Act 1986, which came into force in November 1987, provides that men and women may continue into employment up until the age of 65. See Chapter 6 for a discussion.
64   Case 19/81 *loc. cit.* note 51 p. 566.
65   *Ibid.* p. 589.
66   These aspects are discussed in Chapter 4 below, p. 121.
67   Case 12/81 *Garland* v. *British Rail Engineering Limited* (1982) E.C.R. 359.
68   *Ibid.* p. 369.
69   Case 96/80 *Jenkins* v. *Kingsgate (Clothing Productions) Ltd* (1981) E.C.R. 911.
70   Section 1(3) reads 'An equality clause shall not operate in relation to a variation between the woman's contract and the man's contract if the employer proves that the variation is genuinely due to a material difference (other than the difference of sex) between her case and his'.
71   Case 96/80 *loc. cit.* note 69 p. 917.
72   *Ibid.*
73   *Ibid.* p. 922.
74   *Ibid.* p. 933.
75   *Ibid.* p. 925.
76   *Ibid.* p. 926.
77   *Ibid.* p. 926.
78   For a discussion see Chapter 6 below, pp. 206-12.
79   Case 170/84 *loc. cit.* note 46.
80   *Ibid.* p. 716.
81   *Ibid.* p. 720.
82   Case 171/88 *Ingrid Rinner-Kuhn* v. *FWW Spezial-Gebaudereinigung GmbH and Co.,* judgement of 13 July 1989 (not yet reported). For a summary of the Report of the President of the Third Chamber of the Arbeitsgericht, Oldenberg, see BB 1988, p. 1256 and also O.J. C193/11, 22 July 1988. Two more cases on indirect discrimination are currently before the court; case 33/89 *Kowalska* v. *Freie und Hansestadt Hamburg* (not yet decided) O.J. C68/9, 19 March 1989, case 184/89 *Helga Nimz* v. *Freie und Hansestadt Hamburg* O.J. C163/09, 30 June 1989 preliminary stages.
83   *Ibid.* p. 9.
84   Case 129/79 *Macarthys Ltd* v. *Wendy Smith* (1980) E.C.R. 1275.

85   *Ibid.* p. 1280.
86   *Ibid.* p. 1280.
87   *Ibid.* p. 1288.
88   *Ibid.* p. 1289.
89   Case 157/86 *Mary Murphy and Others* v. *Bord Telecom Eireann* (1987) 1 C.M.L.R. 559. (The original reference.)
90   *Ibid.* p. 561.
91   *Ibid.* p. 565.
92   Case 157/86 *Murphy* v. *An Bord Telecom Eireann* (1988) 1 C.M.L.R. 879.
93   *Ibid.* For a discussion see Chapter 1 above.
94   Case 43/75 *loc. cit.* note 5.
95   O.J. C13/1, 12 February 1974.
96   See cases 29/69 *Stauder* v. *City of Ulm* (1969) E.C.R. 419; 1/70 *Internationale Handelsgesellschaft* (1970) E.C.R. 1125; 4/73 *Nold* v. *Commission* (1974) E.C.R. 491; 44/79 *Hauer* v. *Rheinland-Pfalz* (1979) E.C.R. 3729.
97   Council Directive of 10 February 1975 on the approximation of the laws of the Member States relating to the application of the principle of equal pay for men and women, *loc. cit.* note 1.
98   This definition is found in Article 189 of the Treaty.
99   Case 43/75 (Defrenne II) *loc. cit.* note 5.
100   *Ibid.* p. 469. The Directive is aimed, therefore, at certain aspects of disguised discrimination in the sense of the second Defrenne case.
101   *Ibid.* p. 491.
102   *Ibid.* p. 479.
103   Case 69/80 *loc. cit.* note 30.
104   *Ibid.* p. 791.
105   *Ibid.* p. 807.
106   Case 96/80 *loc. cit.* note 69.
107   *Ibid.* p. 927.
108   Case 235/84 *Rummler* v. *Dato-Druck GmbH* (1987) 3 C.M.L.R. 127.
109   COM (78) 711 final 'Report to the Council on the Implementation of the Principle of Equal Pay for Men and Women', pp. 65–83.
110   Case 235/84 *loc. cit.* note 108 p. 135.
111   *Ibid.* p. 139.
112   *Ibid.* p. 141.
113   The English Court of Appeal ruled in March 1988 in the case of *Bromley* v. *Quick Ltd* (1988) 2 C.M.L.R. 468 that job evaluation schemes based on a so-called 'felt-fair' system were outlawed by UK legislation, thus reinforcing the right provided by Community law to an analytical and unbiased job evaluation scheme. Lord Justice Dillon quoted the Rummler case in his judgement. p. 476.
114   Case 109/88 *Handels-Og Kantorfunktionaernes Forbund I Danmark* v. *Dansk Arbeijdsgiverforening for Danfoss A/S* O.J. C 124/8 11 May 1988.
115   For a full discussion of the proposal, see Chapter 7 below pp 296-300.
116   Cases 58/81 *Commission* v. *Luxembourg* (1982) E.C.R. 2175; 61/81 *Commission* v. *United Kingdom* (1982) E.C.R. 2601; 143/83 *Commission* v. *Denmark* (1986) C.M.L.R. 44; 248/33 *Commission* v. *Germany* (1986) C.M.L.R. 588.
117   C.f. the staff cases on this matter 20/71 *Sabbatini* v. *European Parliament* (1972) E.C.R. 345; 32/71 *Bauduin* v. *Commission* (1972) E.C.R. 363; 21/74 *Airola* v. *Commission* (1975) E.C.R. 221.
118   Case 58/81 *loc. cit.* note 116 p. 2177.
119   *Ibid.* p. 2178.
120   *Ibid.* p. 2181.
121   Case 43/75 *loc. cit.* note 5.
122   For a discussion see Boudard (1986) p. 108.
123   Case 61/81 *loc. cit.* note 116.

124 *Ibid.* p. 2613. It is interesting to note that in the Netherlands value may be assessed on the basis of equity where there is no job classification scheme.
125 *Ibid.* p. 2610.
126 *Ibid.* p. 2611.
127 *Ibid.* p. 2615.
128 *Ibid.* pp. 2616–2617.
129 For a discussion see Szyszczak (1986).
130 Equal Opportunities Commission, *Legislating for Change* (Manchester, EOC, 1986) 5.
131 In the case of *Pickstone and Others* v. *Freemans PLC* (1987) I.R.L.R. 218 before the English Court of Appeal, Lord Justice Nicholls suggested that the 1983 Regulations fell short of the Community standard.
132 Case 143/83 *loc. cit.* note 116.
133 *Ibid.* p. 50.
134 In the UK, the Equal Pay Act requires that a woman choose a comparator who is 'in the same employment'.
135 Case 248/83 *loc. cit.* note 116.
136 See Chapter 4 below, p. 145.
137 Case 248/83 *loc. cit.* note 116 p. 595.
138 *Ibid.* p. 601.
139 *Ibid.* p. 617.
140 In case 102/79 *Commission* v. *Belgium* (1980) E.C.R. 1473, quoted by Advocate General Mancini at p. 593.
141 In case 143/83 *Commission* v. *Denmark loc. cit.* note 116 quoted by Advocate General Mancini at p. 60.
142 For a discussion see Zorbas (1986).
143 Boudard (1986) p. 107.
144 Further difficulties seem to arise all the time – see case 262/88 *Barber* v. *Guardian Royal Exchange Assurance Group,* preliminary reference submitted to the Court of Justice in September 1988. O.J. C279/14, 29 October 1988. See also case 233/89 *Cray Precision Engineers* v. *David William Clarke* O.J. C219/10, 25 August 1989.

4 Equal Treatment Directive

When Ms Defrenne argued that the principle of equal pay for equal work cannot be applied unless there is, to begin with, equality in conditions of employment,[1] she was, of course, right. For, what is the use of the equal pay principle, when women are denied access to certain (well-paid) jobs, when they can be dismissed because of pregnancy or because they are not considered to be the breadwinner for their family? Indeed, if interpreted strictly as the Court of Justice has done, the principle of equal pay has limited value.

At the Community level, this criticism has been met by issuing the Directive on the implementation of the principle of equal treatment for men and women as regards access to employment, vocational training and promotion, and working conditions (Equal Treatment Directive).[2]

However, it would be incorrect to suggest that the Equal Treatment Directive is only a response to the limitations inherent in Article 119. Its origin should be sought in the more general developments within the Community when the social aspects of the common market became a more important theme. The major incentive for Community social policy development came from the summit meeting of October 1972 held in Paris. The final communiqué stated, *inter alia*:

> The Heads of State or Heads of Government emphasized that they attached as much importance to rigorous action in the social field as to the achievement of the Economic and Monetary Union. They thought it essential to ensure the increasing involvement of labour and management in the economic and social decisions of the Community. They invited the institutions, after consulting labour and management, to draw up between then and 1 January 1974 a programme of action providing for concrete measures and the corresponding resources particularly in the framework of the Social Fund.[3]

In pursuance of this communiqué, in 1973 the Commission drafted a proposal for a social programme. On 21 January 1974 the Council of Ministers passed a resolution initiating the Social Action Programme.[4]

The main objectives of this programme were:

- full and better employment at community, national and regional levels, which is an essential condition for an effective social policy;
- improvement of living and working conditions so as to make possible their harmonization while the improvement is being maintained;
- increased involvement of management and labour in the economic and social decisions of the Community, and of workers in the life of undertakings.

As concerns full and better employment the Council called for measures to deal with particular social issues including the need:

> to undertake action for the purpose of achieving equality between men and women as regards access to employment and vocational training and advancement and as regards access to employment and vocational training and advancement and as regards working conditions including pay, and in addition to attempt to reconcile the family responsibilities of all concerned with their professional aspirations.

Acting on this resolution the Commission drew up in 1975 a Memorandum on the situation of working women in the Community and a draft directive which was to meet the main difficulties signalled by the Memorandum.[5] Preceded by several studies[6] and consultations the Memorandum highlights the main characteristics of the position of women. Increasing numbers of women are entering the labour market, but are confined to a narrow range of jobs at a low level with little opportunity for promotion. One of the most pressing problems is the strong 'job segregation' on the labour market. The reasons for these barriers are historical, social and cultural. Practice is reinforced by the educational system, by inadequate and traditional vocational guidance and by the role of women as wives and mothers. Although the Commission recognized that such problems cannot be met by legislative action alone nevertheless it considered legislation as one of the appropriate means to reach the goal of equal treatment. The Social Action Programme itself could not serve as a juridical basis for a directive for Community Directives must be based on an explicit provision of the Treaty.[7] The Commission proposed as legal basis both Article 100 and Article 235 but the Council opted for Article 235 alone. Apparently, the Council took the view that the Directive was action proving necessary to attain, in the course of the operation of the common market, one of the objectives of the Community for which the Treaty had not provided the necessary powers. The Equal Treatment Directive was adopted on 9 February 1976.

Terms of the Equal Treatment Directive

Article 1 describes the purpose and the scope of the Directive. According to this Article the principle of equal treatment of men and women applies to access to employment, including promotion, to access to vocational training and guidance, and to working conditions. More detailed provisions regarding these three areas are elaborated in Articles 3, 4 and 5. Although equal treatment in social security is included in principle, the Directive provides that its gradual implementation will be determined by subsequent legal instruments (Article 1, paragraph 2).[8] This somewhat curious construction may be explained by the fact that the initial proposal of the Commission for the Second Directive concerned social security as well. As the Directive itself makes no explicit distinction, the provisions apply to both private and public sectors and to self-employed workers.[9]

Furthermore, the implementing measures must apply to *de jure* and *de facto* discrimination[10], to both formal provisions and to all discriminatory acts, practices and circumstances in the areas covered by the Directive.

Article 2, paragraph 1 defines the principle of equal treatment. According to this provision 'the principle of equal treatment shall mean that there shall be no discrimination whatsoever on grounds of sex either directly or indirectly by reference in particular to marital or family status'. As the Directive gives no further definition of the terms direct and indirect discrimination problems of interpretation have arisen in some Member States. The absence of a general definition of these concepts may lead to a restrictive interpretation contrary to the Directive either by the legislator when implementing the Directive or by the courts when applying the law. In particular the concept of indirect discrimination reveals problems concerning its content.[11] It may be asked why the Community legislator did not include a definition of both concepts in the Directive. Given the confusion that existed (and probably still exists) with respect to the concept of discrimination[12] it was to be expected that national interpretations would differ. On the other hand, although non-discrimination theoretically seems to be quite a clear concept, problems often arise when it must be applied to a concrete case. Guidelines for the test of discrimination may be very useful as they guarantee to a certain extent a uniform approach, but some scope for interpretation or at least appreciation will always be left.[13]

Within the context of the Equal Treatment Directive *direct discrimination* means different (less favourable[14]) treatment of a person based on sex. In other words, the fact that a person is a woman (or a man) is the ground for different treatment. *Indirect discrimination* occurs when a neutral (i.e. applying equally to both sexes) criterion is used, but *de facto* it mainly affects persons of one sex only. Such a criterion may be discriminatory even if the author did not intend to discriminate. As a possible 'escape' still remains the proof that the use of the criterion was based on reasons objectively justified. It may be assumed that the test for indirect discrimination established by the Court in *Bilka*[15] applies to all forms of indirect discrimination, thus to discrimination under the Equal Treatment Directive as well. Summing up, this test asks the following:

- does the use of a neutral criterion (for example, part-time workers) affect in effect a larger, number of women than men?
- can the use of the criterion be objectively justified?
- has the principle of proportionality been respected?

Some remarks must be made concerning this test. In the first place it is not always easy to demonstrate that only or predominantly one group has been affected. Often, in indirect discrimination cases, statistics may be used to support legal arguments. However, two problems may occur here at least. Sometimes no statistics are available at all. And if statistics are available, what statistics should be used? Statistics of Europe's population? National population? Workers within a company? Or only workers within a branch of the company? It is extremely important to determine which groups must be compared to argue that the given criterion is 'suspect'.[16]

If this first step succeeds, then the burden of proof shifts: the person suspected of discrimination must prove that his or her way of acting is objectively justified. There will only be an objective justification if the objective pursued is a legitimate one (e.g. certain qualities required for a job must be 'job-related', i.e. a person without those qualities cannot perform the function well) and the means must be necessary to achieve the objective. If the objective can be achieved by using other – less or not discriminatory – methods (criteria), there will be no justification. Although the test seems to be quite simple, in practice serious problems may arise. The courts often have to balance the principle of non-discrimination and other interests. How are they to compare the importance of eliminating discrimination with, for example the profitability of a business or a clearly defined redundancy selection criterion? The justification test, being an exception to a fundamental right, must be kept as strict as possible. Moreover, once justified does not mean for always and everywhere justified since the justification is time and context-bounded. A reassessment from time to time seems necessary.

As concerns direct discrimination, it must be pointed out that a distinction need not necessarily be made on the basis of the criterion male or female. Other characteristics related only to one of the sexes and used as bases for different treatment will be directly discriminatory as well: reference to pregnant persons or persons under military duty implies direct discrimination, at least as long as only women can get pregnant and only men are liable for military service.[17] Direct discrimination will also occur when, for instance, a collective agreement contains some more far-reaching guarantees for 'heads of household' and head of household is defined in the agreement itself, or in another text to which the agreement refers, as 'the husband'.

In particular, the reference to pregnancy seems to cause considerable confusion. The Dutch Emancipatieraad and government, for example, considered such a reference as indirect discrimination[18]. Another striking example is *Turley* v. *Allders Department Stores Ltd.* The Employment Appeal Tribunal held that while establishing discrimination, one must compare 'like with like'. As there is no masculine equivalent to a pregnant woman there can be no discrimination.[19] This approach merits some remarks. In general, the principle of equal treatment requires that comparable situations will not be treated differently and, consequently that different situations will not be treated equally. This principle in this form can be found in both national and Community law.[20] However, this same principle implies that an inquiry must be made into the comparability of the situations. On this basis the EAT reasoned that as far as pregnancy is concerned, a man and a woman are not comparable and consequently they may be treated differently. It has been rightly argued that such a comparison denies 'the core reality that sex-based biological differences are related to sex', trying to define a sex-discrimination problem in other terms: a woman is not discriminated against on grounds of her sex but on grounds of her pregnancy.[21] However this may be, under the Directive a comparability test seems irrelevant. It may be argued that the Directive prohibits different treatment on grounds of sex with respect to all matters falling within its scope. The only 'loop-holes' in the Directive are its derogations. There is no space for comparability or justification tests, at least not as far as direct discrimination is concerned. In case of indirect discrimination the justification test does apply. Thus, for instance excluding pregnant women from a selection procedure for a job is in principle contrary to the Directive: women – though a small part of them – are treated less favourably than men and the situation falls within the scope of the Directive. It is exactly this problem of refusing to employ a woman because she is pregnant that was submitted to the Court of Justice in June 1988. The Dutch Hoge Raad asked the Court whether employers are directly or indirectly in breach of the principle of equal treatment laid down in Articles 2, paragraph 1, and 3, paragraph 1, of the Directive if they refused to enter into a contract of employment with a candidate found by them to be suitable for the job because she is pregnant. Moreover, the Hoge Raad wants to know whether a justification can be pleaded in this respect by the employer, other than that under Article 2, paragraph 2, or 4.[22]

Contrary to direct discrimination, indirect discrimination is or can be very tricky. Age limits for entry to certain posts in public service may be indirectly discriminatory as many women in their twenties or thirties are engaged in bearing or bringing up children and cannot consequently comply with such a requirement in many cases. Redundancy of part-time workers or by applying the criterion 'last in, first out' may also be discriminatory as domestic commitments often do not allow women to work full-time or constrain them to enter on the labour market later than men. Requirements of physical strength , geographical mobility, minimum height, all these may constitute indirect discrimination as well. Several traditional practices may be questioned as being potentially indirectly discriminatory.

The reference in the Directive to family or marital status needs special attention. It is a confusing passage. On the one hand, it is true that criteria referring to family status, such as 'head of the household' or 'breadwinner' are often the origin of discrimination against women, as nowadays mainly men qualify for these criteria. However, if women must resign in the civil service upon marriage, or if married nurses cannot be appointed to permanent jobs, or if a woman is not given a job because she has small children, are these cases of indirect discrimination by reference to marital or family status? Such practices are simple direct discrimination of women based on certain biases. According to the Directive men and women must be treated equally regardless of whether they are married or not, have small children or not. The additional characteristics are irrelevant. Consequently apart from criteria such as 'head of the household', 'breadwinner', or possibly 'a person with family responsibilities' which often will be a woman, it is not clear to what situations the passage 'marital and family status' refers. Or it may be understood as a prohibition of discrimination between married and unmarried persons. That, however, may be well beyond the scope of the Directive.

Article 2, paragraph 2 authorizes the Member States to exempt certain occupational activities and the training leading thereto, for which due to their nature or the conditions in which they are performed, sex is a determining factor.

According to the Commission 'the system of derogation is based on this factor alone, so that no derogation is possible unless, for objective reasons to do with its nature, the job can be carried out either only by a man or only by a woman'.[23]

This provision must be interpreted strictly and it should cover the entire field of possible exceptions. Consequently national provisions drawn up in such a way that they could be interpreted in a wide sense are not allowed. Neither is allowed an exclusion of a whole series of jobs 'en masse'[24] or where the exclusion is dependent on a subjective judgement, for instance, of the employer.[25]

In fact, although it does not appear from the Directive at first sight, the Member States are under the duty to draw up a list of excluded professions. According to Article 9, paragraph 2, they must periodically assess the occupational activities excluded in order to decide, in the light of social developments, whether there is justification for maintaining the exclusions concerned. The Commission must be notified of the results of this assessment. The Commission plays an important role in supervising the list of excluded professions,[26] and due to the reluctance of the Member States to perform this obligation, it has begun several enforcement actions.[27]

It may be argued that sex is a determining factor for the performance of occupational activities only in cases where the performance by the opposite sex would lead to certain absurdities or would be impossible. For instance, actor/actress, soprano/bass singer, wet-nurse, fashion model or model for sculptors or painters etc. In those cases the occupational activities are very narrowly linked to *physical characteristics* of one of the two sexes. However, the list of activities excluded in different Member States is quite long and varied.[28] As examples may be mentioned: firemen, civilian employees in the military security department, priests, sales staff for ladies' underwear, some jobs in prisons, technical staff of post and telecommunications, jobs of lady supervisor and boarding-school teacher in certain educational establishments, sailors, midwives, kindergarten teachers, certain departments of the police. Some occupational activities are only to a certain extent open to women. Amongst the reasons given for the exclusion of some of these activities have been the following: personal safety, unpleasant working conditions, reasons of morality and/or decency, religious reasons, social reasons such as the personal relationship between the employer and the employee, etc.[29] Often, the exclusions seem to be determined by the biased view of the role of women within society. The range of occupational activities excluded in the Member States is thus apparently fairly wide and not always of the same tenor. Further, some Member States have made practically no exclusions; some have clearly set out the activities excluded and some have made only general provisions. It is obvious, that if one State is capable of producing a list, another must be equally capable. Moreover, although some provisions in the Member States coincide, other provisions differ. Apparently, the exclusions were determined by historical and social factors, but they seem nowadays to be arbitrary to some extent. Therefore, it should be possible in time to draw up a uniform list that could serve as a guideline in all Member States. Furthermore, it must be pointed out that exceptions based on the context of the work are much more dangerous than those linked to the nature of the job since they may give rise to loose interpretations influenced by social stereotypes.[30]

Article 2, paragraph 2 should be interpreted as strictly as possible. Recruitment should depend on individual aptitude in the first place, and the differentiation between sexes should be permitted only where *biological difference* affects the occupational activity to such an extent that no comparisons can be made between men and women.[31] From this point of view one may question the relevance of 'social developments' mentioned in Article 9, paragraph 2. Social and other reasons for exclusion may create dangerous loopholes in the system of derogations.

Article 2, paragraph 3 provides for the second exception to the principle of equal treatment. Provisions concerning the protection of women as regards pregnancy and maternity are permitted.

In the Commission's view this Article should be interpreted strictly. Protective legislation which forbids the access of women to certain work or provides special specific working conditions fall within the scope of

Article 3, paragraph 2(c), or Article 5, paragraph 2(c). National provisions on leave and other advantages offered for the purposes of bringing up children are working conditions to which the principle of equal treatment applies (Article 5). According to the Commission this paragraph of Article 2 refers only to the protection of women needed because of pregnancy and the bearing of children; in other words, it deals with physical protection. However, in that case, it is not clear what is meant by maternity (the days or weeks following a confinement?). Moreover, the provision refers to 'provisions concerning the protection of women, *particularly* (emphasis added) as regards pregnancy and maternity'. Such wording suggests a wider field of application than the Commission's interpretation. Therefore it is not surprising that the Court of Justice took a different position from the Commission in the *Hoffmann* case[32] which will be discussed later. A possible explanation for the term 'particularly' could be that Article 2, paragraph 3 gives only the general rule, i.e. protective legislation is permitted, and that this rule is elaborated in Article 3, paragraph 2(c), and Article 5, paragraph 2(c): when the protective provisions appear to be discriminatory they must be reviewed if they are no longer well founded. In this perspective Article 2, paragraph 3 and the two other provisions should be interrelated. However, the judgement in *Hoffmann* treats Article 2, paragraph 3 as a distinct exception.

It is noteworthy that in both the New Community Action Programme and the Medium-term Community Programme[33] protection of women during pregnancy or motherhood figures as a specific action. In the Medium-term Programme the Commission has undertaken itself to lay down guidelines for the inprovement of protection of pregnancy and motherhood and for the elimination of discriminatory effects on the employment of women. Unfortunately, until now, the only 'hard' commitment in this field is not very impressive.[34]

Finally, Article 2, paragraph 4 allows for the possibility for positive action. Under this provision measures are allowed 'to promote equal opportunity for men and women, in particular by removing existing inequalities which affect women's opportunities in the area referred to in Article 1, paragraph 1. This provision, being optional only, has not proved to be very dynamic in practice. Positive action may be a powerful device to combat *de facto* inequalities which affect women's opportunities in the labour market, and it may supplement in a very useful way the prohibitive provisions of the Directive. Therefore, supported by the Council,[35] the Commission has developed a fairly comprehensive policy on positive action. The actions put forward for implementation or encouragement in both the private and public sectors cover a wide range of aspects. They include, for instance, the encouragement of recruitment and advancement of women in sectors where they are underrepresented, the dissemination of information and consciousness raising on equality matters, the diversification of vocational choice for women, the adaptation of working conditions and reorganization of working time, the adoption of measures encouraging greater sharing of occupational and social responsibilities, and the creation of special training schemes for women who wish to resume work after an interruption. The list is long and varied.[36] However, what all those actions have in common is that they are relatively innocuous: and to a large extent they fall within the scope of the principle of equal treatment. Until now the Community has not developed proposals for affirmative action of the kind attempted in the United States, where the establishment of quotas for ethnic minorities has given rise to problems for the courts.[37] Nevertheless, as soon as positive measures are adopted which run very clearly contrary to the principle of equal treatment, such as the preferential hiring of a woman over a better qualified man, the exact scope of Article 2, paragraph 4 will probably become an issue. This provision, being a derogation, according to the Court's case-law, must be interpreted strictly. This would imply that the measure concerned should be an *ultimum remedium* in a specific situation, for example, where there is very serious and structural underrepresentation of women, and that it should apply for a limited period only.[38]

Article 3, paragraph 1 concerns the first area of application of the Directive. It prohibits any discrimination whatsoever on grounds of sex 'in the conditions, including selection criteria, for access to all jobs or posts, whatever the sector or branch of activity, and to all levels of the occupational hierarchy'. In other words, it relates to access to employment and promotion. Of course, both direct and indirect discrimination are prohibited (see Article 2) and as has already been mentioned this provision applies to the private sector, the public sector and self-employed occupations. One of the best measures of the degree of compliance with this provision are vacancy notices and job advertisements. According to the Commission, the observation of the principle of non-discrimination in vacancy notices and advertisements depends strongly on the following factors:[39] whether the law specifies the obligation of non-discriminatory vacancy notices or advertisements in detail; whether handbooks indicate clearly how to draft a non-discriminatory vacancy notice; whether the placement offices can intervene to amend any discriminatory notices submitted by employers; whether a campaign has been conducted among those publishing advertisements to ensure that they do more than publish a simple reminder of legal obligations at the head of a page of discriminatory advertisements; and whether there is any control over compliance with legal obligations. If none of these conditions is met, a legal obligation has little effect.

Problems arise also when there is direct recruitment by the employer or when recruitment happens through employment offices. Employment offices used to list vacancies under 'men' and 'women'. Although this practice seems to have been abolished, a systematic control on employment offices is highly desirable so as to ensure that there will not be discrimination of a more subtle nature[40].

In the case of direct recruitment, even where there has been a non-discriminatory advertisement, it may be very difficult to prove that discrimination has occurred. A special problem is the access to employment by pregnant women. Although refusal to employ a woman who is pregnant will amount to direct discrimination,[41] in practice it will often happen. Therefore, it would be very useful – at least for reasons of legal clarity – to include the prohibition of discrimination on grounds of pregnancy in the national legislation.

Article 3, paragraph 2 imposes – so far as it is necessary to comply with paragraph 1 – three obligations on the Member States:

(a) to abolish any laws, regulations and administrative provisions contrary to the principle of equal treatment;
(b) to ensure that any provisions contrary to the principle of equal treatment which are included in collective agreements, individual contracts of employment, internal rules of undertakings or in rules governing the independent occupations and professions shall be, or may be declared, null and void or may be amended;
(c) to revise laws, regulations and administrative provisions contrary to the principle of equal treatment when the concern for protection which originally inspired them is no longer well founded, and to ensure that where similar provisions are included in collective agreements labour and management shall be requested to undertake the desired revision.

Although the provisions under (a) and (b) are apparently quite clear, to trace discriminatory provisions in national legislation and collective agreements and, in particular, in internal rules of enterprises and in rules governing the independent occupations may require an extensive and time-consuming investigation. Strictly speaking, an investigation is not necessary as a Member State may draw up legal provisions prohibiting discrimination on ground of sex in general but, of course, a systematic analysis is preferred.[42] It seems that collective agreements rarely deal with questions of access and promotion. However a Belgian study has pointed out that certain clauses have an indirectly discriminatory effect: some evaluation criteria (such as heavy physical effort) underlying job classifications may indirectly constitute an obstacle to equal opportunity as regards access to employment and promotion. They may suggest that the job in question is in practice only open to a man or a woman.[43]

Further, the nullification of contrary clauses in collective agreements must in almost all cases be ordered by a court. Such a case-by-case approach is quite inefficient as it requires separate anti-discrimination proceedings. Moreover, the sanction of nullity is only effective with respect to legal acts in legally binding agreements. If they are not binding, like collective agreements in the UK, a *de facto* removal seems necessary.[44] The insertion of 'equality clauses' in collective agreements so as to promote awareness of workers' rights within the branches concerned may be a good initiative, but is not obligatory under the Directive.

Whilst the protective legislation as provided for in (c) will be dealt with later in detail, at this point it suffices to observe that the list of national provisions prohibiting the access of women to certain occupational activities is long and varied.[45]

Article 4 deals with the second area of application of the Directive, namely with access to vocational guidance and training. The Member States must take all necessary measures to ensure that any laws, regulations and administrative provisions contrary to the principle of equal treatment shall be abolished and that any provisions contrary to the principle of equal treatment which are included in collective agreements, individual contracts of employment, internal rules of undertakings or in rules governing the independent occupations and professions shall be, or may be declared, null and void or may be amended.

This provision is a logical supplement to equal opportunities as regards access to occupational activities. As long as there is segregation in vocational education, job segregation will not change (and probably vice versa).[46]

Article 4 covers the following types of training:[47] vocational training in secondary and higher education; training and apprenticeship in the liberal professions and the self-employed sector; continuous training; further training and advancement schemes in public and private companies. In the draft directive, general education was included as well but was removed as, in the view of the Council it was not a legitimate area for EEC action.[48] It seems that at the national level some problems occurred concerning the scope of Article 4, especially in those Member States where the distinction between general education and vocational education is not clear.[49] For instance, there seems to exist some uncertainty about the question, whether university education falls within the scope of Article 4.[50]

As previously stated, Article 4 covers only access to vocational training. It is evident that as long as the content of the proposed subjects is not based on principles of equality, equal opportunities will to a certain extent remain illusory. However, equality as concerns the content of education is beyond the scope of the Directive. Finally Article 4 (c) provides that vocational guidance, vocational training, advanced vocational training and retraining shall be accessible on the basis of the same criteria and at the same levels, but an exception is made for private training establishments which enjoy autonomy in some Member States. Although this exception concerns only school institutions and not private companies, nevertheless it may be considered as a weak point in the Directive.

The third field of application, that concerning 'working conditions', is covered by Article 5. Article 5, paragraph 1, prohibits discrimination on grounds of sex with regard to working conditions, including the conditions governing dismissal. Like Article 3, Article 5 provides that the Member States must abolish any laws, regulations and administrative provisions contrary to the principle of equal treatment and must ensure that any provisions contrary to the principle of equal treatment included in collective agreements, individual contracts of employment, internal rules of undertakings or rules governing the independent occupations and professions shall be, or may be, declared null and void or may be amended. The Directive does not define the term 'working conditions'. In the view of the Commission it must be interpreted in the widest sense. The term should cover both social security and pay, but both fields must be considered as excluded from the scope of the Equal Treatment Directive as they are covered by other Community instruments.[51]

In some Member States problems arose as regards the concept of 'working conditions'. Some States interpreted this term more strictly than others.[52] In particular, collective agreements have caused some difficulties. Here again, the proper remedy is a systematic analysis and subsequent amendment of offending provisions rather than a review by the courts on a case-by-case basis. The main forms of discrimination in this area included in collective agreements seem to be working conditions linked to family status and to the concept of women as being solely responsible for bringing up children.[53] A fine, though perhaps atypical, example can be found in France. A French law of 13 July 1983 amended the Labour Code in order to comply with the Second Directive. A number of new general provisions on equality for men and women in professional matters were inserted into the Code. However, the new law provided that the aforesaid provisions on equality do not prohibit the application of usages, terms of contracts of employment or of collective agreements in force at the date on which the law was promulgated granting particular rights to women. The law obliged employers and trade unions to proceed, by collective negotiation, to bring such terms into conformity with the principle of equal treatment, but it did not mention any time limit. The special rights which apparently existed already and were allowed to continue to exist were, *inter alia*, the extension of maternity leave, the reduction of working hours, the obtaining of specific holidays (additional holiday for each child, days off at the start of the school year and holidays when a child is ill), the payment of an allowance for a crèche or babysitter, the reduction of the retirement age and the award of additional benefits for children. It is clear that these rights are inspired by the traditional role of women in regard to the health and education of children within the family unit. From the point of view of equal treatment several of these working conditions must be available to both female and male workers.[54]

Article 5, paragraph 2 (c), refers to protective legislation. The legislation covered by this provision concerns 'special working conditions for women'.

The (not exhaustive) list of these working conditions is – again – long and the items included differ from Member State to Member State.[55]

Protective legislation (Article 3, paragraph 2 (c), and Article 5, paragraph 2 (c)) can thus, in general, be divided into two groups of measures: provisions governing access to employment and specific working conditions. Both types of protective legislation seem to be qualified as 'suspect' under the Directive: they are not compatible with the principle of equal treatment 'when the concern for protection which originally inspired them is no longer well founded'. Such provisions must be revised. According to Article 9, paragraph 1, 'the Member States shall carry out a first examination and if necessary a first revision of the laws, regulations and administrative provisions...within four years of notification of [the] Directive', i.e. by 12 February 1980. From a general survey made by the Commission it appears that 'there are no common, permanent requirements concerning the specific protection of women which have proved imperative in all countries in identical circumstances'.[56] On the contrary, the existing protective provisions vary considerably from Member State to Member State. Some activities prohibited in one Member State are covered by special working conditions in another and vice versa. A good example is the prohibition of night work: in some countries women are excluded from jobs which may involve night work; in other countries those jobs are open to women in principle, but specific provisions on working hours apply.[57] Even more confusing is the fact that night work is considered harmful to women in industry but not, for example, in nursing.

As regards the abolition or revision of protective legislation, some resistance from, in particular, the trade unions has arisen since they regard certain protective provision as beneficial to female workers. However, it is not often considered that the effects of certain activities may be harmful to men as well as to women. Obviously, equal treatment especially in this area can be realized in several ways: by bringing the standard down, i.e. the lower standard of protection applicable to men will apply to women as well, by raising the working conditions of men to the same level as that of women or by drawing up new working conditions applicable to both. Naturally, the most proper solution will depend on the nature of the activities concerned. However, it must be pointed out that the tendency perceptible in some Member States is to lower the standard of treatment of women or even of both sexes. Furthermore, in the area of protective legislation the problem of conflicting international obligations may arise as the Member States are parties to several ILO Conventions which also deal with protective legislation.[58]

In a Commission's study on protective measures, several categories of prohibited jobs are mentioned:[59] underground work in mines and quarries, work in compressed air caissons, handling chemicals, German blast furnaces, Dutch and Greek docks, dirty work in several countries, exposure to lead and exposure to ionizing radiation. Some prohibitions are

well-founded for reasons of protection of the foetus or the reproductive
capacity of the female worker in a more general sense. However, the
protection of the reproductive functions of men is sometimes neglected.[60]
Other prohibitions are based on the misconception that women are
biologically unsuited to perform certain activities,[61] or out of a concern
with morality or social considerations, such as the idea of the traditional
sharing of duties between the sexes within the family, or ideas that
women should be spared certain difficult, unpleasant and dirty jobs.

As concerns working conditions, the study divides them into two main
groups.[62] The first group of measures aims to protect family life. These
measures are to a large extent based on traditional ideas about the
need to protect the mother or the woman's role of mother and wife.
Such measures include limits on the length of time or qualitative limits
on the time women work. The second group aims at making certain
difficult conditions less unpleasant for women. These measures protect
the female worker 'for her own sake'. As examples can be mentioned
lower retirement ages, the ban on women handling dangerous machinery,
the provision of seats for female workers in shops, and the prohibition of
manual shifting of loads.[63] These working conditions are often based on
stereotyped ideas about women. Why should only women have a seat
at work? Is dangerous machinery not equally dangerous to both sexes?
Moreover, real equal opportunities in the labour market presuppose the
're-sharing' of duties at home. Although this problem cannot be directly
solved by legislation, the legislation governing working conditions can at
least ease the 'new division of labour' within the family by providing, for
example, for less, or more suitable, working hours for both sexes.

Furthermore, it must be observed that, indeed, the adoption of specific
working conditions should be preferred over the exclusion of women
from certain jobs. However, it must be kept in mind that in certain
circumstances these conditions may in fact amount to an exclusion because
an employer may prefer to engage a person to whom no special working
conditions apply.

In summary, the conclusion may be drawn that the delimitation between
protective measures covered by Article 3, paragraph 2, and those falling
within the scope of Article 5, paragraph 2, is not clear in practice. This is due
to the complexity and case-by-case approach of the national legislatures of
the Member States. Protective legislation prohibiting employment should
be abolished in all those cases where satisfactory protection – if needed
at all and only for reasons narrowly linked to the reproductive function
of women – can be guaranteed by specific working conditions. All other
protective measures should apply equally to men and women.

Furthermore, it must be pointed out that the whole system of derogations
to the principle of equal treatment is rather confusing. As has already been
mentioned, the justifications for exemption under Article 2, paragraph
2 (sex as a determining factor) are often the same as under Article 3,

paragraph 2, for instance, moral and social grounds, reasons of personal safety. The exclusions under Article 2, paragraph 2, are to a large extent protective measures which should fall within the scope of Article 3, paragraph 2. This position has the following consequences: exclusions under Article 3 are classified as 'suspect'; under Article 2, paragraph 2 they are not; Article 2, paragraph 2 should be confined to a very limited group of occupational activities where the sex is a vital requirement; if the access to a job is prohibited under Article 3 the preferred option of Article 5, paragraph 2 should be kept in mind.

The second confusion may be caused by the unclear relation between Article 2, paragraph 3 (protection of women as regards pregnancy and maternity) and Article 5, paragraph 2. The Court of Justice interprets Article 2, paragraph 3 in a wider sense than simply protecting the woman for physical reasons. However, it would be more sensible to qualify all other than biological protective measures as falling within the scope of Article 5. Protective working conditions must be examined and revised under Article 9. No such obligation exists in relation to Article 2, paragraph 3 and, if the conditions are no longer well founded, they must apply equally to men and women. So, leave for women with very small children, which may be regarded as a provision concerning the protection of women as regards maternity in an extensive interpretation, should be considered as a working condition. As a justification on biological grounds may not be expected, such leave should be guaranteed to men and women equally.

Protective legislation is a subject of constant concern to the Commission, whereas the Member States seem to take their time in reviewing it. The review of protective legislation figured in the New Action Programme and is included again in the Medium-term Programme.[64] In 1987 the Commission submitted a communication on protective legislation for women to the Council.[65] However, as appears from this communication, it is improbable that protective legislation will be reassessed in the near future. This may be regretted, for these measures often have negative influence on women's employment. On the other hand, it may be asked how much women will gain if the review of protective legislation results in an 'equalize-down' solution.[66] Unfortunately, there is probably no 'hard' obligation under Community law to equalize up, unless the provisions of the Treaty aiming at improvement of the living and working conditions can be interpreted as a guarantee against deterioration.[67]

However well drafted the law may be, it is of little use if an individual has no opportunity to seek legal redress. Therefore, Article 6 of the Equal Treatment Directive provides for legal remedies. The Member States are under the duty to introduce into their national legal systems such measures as are necessary to enable all persons who consider themselves discriminated against within the meaning of the Directive, to pursue their claims by judicial process after possible recourse to other competent authorities. In some Member States, the implementing legislation provides expressly for a legal remedy; in other Member States the persons concerned have legal redress under a general action to claim a legal remedy. From an expert report on the provisions for legal redress in the Member States[68] it appears that despite the divergence in legal systems, there are several problem areas common to all Member States. These are the questions of representation and assistance, time limits, the obtaining of information prior to a hearing, the presentation of a case, the burden of proof, the remedies or sanctions available on proof of a claim and the presence or absence of protection from victimization.

It has already been pointed out that the proof of discrimination may frequently be difficult. The collection of evidence seems to be one of the biggest problems in applying the law.[69] Therefore the report recommends the appointment of Equality Officers in each Member State with sole responsibility for investigating complaints of discrimination, collecting evidence and writing a report which would be available to both parties and to a court. Furthermore, a system of using rapporteurs for the determination of what evidence and witnesses are necessary should be adopted. The second serious problem is that the initial burden of proof is generally on the complainant. Therefore, to assist an action against discrimination, the burden of proof should be formally altered.[70] An essential condition for adequate judicial protection is likewise that the remedies should be clear, designed to be effective and made known to the workforce.

It is striking that a relatively small number of cases concerning discrimination has been brought in the courts. This must probably be ascribed to the difficulties already mentioned, as well as to the costs and the inflexibility of procedures and pressure exerted by the employers.[71] Therefore, provisions should be made for the establishment of a representative action by, for example, trade unions or other organizations.[72] Moreover, it appears that in Member States in which special bodies offering advice and assistance exist, such as the Equal Opportunities Commission in the UK, a greater number of cases has been brought in the courts.[73] Such bodies should also be given powers to start an investigation regardless of whether there has been a complaint or not.[74]

The Equal Treatment Directive does not oblige the Member States to provide for a certain type of sanction. National legislation provides for fines under penal law or under administrative law, for compensation for damages or for a combination of both.[75] The rates of compensation available seem to vary considerably. The expert report therefore recommends that a standard sum should be awarded on proof of discrimination even without proof of damage.[76]

As far as victimization is concerned, Article 7 of the Directive provides that Member States shall take the necessary measures to protect employees against dismissal by the employer as a reaction to a complaint within the undertaking or to any legal proceedings aimed at enforcing compliance with the principle of equal treatment. This is a limited requirement as it does not protect a person applying for a job or a person who is moved to a less satisfying job because of a complaint. Nor does it protect witnesses.[77]

Under Article 8 the Member States must take care that the provisions adopted pursuant to the Directive, together with the relevant provisions already in force, are brought to the attention of employees by all appropriate means, for example at their place of employment. In other words, this Article calls for an information campaign.

The deadline for the implementation of the Directive was 12 August 1978.[78] Four Member States passed laws within the prescribed period (Belgium, Denmark, Ireland and Italy). The Netherlands, Germany, Luxembourg and Greece have trespassed the time limit. The UK already had a law covering the aims of the Directive. In France two existing laws dealt with the problem in part. Therefore a number of supplementary laws was needed. Although considerable progress has been achieved in the Member States since implementation, inadequate legislation still exists as will be seen in the next two sections.

Case-law of the Court of Justice: preliminary rulings

The first preliminary ruling concerning the Equal Treatment Directive was requested by the Employment Appeal Tribunal in consequence of a proceeding initiated by a man against British Railways Board.[79]

Mr Burton was an employee of the British Railways Board. As a result of an internal reorganization, the Board made an offer of voluntary redundancy to some of its employees. Under the redundancy scheme agreed upon between the management of the Board and the recognized trade unions, female employees could avail themselves of the opportunity offered by the voluntary redundancy scheme at the age of 55, while a male employee was eligible for redundancy at the age of 60. The principal advantage accompanying the voluntary redundancy consisted in the enjoyment of benefits equal to the pension payable at pensionable age for a maximum period of five years prior to the attainment of that age. Mr Burton applied for voluntary redundancy, but his application was rejected on the ground that he was 58, thus under the minimum age provided for male employees under the redundancy scheme. Mr Burton complained to an Industrial Tribunal against the decision to refuse to grant him the benefit payable under the redundancy scheme. The Tribunal dismissed the complaint since both the Equal Pay Act and the Sex Discrimination Act did not apply. Mr Burton appealed to the Employment Appeal Tribunal and relied on Article 119 EEC, the Equal Pay Directive and the Equal Treatment Directive. The Tribunal then submitted some questions of interpretation to the Court of Justice, wanting to know mainly whether the voluntary redundancy benefit fell within the scope of Article 119 and the Equal Pay Directive, or whether alternatively it fell within the scope of the Equal Treatment Directive.

According to the Court of Justice the question referred to it did not concern the benefit itself, but whether the conditions of access to the voluntary redundancy scheme were discriminatory. This matter is covered by the Equal Treatment Directive and *not* by Article 119 or the Equal Pay Directive.

The Court considered that, in the context of the Equal Treatment Directive, the term 'dismissal' in Article 5, paragraph 1 must be widely construed so as to include termination of the employment relationship between a worker and his or her employer, even as part of a voluntary redundancy scheme. However, in deciding whether the difference in treatment is discriminatory within the meaning of the Directive, account must be taken of the relationship between measures such as the voluntary redundancy at issue and national provisions on normal retirement age. In the UK the minimum qualifying age for a state retirement pension is 60 for women and 65 for men. This difference in minimum pensionable age for social security purposes does not amount to discrimination prohibited by Community law for the Third Directive provides in Article 7 that the Directive shall be without prejudice to the right of Member States to exclude from its scope the determination of pensionable age for the purposes of granting old age and retirement pensions and the possible consequences thereof for other benefits. The access to the voluntary redundancy at issue is tied to the retirement scheme governed by UK social security provisions. Thus the difference between the benefits for men and women under the voluntary redundancy stems from the fact that the minimum pensionable age under the national legislation is not the same for men as for women. This latter not being discriminatory, the difference in age under the voluntary redundancy is not discriminatory either.

The judgement resembles strongly a miscellany of incoherent thoughts causing considerable confusion as to the scope of the Equal Treatment Directive. It suggests that conditions of access to voluntary redundancy benefits fall within Article 5 of the Directive as being 'conditions governing dismissal'. However, because there is a link between the access to the benefits in question and the discriminatory age limits which are permitted to continue by virtue of Article 7 of the Social Security Directive, there is no discrimination prohibited by Community Law.

It is certainly not obvious, neither is it explained by the Court, why an exception provided for in the Third Directive should be extended to the Equal Treatment Directive. The link between the two Directives is Article 1, paragraph 2 of the Equal Treatment Directive excluding social security matters from its scope. After it has been established that an issue is covered by the Third Directive and *not* by the Second, an exception of the former Directive may apply.[80] Nevertheless, the Court did not make any effort to consider this point. Apparently, it was deemed sufficient that there was a link between access to voluntary redundancy and national provisions on normal retirement age to have the exception applied. Fortunately, in three other cases which will be discussed next it was made clear by the Court how to understand *Burton*.

On 26 February 1986 the Court of Justice gave three judgements[81] which – in essence – concerned the same problem, namely the difference in retirement age for men and women. These cases will be discussed here together as far as possible. The facts leading to the preliminary rulings may be summarized as follows:

- Ms Marshall worked as a dietician with the Southampton and South West Hampshire Area Health Authority. At the age of 62 she was dismissed, notwithstanding that she had expressed her willingness to continue in employment until she reached the age of 65. The sole reason for her dismissal was the fact that she was a woman who had passed the retirement age. The Health Authority followed a general policy that the normal retirement age will be the age at which social security pensions become payable in the UK, at 65 to men and at 60 to women. However, there is no statutory obligation to retire at the age at which the state pension becomes payable. Where an employee continues in employment after that age, payment of the state pension or of the pension under an occupational pension scheme is deferred.

  Ms Marshall instituted proceedings against the Health Authority contending that her dismissal constituted discriminatory treatment on the ground of sex contrary to the Sex Discrimination Act and Community law.

  The Industrial Tribunal dismissed her claim in so far as it was based on infringement of the Sex Discrimination Act. Under this Act discrimination on the ground of sex is permitted where it arises out of 'provisions in relation to retirement'. It however upheld the claim that the principle of equal treatment laid down by the Equal Treatment Directive had been infringed. On appeal to the Employment Appeal Tribunal the second point of the decision was set aside, since – according to the Tribunal – an individual could not rely upon a violation of the Equal Treatment Directive in proceedings before a British court or tribunal. The Court of Appeal to which Ms Marshall appealed referred two question to the Court of Justice. It wanted to know whether the dismissal policy followed by the Health Authority was contrary to the Equal Treatment Directive and whether that Directive could be relied upon by individuals in national courts or tribunals.

- The case of Ms Beets-Proper was very similar to that of Ms Marshall. Ms Beets-Proper was employed as a secretary by Van Lanschot Bankiers (hereafter referred to as 'the bank'). After she had reached the age of 60, the bank considered the contract of employment terminated, notwithstanding Ms Beets-Proper had expressed a wish to continue her employment.

  The contract was considered terminated by the bank for similar reasons as in the Marshall case: the retirement age under the occupational pension scheme, of which Ms Beets-Proper was a member, was 60 years for women and 65 years for men. The bank reasoned that the date on which Ms Beet-Proper was entitled to the payment of the pension was also a date at which she could be dismissed. Consequently, the bank refused access to Ms Beets-Proper to her office. Ms Beets-Proper instituted proceedings against the bank. The Dutch Supreme Court, dealing with this case in cassation, referred one question to the Court of Justice. Stated simply, the Court wondered whether the term 'working conditions' in the Equal Treatment Directive also includes the conditions governing dismissal when these conditions are narrowly linked to the pensionable age.

- In the last case Ms Roberts was employed by Tate & Lyle Industries Limited at their Liverpool depot. Under a mass redundancy, she was made redundant at the age of 53. She was a member of an occupational pension scheme which provided for compulsory retirement with a pension at the age of 65 for men and 60 for women. Under the redundancy scheme all employees made redundant were to be offered either a cash payment or an early pension out of the pension scheme up to five years before the date of their entitlement under the scheme. The pension was therefore payable immediately to women over the age of 55 and men over the age of 60. As a result of representations made by male employees against the allegedly discriminatory nature of those arrangements, Tate & Lyle amended them by agreeing to grant an immediate pension to both men and women over the age of 55, with the amount of their cash payment reduced. Ms Roberts brought proceedings against Tate & Lyle claiming that her dismissal constituted discrimination contrary to the Sex Discrimination Act and to Community law since, under the new arrangements, a male employee was entitled to receive an immediate pension ten years before the normal retirement age for men whereas a female employee was not so entitled until five years before the normal retirement age for women.

  The part of the claim based on the Sex Discrimination Act was dismissed for the same reasons as in the Marshall case. After the second part of her claim had been dismissed by the Industrial

Tribunal and the Employment Appeal Tribunal, the Court of Appeal referred the following questions to the Court of Justice:

- whether or not the redundancy scheme constituted discrimination under the Equal Treatment Directive;
- whether or not the Equal Treatment Directive can be relied upon by an individual in national courts and tribunals.

The central question in these three cases was whether or not a *dismissal narrowly linked to the pensionable age* must be considered as a 'working condition' or, in particular, 'condition governing dismissal' within the meaning of Article 5 of the Equal Treatment Directive.

The defending parties (Health Authority, Van Lanschot Bankiers) supported by some governments (UK, The Netherlands, Denmark), and Ms Roberts relied heavily on *Burton*. They argued that account must be taken of the link existing between the ages at which retirement and old age pensions become payable and the ages imposed in the context of a dismissal policy. The fixing of different retirement ages linked to the different pensionable ages for men and women should not constitute an unlawful discrimination, since the difference *derives from* the different pensionable ages which are allowed under Community law.

However, the Court decided otherwise. It observed in the first place that the question referred to did not concern access to a statutory or occupational retirement scheme, that is to say the conditions for payment of an old age or retirement pension, but the fixing of an age limit with regard to the termination of employment. The question therefore related to the conditions governing dismissal and fell to be considered under the Equal Treatment Directive. In its judgement in *Burton* the Court had already stated that the term 'dismissal' contained in Article 5, paragraph 1 of the Directive must be given a wide meaning. Consequently, an age limit for compulsory dismissal falls within 'conditions of dismissal' within the meaning of the Equal Treatment Directive, even if the dismissal involves the grant of retirement pension. The Court continued as follows:

> As the Court emphasized in judgment in the Burton case, Article 7 of Directive n° 79/7 expressly provides that the Directive does not prejudice the right of Member States to exclude from its scope the determination of pensionable age for the purpose of granting old-age benefits falling within the statutory social security schemes.
>
> The Court thus acknowledged that benefits tied to a national scheme which lays down a different minimum pensionable age for men and women may lie outside the ambit of the aforementioned obligation.
>
> However, in view of the fundamental importance of the principle of equality of treatment, which the Court has reaffirmed on numerous occasions, Article 1(2) of Directive n° 76/207, which excludes social

security matters from the scope of that Directive, must be interpreted strictly. Consequently, the exception to the prohibition of discrimination on grounds of sex provided for in Article 7 (1) (a) of Directive n° 79/7 applies only to the determination of pensionable age for the purposes of granting old-age and retirement pensions and the possible consequences thereof for other benefits.

In that respect it must be emphasized that, whereas the exception contained in Article 7 of Directive n° 79/7 concerns the consequences which pensionable age has for social security benefits, this case is concerned with dismissal within the meaning of Article 5 of Directive n° 76/207.[82]

It follows that both the dismissal of Ms Marshall and Ms Beets-Proper were contrary to the Equal Treatment Directive. The difference in age which men and women could be dismissed constituted a discriminatory working condition prohibited by Article 5, paragraph 1. On the other hand, in the case of Ms Roberts no discrimination was established. According to the Court the grant of a pension to persons of the same age who are made redundant amounts merely to a collective measure adopted irrespective of the sex of the persons concerned in order to guarantee them all the same rights. Article 5, paragraph 1 of the Equal Treatment Directive must be interpreted as meaning that a contractual provision which lays down a single age for the dismissal of men and women under a mass redundancy involving the grant of an early retirement pension, whereas the normal retirement age is different for men and women, does not constitute discrimination on grounds of sex, contrary to Community law.

It appears from these three judgements that the Court of Justice is willing to draw a sharp distinction between age limits for dismissal on the one hand and the pensionable age, i.e. the age at which a person is entitled to the payment of a pension, on the other. The reasoning of the Court may be summarized as follows: the term 'conditions governing dismissal' must be given a wide meaning. Article 1, paragraph 2 of the Equal Treatment Directive which excludes social security matters from its scope must be construed strictly. Thus Article 7 of the Third Directive concerns only the determination of pensionable age for the purposes of *granting* pensions. If a case does not concern age as a condition for payment of a pension, but the age limit with regard to the termination of employment, the exception does not apply. Consequently the age limit falls within the scope of the Equal Treatment Directive and constitutes a 'condition governing dismissal'. Although the judgements of the Court are satisfactory from the viewpoint of equal treatment, they have some odd consequences. Women can – from the financial point of view – stop working a few years earlier than men since they are entitled to the payment of a pension earlier. It is not clear what would happen if a man claims to terminate his employment before the age of 65. Moreover, what will be the consequences if a woman decides to work a few years more? Contributions towards pensions are often based on the presupposition that women retire earlier than men. It seems obvious that the only remedy for these and other, related, problems is the equalization of the pensionable ages of men and women.[83]

Apart from the substantive aspects of *Marshall*, the case is important since in it the Court decided that directives have no horizonal direct effect. In brief,[84] the Court considered that the basis for reliance on a directive in the national courts as against a Member State lies in the fact that, according to Article 189 of the Treaty, a directive is binding in relation to Member States. As it is not binding on individuals, a directive may not of itself impose obligations on individuals and, consequently, may not be relied upon against such persons. However in *Marshall*, the Court of Appeal had already stated that the health authority was a public authority and not a private employer. Since Article 5, paragraph 1 of the Directive was found sufficiently precise and unconditional, the Court held that this provision may be relied upon as against a State authority acting in its capacity as employer, in order to avoid the application of any contrary national provision.

Another case bringing up – although very summarily – the problem of the scope of the Second Directive in relation to social security is *Newstead*.[85] Mr Newstead was a member of an occupational scheme for civil servants. Under this scheme, male civil servants were obliged to contribute to a widows' pension fund, whatever their marital status, while no such obligation existed for female civil servants. Mr Newstead, who was unmarried, argued that the obligation to contribute to the widows' pension fund has the effect of discriminating against him in comparison with a female civil servant in an equivalent post. Before the English courts he relied, *inter alia*, on Article 119, the Equal Pay Directive and the Equal Treatment Directive. The Employment Appeal Tribunal referred the question to the Court of Justice. The latter, after having determined that the case did not fall within the scope of Article 119 and the Equal Pay Directive,[86] turned to the applicability of the Equal Treatment Directive. Without having established whether the scheme in question was covered by the Social Security Directive or the Occupational Schemes Directive, the Court decided that, according to its Article 1, paragraph 2, the Equal Treatment Directive is not intended to apply to social security matters. Furthermore, none of the Directives adopted by the Council relating to social security applies to survivors' pensions, whether they are provided for under a statutory social security scheme or under an occupational scheme.[87]

The next two preliminary rulings to be discussed elucidate to some extent the scope of the exceptions of the Equal Treatment Directive.

The case of *Hofmann*[88] concerned, in particular, the interpretation of Article 2, paragraph 3, protection of women as regards pregnancy and maternity. German legislation provides for two successive periods of leave for a woman after the birth of her child. The first leave ('Schutzfrist') is compulsory and covers a period of eight weeks from childbirth. During that period a woman is relieved of all her duties at work and continues to receive her net remuneration, which is paid by the sickness fund and/or the employer.

The second leave ('Mutterschaftsurlaub') is optional. A mother is entitled to a maternity leave beginning after the expiry of the first compulsory leave and till the day on which the child reaches the age of six months. Throughout that leave, the mother is relieved of her duties at work and the state, through the intermediary of the sickness fund, pays her a daily allowance not exceeding DM 25. On the expiry of her leave, she enjoys a guaranteed right to resume her employment on the same conditions as before.

The second – optional – leave comes to an end three weeks after the death of the child and not later than the day on which the child would have reached the age of six months. The leave similarly comes to an end if the child dies during the compulsory leave, and is not granted if death occurs more than three weeks before expiry of the compulsory leave. Moreover, the leave is granted only to women who have been in employment for a period of, generally speaking, nine months before the birth.

Ulrich Hofmann, the father of an illegitimate child of which he acknowledged paternity, obtained from his employer unpaid leave for the period between the expiry of the mother's compulsory leave and the day on which the child reached the age of six months. During that period he looked after the child while the mother resumed employment as a teacher. On 1 August 1979 Ulrich Hofmann submitted to the 'Barmer Ersatzkasse', the competent sickness fund, a claim for the above-mentioned daily maternity allowance. The sickness fund refused the claim. Hofmann lodged an administrative appeal against that refusal, but without success: the 'Sozialgericht Hamburg' dismissed the action on the ground that the wording of the relevant provision of German law and the intention of the legislature indicated that only mothers could claim maternity leave. It was the deliberate intention of the legislature not to create 'parental leave'. Hofmann lodged an appeal against this judgement. The Landessozialgericht Hamburg took the view that the dispute raised the question whether the German legislation was in conformity with the Equal Treatment Directive. In the preliminary reference it required the Court to define the scope of the principle of equal treatment as laid down in Article 2, paragraph 1 of the Directive and the exception contained in Article 2, paragraph 3. More precisely, the question was whether the optional leave was a measure to protect women. If the leave did not fall within the scope of this exception, it must be considered as a working condition under Article 5 to which the principle of equal treatment applies.

According to the Court of Justice, it appears from the analysis of the Directive that it is not designed to settle questions concerned with the organization of the family, or to alter the division of responsibility between parents. Furthermore, the Directive recognizes the legitimacy of protecting a woman's needs by reserving, under Article 2, paragraph 3 to Member States the right to retain or introduce provisions which are intended to protect women in connection with 'pregnancy and maternity'. The protection envisaged by Article 2, paragraph 3 is twofold. In the first place it concerns the protection of a woman's biological condition during pregnancy, and thereafter until such time as her physiological and mental functions have returned to normal after childbirth; in the second place the special relationship between a woman and her child may be protected by preventing that relationship from being disturbed by the multiple burdens which would result from the simultaneous pursuit of employment. Therefore an optional maternity leave falls within the scope of Article 2, paragraph 3, as it seeks to protect a woman in connection with the effects of pregnancy and motherhood. The leave may legitimately be reserved to the mother to the exclusion of any other person as it is only the mother who may find herself subject to undesirable pressures to return to work prematurely.

Finally, the Court pointed out

> that the Directive leaves Member States with a discretion as to the social measures which they adopt in order to guarantee, within the framework laid down by the Directive, the protection of women in connection with pregnancy and maternity and to offset the disadvantages which women, by comparison with men, suffer with regard to the retention of employment. Such measures are (.....) closely linked to the general system of social protection in the various Member States. It must therefore be concluded that the Member States enjoy a reasonable margin of discretion as regards both the nature of the protective measures and the detailed arrangements for their implementation.[89]

This judgement of the Court is disappointing but, after the judgements in two enforcement actions[90] not very surprising. The Court affirmed in *Hofmann* its former view on the interpretation of exceptions to the principle of equal treatment. As regards Article 2, paragraph 3, it leaves the Member States much more discretion than is thought desirable by the Commission, who advocated a very strict interpretation. It may be asked whether the *Hofmann* decision is sensible at all. Hofmann claimed that the main object of the disputed German provisions is not to give protection to the mother on biological and medical grounds but to the child. This follows in particular from the fact that the leave is withdrawn in the event of the child's death, from the optional nature of the leave and from the requirement that the woman should have been employed for a minimum period prior to childbirth. The German Government and the 'Barmer Ersatzkasse' argued that the protection afforded by the disputed legislative provision aims to reduce the conflict between a woman's role as a mother and her role as a wage-earner, in order to preserve her health and that of the child. The optional maternity leave is justified for reasons which are connected with a woman's biological characteristics, since it aims to avoid placing the mother, on expiry of the compulsory leave, under an obligation to decide whether or not to resume her employment.

The Court of Justice supported the German government's arguments. Under Article 2, paragraph 3, two aims may be sought: the protection of a woman's biological conditions, her physiological and mental functions, and the protection of the special relationship between a woman and her child which can be jeopardized by the multiplicity of burdens imposed by motherhood and employment. It is quite clear that as the disputed German leave is optional it is not created to meet imperative biological or medical needs. There seems to be no agreement on the length of time for which a woman should enjoy special treatment following pregnancy and childbirth. Moreover, this period may vary from woman to woman. However, compared to other European countries,[91] the German compulsory leave may be considered long enough for the physiological and mental recovery. Further, if the young mother is unable to resume her employment it seems logical that *she* would take the optional leave instead of the father if this leave was left at the discretion of the parents. The second aim mentioned by the Court of Justice, a security against the multiplicity of burdens, also can be achieved by leave for the father. If he takes care of the child the burden for the woman is much smaller. Therefore, the conclusion must be that the second kind of protection can be achieved by other, non-discriminatory, means: both parents should be eligible for the optional leave and choice should be left at their discretion.[92] Such a solution agrees with the objective of the Equal Treatment Directive.

Finally, it must be observed that the Directive is not designed to settle questions concerned with the organization of the family. It is left to the discretion of the parents how they will divide responsibilities. However, legal (Community) provisions dealing with the access to employment and working conditions must be drafted and interpreted in such a way as *to make a choice possible* regarding the division of work at home because of the link between the division of labour at home and in employment.

On 15 May 1986 the Court of Justice gave a judgement in the case of *Johnston*.[93] The Chief Constable of the Royal Ulster Constabulary, the competent authority for appointing reserve constables to the RUC Reserve in Northern Ireland and to full-time posts in the RUC full-time Reserve, refused to renew Ms Johnston's contract as a member of the RUC full-time Reserve and to allow her to be given training in the handling and use of fire-arms. He did so for the following reasons. Because of the high number of police officers assassinated in Northern Ireland over a number of years, the Chief Constable decided that in the RUC and the RUC Reserve, men should carry fire-arms in the regular course of their duties but that women would not be equipped with them and would not receive training in the handling and use of fire-arms. The Chief Constable considered that, if female officers were armed, it would increase the risk that they might become targets for assassination. Moreover, according to him, armed women officers would be less effective in certain areas for which women are better suited, in particular welfare-type work which involves dealing with families and children. Finally, he considered that, if women as well as men were to carry fire-arms in the regular course of their duties, it would be regarded by the public as a much greater departure from the ideal of an unarmed police force. In 1980 the Chief Constable decided that the number of women in the RUC was sufficient for the duties generally assigned to women members. He took the view that general police duties, frequently involving operations requiring the carrying of fire-arms, should no longer be assigned to women since they were not allowed to carry fire-arms. Consequently, he decided not to offer or renew any more contracts for women, except where they had to perform duties assigned only to women officers. However, as previously stated, the number of women in the RUC was sufficient for the performance of those tasks.

Following the refusal of the Chief Constable, Ms Johnston complained to the Industrial Tribunal of Northern Ireland. She contended that she had suffered unlawful discrimination prohibited by the Sex Discrimination Order.[94]

In the proceedings before the Industrial Tribunal, the Chief Constable produced a certificate issued by the Secretary of State in which the latter certified in accordance with Article 53 of the Sex Discrimination Order, that 'the act consisting of the refusal of the Royal Ulster Constabulary to offer further full-time employment to Mrs Marguerite I. Johnston in the Royal Ulster Constabulary Reserve was done for the purpose of (a) safeguarding national security; and (b) protecting public safety and public order'.[95] Article 53, paragraph 1, of the Sex Discrimination Order provides that none of its provisions prohibiting discrimination 'shall render unlawful an act done for the purpose of safeguarding national security or of protecting public safety or public order'. Article 53, paragraph 2 provides that 'a certificate signed by or on behalf of the Secretary of State and certifying that an act specified in the certificate was done for a purpose mentioned in paragraph 1 shall be conclusive evidence that it was done for that purpose'. By virtue of these provisions of the Sex Discrimination Order, the issue of the certificate would have had the effect of depriving Ms Johnston of any remedy. However, she also relied on the provisions of the Equal Treatment Directive. Subsequently, in order to be able to rule on the dispute, the Industrial Tribunal referred several questions to the Court of Justice for a preliminary ruling.

The first essential question was whether, and under what conditions, men and women employed with the police could be treated differently on grounds of the protection of public safety. It was argued before the Court of Justice that, on the basis of certain safeguard clauses of the EEC Treaty, derogations from the principle of equal treatment might be justified in order to protect public safety.

However, the Court held that only Articles 36, 48, 56, 223 and 224 of the EEC Treaty provide for derogations applicable in situations involving public safety. These articles deal with exceptional and clearly defined cases. They are of limited character and do not lend themselves to a wide interpretation. It is not possible to infer from them that there is inherent in the Treaty a general proviso covering all measures taken for reasons of public safety. Such a presumption would impair the binding nature of Community law and its uniform application. It follows that the application of the principle of equal treatment is not subject to any general reservation. If an act is discriminatory for reasons related to the protection of public safety, such an act must be examined in the light of the exceptions laid down in the Equal Treatment Directive only.

The first exception was then Article 2, paragraph 2, the derogations allowed on account of the context in which the occupational activity is carried out. In particular, the question was whether, owing to the specific context in which police activity is carried out in Northern Ireland, the sex of the person carrying out that activity constitutes a determining factor. The Court held that Article 2, paragraph 2, being a derogation from an individual right, must be interpreted strictly. However, the context in which the occupational activity of members of an armed police force is carried out is determined by the environment. In this regard, the possibility cannot be excluded that in a situation characterized by serious internal disturbances the carrying of fire-arms by policewomen might create additional risks of assassination and might therefore be contrary to the requirements of public safety. Consequently, the context of certain police activities may be such that the sex of police officers constitutes a determining factor in carrying them out. Further, the Court pointed out that there are certain limitations even if a case is covered by the derogation concerned. First, by virtue of Article 9, paragraph 2, the Member States are under the duty to assess periodically the activities concerned in order to decide whether, in the light of developments, the derogation from the general scheme of the Directive may still be maintained. Second, in determining the scope of any derogation from an individual right, the principle of proportionality must be observed. This principle requires that derogations remain within the limits of what is appropriate and necessary for achieving the aim in view. In the case of Ms Johnston, the principle of proportionality required that the principle of equal treatment should be reconciled as far as possible with the requirements of public safety. According to the Court of Justice it is – under Article 177 EEC Treaty – for the national court to say whether the decision of the Chief Constable is well founded and justified and whether the principle of proportionality is observed. Moreover, the national court has to determine whether the refusal to renew Ms Johnston's contract could possibly be avoided by allocating to women duties which, without jeopardizing the aims pursued, could be performed without fire-arms.

The second possible exceptions could be Article 2 paragraph 3, and Article 3, paragraph 2 (c), derogations allowed on the ground of a concern to protect women. The Court considered that Article 2, paragraph 3, which also determines the scope of Article 3, paragraph 2 (c), must be interpreted strictly. The Equal Treatment Directive was intended to protect a woman's biological condition and the special relationship which exists between a woman and her child. This was, according to the Court, clear from the express reference to pregnancy and maternity in the aforementioned provision. This provision did not therefore allow women to be excluded from a certain type of employment on the ground that public opinion demands that women be given greater protection than men against risks which affect men and women in the same way. A total exclusion of women from an occupational activity which, owing to a general risk not specific to women, is imposed for reasons of public safety, does not fall within the scope of Article 2, paragraph 3. Consequently, this exception to the principle of equal treatment is not applicable.

With regard to Article 2, paragraph 3, the Court thus reaffirmed that it provides for the protection of the biological condition and the special relationship existing between the mother and her child.[96] Apparently, the provision cannot be invoked in situations in which a danger exists for men and women equally. The Court obviously wished to cancel the image of weak and helpless women from Hollywood movies. However, it may be asked whether this same image of a weak woman in need of protection did not in fact influence the Court's interpretation of Article 2, paragraph 2.

From the consideration concerning Article 2, paragraph 2 it appears that, when dealing with the question whether the sex of a worker is a determining factor in the performance of certain occupational activities, not only do biological characteristics play a part, but that other grounds – such as the environment in which the activities are carried out – may be invoked. In the present case this meant the specific environment in Northern Ireland. However unpleasant and dangerous the situation there might be, this fact does not provide any explanation why policewomen might be more likely to be assassinated than policemen. Or do female armed police officers provoke more violence than males? Or does the Court suggest that policewomen may prove less capable of using their weapons to defend themselves? In brief, the reasons given by the Chief Constable are questionable and the Court did not want to get its fingers burnt.

Finally, one consideration of the Court raises several questions. The Court held that Article 2, paragraph 3 also determines the scope of Article 3, paragraph 2 (c). Article 2, paragraph 3 provides for an exception to protect women as regards pregnancy and maternity. It seems that, under this provision, the Member States have the option of excluding women from certain occupational activities for reasons of protection.[97] However, protective legislation that prohibits the access of women to certain jobs may also fall within the scope of Article 3, paragraph 2 (c). As stated above,[98] the reasons for protective measures under this provision are rather diverse: they include moral, social, religious and other grounds. Now, if it is assumed that Article 2, paragraph 3 also determines the scope of Article 3, paragraph 2 (c), it is not clear what the difference between those two provisions is.[99] Does it mean that exceptions under Article 3, paragraph 2 (c) are only justified if based on concerns relating to women because of pregnancy and maternity? What is then the function of Article 3, paragraph 2 (c)? Does this article mean that all derogations to the principle of equal treatment with regard to access to employment and vocational training *must* be revised under Article 3, paragraph 2 (c), in conjunction with Article 9, paragraph 1, except those relating to the protection of women in connection with pregnancy and maternity? Would it not be more sensible to say that *all* exceptions under Article 3, paragraph 2 (c) must finally disappear and that the only exceptions allowed will be those falling within the scope of Article 2, paragraph 3? Or does it mean that there is an interrelation between the two articles in the sense that, as already suggested, Article 2, paragraph 2 is the general rule and Article 3, paragraph 2(c) is elaborating it? The consequences of the suggested link between Article 2, paragraph 3, and Article 3, paragraph 2 (c), are obscure. Moreover, the confusing relations between the several exceptions becomes even more chaotic.

The second important problem in *Johnston* was that, due to Article 53, paragraph 2 of the Sex Discrimination Order, the national court was effectively prevented from fully exercising its powers of judicial review. The Court held that it follows from Article 6 of the Equal Treatment Directive that the Member States must take measures which are sufficiently effective to achieve the aim of the Directive and that they must ensure that the rights thus conferred may be effectively relied upon before the national courts. The Court underlined the fundamental character of this provision by a reference to, *inter alia*, the constitutional traditions common to the Member States and Articles 6 and 13 of the European Convention for the Protection of Human Rights and Fundamental Freedoms, where the principle of effective judicial control is laid down. By virtue of Article 6, all persons have the right to obtain an effective remedy in a competent court when they consider themselves wronged by discrimination contrary to the Equal Treatment Directive. The Member States are under a duty to ensure effective judicial control as regards compliance with the applicable provisions of Community law and of national legislation intended to give effect to the rights for which the Directive provides. Consequently, a provision like Article 53, paragraph 2 of the Sex Discrimination Order is contrary to the principle of effective judicial control laid down in Article 6 of the Directive, since a certificate issued under that former provision deprives an individual of the possibility of asserting by judicial process the rights conferred by the Directive.

Furthermore, the Court dismissed some arguments based on Article 224 of the Treaty.[100] It held that this derogation from the obligations imposed on the Member States by Community law in the event of internal disturbances affecting the maintenance of law and order was not applicable. None of the facts before the Court and none of the observations submitted to it suggested that the serious internal disturbances in Northern Ireland made judicial review impossible, or that measures needed to protect public safety would be deprived of their effectiveness because of such a review by the national courts.

The final question was concerned with the effects of the Equal Treatment Directive,[101] more particularly with Articles 2 and 6. As far as the latter is concerned, the Court held that Article 6 of the Equal Treatment Directive has direct effect. The provision is sufficiently precise and unconditional to be capable of being relied upon as against a Member State which has not ensured in its internal legal order that all persons who consider themselves wronged by sex discrimination must have an effective judicial remedy. Considering the fundamental importance the Court apparently attaches to this provision it may be assumed that not only the denial of a judicial remedy but a limited opportunity to legal redress must also be considered contrary to the Equal Treatment Directive.

More recently, in a case concerning free movement of workers,[102] the Court emphasized again the fundamental importance of legal remedies. It considered that the existence of a legal remedy against any decision by a national authority refusing to recognize a Community law fundamental right is essential to guarantee the individual concerned effective protection of this right. Then the Court went even further when it held that the national authority must make known the reasons for its decision. The Court found it necessary that the person concerned should be able to defend his or her right in the best possible circumstances and to be enabled to decide, with full knowledge of the reasons behind the decision, whether it is appropriate to bring the case before a court. It may be assumed that the same applies in the area of equal treatment of men and women, since on several occasions it has been recognized as a fundamental right by the Court.[103]

With respect to Article 2, paragraph 2, the Court confirmed that this provision has no direct effect, since it constitutes an option for the Member States.[104] The national court must see whether that option has been exercised in provisions of national law and construe the content of those provisions. Should it appear that the national derogation goes beyond the limits of the exceptions permitted by Article 2, paragraph 2, then the question of direct effect arises. The Court first referred to its established case-law and in particular to *Marshall*,[105] and then it found that Article 3, paragraph 1, and Article 4, paragraph 1, both in conjunction with Article 2, paragraph 1, which defines the principle of equal treatment, do have direct effect. These provisions may thus be relied upon before a national court to set aside a derogation under national legislation when this latter goes beyond the limits of the exceptions permitted by Article 2, paragraph 2. Moreover, the Court pointed out that, while determining the scope of Article 2, paragraph 2, or any other derogation from individual rights, the principle of proportionality must be observed.

The fact that directives have no horizontal direct effect did not cause any problem. The Court observed that the Chief Constable must be considered as a public authority not acting as a private individual. He may not take advantage of the failure of the state, of which he is an emanation, to comply with Community law.

However, before the Court dealt with the question of direct effect, it held that national courts are under a duty to interpret their national law in the light of the wording and the purposes of the Directive. In case that this so-called 'concurring interpretation' would seem impossible, the direct effect becomes relevant. This obligation of concurring interpretation has been developed by the Court in the Von Colson and Kamann and Harz cases[106] to which we will turn now.

In the *Von Colson and Kamann* case the following facts gave rise to the need for preliminary questions by the Arbeitsgericht Hamm: Sabine Von Colson and Elisabeth Kamann were both social workers who applied for two posts in Werl prison. The prison is administered by the Land of Nordrhein-Westfalen. The two women were not offered the posts and two less qualified male candidates were appointed. The authorities justified this choice by citing the problems and risks connected with the appointment of women in a prison reserved for male offenders. According to the Arbeitsgericht Hamm which dealt with this case, it was clear that the two female candidates had been discriminated against. Nevertheless the redress available under German law caused serious difficulties. The plaintiffs claimed that the defendant Land should be ordered to offer them a contract of employment in the Werl prison or, as an alternative, to pay them damages amounting to six months' salary. Moreover, Von Colson claimed the reimbursement of travelling expenses occurred by her in pursuing her application for the post. However, the Arbeitsgericht considered that under German law only the claim for the travelling expenses could be allowed. According to the Court, the only sanction applicable for discrimination in respect of access to employment is compensation for 'Vertrauensschaden', that means the loss incurred by candidates who are victims of discrimination in the establishment of the employment relationship. Such compensation is provided for under paragraph 611a(2) of the German Civil Code, which purports to implement the Equal Treatment Directive.

In the *Harz* case the same problem rose. Dorit Harz, a graduate in business studies, had applied for a post advertised by Deutsche

Tradax GmbH. However, the manager of Deutsche Tradax returned her application papers and informed her that only male applicants would be considered for the position. The Deutsche Tradax buys and sells agricultural raw material, a business in which, they argued, only men should be employed. Moreover, it supplies large quantities of cereals to Saudi Arabia where the social and religious structures prevailing preclude a woman from establishing business contacts and maintaining existing business relationships. The Arbeitsgericht Hamburg took the view that there had been discrimination in the selection procedure but it could not allow the required redress: engagement of Ms Harz by Deutsche Tradax or damages in the sum of DM 12 000. The Arbeitsgericht could only order under the provisions of Paragraph 611a(2) of the Civil Code the payment of a minimal compensation of DM 2,31 in respect of expenses incurred by Ms Harz in relation to her application. It considered that such compensation was not sufficient to ensure compliance with the Equal Treatment Directive, since it would not serve to ensure that employers conduct themselves in conformity with the law.

Both courts, being in doubt as to whether such minimal compensation was in conformity with the Equal Treatment Directive, submitted several questions to the Court of Justice for a preliminary ruling. The questions were framed in similar terms and concerned the following problems:

1.   Does the Directive confer on the candidate discriminated against a right to the conclusion of an employment contract as a sanction imposed on the offending employer?
2.   Is it possible to infer from the Directive any sanction in the event of discrimination other than the right to the conclusion of a contract of employment?
3.   Has the Equal Treatment Directive and in particular Articles 1, 2 and 3 thereof direct effect?

The Court of Justice ruled on those questions as follows: First, it referred to Article 189 of the Treaty. This provision leaves Member States to choose the ways and means of ensuring that the Directive is implemented. But, according to the Court, this freedom does not affect the obligation imposed on all the Member States to which the Directive is addressed to adopt, in their national legal systems, all the measures necessary to ensure that the Directive is fully effective, in accordance with the objective it pursues. The objective of the Equal Treatment Directive is to implement the principle of equal treatment for men and women, in particular by giving males and females real equality of opportunity as regards access to employment. Article 3, paragraph 2 (a) obliges the Member States to take the measures necessary in this respect. Furthermore, from Article 6 it follows that they are required to adopt measures which are sufficiently effective to achieve the objective of the Directives and to ensure that those measures may in fact be relied on before the national courts by the persons concerned. The Court found that such measures may include, for example, provisions requiring the employer to offer a post to the candidate discriminated against or giving the candidate adequate financial compensation, backed up where necessary by a system of fines. However, the Directive does not prescribe a specific sanction. The Member States are free to choose between the different solutions suitable for achieving its objectives.

While dealing with the other two questions, the Court of Justice elaborated further on the problem of effective sanctions. It held:

> It is impossible to establish real equality of opportunity without an appropriate system of sanctions. That follows not only from the actual purpose of the Directive but more specifically from Article 6 thereof which, by granting applicants for a post who have been discriminated against recourse to the courts, acknowledges that those candidates have rights of which they may avail themselves before the courts.[107]

According to the Court it follows that, although no specific sanction is required, the sanction chosen by the Member State must be such as to guarantee real and effective judicial protection. Moreover, it must also have a real deterrent effect on the employer. Consequently, where a Member State chooses to penalize the breach of the prohibition of discrimination by the award of compensation, that compensation must in any event be adequate in relation to the damage sustained.

It will not come as a surprise that the Court found the reimbursement of expenses incurred in submitting the application failed to satisfy the requirements of an effective transposition of the Directive. Yet, in the oral procedure before the Court, the German government maintained that provision at issue, i.e. Paragraph 611a(2) of the Civil Code, did not necessarily exclude the application of the general rules of law regarding compensation. In this respect, the Court of Justice held that it is for the national court alone to rule on that particular question concerning the interpretation of its national law. However, it added a crucial consideration:

> the Member States' obligation arising from a directive to achieve the result envisaged by the Directive and their duty under Article 5 of the Treaty to take all appropriate measures, whether general or particular, to ensure the fulfilment of that obligation, is binding on all the authorities of Member States including, for matters within their jurisdiction, the courts. It follows that, in applying the national law and in particular the provisions of a national law specifically introduced in order to implement Directive n° 76/207, national courts are required to interpret their national law in the light of the wording and the purpose of the Directive in order to achieve the result referred to in the third paragraph of Article 189.[108]

As has been already mentioned the judgements in the *Von Colson* and *Kamann* and the *Harz* cases are not only of considerable importance for EEC sex discrimination law, but also for Community law in general.[109] In particular the message of the Court on the issue of sanction for the violation of the principle of equal treatment is clear. Although the Equal Treatment Directive requires no *specific* sanction, the Member States, choosing from the different solutions available, must take care that the sanction is effective. From the purpose of the Directive and in particular from Article 6, it follows that a sanction must be such as to guarantee real and effective judicial protection, and have a real and deterrent effect on the employer. If a Member State decides to penalize the violation of the equal treatment principle with compensation, such compensation must be *adequate in relation to the damage sustained*. On the other hand, where the law does not provide for sanctions or compensation at all, neither specific nor more general sanctions or compensation, the Directive will be of no help for the person who has been discriminated against.

Case-law of the Court of Justice: enforcement actions

It is not only actions started by individuals in national courts which have given rise to interpretation of the Equal Treatment Directive by the Court of Justice. The Commission, entrusted under the Treaty of Rome with ensuring that Community law provisions are properly implemented by the Member States,[110] started several enforcement actions concerning the implementation of the Equal Treatment Directive. Some of those actions resulted in judgements of the Court of Justice which provide further interesting evidence of the Court's interpretation of the Directive.

Some of the enforcement actions have never reached the Court of Justice when disagreements between the Commission and a Member State have been solved prior to any involvement of the Court, or they have been withdrawn while pending. The Commission's files concerning the pre-judiciary stage of enforcement proceedings are not accessible to outsiders. Nevertheless, some examples can be given here.[111] The Belgian law of 4 August 1978, implementing the Equal Treatment Directive, provided that the meaning of 'vocational guidance and training' for the purposes of the law will be determined by an executive decree. When, in 1980, no such a decree had been adopted, the Commission started an enforcement action and, subsequently, brought the matter before the Court of Justice. Another Belgian decree, of 26 May 1975, relating to prolonged absences justified by family reasons, granted to female state employees only the right to be absent for a maximum period of two years to take care of their children. Although the explanatory memorandum of the above-mentioned law of 1978 stated that benefits granted to female workers in the public sector to enable them to exercise their family responsibilities should be applicable to both men and women, the Commission took the view that by not extending this leave to male employees explicitly, Belgium did not comply with Article 5 of the Directive.

A Danish law of 12 August 1978 implemented Articles 4 and 5 of the Equal Treatment Directive in a rather restricted way. Equality of treatment with respect to guidance, conditions of employment etc. applied only to men and women who were employed in the same place of work.

The Irish legislation gave rise to a considerably longer procedure with the Commission. This legislation concerned the exclusion of activities from the ambit of the equality principle where the sex of the person was a determining factor. It was possible to reserve entry to training and employment for midwives and public health nurses to persons of one sex. Another series of exclusions was possible for jobs in institutions which provided specific care to persons of a particular sex. Either the nature of the institution or the type of care and supervision provided there could mean that only persons of a determined sex were appointed. Another group of exempted jobs concerned employment in the armed forces, the police, prisons, and jobs carried out either in private residences or with close relations. The Commission took the view that the exceptions were too general. They made it possible to exclude a whole series of jobs *en masse* and could be interpreted in a very wide sense.

A fine example of indirect discrimination could be found in a Belgian decree from 1984 creating a job promotion programme. Under this decree the concept of 'head of household' was used to give priority for access to certain jobs.

Finally, in Belgium in 1980 women were admitted for training and for the career of deck officer, including sea captain. Nevertheless they were still unable to enter the 'engine section' of the Naval Training College. The admission to this section had to be preceded by a practical course on board ship which involved activities women were forbidden to carry out under certain protective legislation provisions (in particular, prohibition of painting work involving the use of ceruse and work involving the carrying of loads by hand). However an examination revealed that there no longer existed any justification for barring access to the practical course. Ceruse was hardly used in the engine room and the job of mechanical officer rarely required the officer to carry loads over 27 kg.

The Commission seems to have been quite successful in several actions against the Member States. Apparently they complied with the Commission's views on the proper implementation of the Directive without a judgement of the Court being necessary. However, in a number of cases the Commission was doing rather less well: the actions ended with judgements of the Court which on several occasions dismissed some of the Commission's complaints.

The first case which was brought before the Court of Justice was an enforcement action against *Italy*.[112] In this case the Commission made three charges. The first concerned a breach of Article 5 of the Equal

Treatment Directive. The Italian law no. 903 of 9 December 1977 which was intended to transpose the provisions of Article 5 into national law was not in conformity with the spirit and the letter of the Directive. The Commission alleged that the Italian government had only partially implemented the principle of equal treatment with regard to working conditions as the law no. 903 applies the principles only in respect of *certain* working conditions such as remuneration, retirement age and the right to take leave from work in the case of adoption. It does not cover all working conditions, notwithstanding the much wider nature of the provision contained in Article 5 of the Directive.

The second charge concerned a failure to implement Article 6 of the Directive properly. Article 15 of the law no. 903 provides for a special procedure only in relation to breaches of Articles 1 (access to employment) and 5 (prohibition of women's working at night) thereof. The Commission complained that by not extending the procedure to *all* matters referred to in the Directive the Italian government restricted the legal remedies and therefore did not comply with Article 6 of the Directive which provides for remedies for all persons who consider themselves wronged by the non-application to them of the principle of equal treatment within the meaning of Articles 3, 4 and 5 of the Directive.

In the third place the Commission criticized Article 6 of the law no. 903 dealing with leave in the event of adoption. According to Article 6 only women and not men are eligible, by analogy with the scheme provided for in the case of maternity, for three months' compulsory leave after a child had been adopted into the family if the child is less than six years of age at the time of adoption. The Commission alleged that such different treatment amounts to discrimination in working conditions prohibited by Article 5 of the Directive.

The Commission's action was not successful since the Court dismissed the application in its entirety. As to the first complaint, the Court held that Article 189 of the EEC Treaty provides that a directive is binding as to the result to be achieved, but it leaves to the national authorities the choice of form and methods. The Italian government had pointed out during the procedure before the Court that the Italian legislation contains a very general provision[113] which constitutes a sufficient guarantee against all forms of discrimination which are not covered by a specific provision. Therefore the Italian legislature cannot be criticized for having adopted a number of specific provisions in relation to the most important working conditions only. It can confine itself in relation to all other working conditions to a general provision. The Italian Republic would only fail to fulfil its obligation under the EEC Treaty if it could be shown that the result sought by the Directive has not in fact been attained. Since the Commission had not shown that the specific provisions, combined with a general supplementing provision, had left some areas of the scope of the Directive unprovided for, the first complaint could not be upheld.

The second complaint was dismissed on comparable grounds to the first. The Italian government contended that Article 700 of the Italian Code of Civil Procedure may be relied on in all areas where the Directive applies and which are not covered by Article 15 of law no. 903. Moreover, Article 24 of the Italian Constitution provides that any person may bring proceedings to protect his or her rights and lawful interests. Workers suffering discrimination may rely on that constitutional provision which is of direct application to ensure observance of the provisions of law no. 903 by means of a court action. As the Commission had not contested these explanations, the complaint could not be upheld.

As regards the third charge, the Court held that the distinction is justified by the legitimate concern to assimilate as far as possible the conditions of entry of the child into the adoptive family to those of a newborn child in the family during the very delicate initial period. The difference in treatment criticized by the Commission could not therefore be regarded as discrimination within the meaning of the Directive.

From this judgement two conclusions may be drawn. In the first place the Equal Treatment Directives does *not* require *specific* implementing measures for the transposition of Articles 3, 4 and 5. The Member States can confine themselves to *general* provisions in national legislation. The Commission had contended that the Directive required *special* means of action against discrimination in view of its special and difficult social and economic context. The same conclusion applies to the implementation of Article 6: a *general* provision for legal remedies is sufficient. Accordingly it is to the discretion of the Member States how they implement the Directive as long as the result sought by it is achieved in fact. However, if it appears that the national system does not provide adequate legal remedies, the Member State would be in breach of its obligations under Community law. Although the Court decided that Italy complied formally with the Directive, it is possible that the Equal Treatment Directive is not properly implemented and in concrete cases before Italian courts the deficiencies in the system may appear.

The second conclusion concerns leave for adoptive mothers. In this matter the judgement is both poor and disappointing. The Court simply states that the distinction between adoptive fathers and adoptive mothers is justified by the concern to assimilate the situations when a child is adopted and when a child is born. It does not explain, however, how this difference in treatment fits within the system of the Directive. The matter was discussed more profoundly by Advocate General Rozès. According to her, the key question was whether or not the leave granted to settle a child in the family adopting it is a working condition in the sense of Article 5 of the Directive. The Italian government argued that the leave for adoption does not fall within the concept of working conditions, but appertains to 'provisions concerning the protection of women, particularly as regards pregnancy and maternity' referred to in Article 2, paragraph 3. National provisions falling within the scope of this Article – one of the exceptions of the Equal Treatment Directive – do not come within the ambit of the Directive and consequently the principle of equal treatment does not apply to them. The Commission, on the other hand, stresses that Article 2, paragraph 3, being an exception, must be interpreted strictly to cover only measures relating to pregnancy and maternity. According to Advocate General Rozès, the leave which is granted after childbirth to allow the mother to rest may rightly be regarded as a provision to protect women in relation to maternity. The leave after adoption, however, benefits the child above all in so far as it is intended to foster the emotional ties necessary to settle the child in the family adopting it. Moreover, from the provisions of Italian law it appears that the interests of the child to be adopted are predominant. The Advocate General therefore considered adoption-leave as a working condition within the meaning of Article 5 of the Directive. Consequently, adoptive fathers must be entitled to it on the same basis as their working wives. From the point of view of the elimination of sex-based discrimination, the position taken by the Advocate General is much more satisfactory than the decision of the Court. Furthermore, the case discussed here is a very good example of the imperfections of Article 2, paragraph 3 of the Equal Treatment Directive already mentioned,[114] namely the unclear scope of the term 'maternity'.

In case 165/82 the Commission made three charges against the UK.[115] First, the Commission claimed that the UK legislation did not contain any provision ensuring that provisions contrary to the principle of equal treatment included in collective agreements, internal rules of undertakings or rules governing the independent occupations and professions are or may be declared null and void or may be amended by the courts. Consequently, UK had failed to comply with Article 4 of the Equal Treatment Directive.

Second, the Commission considered that the terms of Section 6 (3) of the Sex Discrimination Act, which provided that the prohibition of discrimination does not apply to employment in a private household or to small undertakings where the number of persons employed by an employer does not exceed five, were contrary to the terms of the Directive, in particular Articles 3, 4 and 5. These exceptions could not fall within the scope of Article 2, paragraph 2 of the Directive. This Article, being an exception to the principle of equal treatment, must be interpreted strictly. Only *certain* occupational activities may be excluded from its field of application. The UK provision referred to the extremely imprecise concept of 'employment...for the purposes of a private household' without limitation as to numbers, and adopted the entirely arbitrary figure of five persons in connection with all kinds of employment. Furthermore, no guidance was given as to what is a 'household' or when it is to be considered 'private'.

Finally, the Commission complained that the UK did not comply with the Directive as the prohibition of discrimination based on sex did not apply to the employment, promotion and training of midwives. The Commission did not accept the UK's contention that the occupation of midwife is covered by the exclusion of Article 2, paragraph 2 of the Directive, namely by reason of its nature or the context in which it is carried out.

As to the first charge, the UK government put forward several arguments in defence of its position. However, according to the Court of Justice, it did not meet all the complaints made by the Commission. The central argument of the UK, which turns on the point that collective agreements, being non-binding, were not covered by the Directive, was not accepted by the Court. The Court held that the Directive covers *all* collective agreements without distinction as to the nature of their legal effects. Even if they are not legally binding, nevertheless collective agreements have important *de facto* consequences for the employment relationships to which they refer. Therefore any clauses contrary to the principle of equal treatment must be rendered inoperative, eliminated or amended by appropriate means. Furthermore, the Court affirmed that the UK legislation neither complied with Article 4(b) of the Directive as far as discriminatory provisions are concerned in internal rules of undertakings nor in the rules governing independent occupations or professions.

The Commission's second complaint was also successful. As regards the reference to employment in a private household, the Court recognized that a reconciliation of the principle of equality of treatment and the principle of respect for private life is one of the factors which must be taken into consideration in determining the scope of the exception provided for in Article 2, paragraph 2 of the Directive. However, that consideration may be decisive only for *certain* kinds of employment in private households and not for all kinds. As far as small undertakings with not more than five employees are concerned, the Court held that the UK had not put forward any argument to show that in such cases the sex of the worker would be a determining factor by reasons of the nature of his or her activities or the context in which they are carried out. The Court concluded that by reasons of *its generality* the exclusion of the principle of equal treatment in UK legislation goes *beyond* the objective which may be lawfully pursued within the framework of Article 2, paragraph 2 of the Directive.

The Commission's third allegation, however, was dismissed by the Court. First, the Court referred to Article 9, paragraph 2 of the Directive which requires Member States periodically to assess the occupational activities referred to in Article 2, paragraph 2 in order to decide, in the light of social developments, whether there is any justification for maintaining the permitted exclusions. Then it examined whether or not the UK had exceeded the limits of the power granted to the Member States by those articles. The conclusion was that the UK stayed within the limits as 'at the present time personal sensitivities may play an important role in relations between midwife and patient'.[116]

In the first place it should be observed that, according to Advocate General Rozès, the exclusion of men from employment and training as midwives is contrary to the Directive. The Advocate General held the view that the nature of midwifery and the context in which it is carried out is not so peculiar that it could justify the non-applicability of the equal treatment principle. The difficulties against male midwives can be sufficiently met by the fact that a woman is free to choose a midwife she prefers. However, the Court decided otherwise, giving Article 2, paragraph 2 a broader interpretation. Apparently the social developments mentioned in Article 9, paragraph 2 may play an important part in the decision whether or not the sex of the worker is a determining factor.

Further, as Article 2, paragraph 2 gives little indication of when sex may be a determining factor for an occupational activity, this provision leaves the Member State a margin of appreciation. However, this discretion is fairly fettered. Exceptions to the principle of equal treatment which are worded in general terms go beyond the limits of Article 2, paragraph 2, which must be interpreted strictly. As far as collective agreements are concerned, the Court underlined in this judgement that under the Directive both *de jure* and *de facto* discrimination are prohibited. Although collective agreements are not legally binding in the UK their provisions have considerable effect in practice. A discriminatory provision in a collective agreement might at the very least lead to an ambiguous situation and to misapprehensions not acceptable from the viewpoint of legal certainty.[117]

The Federal Republic of Germany adopted on 13 August 1980 the 'Arbeitsrechtliches EG-Anpassungsgesetz' in order to implement the Equal Treatment Directive and the Equal Pay Directive. The purpose of that law was to insert a series of new paragraphs in the German Civil Code. The Commission brought an enforcement action[118] before the Court of Justice charging Germany essentially with restricting the measures so adopted to employment relationships governed by private law and, moreover, with failing to give adequate legal effect to a specific provision of the law mentioned. More specifically, the Commission lodged five separate complaints, which may be summarized as follows:

1. Failure to transpose the Equal Treatment Directive with regard to employment relationships in the public service;
2. failure to transpose the Equal Treatment Directive with regard to the rules governing the independent professions;
3. failure to define the scope of the exceptions referred to in Article 2, paragraph 2 of the Equal Treatment Directive;
4. failure to comply fully with the Equal Treatment Directive when adopting the provisions concerning offers of employment;

5. failure to transpose the Equal Pay Directive with regard to remuneration in the public service.[119]

The Court of Justice rejected the two first complaints for the following reasons. Although, according to the Court, both the Equal Treatment Directive and the Equal Pay Directive are of general application, which means that they apply, *inter alia*, to employment in the public service, the first complaint could not be upheld. In the first place the Commission had not established, or even attempted to establish, that discrimination on grounds of sex exists, either in law or in fact, in the public service in Germany. In the second place, the German Basic Law affirms the equality of men and women before the law and guarantees the principle of non-discrimination on grounds of sex and equal access to employment in the public services for all German nationals.[120] The rights defined in the Basic Law are directly conferred on individuals and give rise, where they are infringed by public authorities, to a right of action before the administrative courts and eventually before the Constitutional Court.[121] Therefore, the Court of Justice found that the constitutional provisions constitute, in conjunction with the existing system of judicial remedies, including the possibility of instituting proceedings before the Constitutional Court, an adequate guarantee of the implementation, in the field of public administration, of the principle of equal treatment. Furthermore, the Court pointed out that the legislation concerning the German public service contained the same guarantees: it expressly lays down that appointment to posts in the public service must be based on objective criteria, without any distinction on grounds of sex.[122] Consequently, according to the Court, the object of the Directive had already been achieved in Germany as regards employment in the public service. In this context the Commission argued that the requirement of 'aptitude' of the applicants for employment in the public service makes it possible to reintroduce discrimination on grounds of sex. The Court did not agree. It was of the opinion that the criterion of 'aptitude' for office in the public service covers a wide variety of criteria of assessment which, having regard to the broad range of duties performed by the public administration, are entirely unconnected with the question of a person's sex, and besides, the Commission had not established that the criterion had been applied in practice in such a way as to lead to discriminatory appointments in the public service.

The second complaint concerning the independent professions was rejected for similar reasons as the first. The Commission – again – had not produced evidence from which it might be inferred that the rules governing the independent professions in Germany gave rise to discrimination. The guarantees provided by the Basic Law and the existing system of judicial remedies as regards the freedom for all German nationals to take up an independent profession, subject only to certain qualifications that are objectively determined without any reference to sex, result in, as far as the rules governing the independent professions are concerned, the object of the Equal Treatment Directive being achieved.

The complaint concerning the implementation of Article 2, paragraph 2, and Article 9, paragraph 2 of the Equal Treatment Directive was well founded. The German Civil Code makes it possible to derogate from the principle of equal treatment where a person's sex constitutes a condition for carrying out a given occupational activity. The Commission considered this provision inadequate since it did not contain a catalogue setting out precisely the exceptions permitted. Moreover, Germany did not create an adequate basis for enabling the Commission to exercise the right of supervision which is conferred upon it by Article 9, paragraph 2 of the Directive. The Court pointed out in the first place that the purpose of Article 2, paragraph 2 is not to oblige but to permit the Member States to exclude certain occupational activities from the field of application of the Directive. It does not require the Member States to exercise that power of derogation in a particular way. However, another Article of the Directive, Article 9, paragraph 2, does impose certain obligations on the Member States. It provides for supervision in two stages: a periodic assessment by the Member States themselves of the justification for maintaining exceptions to the principle of equal treatment, and supervision by the Commission based on the notification of the result of that assessment. This twofold supervision serves to eliminate progressively existing exceptions which no longer appear justified, having regard to the criteria laid down in Article 2, paragraphs 2 and 3. The Court deduced from this system of supervision the obligation for the Member States to compile a complete and verifiable list, in whatever form, of the occupations excluded and to notify the results to the Commission. The Commission, for its part, has the right and duty, by virtue of Article 155 of the EEC Treaty, to adopt measures necessary to verify the application of that provision. As Germany had not adopted the necessary measures to create even a minimum of transparency with regard to the application of Article 2, paragraph 2, and Article 9, it prevented the Commission from exercising effective supervision and made it more difficult for persons wronged by discriminatory measures to defend their rights. Therefore, Germany was found to have failed to fulfil its obligations under the EEC Treaty.

The next complaint, which was rejected by the Court, concerned a provision of the Civil Code dealing with the advertisement of offers of employment. Although according to this provision advertisements should be 'impartial' as regards the sex of the employees, the provision was not binding. The Commission argued that Germany, by failing to give legal effect to the provision, did not satisfy the requirement laid down in Article 6 of the Equal Treatment Directive. Germany argued that since offers of employment precede access to employment, they do not come within the scope of the Directive. The Court held that offers of employment cannot be excluded *a priori* from the scope of the Equal Treatment Directive, inasmuch as they are closely connected with access to employment and can have a restrictive effect thereon. However,

> the Directive imposes no obligation on the Member States to enact general legislation concerning offers of employment, particularly as this question is in turn closely linked to that of the exceptions permitted by Article 2 (2) of the Directive, given that the application of Article 9 (2) in full will have the effect of creating the necessary transparency also as regards offers of employment.[123]

The contested provision must be regarded as an independent legislative measure adopted for the purpose of giving effect to the principle of equal treatment, and not as implementing an obligation imposed by the Directive.

The Court dealt very briefly with the last complaint. The Commission charged Germany with not having transposed the Equal Pay Directive into national law with regard to remuneration in the public service. But, as the Commission did not provide the slightest evidence of sex discrimination with regard to the remuneration of public servants in Germany and as the remuneration is based exclusively on post and grade, regardless of the sex of the officials, the complaints could not be upheld.[124]

This case brought by the Commission before the Court of Justice must be considered to a great extent a matter of principle. Of course the Commission was informed about the Basic Law provisions which cover the public service and independent professions. However, it considered the existing legal situation as not providing sufficient clarity and certainty for legal purposes to satisfy the requirements of the Directive. In the Commission's view, the provisions in question needed to be given concrete form and be implemented by ordinary legislation to be effective in practice. On the other hand, the Commission did not succeed in establishing that discrimination in those areas existed in Germany. It may be asked whether such proceedings are not a waste of time and labour if the Commission is not able to give concrete examples of discrimination. However, the judgement of the Court must be considered within the context of the German situation. The German provisions applicable define clearly the equal treatment principle and confer directly rights on individuals. The persons concerned can rely on these rights in administrative courts and, if necessary, before the Constitutional Court. The German system of judicial remedies as regards the fundamental rights with the possibility of 'Konkretes Normenkontrollverfahren' and 'Verfassungsbeschwerde'[125] constitutes a far-reaching guarantee for the observance of non-discrimination. There is no doubt that if similar proceedings should be instituted against a Member State which does not have such guarantees, for instance, where the review of legislation by courts is impossible, the judgement would be completely different.

The decision of the Court with regard to Article 2, paragraph 2 must be welcomed. It has been already observed[126] that the national exceptions falling – according to the Member States – within the scope of Article 2, paragraph 2 vary considerably. Moreover, the compatibility of several of those exceptions with the Equal Treatment Directive may be questioned. On the one hand the Court leaves the Member States a margin of appreciation under Article 2, paragraph 2,[127] but on the other hand, it puts the Member States under the duty to compile a complete and verifiable list of the occupations excluded to enable the Commission to exercise supervision. If the Commission establishes that certain exclusions are no longer justified in the light of social developments, it may institute enforcement proceedings against the Member State(s). And, of course, such a list is from the viewpoint of legal certainty and clarity extremely important for the individuals within the Member State.

Moreover, it is interesting to observe that the Court referred not only to Article 2, paragraph 2, but also to paragraph 3. The obligation stated in Article 9, paragraph 2 concerns only the exceptions based 'on sex as a determining factor'. The reference by the Court to paragraph 3 (protection of women, particularly as regards pregnancy and maternity) suggests that a Member State must include in the list of excluded occupations both the activities for which sex constitutes a determining factor and which are excluded in order to protect women. This decision could imply that the ideas about the protection of women depend on social developments which may vary from Member State to Member State. Viewed in the light of the former case-law,[128] which leaves, with regard to Article 2, paragraph 3 the Member States a considerable margin of appreciation, this is not surprising. Moreover, it implies a recognition by the Court that women may be excluded from some occupations and professional activities under Article 2, paragraph 3 for their protection, a wider interpretation than that advocated by the Commission.

One last remark concerns advertisements. It has been pointed out above[129] that the Commission attaches great importance to neutrally drafted job advertisements. The Court recognized that offers of employment may fall within the scope of the Equal Treatment Directive 'inasmuch as they are closely connected with access to employment and can have a restrictive effect thereon',[130] but on the other hand the Member States are not under the obligation to enact general legislation concerning offers of employment. The reasons for this decision are quite unclear. It cannot be denied that discriminatory advertisements have *some* restrictive effects on access to employment. Would a woman apply for a job where an advertisement specifies that a man is required, even if she knows that discrimination is prohibited at the moment of selection? Although an obligation for the Member States to enact legislation concerning job advertisements is not specifically mentioned in Article 3, it may be argued that such legislation is necessary to achieve the objective of the Directive and that such legislation must be enforceable. The Court expects the necessary transparency as far as the offers of employment are concerned from the list compiled under Article 9, paragraph 2. However, how can a list *in whatever form* guarantee that there will be no discriminatory job advertisements? On this point, the reasoning of the Court is not very convincing.

In case 318/86[131] the Commission claimed that France did not comply with the Equal Treatment Directive as far as access to employment in the civil service was concerned. In France officials in the civil service are recruited by competition. From time to time, administrative competitions are organized for certain posts. In each competition, a number of posts are available and are distributed among the candidates found to be suitable. Civil servants are not recruited for a specific post. They have to occupy any post corresponding with their grade in their corps. The civil servants may be promoted to a higher grade in the course of their career. Usually, a single competition is held for female and male candidates and the sole criterion for recruitment is the grading of the candidate, regardless of sex. However, certain exceptions have been provided for. Article 21 of law no. 84-16 of 11 January 1984 laying down statutory rules on the state civil service provides as follows:

> For certain corps a list of which will be drawn up by decree of the Conseil d'Etat...separate recruitment may be organized for men and women if belonging to one or other sex constitutes a determining factor for the performance of the duties carried out by persons in such corps.

The above-mentioned list specified the following corps for which separate recruitment could be organized: police superintendents, captains and officers, inspectors, investigators and police constables and policemen in the national police force; assistants at the Maison d'Education of the Légion d'Honneur; corps in the external departments of the prison service, namely management, technical and vocational training and custodial staff, including governors of small prisons; customs inspectors, investigators and officers; teachers; physical education and sports teachers and assistant teachers. However, during the procedure with the Commission and while the case was pending before the Court several of these corps have been removed from the list. Ultimately, the Commission's action remained directed at the five corps in the national police force and the governors of certain small prisons.[132]

The separate recruitment with which the Commission did not agree from the point of view of equal treatment, did *not* involve the organization of separate competitions, with separate sittings, examinations and selection boards as the term suggests. There was a single competition but the decision ordering the holding of a competition fixed in each case the percentage of posts to be allotted to men and women respectively. In other words, it was a system of quota, but the quota itself (x posts to men, y posts to women) was determined *ad hoc* and without it being made clear according to which criteria.

The Commission claimed that in principle separate recruitment was contrary to the principle of equal treatment. By determining in advance the number of posts to be allocated to candidates of each sex, the French rules made the candidates' sex a criterion for his or her appointment. The French government tried to contradict the Commission's position first, but then it confined itself to arguing that separate recruitment was justified on the basis of Article 2, paragraph 2 of the Directive since, for several activities carried out by the corps concerned, sex would be a determining factor. The Commission disagreed. It recalled that Article 2, paragraph 2 must be interpreted strictly: a derogation is compatible with the Directive only for objective reasons relating to the very nature of the occupational activity concerned or the context in which it is carried out and showing that, with regard to the specific duties involved, it may be pursued by persons of a specific sex only. Further, the Commission recognized that with respect to certain posts within a corps, sex may constitute a determining factor. But that can never be a justification for applying discriminatory conditions of recruitment to those corps, treating them as a whole and without regard for the nature and context in which particular duties entrusted to successful candidates are carried out.

The French government replied that the system of separate recruitment resulted from the special organization of the French civil service. A civil servant is appointed to a grade rather than to a particular post; he or she has to occupy posts which often cover very different occupational activities and once appointed he or she may not be subject to any measure based on sex. Discrimination between men and women is prohibited by regulations concerning the civil service. Thus it would be impossible to take into consideration some specific duties performed by a civil servant instead of the particular corps to which he or she is appointed.

As far as the national police is concerned, the French government contended that a great proportion of women in these corps would seriously damage its credibility. In particular, the maintenance of public order requires a display of the capacity to use force at all times, which would be disrupted by a large-scale recruitment of women. The need to dissuade potential troublemakers and the physical dangers of the job should justify recruiting only a limited proportion of women. The French government accepted that many police activities may be carried out by either sex. But because under the French system of civil service, police officers have to be interchangeable, separate recruitment had to be maintained. Moreover, the French government mentioned some other practical difficulties in employing women with the police, such as the fact that a relatively large proportion of the women recruited have requested part-time work and the fact that a pregnant police officer can no longer wear a uniform and so has to be given a desk job.

The case of governors of small prisons[133] was slightly different. These posts were not filled by recruitment but they were part of the career of prison wardens and were filled by way of promotion. The Commission accepted that custodial staff, i.e. wardens, may be recruited on the basis of sex. Sex should be a determining factor for the employment of prison staff who carry out custodial duties. However, since governors no longer exercise custodial duties but administrative ones, Article 2, paragraph 2 of the Directive could not apply. Thus in the Commission's view the appointment of governors from amongst staff originally recruited separately by sex was itself vitiated by discrimination notwithstanding the fact that the separate recruitment for custodial staff was justified under Article 2, paragraph 2.

The Court dismissed the Commission's complaint as far as the governors of small prisons were concerned. The Court found that in a corps in which the separate recruitment of female and male candidates was regarded as justified under Article 2, paragraph 2 of the Directive and in which promotion to a higher grade was not discriminatory, the fact that certain activities corresponding to a higher degree did not necessarily have to be carried out by persons of one or other sex did not make Article 2, paragraph 2 inapplicable. In particular, the Court held that there might be reasons for allowing the duties of a governor to be exercised only by persons who had been prison wardens in the past and so acquired the necessary experience for the post of a governor. The Commission had not established that such considerations were invalid.

From a very formal point of view the Commission was perhaps right. As Advocate General Slynn has pointed out, there remained in force a legislative provision allowing for separate recruitment to the post of governor inasmuch as that post was comprised in the corps of custodial staff mentioned in the list, while the activities of a governor did not necessarily have to be performed by a man or a woman. On the other hand, the Commission fully agreed with separate recruitment for the custodial staff as such. Its complaint was that the separately recruited wardens could be promoted to certain – in number very limited – posts where the sex was not a determining factor any more. However, the Commission did not clearly take into account that the prior experience as warden made those persons eligible for the post of governor of a small prison.

The complaint concerning the police was upheld. The Court held, in particular, that Article 2, paragraph 2 could only cover specific activities and together with Article 9, paragraph 2 it required a certain degree of transparency enabling effective supervision on the part of the Commission. With respect to the recruitment of police officers, the required transparency did not exist at all. The percentage fixing the distribution of posts to male and female candidates was not governed by any objective criterion laid down in legislation or regulation. The system of recruitment as it existed in France prevented any form of supervision on the part of the Commission and the courts, as well as on the part of persons adversely affected by discriminatory measures, to determine whether the percentage laid down for separate recruitment in fact corresponded to the specific activities for which the sex of the person carrying them out constituted a determining factor. Also the justification based on the basic principles governing the French civil service found no favour in the eyes of the Court. It recalled that the principle of proportionality required that, as far as possible, equal treatment of men and women should be reconciled with the requirements which were determining factors for the carrying out of the specific activity at issue. The organization of the civil service may not lead to exceptions to an individual right which would exceed the limits of what was necessary to attain the lawful aim pursued.

The Court did not deal with the question whether and what police activities may be exclusively assigned respectively to male and female police officers. It left aside for the moment what exactly should be considered as the lawful aim pursued by the derogation. However, the Court did not have to consider this problem, since the French recruitment system was unverifiable and over-broad, which was sufficient to declare that France has failed to fulfil its obligations. On the other hand, this judgement reaffirms that the Court is prepared to accept that sex may be a determining factor for certain policing activities. The Advocate General discussed the question in more detail. He held that for certain police activities sex may be a determining factor, but not simply because average men are bigger and stronger than women, but because potential delinquents regard men as more ready to use force and perhaps because men are more willing to use force. However, he doubted whether such a perception could justify the exclusion of women from certain police units dealing with violence as it was not established that they cannot cope with violence in a satisfactory manner. This latter was apparently exactly what the French government contended when arguing that police duties which involve the display of force are unsuitable to be carried out by women, forgetting that selection should depend on individual merit and not on generalized and stereotyped assumptions about the group of individuals to which the candidate belongs. Moreover, it became clear that a derogation to the principle of equal treatment can not be justified with arguments based on the existing organization of the civil service and the convenience of the French authorities.

The last case to be discussed is also an infringement proceedings against France.[134] On 13 July 1984, the French Republic adopted law no. 83-635 amending the Labour Code and the Criminal Code as regards equality at work between women and men. Article L 123-1(c) of the Labour Code, as then amended, laid down a general prohibition on adopting any measure on grounds of sex, particularly in regard to remuneration, training, assignment, qualification, classification, professional advancement or transfer. Article L 123-2 prohibited the insertion of any term reserving the benefit of any measure to one or more employees on the grounds of sex in any collective agreement or contract of employment, except where such a clause is intended to implement certain articles of the Labour Code which provide for the protection of women by reasons of pregnancy, maternity and nursing. However, Article 19 of law no. 83-635 provided the following:

> The provisions of Articles L 123-1(c) and L 123-2 of the Labour Code do not prohibit the application of usages, terms of contracts of employment or of collective agreements in force at the date on which this law is promulgated granting particular rights to women.
>
> However, employers, groups of employers and groups of employed persons shall proceed, by collective negotiation, to bring such terms into conformity with the provisions of the abovementioned Articles.

In the written procedure, the French government indicated that the special rights, to which Article 19 refers, include, among others, the extension of maternity leave, the reduction of working hours, the obtaining of specific holidays for each child (additional holidays at the start of the school year and holidays when the child is ill), the payment of an allowance for a crèche or babysitter, the reduction of the retirement age and the award of additional benefits for children. The government explained further that the trade unions induced the employers to place those special rights in contracts of employment and collective labour agreements in order to provide additional protection for working women. According to French social tradition, women play an essential role in regard to the health and education of children within the family unit. The rights in question were designed to permit them to reconcile that role with the social interest represented by working women. Furthermore, the special advantages should contribute to increasing the birth rate, which is in France, with 60 per cent of working women being mothers, traditionally low.

The Commission's action was concerned essentially with two points. First, Article 19, paragraph 1 of law no. 83-635 was, in the Commission's view, contrary to Article 5, paragraph 2(b) of the Equal Treatment Directive, since it permitted the continuance of certain rights which were incompatible with the principle of equal treatment. Second, the Commission challenged the second paragraph of Article 19, which left it to management and labour to bring the provisions into line without imposing a time limit or any effective sanction if the provisions are not amended within a reasonable time.

The French government argued, as to the first point, that the continuance of special rights in favour of women was justified by the organization of the family and division of responsibilities therein, in particular, the role of the woman as mother, and by the need to smooth out *de facto* inequalities. The government referred in this respect to the Court's judgement in *Hofmann*[135] and to the fact that Article 2, paragraph 3 of the Directive provides for an exception to the principle of equal treatment when a provision aims at protection of women, *particularly* as regards pregnancy and maternity. Further, the government maintained that the concepts of 'equal opportunity' and 'existing inequalities' in Article 2, paragraph 4 must not be understood solely in the context of the work environment but also in an overall social context including, in particular, the way in which family responsibilities are divided.

To the second complaint the French government responded that the immediate implementation of all the provisions of the Directive was difficult to imagine having regard to the importance of the social rights at issue and the fact that the two sides of industry were anxious to maintain advantages which had been acquired. The government stressed that collective bargaining was the only way to bring about the abolition of special rights for women and that it was better able to influence the actual conduct of the persons concerned than a legislative measure. Furthermore, the government held that an elimination of offending provisions could be ensured in the approval procedure to which all new collective agreements were submitted.

The Court dealt with the French arguments in a relatively short and somewhat vague way. In relation to Article 2, paragraph 3 of the Directive, the Court recalled that, according to its judgement in *Hofmann*, the purpose of this provision is to provide protection for the special relationship between mother and child during the period following pregnancy and childbirth by ensuring that that relationship is not disturbed by the cumulative effect of the burdens resulting from the simultaneous exercise of a professional activity. The French provisions at issue could not be justified under Article 2, paragraph 3; the terms of the French legislation, which deals with maintenance of any term granting 'special rights to women', were found to be too general. Furthermore, it followed from the examples of special rights that some of them provide protection for women as older workers or parents, characteristics which could be attributed either to male or female workers.

As far as Article 2, paragraph 4 was concerned, the Court held that the precise and limited purpose of this exception is to authorize measures which, although discriminatory in appearance, are actually intended to eliminate or reduce inequalities which may exist in everyday life. However, in the case before the Court no factor in the file allowed the conclusion to be drawn that the general maintenance of special rights for women in collective agreements corresponded to the situation envisaged by Article 2, paragraph 4.

Finally, the Court considered that even if the French argument that collective bargaining was the best way to abolish discrimination was correct, it did not justify national legislation which, several years after the expiry of the time limit laid down for the implementation of the Directive, leaves the abolition of certain inequalities to the two sides of industry without imposing a time limit on them for compliance with that obligation. The Court referred in this respect to the fact that during the period from 1984 to 1987 sixteen collective agreements had been renegotiated. Compared to the total number of collective agreements concluded every year in France (in 1983: 1050 agreements covering an occupational branch and 2400 agreements concluded within individual undertakings), the number was very modest.

The Court's judgement is drafted in such vague and general terms that it hardly permits to draw some meaningful conclusions on the interpretation of the Directive. As far as Article 2, paragraph 3 is concerned it may be argued that the Court followed strictly its case-law on the narrow constructions of exceptions to the principle of equal treatment. First, although the word 'particularly' seems to indicate that situations other than pregnancy and maternity may fall within the scope of the above-mentioned paragraph, the Court did not accept the French argument based on the traditional role of women as mothers. Special rights which are not directly connected with pregnancy and maternity do not apparently fall within the scope of Article 2, paragraph 3. Second, this judgement may suggest that the term 'maternity' must be understood as the special relationship between mother and child during the period following pregnancy and childbirth. Everything that goes beyond this period is not maternity any more and consequently special rights must be accorded to both mother and father. Thus, although in *Hofmann* the Court construed Article 2, paragraph 3 in an unnecessarily broad way,[136] from this judgement it appears that the Court is willing to apply this construction strictly.

The considerations concerning Article 2, paragraph 4 are even more non-committal. What kind of inequalities in everyday life is the Court aiming at? Situations at the workplace, like under-representation of women in certain branches of industry or in certain functions? Or at more general problems like family responsibilities which may affect women's opportunities in the labour market? Perhaps the Court dismissed the French arguments not only because of the very general character of the provision and the fact that it was open-ended, but perhaps also because of the contrary effects which special rights may have in the long run. It is undoubtedly true that women's opportunities are still restricted by family responsibilities and that their chances may increase when special rights or, at least, facilities are provided. However, it is a very delicate task to find the appropriate balance between short and long-term achievements. Special rights such as those at issue in the present case will have harmful effects on the position of women since they perpetuate and even legitimize the traditional division of roles between men and women. Moreover, this type of legislation makes it less attractive for parents to share family responsibilities or to change the roles completely, and it discriminates against single-parent families with a man as the sole breadwinner. On the other hand, in the past, the Court seemed to be prepared to take into account the traditional division of roles between men and women when interpreting Community equality law. The same philosophy may possibly determine the exact scope of Article 2 paragraph 4.

Finally, this case raised a more general problem concerning the level of equality to be established. The French government argued that the application of the principle of equal treatment to the special rights at issue will probably lead to a withdrawal from women of the rights concerned, which would be a socially retrograde step. Unlike the Court, the Advocate General examined this point, though he did so only briefly.[137] The Advocate General supported the Commission's proposition that equality should be achieved by a levelling-up process, i.e. by applying the same benefits to men. He found such an approach in accordance with the terms and spirit of the Directive, the third recital of which sets out the aim of furthering the harmonization of living and working conditions 'while maintaining their improvement'. As the Advocate General understood it, Community law merely requires the benefits to be offered to men and women on equal terms.

Conclusions

The case-law of the Court of Justice with regard to the Equal Treatment Directive is, compared with other areas of Community law, not extensive. Nevertheless, from the judgements discussed in the preceding pages some more general conclusions on the interpretation of the Equal Treatment Directive can be drawn.

The first conclusion concerns Article 2, paragraph 2, the exception to the principle of equal treatment because of sex as a determining factor for the performance of certain occupational activities. Although this provision, being an exception, must be interpreted strictly, the Court of Justice has left the Member States a margin of appreciation. It seems that it has done so because social developments (mentioned in Article 9, paragraph 2) may vary from Member State to Member State. Thus not only are biological differences between the two sexes decisive, but social considerations of character and the environment in which the activities are carried out may also be taken into account. Moreover, other fundamental rights may play a part when answering the question whether or not the exclusion of one of the sexes is justified. However, the discretion under Article 2, paragraph 2 is not unlimited. Exclusions drawn up in general terms go beyond the limits of this provision. The Member States are even – by virtue of Article

9, paragraph 2 – under the duty to draw up a complete and verifiable list of the occupational activities excluded. The list is subject to the supervision of the Commission.

Second, as far as the exception of Article 2, paragraph 3 is concerned, the protection of women in connection with pregnancy and maternity, the Court is very, perhaps too, cautious. The Court has given this provision quite a wide interpretation. This Article provides for twofold protection. In the first place it seeks to protect the woman's biological condition during and after pregnancy. In the second place it concerns the protection of the special relationship between a mother and her child during the period following childbirth. The same reasoning applies under certain circumstances to the adoptive mother as well. Moreover, the margin of appreciation left to the Member States under this Article is quite wide as regards the nature and the arrangements for implementation of the protective measures. It even seems that Member States have a discretion under Article 2, paragraph 3 to exclude some occupational activities in order to protect women. One may wonder how such a position can be reconciled with the objectives of the Equal Treatment Directive. The period of pregnancy and maternity, in the strict sense as advocated above,[138] is a relatively short one in a woman's life. Therefore it is difficult to understand why a woman should be excluded for her whole life from certain jobs. If a protection is needed because of her procreative functions, a wider concept than pregnancy and maternity, sufficient protection can be reached by special working conditions under Article 5.

More generally, it must be observed here that the case-law of the Court does not contribute to the necessary delimitation between the several derogations provided for by the Directive; on the contrary it seems to have confused the matter even more. On the other hand, there is one positive observation on the problem of exceptions: the Court has required the observance of the principle of proportionality when dealing with the question of whether or not a derogation is justified. This requirement may in concrete situations limit the scope of a derogation considerably.

The third conclusion concerns Article 5, in particular the term 'dismissal'. This term must be interpreted widely. It includes among other things, the termination of the employment relationship under a voluntary redundancy scheme. A strict distinction must be made between 'dismissal' and the entitlement to retirement and old age pension or the access to a retirement scheme. As far as the latter is concerned, difference in pensionable age constitutes no discrimination under Community law as it stands now. On the other hand the use of different ages in relation to dismissal is discriminatory under the Equal Treatment Directive even if this difference is due to the unequal pensionable ages. It has been pointed out already that this approach – however welcome it may be – may raise several problems.

Furthermore, it may be concluded that, although the Equal Treatment

Directive does not require a *specific* sanction in case of violation of the principle of equal treatment, in order to implement the Directive effectively, the Member States must provide for *a* sanction which guarantees real and effective judicial protection and which has a real and deterrent effect. The sanction must be adequate in relation to the damage sustained.

Finally, it must be pointed out that the Court considered Article 3, paragraph 1, Article 4, paragraph 1, Article 5, paragraph 1 (all in conjunction with Article 2, paragraph 1) and Article 6 as having direct effect.

The overall impression is that the case-law, although it may be criticized on several points, is extremely important. Not only for sex-discrimination law, but for the Community law in general. In this context the issues concerning judicial protection and the effective implementation of directives[139] must be borne in mind. On the other hand, it is no exaggeration to state that while answering several questions the Court has raised new problems as well.

Notes

1   Case 149/77 *Defrenne* v. *Sabena* (1978) E.C.R. 1365.
2   Council Directive 76/207 of 9 February 1976, O.J. L39/40, 14 February 1976.
3   Sixth General Report on the Activities of the Communities, p. 11.
4   O.J. C13/1 12 February 1974.
5   COM (75) 36 final. Proposal for a directive was annexed to the memorandum.
6   In particular, *Les conditions de travail des femmes salariées dans les six Etats membres de la Communauté Européenne* (six studies on the situation of working women in the separate Member States), Brussels 1972, doc. V/164/73 – V/169/73; Cornu, *Women and employment in the United Kingdom, Ireland and Denmark*, Brussels 1974, V/649/75.
7   See Chapter 2, p.43
8   See Directive 79/7, discussed in Chapter 5 and Directive 86/378, discussed in Chapter 7.
9   Compare Report from the Commission to the Council on the situation at 12 August 1980 with regard to the implementation of the Equal Treatment Directive (hereafter: Commission Report), COM (80) 832 final, p. 6.
10   *Ibid.* pp. 32–3.
11   See Quintin (1985) p. 310, Sousi-Roubi (1981) p. 167, who points out that the concept of indirect discrimination was as such unknown in French law, and Commission document 'Implementation of the equality directives', Luxembourg 1987, p. 2 and p. 16.
12   See Chapter 1, p. 15 and Chapter 3, p. 71.
13   In 1981, in the New Action Programme (see below note 33), the Commission announced a study into the problem of indirect discrimination and a subsequent Community definition. Further, a tentative formulation of the concept was given in an interim report on the application of the quality principle in the field of social security (COM(83)793 final). More guidance has meanwhile been provided by the Court of Justice, in case 170/84 *Bilka-Kaufhaus* v. *Weber von Hartz* (1986) E.C.R. 1607, discussed in Chapter 3, p. 74 and in case 30/85 *Teuling* v. *Bedrijfsvereniging voor de Chemische Industrie*, (1988) 3 CMLR 789, discussed in Chapter 5, p. 192. On the concept of indirect discrimination, in particular, in the UK see the very informative report of Byre (1987). It was not until May 1988 that the Commission

gave a definition of indirect discrimination in a draft directive on the burden of proof. See Chapter 7, p. 299.

14 It is not clear whether it is sufficient that there is *different* treatment or whether *less favourable* treatment is required.

15 Case 170/84, *loc. cit.* note 13.

16 Compare Byre (1987) p. 32.

17 Vice versa, an advertisement asking for persons not liable to military service may be indirectly discriminatory as only few men will qualify.

18 Weele (1983) p. 60. Compare also Treu, in Verwilghen (ed.) (1987) p. 140. More recently, however, an amendment has been accepted by the Dutch Parliament to a bill concerning reform of the legislation on equal treatment of men and women. According to this amendment, discrimination on grounds of pregnancy is a form of direct discrimination. See N.J.B. (1988) p. 1248.

19 (1980) I.L.R. 4. The E.A.T. reversed *Turley* in *Hayes* v. *Malleable Working Men's Club and Institute* and in *Maughan* v. *NE London Magistrates Court Committee* (1985) I.C.R. 703 and treated the appropriate comparator as being a sick man. Furthermore, in a recent Industrial Tribunal case in Glasgow, *Jennings* v. *Burton* (unreported), the I.T. treated dismissal on the grounds of pregnancy as sex discrimination *(The Glasgow Herald* 31 August 1988).

20 For example Article 1 of the Dutch Constitution states: 'In the Netherlands all persons shall be treated equally in equal circumstances...' See further on the unwritten principle of equality the Dutch report for the 12th FIDE Congress 1986, by Prechal and Heukels (1986), pp. 263–64. Compare for the 'community principle' joined cases 117/76 and 16/77 *(Ruckdeschel)* (1977) E.C.R. 1753.

21 Curtin (1987) pp. 134–35.

22 Case 177/88 *Dekker* v. *Stichting Vormingscentrum voor jong volwassenen plus*, O.J. C 211/11, 11 August 1988. Furthermore, in July 1988 a question was submitted to the Court of Justice by the Højesteret, Danish Supreme Court, concerning dismissal of a female employee on grounds of long absence which was due to illness. Such a dismissal seems to be possible under Danish law under certain circumstances. However in this particular case the illness was caused by pregnancy. Thus the problem the Court has to deal with is whether such a dismissal must be considered as contrary to Article 5, paragraph 1 of the Equal Treatment Directive. (Case 179/88 *Hertz* v. *Aldi Marked*, O.J. C 205/6, 6 August 1988).

23 Commission Report, *loc. cit.* note 9, p. 39.

24 Compare Zorbas (1986) p. 139.

25 *Ibid.* p. 136.

26 See case 248/83 *Commission* v. *FRG* (1985) E.C.R. 1459, discussed below, p 145.

27 See below, p. 139 *et seq.*

28 Commission Report, *loc. cit.* note 9, p. 39–61.

29 See Report on protective measures and the activities not falling within the fields of application of the Directive on Equal Treatment, V/707/3/82.

30 Compare Sousi-Roubi (1981) p. 170.

31 Commission Report, *loc. cit.* note 9, p. 55.

32 Case 184/83 *Hofmann* v. *Barmer Ersatzkasse* (1984) E.C.R. 3047. See below, p. 127.

33 The New Community Action Programme on the Promotion of Equal Opportunities for Women (1982–1985), COM (81) 758 final, and the Medium-term Community Programme on the Promotion of Equal Opportunities for Women (1986–1990), COM (85) 801 final.

34 In Article 8 of Directive 86/613, (the 'Self-Employed Women Directive', see Chapter 7, p. 290) the whole problem of protection of self-employed women during pregnancy and motherhood is reduced to an obligation for the Member States to undertake certain studies.

35 See Council Recommendation of 13 December 1984 on the promotion of positive action for women, O.J. L 331/34, 19 December 1984.

36   See for example the two Action Programmes, *loc. cit.* note 33, Raetsen in Quintin *et al.* (1986) pp. 76–87, Docksey, in McCrudden (ed.) (1987) p. 14, and Report on the implementation of the Council Recommendation of 13 December 1984 on the promotion of positive action for women, COM(88)370 final. More specifically for the UK see McCrudden (1986) and for some other European countries Vogel-Polsky (1985). More recently an EEC positive action guide has been announced in EIRR (1988) p. 29.

37   See *inter alia*, *Regents of the University of California* v. *Allan Bakke*, 438 U.S. 265 (1978), *United Steel-workers of America* v. *Weber*, 443 U.S. 193 (1979) and *Fullilove* v. *Klutznick*, 448 U.S. 448 (1980). Within the EC no case concerning comparable problems has been submitted to the Court of Justice yet. However, on the national level the uncertainties on compatibility of positive measures with the principle of equal treatment has emerged. See for instance McCrudden (1986) p. 228 *et seq*, Sloot (1986) p. 190, and 'Implementation of the equality directives', *loc. cit.* note 11, p. 49.

38   Compare Sloot (1986) pp. 131 and 259, and Docksey, in McCrudden (ed.) (1987) p. 17.

39   Commission Report, *loc. cit.* note 9, p. 106.

40   See Annex to the European Parliament Report on the position of women in Europe (Rodano-report), Doc. 1-1229/83, p. 45–46.

41   See above, p. 108.

42   Compare Commission Report, *loc. cit.* note 9, pp. 35–36. Moreover, the maintenance *de facto* of discriminatory provisions – even when they are not binding any more – may give rise to an ambiguous situation, contrary to legal certainty and to community law as well. See Chapter 2, p. 43.

43   See Commission Report, *loc. cit.* note 9, p. 93.

44   See case 165/82 *Commission* v. *UK* (1983) E.C.R. 3431, discussed below, p. 143.

45   See Commission Report, *loc.cit.* note 9, p. 162–165 and, more recently, Commission's communication on protective legislation for women in the Member States, COM (87) 105 final.

46   See for some self-evident figures Commission Report, *loc. cit.* note 9, p. 132–138.

47   *Ibid.* p. 111–112.

48   In case 293/83 *Gravier* v. *Ville de Liège et al.* (1985) E.C.R. 593, the Court indeed held that 'the conditions of access to vocational training fall within the scope of the Treaty'. It appears, in particular, from case 26/88 *Blaizot et al.* v. *Université de Liège et al.*, (1989) 1 CMLR 57 that general education as such is not covered by the Treaty.

49   See Quintin (1985) p. 310.

50   Compare however on this point case 26/88, *loc. cit.* note 48, where the Court held that, in general, university education should be considered as vocational training since it prepares for qualification for a particular profession, trade or employment or it provides the necessary training and skills for such profession, trade or employment.

51   See Commission's Report, *loc. cit.* note 9, p. 139. At first sight such approach does not seem to make a lot of sense. Nevertheless, such a broad interpretation of the Equal Treatment Directive means that, for instance, the exclusion of social security must be interpreted strictly, and that so many aspects of an employment relation as possible will then be covered by the Directive. See for a comparable approach case 152/84 *Marshall* v. *Southampton and South West Hampshire Area Health Authority* (1986) E.C.R. 723, discussed below, p. 122.

52   *Ibid.* p. 145.

53   *Ibid.* p. x.

54   Because of this 'permissive legislation', the Commission brought a case against France before the Court of Justice (case 312/86). However, the Commission's primary concern was the law amending the labour code itself and not directly the several special rights for women. See for further discussion of this case below, p. 153.

55   See Commission Report, *loc. cit.* note 9, p. 165–168 and Commission communication
      on protective legislation, *loc.cit.* note 45.
56   Commission Report, *loc.cit.* note 9, p. 161
57   *Ibid.* p. 169.
58   For instance ILO Convention nos 4 and 41 (Nightwork for Women), ILO Convention
      no. 127 (Maximum weight of loads to be shifted by one worker), ILO Convention
      no. 136 (Protection against benzene poisoning) and ILO Convention no. 149
      (Employment and labour and legal conditions of nursing staff). This conflict must
      be solved in accordance with Article 234 EEC.
59   See Report on protective measures, *loc.cit.* note 29, p. 47.
60   *Ibid.* p. 69.
61   For instance, in various sectors 'heavy work' remained barred to women in spite of
      rapid changes in the production process using new technologies which make the
      requirements of physical strength superfluous.
62   Report on protective measures, *loc.cit.* note 29, p. 81.
63   A very special working condition is included in the Rhine Navigation Regulations: it
      is prohibited for women to wear tight clothes during working hours. Protection 'for
      her own sake'?
64   *Loc. cit.* note 33. From the Commission report on the implementation of the New
      Community Action Programme, COM (85) 641 final, it appears that the changes
      in protective legislation by the Member States were more or less incidental and
      isolated.
65   *Loc.cit.* note 45. Subsequently, the Council adopted conclusions on protective
      legislation for women in the Member States, O.J. C 178/4, 7 July 1987 and
      requested, *inter alia*, the Member States and both sides of industry to review the
      protective legislation.
66   Compare Conaghan, in McLaughlin (ed.) (1987) p. 61.
67   In particular Articles 2 and 117 of the Treaty. Compare in this respect case 43/75
      Defrenne v. *Sabena* (1976) E.C.R. 455, in particular considerations 10 and 11. It may
      be asked whether the same 'social' principles inspiring Defrenne II should not be
      used when interpreting the Equal Treatment Directive. Moreover, the preamble of
      the Equal Treatment Directive sets out the aim of furthering the harmonization of
      living and working conditions 'while maintaining their improvement'. See however
      also Chapter 5, p. 168 and p. 195.
68   Report of a comparative analysis of the provisions for legal redress in Member States
      of the EEC in respect of Article 119 of the Treaty of Rome and the Equal Pay, Equal
      Treatment on Social Security Directives, V/564/84.
69   *Ibid.* p. 27.
70   *Ibid.* p. 80. Compare also the Medium-term programme, *loc.cit.* note 33. See also
      'Implementation of the quality directiveness', *loc.cit.* note 11, p. 9. On 13 May 1988
      the Commission adopted a proposal for a Council Directive on the burden of proof
      in the area of equal pay and equal treatment for women and men, COM (88) 269
      final. See for discussion Chapter 7, p. 296.
71   See New Action Programme, *loc. cit.* note 33, Action 2.
72   See Report on legal redress, *loc.cit.* note 68, p. 82 and Sousi-Roubi (1981) p.
      172.
73   Commission Report, *loc.cit.* note 9, p. 198–200, and the New Community Action
      Programme, *loc.cit.* note 33, Action 2.
74   These bodies (the equal opportunities commissions) are the 'other competent
      authorities' within the meaning of Article 6. Their functions and powers vary from
      Member State to Member State. See Commission Report, *loc.cit.* note 9, pp. 194–197.
      See also Sousi-Roubi (1981) pp. 170–171.
75   *Ibid.* p. 201. The sanctions depend heavily on the powers conferred upon a
      Court under the domestic law. While in one Member State only a relatively
      small compensation is possible, in another Member State the Court may order

reinstatement in case of a discriminatory dismissal. For an informative comparative review of several national legal provisions see also Hanau in Gamillscheg *et al.* (eds.) (1980) pp. 458–464.

76   Report on legal redress, *loc.cit.* note 68, p. 81.

77   *Ibid.* pp. 62–64.

78   1 January 1981 for Greece and 1 January 1986 for Spain and Portugal.

79   Case 19/81 *Burton* v. *Railways Board* (1982) E.C.R. 555. At present a case very similar to *Burton* is pending before the Court: Case 262/88 *Douglas Harvey Barber* v. *Guardian Royal Exchange Assurance Group*, O.J. C279/14, 29 October 1988. Also compare case 233/89 *Cray Precision Engineers* v. *David William Clarke* (not yet decided) O.J. C219/10, 25 August 1989.

80   It is however very probable that the voluntary redundancy scheme in question was not covered by the Third Directive. Advocate General VerLoren van Themaat found in his opinion to this case, *loc.cit.* note 79, pp. 587–588, that the payments were not due under a statutory scheme but under voluntary agreements between the employers and workers. Nowadays such a scheme would be probably covered by the Fourth Directive (Equal treatment in occupational social security schemes, see Chapter 7, p. 276). Since the Court found that Article 119 did not apply, at the moment Burton was pending, there was in fact no relevant Community law dealing with conditions for access to occupational schemes. Only Article 3, paragraph 3 of the Social Security Directive provided that with a view to ensuring implementation of the principle of equal treatment in occupational schemes the Council will adopt provisions defining its substance, its scope and the arrangements for its application.

81   Case 152/84 (Marshall), *loc.cit.* note 51, case 262/84 *Beets-Proper* v. *Landschot Bankiers* (1986) E.C.R. 773 and case 151/84 *Roberts* v. *Tate & Lyle Industries* (1986) E.C.R. 703.

82   Case 152/84 (Marshall), *loc.cit.* note 51, p. 746.

83   Already in 1982 the Council recommended the progressive introduction of flexible retirement. O.J. L 357/27, 18 December 1982.

84   See for a more detailed discussion Chapter 2, p. 30.

85   Case 192/85 *Newstead* v. *Department of Transport and H.M. Treasury* (1988) 1 CMLRep 219.

86   See for this part of the judgement Chapter 3, p. 64.

87   Article 3, paragraph 2 of the Social Security Directive, and Article 9 of the Occupational Schemes Directive.

88   Case 184/83, *loc.cit.* note 32.

89   *Ibid.*, p. 3075-3076.

90   Case 165/82 and, in particular, case 163/82. See below, p. 140 and p. 143 respectively.

91   Compare a survey on maternity leave legislation in the Member States, in EIRR (1985) no. 141, pp. 18–22.

92   This was the basic idea of the Commission's proposal for a directive on parental leave and leave for family reasons, O.J. C333/6, 9 December 1983, and an amended proposal in O.J. C316/7, 27 November 1984. However this draft directive appears to be blocked within the Council. See Chapter 7, p. 300.

93   Case 222/84 *Johnston* v. *Royal Ulster Constabulary* (1986) E.C.R. 1651.

94   In 1976, in Northern Ireland, the Sex Discrimination Order put into effect similar provisions as are contained in the Sex Discrimination Act.

95   *Loc.cit.* note 93, p. 1678.

96   See case 184/83 (Hofmann), *loc.cit.* note 32.

97   Compare case 248/83 *Commission* v. *FRG*, *loc. cit.* note 26.

98   See above, p. 116.

99   For the importance of a clear distinction see above, p. 118.

100   This Article runs as follows: 'Member States shall consult each other with a view to taking together the steps to prevent the functioning of the common market being affected by measures which a Member State may be called upon to take in the event

of serious internal disturbances affecting the maintenance of law and order, in the event of war, serious international tension constituting a threat of war, or in order to carry out obligations it has accepted for the purpose of maintaining peace and international security.'

101   See also Chapter 2, p. 35.
102   Case 22/86 *Heylens* v. *UNECTEF*, (1989) 1 CMLR 901.
103   See, for instance, consideration 36 in case 152/84 (Marshall), *loc.cit.* note 51, or consideration 27 in case 149/77 *Defrenne* v. *Sabena* (1978) E.C.R. 1365.
104   See case 248/83 *Commission* v. *FRG*, *loc.cit.* note 26.
105   Case 152/84, *loc.cit.* note 51.
106   Case 14/83 *Von Colson and Kamann* v. *Land Nordrhein-Westfalen* (1984) E.C.R. 1891, and case 79/83 *Harz* v. *Deutsche Tradax* (1984) E.C.R. 1921.
107   Case 14/83, *loc.cit.* note 106, p. 1908.
108   *Ibid.* p. 1909.
109   See for more details Chapter 2, p. 35.
110   See also Chapter 2, p. 41.
111   Those cases have been discussed by Zorbas, in Quintin *et al.* (1986) pp. 127–153.
112   Case 163/82 *Commission* v. *Italy* (1983) E.C.R. 3273.
113   Article 15 of law no. 300 of 1970 on working conditions as amended in 1977.
114   See above, p. 111.
115   *Loc. cit.* note 44.
116   *Ibid.* p. 3449.
117   Compare in this respect case 143/83 *Commission* v. *Denmark* (1985) E.C.R. 427, discussed in Chapter 3, p. 94.
118   Case 248/83 *Commission* v. *FRG*, *loc.cit.* note 26.
119   The problem of remuneration has been discussed in Chapter 3, p. 96. Moreover, initially the Commission lodged another complaint concerning maternity leave which was at issue in Hofmann, *loc.cit.* note 32. After the ruling in this latter case the Commission withdrew it.
120   Paragraphs 2 and 3 of Article 3 of the Basic Law provide that:

- Men and women shall have equal rights.
- No one may be prejudiced or favoured because of his sex...

Article 33, paragraph 2, provides that:

- Every German shall be equally eligible for any public office according to his aptitude, qualifications and professional achievements.

Article 1, paragraph 3, states that:

- The following basic rights shall bind the legislature, the executive and the judiciary as directly enforceable law.

121   The law of 13 August 1980 was nevertheless necessary for employment relations under private law as it was uncertain whether the constitutional provisions on equal treatment of men and women could create direct rights between private individuals (the so called 'Drittwirkung' which may be compared with the concept of horizontal direct effect).
122   Paragraph 7 of the Beamtenrechtsrahmengesetz and paragraph 8 of the Bundesbeamtengesetz.
123   *Loc.cit.* note 26, p. 1488.
124   See for more details Chapter 3, p. 96.
125   As far as 'Verfassungsbeschwerde' are concerned, Article 93, paragraph 1, sub 4a of the German Basic Law provides that the Federal Constitutional Court shall decide on

complaints of unconstitutionality, which may be entered by any person who claims that one of his basic rights (and a number of other rights) has been violated by public authority. The 'Konkretes Normenkontrollverfahren' (Article 100 of the Basic Law) can be compared, to a certain extent, with preliminary proceedings: if a court considers unconstitutional a law the validity of which is relevant to its decision, the proceedings shall be stayed and a decision shall be obtained from the Federal Constitutional Court if the basic law is held to be violated.

126   See above, p. 110.
127   See case 224/84 (Johnston), *loc.cit.* note 93 and case 165/82 (*Commission* v. *UK*), *loc. cit.* note 44.
128   See case 184/83 (Hofmann), *loc. cit.* note 32.
129   See above, p. 112.
130   Consideration 43, *loc. cit.* note 26, p. 1488.
131   Case 318/86 *Commission* v. *France,* judgement of 30 June 1988 (not yet reported).
132   Formally, Commission's action also concerned management staff and technical and vocational training staff in the external departments of the prison service. However, the French government agreed that separate recruitment for these categories of civil servants could not be justified on the basis of Article 2, paragraph 2. They told the Court the legislation was in train to remove them from the list.
133   It concerns prisons of less than 100 places.
134   Case 312/86 *Commission* v. *France,* (1989) 1 CMLR 408. However, a new case based on Article 169 EEC has been instigated recently against the UK. See case 202/89 *Commission* v. *UK* O.J. C192/13, 29 July 1989.
135   Case 184/83, *loc. cit.* note 32.
136   See above, p. 129.
137   Case 312/86, *loc. cit* note 134, pp. 414-15.
138   i.e. the period following directly on confinement. See above, p. 111.
139   See Chapter 2, p. 35.

5 The Social Security Directive

When researching the origins of the Social Security Directive in the literature repeated references are found to the Equal Treatment Directive, since this Directive provides in Article 1, paragraph 2 that to ensure the progressive implementation of the principle of equal treatment in matters of social security the Council will adopt provisions defining its substance, its scope and the arrangements for its application. Initially, social security was included in the Commission's draft for the Equal Treatment Directive and the principle of equal treatment in social security is still mentioned as one of its purposes. Only its implementation was deferred. Social security was probably omitted as it became clear that its inclusion would considerably reduce the chances of adoption of the Equal Treatment Directive by the Council. This is evidenced by the different implementation periods, 30 months for the Equal Treatment Directive and six years for the Social Security Directive, plus the fact that the Equal Treatment Directive, compared to the Social Security Directive, did not entail great expenses upon the Member States. Moreover, the Council required a further study of the discriminatory provisions in social security schemes first before they were willing to commit themselves.[1]

The origins of the Social Security Directive date back to the early 1970s. As has been already stated in Chapter 3, in the first *Defrenne* judgement the Court had excluded statutory social security schemes from the concept of 'pay' in Article 119. However, *a contrario* the Court's line of reasoning, and in the light of the clear opinion of the Advocate General in that case, the conclusion arises that occupational schemes are covered by Article 119. So, during the drafting of the Equal Pay Directive, the question arose whether occupational schemes should be included. In the end they were omitted. Since occupational schemes are as a rule complementary to, substitutive of, or cumulative to statutory schemes, it appeared difficult to ensure equality in the first without doing so in the latter.[2] Viewed in this light, implementation of the equal treatment principle in social security schemes seems to be a precondition for a meaningful implementation of this principle in occupational schemes. Certainly, the situation is highly paradoxical: Article 119, including occupational schemes, had to be implemented by 1 January 1962, at least by the original six Member States. However, real equality in occupational schemes is thought to depend on equality in statutory social security schemes. The latter had to be accomplished by 23 December 1984. The Directive on the implementation of the principle of equal treatment in occupation schemes, which is dealt with in the next chapter, has to be fully implemented by 1993.

Originally, occupational schemes were included in the Social Security Directive here under discussion. Again, at the instigation of the Member States, who considered the statutory social security operation complicated and costly enough, occupational schemes were omitted. In the final version of the Social Security Directive, Article 3, paragraph 3 provides that with a view to ensuring implementation of the principle of equal treatment in occupational schemes the Council, acting on a proposal from the Commission, will adopt provisions defining its substance, its scope and the arrangements for its application.

The Social Security Directive pursues the social policy objectives of Article 117 and 118 of the EEC Treaty. Since those articles do not confer the necessary powers, nor does Article 100,[3] the Council resorted, as in the case of the Equal Treatment Directive, to Article 235. Due to the diversity and complexity of the social security provisions already in existence in the Member States to which it is to apply and, undoubtedly due to its compromise character, the Directive seems an ambiguous instrument, full of important exceptions.

Terms of the Social Security Directive

Article 1 of the Directive elaborates its purpose, that is to say the progressive implementation, in the field of social security and other elements of social protection provided for in Article 3, of the principle of equal treatment for men and women in matters of social security. The reference to 'other elements of social protection' was included at the request of France. In French law the term 'sécurité sociale' has, compared to other Member States, a narrow meaning. For example, it does not cover unemployment benefits and social assistance. So, to ensure the scope of the Directive will be the same in all Member States the above-mentioned phrase was inserted.

Some uncertainty might be caused by the word 'progressive'. Why is the purpose the 'progressive implementation' and not just 'implementation'? The term 'progressive' certainly does not mean that the Directive is in the nature of a programme which could possibly be used as an argument against the direct effect of its provisions.[4] It should be rather understood as the announcement of a first step in the sphere of equal treatment in social security. In the Commission's initial proposal it was envisaged that the Directive would apply to both statutory and occupational schemes.

The draft envisaged a two-year period for implementation in respect of Statutory schemes, three years for increases in respect of dependants and four years for occupational schemes. Even though the final version deals only with statutory social security schemes, the Directive remains a first step. The follow-up took shape in the Occupational Schemes Directive. Moreover, a Commission proposal for a new Directive dealing with social security matters not covered by the Social Security Directive, such as retirement age, family allowances and survivors' pensions was published in November 1987.[5]

Furthermore, it must be mentioned here that during the implementation period (i.e. between December 1978 and December 1984), two Member States succeeded in a kind of 'regressive implementation'. Early in the 1980s, the Commission received two complaints, one from Belgium and one from the Netherlands. The Belgian complaint (1981) concerned a Royal Decree relative to employment and unemployment and a ministerial decree implementing it. The two decrees resulted in higher unemployment benefit rates for workers who were heads of household. The notion of head of household was defined in such terms that many women were seriously disadvantaged. The Commission took the view that this was probably a case of indirect discrimination and started an infringement procedure against Belgium, even though the implementation period of the Directive had not expired. The matter was apparently settled during the administrative stage.[6] The Dutch complaint (1983) dealt with the introduction of increases in benefit for breadwinners in a disablement scheme, whereas no reference to such a criterion had previously been made. In this case, the Commission did not start an infringement procedure. Nevertheless, the Court has dealt with this problem in the *Teuling* judgement in another context.[7]

The adoption of provisions at the national level during the implementation period which cause new discrimination or worsen existing discrimination is prohibited. In fact, during this period, the Member States have two obligations: to take the measures necessary for the implementation of the Directive and not to undertake anything that would run counter to the pursuit or achievement of the Directive's objective. This is not only logical (a kind of 'recouler pour mieux sauter' is unknown in Community law), but it is also required by Article 5 of the Treaty, according to which: 'The States shall abstain from any measure which could jeopardise the attainment of the objectives of this Treaty'. This obligation applies to secondary Community legislation as well.[8] Thus, the 'steps backwards' can give rise to an infringement procedure by the Commission, namely because of the infringement of Article 5. On the other hand, according to the well established case-law of the Court, an individual may not invoke the Directive before a national court, as long as the implementation period is not expired.[9]

It should be noted that the adoption of discriminatory provisions in national legislation during the implementation period must be distinguished from the deterioration of social security schemes in general, for everybody. Indeed, equal treatment can be achieved by abolishing certain benefits altogether instead of giving women an entitlement to allowances previously received only by men. The legislator may equally well level down the benefits, shorten the duration of the allowances, and make the conditions of access to the schemes harder for everyone. This is a possible way of creating equality, certainly, but is it a correct one? Unfortunately it is exactly what has happened in some Member States.[10] The Directive does not seem to oppose such 'equal but worse-operations', unless it can be argued that 'progressive implementation' means 'equality by improvement'. Neither do the Treaty provisions, in particular Article 2 and Article 117 proclaiming the improvement of living standards as one of the objectives of the Treaty, oblige the Member States to achieve equality by levelling up social security. Although from the second *Defrenne* judgement it appears that the principle of equal pay can be achieved only by raising the lowest salaries, in recent case-law there are indications that as far as social security is concerned the Court holds a different opinion.[11]

Article 2 defines the personal scope of the Directive which applies to the working population, whether wage-earners or self-employed persons. It includes persons whose activity is interrupted by illness, accident or involuntary unemployment, persons seeking employment, and retired or invalid workers and self-employed persons. Persons who are not employed, such as those involved in unpaid domestic tasks, persons who cannot be employed, children for example, and persons who do not want to be employed, are not covered by the Directive. Because of its broad definition, the personal scope of the Directive should not cause serious problems. Nevertheless, if difficulties should arise, the solution should be sought at Community law level, if necessary by means of a preliminary reference, rather than at national level.[12] For example, if a national unemployment scheme provides for benefits for persons seeking employment, and a person seeking employment is defined as somebody available for full-time work, women seeking – for family reasons – a part-time job will be excluded.[13] This is an example of possible indirect discrimination as concerns the conditions of access to a scheme. However, if the Directive's notion of 'persons seeking employment' were to be given a national meaning, it could be argued that since a person seeking employment is only a person seeking full-time employment, a person seeking part-time employment does not fall within the scope of the Directive. Consequently, because the Directive does not apply, any possible indirect discrimination would not be examined at all. This is obviously a highly undesirable result due to a legislative technique, depending on national definitions of notions such as worker, self-employed, persons seeking employment etc. Therefore it is imperative that the categories of persons mentioned in Article 2 should be defined in Community terms.

According to Article 3, paragraph 1, the Directive applies to statutory schemes which provide protection against sickness, invalidity, old age, accidents at work and occupational diseases, unemployment, and to social assistance, in so far as it is intended to supplement or replace the aforementioned schemes.

What is meant by statutory schemes providing protection against the listed contingencies seems to be clear. However, it is not as easy as it seems. Certainly, the Directive concerns any protection of the working population which is organized by legislation creating statutory schemes. Moreover, it concerns social aid measures, which may be accorded to *anyone*, working and not working, in so far as these measures supplement or replace the statutory schemes. Thus both statutory schemes and social assistance are included as far as they protect the working population. Nevertheless, there is a 'grey area' of schemes which may raise doubts, for example, 'special' schemes of social security or 'contracted-out schemes'.

In the first *Defrenne* judgement,[14] the Court excluded from the scope of Article 119 social security schemes directly governed by legislation without any element of agreement within the undertaking or the occupational branch concerned, which are obligatorily applicable to general categories of workers. Furthermore, the Court held that these schemes assure for the workers the benefit of a legal scheme, to the financing of which workers, employers and possibly the public authorities contribute in a measure determined less by the employment relationship between the employer and the worker than by considerations of social policy. The worker will normally receive the benefits legally prescribed not by reasons of the employer's contribution but solely because the worker fulfils the legal condition for the grant of benefits.

This judgement gives several indications for the characteristics of a statutory social security scheme:

- the scheme is directly governed by legislation;
- the scheme does not involve any element of agreement between the employer and the employee (the latter may be of course represented by, for example, a trade union);
- the scheme applies to the person concerned because of his or her status as a worker and not because he or she is employed by a particular employer;
- the scheme is financed by workers, employers and eventually by the state;
- there is no link between the contributions and the benefits (often the contributions are treated as tax or the whole scheme is brought into the budget).[15]

According to the Court, social security schemes having these characteristics do not fall within the scope of Article 119 but within the 'broader headings' in Article 118.[16] To implement those two Articles further community legislation is required. And this is exactly what the Social Security Directive is supposed to do.

To date, it seems that the case-law provides a reasonable answer to the question as to what schemes should be considered as statutory. Unfortunately, as already said, some uncertainties still remain.

In several Member States there exist so-called special schemes of social security. These schemes provide protection for certain categories of workers, such as railroad personnel, the military and civil servants. They are established by legislation and replace (partly) the general schemes. According to Advocate General Dutheillet de Lamothe[17] all these schemes have two main characteristics:

- they are closely and intimately linked with the general scheme of social security either because payment of benefits is made by the same fund as the general scheme or, when it is made by special funds, because these funds are financially and administratively linked with the institutions of the general scheme and are often even dependent on them. Their function thus comes within the general system of equalization laid down at a national level;
- they obtain certain special advantages for employed persons in certain posts and, in return, they provide for a contribution from employer and employee usually at a higher rate than that of the general scheme.

In particular, because of the 'close and intimate link' the Advocate General concluded that the 'special schemes' just like the general schemes fall outside the scope of Article 119.

However this may be, the fact is that a special scheme does not apply to general categories of workers, but to persons employed by a particular employer, the state for example. Moreover, although the scheme is directly governed by legislation, this should not imply that the scheme does not originate from an agreement. The state may often adopt legislation in respect of its 'employees' to deal with their position, but in fact such legislation only governs the employment relationship in the same way as an agreement does in the private sector.[18] Furthermore, such legislation may be the result of negotiations between the authorities and the civil service union. Moreover, to equate special schemes with general schemes may result in an inequitable difference in treatment of various categories of employees: if an employer operates a 'normal' occupational scheme Article 119 applies,[19] whilst if he or she operates a special scheme, employees could not rely on Article 119. It is unacceptable from the point of view of Community law to make the applicability of Article 119 dependent on the choice of the employer.[20] Unfortunately, in the first *Defrenne* case the Court equated special schemes with general schemes and it did so without any statement of reasons.[21]

Contracted-out schemes may also cause difficulties.[22] According to British social security legislation a contracted-out occupational security scheme replaces the earnings-related part of the state pension scheme. Although these schemes are occupational, often products of collective bargaining and of voluntary origin, the fact that they substitute for a part of the state scheme led Advocate General Warner in the *Worringham* case to conclude that the contracted-out scheme under consideration in that case fell outside the scope of Article 119. He deemed the connection between the two schemes very close. However, the Court avoided the problem of the relationship between the contracted-out scheme and the state scheme. It held that Article 119 applied, because the contributions in question affected the determination of gross salary. In *Newstead*[23] the British government invoked the reasoning of Advocate General Warner with a view to excluding the contracted-out scheme from the scope of Article 119. It is not clear whether or not the Court accepted this argument. Consideration 15 of the judgement suggests it did. The Court held:

> The disparity at issue is in fact the result of the deduction of a contribution to an occupational pension scheme. That scheme contains some provisions which are more favourable than the statutory scheme of general application and is a substitute for the latter. Such a contribution must therefore, like a contribution to a statutory social security scheme, be considered to fall within the scope of Article 118 of the Treaty, not of Article 119.

It must be borne in mind that the case concerned an obligatory *contribution* by male employees to the scheme. The judgement does not necessarily imply that all contracted-out schemes as a whole or at least the benefits paid under these schemes do not fall within the scope of Article 119. Some other considerations of the judgement indicate that the Court did not want to solve the problem yet. When it is dealing with 'survivors'' pensions, the cause of the discrimination of Mr Newstead, the Court refers in detail to the provisions in both the Social Security Directive and the Occupational Schemes Directive which exempt survivors' benefits from their substantive scope. If the Court had accepted that contracted-out schemes must be equated to statutory social security schemes, the reference to the Occupational Schemes Directive would have been superfluous (and vice versa). The last reference indicates that Article 119 may apply, since the Occupational Schemes Directive covers matters falling within the scope of Article 119.[24]

There are several reasons not to consider the contracted-out schemes as statutory. It should be noted that such schemes are obviously occupational: they are of voluntary origin; the contributions and the benefits are governed by the rules of the scheme and not by legislation; the Social Security Act 1975 when referring to contracted-out schemes uses the term 'occupational pensions schemes'; the fact that a contracted-out scheme must meet certain statutory conditions cannot lead to the conclusion that the schemes should be considered as statutory, since 'normal' occupational schemes must comply with the law as well. Moreover, the Occupational Schemes Directive clearly provides – in Article 2 – that occupational schemes intended to replace statutory social security schemes fall within its scope. This means that contracted-out schemes should not be considered statutory. And this means as well, as has been stated above, that they may fall within the scope of Article 119. Furthermore, if it is accepted that contracted-out schemes are statutory, this would mean that the great majority of pension schemes in the UK would not be covered by Article 119, which is questionable from the point of view of Community law. If individuals in other Member States may rely on Article 119 as far as occupational schemes are concerned, it would be unfair for UK citizens not to be able to do so as regards their occupational (contracted-out) schemes. The applicability of Article 119 should not depend on peculiarities of the national legislation.

It seems to be clear that, when applying the first *Defrenne* judgement criteria, contracted-out schemes are not statutory. The crucial problem seems to be that it is difficult to accept, for the Commission, for Advocates General and maybe even for the Court, that the state schemes are not subject to Article 119 and that occupational schemes substituting the state schemes should be.[25] However, this seems to be an argument of a mainly practical nature. First, Article 119 provides that 'each Member State shall...maintain the application of the principle that men and women should receive equal pay for equal work'. If 'pay' includes, among others, the employer's contribution to or the benefits of an occupational scheme, it is an obligation for the Member States to ensure – by legislation – that there is no sex-based discrimination as far as these contributions or benefits are concerned. The fact that the Member States were and still are allowed to a certain extent to discriminate in statutory schemes seems irrelevant. Second, Article 119 has horizontal direct effect. This means that an employer is under the duty to respect the equal pay principle, even if the national provisions require him or her to do something else.

If the Court really decided in *Newstead* that contracted-out schemes must be equated to statutory schemes, then it is, like the first *Defrenne* judgement, another unfortunate decision, without any explanation and any statement of reasons.

Finally, it must be stressed here how important the qualification of a scheme is: if it is statutory, it means that Article 119 does not apply and the door is open for the application of the discriminating exceptions of the Social Security Directive.

Paragraph 2 of Article 3 excludes two areas from the substantive scope of the Directive: benefits for survivors and family benefits.

It should be noted that both survivors and family benefits are listed in the ILO Convention no. 102 concerning minimum standards of social security, and that they are covered by the Community legislation on migrant workers.[26]

As regards survivors' benefits, in the majority of Member States' statutory social security schemes provide for widows' pensions, but widowers' pensions are either unknown or very limited. For example, a widower's pension is only allowed if the man is disabled and financially dependent on the deceased wife.[27] The reason behind this discrimination against men is obvious. In the traditional family model the death of the husband, the sole breadwinner, causes financial problems to the wife and children. The widow's pension is intended to alleviate such financial hardship. The origin of the widow's pension is based on an outdated idea about how a family is or should be organized. Moreover, the refusal to introduce a widower's pension ignores the fact that the financial position of widowers, particularly when they are responsible for children, may be as bad, or even worse, than that of widows. Since no plausible justification for the exclusion of survivors' benefits from the scope of the Directive seems to be available, the only reason must be that it was deemed just too expensive to grant widowers the benefit. However, even that argument, which is in fact unacceptable, is not convincing: the costs may be minimized in a variety of ways.[28]

The exclusion of family benefits, such as child allowances, single-parent benefits, is likewise dubious. The official explanation is that such benefits concern family policy rather than working conditions.[29] However, if family benefits are granted by way of increase in benefits due in respect of the risks listed in Article 3, paragraph 1a (sickness, invalidity, old age, accidents at work, occupational diseases and unemployment), the Directive does apply. These increases will be discussed below.

Finally, paragraph 3 of Article 3 explicitly postpones the implementation of the equal treatment principle in occupational schemes of social security.

Article 4, paragraph 1 defines the principle of equal treatment. The wording is the same as in Article 2 of the second directive: no discrimination whatsoever on ground of sex either directly, or indirectly by reference in particular to marital or family status. The paragraph states further that discrimination is forbidden in particular as concerns:

- the scope of the schemes and the conditions of access thereto,
- the obligation to contribute and the calculation of contributions,
- the calculation of benefits including increases due in respect of a spouse and for dependants and the conditions governing the duration and retention of entitlement to benefits.

This list is not exhaustive and consequently does not cover all eventualities.

The concept of direct discrimination does not cause serious problems.

This form of discrimination can be easily detected, since the discriminating criteria are the terms men or women (or other clear equivalents such as husband and wife). So, if all men and single women qualify for certain benefits but married women are explicitly (or even implicitly) excluded, such difference in treatment amounts to direct discrimination. It should be noted that, as the majority of the social security schemes are based on the traditional family model, the major instances of discrimination in social security, both direct and indirect, concern in particular married and cohabiting women.

Indirect discrimination, on the contrary, deserves more attention, in particular because several Member States may have replaced the directly discriminatory provisions in their social security legislation by indirect ones.[30] Moreover, the Directive seems to be ambiguous on this point.

As has been already said,[31] indirect discrimination occurs when a neutral criterion is used, but de facto its application mainly affects persons of one sex only. In other words, the difference in treatment does not appear to be directly based on gender, but the apparently neutral measure in reality predominantly affects persons of a given sex. Once it is established, by means of numerical data, that women (or men) are affected, the difference in treatment is 'suspect' and the burden of proof reverses. The author of the allegedly discriminatory measure must prove that the measure is objectively justified. This means, in the first place, that the objective pursued by the measure must be a legitimate one, and that such an objective ought to take priority over the principle of non-discrimination. Thus, a weighing of interests must be made, which may be sometimes rather difficult. For example if the purpose of a measure is the preservation of the traditional family model, it is quite obvious that such an objective should not have priority over the principle of equal treatment. On the other hand, if the purpose is to guarantee a social minimum income for a family, the weighing of interests at stake may turn out to be very delicate. But even if the objective pursued is considered to be more important than the principle of equal treatment, a second question arises: was it not possible to achieve the objective in another less discriminatory way? If it was, the objective justification test will not succeed.

In this context, it must be noted that if a measure is objectively justified at a certain moment, it does not mean it is justified for ever. What may constitute an objective justification in a particular set of circumstances and at a particular time may change. Moreover, the fact remains that the justified measures have an adverse impact on persons of a given sex. Consequently, the justifications should be considered regularly, within the context of a given situation.

As regards the Social Security Directive, the following categorizations can give rise to indirect discrimination: head of household, breadwinner, part-time workers, persons involved in domestic tasks or maybe even domestic staff. However, special attention must be paid to the definition of those concepts first. A social security statute may accord certain benefits to the head of the household or the breadwinner only. If in the same statute (or in another to which this statute refers) the head of household is defined as 'the husband', the discrimination is direct. If it is defined as 'an insured person with a dependent spouse', the discrimination is indirect, at least if it appears 'that a person with a dependent spouse' is in the majority of cases the man. The same may happen to the notion of breadwinner: if there is a presumption in the statute that the man is a breadwinner, while a woman has to prove it (for example she has to prove she earns more than 50 per cent of the family income), the discrimination is direct. The man has to do nothing to get the benefit; the woman must produce evidence first. The conditions governing the entitlement to benefits are discriminatory. On the other hand, if the notion of breadwinner is defined as 'the spouse having the highest salary', the discrimination will be indirect, if it appears that in general men earn more than women. So it is a matter of definition: if the concepts are defined in an apparently discriminatory way, the discrimination is direct. A case concerning this kind of discrimination will be relatively easy since it is clearly forbidden by the Directive (of course if it falls within the scope etc.). If the concepts are defined neutrally it certainly does *not* mean there is no discrimination.[32] The result depends on the indirect discrimination test.

An example of such a neutrally drafted reference which, however, may give rise to indirect discrimination, is included in the Directive itself. The Directive prohibits direct and indirect discrimination as concerns increases due in respect of a spouse and for dependants. Thus if a social security scheme provides for increases of the benefits for married persons or cohabiting persons (if such a situation gives rise to equivalent legal effects)[33] or for persons who financially support others (often the children), men or women must be allowed to claim them. In practice, however, the beneficiary of such increase will in most cases be a man. Although the Directive covers increases due in respect of a spouse in general, in practice this means increases for a dependent spouse. After all, it is difficult to imagine – certainly not in times of budgetary cuts – that a man or a woman may receive automatically an increase in his or her benefit only because of being married and regardless of the income of his or her spouse. On the contrary, the income of the other spouse often results in a cut-back in the benefit. So, in a situation where practically all men have an occupation, whereas many women remain at home or have a negligible income, only a few women will be able to claim that they have a dependent spouse. Consequently, this neutrally drafted criterion for the increased allowance gives rise to a presumption of indirect discrimination, perfectly in line with the Directive itself: it is indirect discrimination by reference to marital status. However, the Commission argues that under certain circumstances the differing treatment can be objectively justified, namely if the increases guarantee a social minimum for a household.

This implies the absence of any other occupational income within the household.[34]

On the other hand, increases in benefits which are proportional to remuneration are regarded as being indirectly discriminatory without any justification, since the remuneration itself is not subject to increases in respect of dependent spouses.[35]

Apart from the presupposition that increases for dependent spouses which guarantee a social minimum may be justified, it is unclear which other increases are compatible with the Directive. This may be the case with the above-mentioned – quite imaginary – increases accorded to a married man or woman regardless of the income of the spouse. Contrary to the first situation of increases for a dependent spouse, this second case will probably not give rise to indirect discrimination on grounds of sex. In the first case, the presumption of indirect discrimination was caused by the fact that only a few women have a dependent spouse. In the second case, however, the only thing to be demonstrated is that the person concerned is married. This test does not seem to affect women more than men. Indeed, such a system of increases will result in unequal treatment of married and single persons. But that is, as such, not contrary to the Directive. The only thing which is prohibited by the Directive is that a reference to marital (or family) status should give rise to discrimination on grounds of sex.[36]

Another source of indirect discrimination may be the reduction of benefits in cases where the entitlement is subject to a family-based (or even cohabiting unit based) means test. In some social security systems the entitlement to benefits of a person depends on the existence of other means, such as an income, within the unit in which the person lives. If such other means exist, the benefits of the person will be reduced, often to zero. So, if a person receiving, for example, social assistance benefits marries (or cohabits) and her or his spouse has an occupational income (or another benefit not subjected to the means test), she or he will lose the benefit. This test often results in the exclusion of previously self-supporting women from benefits since their husband or partner will have a professional income.

The final result is that women *are made* dependent on their husband or partner. The reasoning is that the benefit concerned is a guarantee of a social minimum of subsistence for the (family) unit. If there is somebody else to provide for that minimum, the benefit may be reduced or withdrawn. In practice, such a reasoning may lead to strange situations. For example, under the Dutch civil code the spouses are obliged to support each other. Theoretically the wife (or husband) may claim money from her (or his) spouse; she or he does not 'really' need the benefit. On the other hand, there is no such obligation for cohabiting partners. Thus, the non-earning partner has no right to assert *vis-à-vis* her or his partner, but she or he will get no benefit either since she or he is cohabiting.[37] It is not clear how such a system, which may affect predominantly women, may be objectively justified.

Article 4, paragraph 2, provides that the principle of equal treatment shall be without prejudice to the provisions relating to the protection of women on the grounds of maternity. Although this exemption seems clear at first sight, its scope is in fact quite uncertain.

At first sight, this provision seems to aim at benefits accorded to working women during maternity leave.[38] It must be assumed that the term 'maternity' includes pregnancy. Maternity leave starts, often obligatorily, a few weeks before confinement, during pregnancy, and continues up to several weeks after the delivery. Consequently, as these benefits are accorded with a view to protecting women during maternity leave, that is to say to guarantee them a certain income, to exclude the period before confinement would lead to unacceptable results. Nevertheless, as far as those benefits are concerned, it may be that Article 4, paragraph 2 is superfluous. After all, maternity is not listed amongst the contingencies of Article 3. Thus, the Directive does not apply either. Why then this provision? Or should maternity be regarded as a sickness or accident at work or a kind of unemployment? That seems to be a rather ridiculous assumption.[39]

Another interpretation may be, that under Article 4, paragraph 2 the Member States are allowed to consider maternity leave as a period of employment for social security purposes.[40] Such a measure seems to touch on the limits of the principle of equal treatment. However, at a certain point men and women are not and will never be equal since only women can get pregnant and give birth to children. The remedy is no longer the prohibition of discrimination, but rather a necessary differentiation, in this case in favour of women. Such a differentiation should be possible under Article 4, paragraph 2. But even then Article 4, paragraph 2 will probably have limited scope since it can be argued that when maternity leave is organized as a leave during employment, this period must count for social security purposes. An exclusion of the leave from the employment record would mean that there is discrimination under the Directive since the sex of a worker (maternity leave being a leave exclusively for women) becomes a criterion for, for instance, the calculation of benefits.[41] Thus the aforementioned interpretation has merits only in cases when taking up maternity leave means that the contract of employment ends, like in the UK.

Finally, it may be asked whether this provision should not be given a broader meaning, in the sense that it allows certain positive measures in respect of women who interrupt their employment for reasons of child care. It should be noted that, contrary to the Second Directive, the Social Security Directive does not contain a provision allowing for positive action. Moreover paragraph 2, being an exception to the principle of equal treatment, should be interpreted strictly. Nonetheless, in the preamble of the Directive there is an indication that Article 4, paragraph 2 should be interpreted in very broad terms. The third recital of the preamble runs as follows:

> Whereas the implementation of the principle of equal treatment in matters of social security does not prejudice the provisions relating to the protection of women on the ground of maternity; whereas, in this respect, Member States may adopt specific provisions for women to remove existing instances of unequal treatment.[42]

Whatever may be the background of both this recital and also of Article 4, paragraph 2, a sincere concern about the position of women or just a worry about declining birth rates, a cautious approach should be taken to positive measures within the sphere of social security. Only those measures should be allowed which are linked to maternity or maternity leave *stricto sensu*. If national legislation provides for leave for bringing up children, under the Second Directive such leave must be accorded to both men and women. If this period counts for social security purposes, the measure must apply to men and women. To exempt such periods from the scope of the Directive invoking the argument of the protection of maternity would in fact undermine its purpose and even the purpose of the Second Directive. The result will be that existing inequalities will be reinforced: mother will stay home. In fact, it follows from article 7, paragraph 1b that a measure prescribing or permitting to take into consideration, for social security purposes, periods spent at home in order to bring up children is not covered by Article 4, paragraph 2.[43]

Article 5 provides that the Member States shall take the measures necessary to ensure that any laws, regulations and administrative provisions contrary to the principle of equal treatment are abolished. Compared to the Equal Treatment Directive the obligation imposed upon the Member States seems to be easier to comply with. The Equal Treatment Directive obliges the Member States not only to guarantee the principle of equal treatment in the above-mentioned rules, but also to ensure that the principle will be observed in the private sector.[44] This apparent simplicity is deceptive, since the implementation of the Third Directive, undoubtedly because of budgetary implications, proceeded with much more difficulty and is not yet finished. On the other hand there is one bright spot: statutory social security schemes concern relations between individuals and public authorities. That is the reason why Article 5 refers to laws, regulations and administrative provisions only. This means that if an individual claims benefits under the statutory scheme the problem of horizontal direct effect will not rise: the individual may rely upon the Directive if he or she thinks the principle of equal treatment has been violated.[45]

Article 6 stipulates that there shall be judicial remedies as far as the non-application of the principle of equal treatment is concerned. The

Member States are obliged to introduce into their national legal systems such measures as are necessary to enable all persons who consider themselves wronged by failure to apply the principle of equal treatment to pursue their claims by judicial process, possibly after recourse to other competent authorities. This provision does not seem to bring drastic changes within the legal orders of the Member States. The already existing machinery for the settlement of grievances about social security matters will be used. The persons concerned may pursue their claims before the competent administrative bodies first, and subsequently before the courts. However, it should be noted that in *Johnston*[46] the Court of Justice held that it follows from Article 6 of the Second Directive (equivalent provision to the article under discussion here) that the Member States must take measures which are sufficiently effective to achieve the aim of the Directive and that they must ensure that the rights thus conferred may be effectively relied upon before the national courts. The Court added that the requirement of judicial control stipulated by the provision of the Second Directive reflects a general principle of law which underlies the constitutional traditions common to the Member States. Moreover, it referred to Article 6 of the European Convention of Human Rights. It follows both from the wording of Article 6 itself and from the importance which the Court of Justice attaches to effective judicial review, that the final national body dealing with the problem of equal treatment must be 'an independent and impartial tribunal established by law' within the meaning of Article 6 of the European Convention of Human Rights. Moreover, according to this provision the individual is entitled to a fair and public hearing. The danger that a social security procedure may be in breach of Article 6 of the Convention is not imaginery at all. In *Feldbrugge*[47] the European Court for Human Rights held that a simplified procedure established under the Dutch Appeals Act did not comply with the requirements of Article 6 of the Convention. The procedure under discussion was used in certain circumstances to decide whether or not a person is entitled to an allowance under the Health Insurance Act.

Article 7, paragraph 1 contains a whole list of permissive exclusions.[48] Under this provision the Member States have the right to exclude from the scope of the Directive several social security matters. The exceptions listed relate to specific provisions already in existence in several Member States at the time the Directive was adopted. However, they are not intended to be permanent. Under paragraph 2 of Article 7 the Member States are obliged to examine periodically those excluded matters in order to ascertain, in the light of social developments, whether there is any justification for maintaining the exclusion concerned. On this ground, and because of the Directive aims at the progressive implementation of the principle of equal treatment in matters of social security, it may be concluded that the Member States are allowed to maintain the exceptions, but *not* to introduce new ones.

The first exclusion (a) concerns the determination of pensionable age for the purposes of granting old age and retirement pensions and the possible consequences thereof for other benefits. In the majority of the Member States differences between men and women exist at this point and they have been maintained. In general, the pensionable age for men is 65 and for women 60, or the women may at least opt for an earlier retirement age. The rationale behind this difference in treatment seems to be the 'double burden' for working women: occupational activities and domestic tasks.[49] This reason may seem very praiseworthy, but it does not make a great deal of sense. If it is desired to relieve the working woman, is it not more logical to do so during the more demanding period in her life which usually will be *before* her sixtieth anniversary? Moreover, it is not clear what exactly should be understood by the phrase 'and the possible consequences thereof for other benefits' and, in particular, what those 'other benefits' should be. Does it refer to other benefits *within* the social security scheme, or to early retirement more in general, or perhaps to benefits under occupational schemes? The latter seems unrealistic: occupational schemes are not covered by the Third Directive.[50]

The second exclusion (b) deals with the advantages in respect of old age pension schemes granted to persons who have brought up children, and the acquisition of benefit entitlements following periods of interruption of employment due to the bringing up of children. Under this exclusion it is, for example, allowed to consider the periods a woman has spent at home to bring up children as a period of active employment for pension purposes. Here again women are given preferential treatment to men. It should be noted that such measures apparently do not fall within the scope of Article 4, paragraph 2. The raising of children can be done by both the man and the woman. A strict application of the principle of equal treatment would require to accord the above-mentioned advantages to both sexes. The exclusion has been apparently included to compensate women for their rearing activities, since nowadays it is primarily the mother who interrupts or reduces her professional activities to bring up children. This exclusion, deemed to have a temporary character only, indicates that the term 'maternity' in Article 4, paragraph 2 must be interpreted strictly.

The third exclusion (c) allows states to grant old age or invalidity benefit entitlements by virtue of the derived entitlements of a wife. This obscure text seems to refer to independent rights granted to women included in the insurance schemes of their husbands, such as the 'pension de réversion' in France. Generally speaking, under such a system the old age or invalidity benefits are accorded to the wife instead of the husband, that is to say if he has died. Such benefits are *not* survivors' benefits within the meaning of Article 3, paragraph 2. Otherwise this exclusion would not be necessary.

Under the fourth exclusion (d) increases in long-term invalidity, old age, accidents at work and occupational diseases benefits for a dependent wife may be granted, an obvious example of direct discrimination. Compared to Article 4, paragraph 1, which refers to *a spouse* and which will give rise to (at least presumption of) indirect discrimination as has been pointed out above, this provision refers to *a wife*.

Finally, the fifth exclusion (e) provides for the consequences of the exercise, before the adoption of the Directive, of a right of option not to acquire rights or incur obligations under a statutory scheme. This provision applies only to the UK and it concerns the consequences of the exercise of a right of option which was restricted to married women. Under certain circumstances a married woman could decide to pay only reduced contributions which resulted in limited benefits. This right of option was abolished in 1977.

At first sight all these exclusions seem to have one feature in common: they allow preferential treatment of women. However, this treatment is based on the traditional family model and division of roles between men and women. At the moment, the abolition of certain provisions allowed under this article would cause financial hardship. 'Levelling up' may be too costly and consequently the Member States would opt for abolition as they have done in other areas. For a large part the 'fairness' of those provisions depends on other developments, such as the availability of child-care facilities and an increased participation of women in the labour process. It must be noted that such 'women-friendly' provisions within social security do not really stimulate the necessary changes. On the contrary, to a certain extent, they reinforce the existing situation of inequalities. As in the present economic situation no important steps in this field may be expected, the Member States could begin with some 'small steps', for example by extending the provisions falling under paragraph 1b to young couples, thus to the man as well, which will stimulate women to participate in the labour process making them economically independent, and abolish the increases for dependent wives for younger men. After all, it is to be hoped that the younger generation of women will prefer employment above domestic tasks and that they will have better chances of entering the labour market. Moreover, a certain minimum guarantee will remain in the form of increases for dependent spouses.

Article 8, paragraph 1 provides that the implementation period will be six years after the notification of the Directive. It therefore came into force on the 23 December 1984. Under paragraph 2, the Member States are obliged to communicate to the Commission the text of laws, regulations and administrative provisions they adopt in the field covered by the Directive, including measures adopted pursuant to Article 7, paragraph 2. Moreover, they must inform the Commission of their reasons for maintaining any existing provisions on the matters referred to in Article 7, paragraph 1, and of the possibilities for reviewing them at a later stage.

On the basis of this information the Commission will try to ensure that no abuses occur. This is not an easy task if the unclear language of Article 7 and the fact that the test for maintaining the exclusions is 'social development' are taken into consideration. The latter criterion is very tricky indeed.

Finally, Article 9 provides that within seven years of notification of the Directive, Member States shall forward all information necessary to the Commission to enable it to draw up a report on the application of the Directive for submission to the Council and to propose such further measures as may be required for the implementation of the principle of equal treatment. This report was published on 16 December 1988 and covers the situation at 22 December 1985.[51] The report shows that the majority of the Member States did not implement the Directive within the implication period. Italy, Germany, Denmark and France seem to have a much better record than the other Member States. Moreover, it appears that some Member States introduced the principle of equal treatment in areas which are excluded from the scope of the Directive, such as survivors' benefits. It may be asked if this can be accomplished in one Member State, why not in another? Furthermore, the Commission observes that important progress has been made with the principle of equal treatment in matters of social security. However, the situation is still inadequate, especially in certain Member States, in the field of direct discrimination. Where indirect discrimination is concerned, the implications of the Directive are still far from being fully assessed. The Commission notes that there is even some evidence of retrograde steps.[52] Finally, the Commission points out that new initiatives have been taken to fill the remaining gaps and to complete the legislation on equal treatment in matters of social security.[53]

The case-law of the Court of Justice

The first case before the Court concerning the interpretation of the Social Security Directive was *Drake*.[54] Section 37(1) of the British Social Security Act provided for the payment of an invalid care allowance under the following conditions: the applicant was to be regularly and substantially engaged in caring for a severely disabled person; the applicant was not to be gainfully employed; the severely disabled person was to be such a relative of his or such other person as might be prescribed by the law. Section 37(2) defined 'severely disabled person' as a person entitled to an attendance allowance under Section 35 of that Act or any other benefit of the same nature. Under Section 37(3) the invalid care allowance was not paid to any person who was under the age of 16 or was engaged in full-time education; to a married woman who lived with her husband or to whose maintenance her husband contributed a weekly sum not less than the weekly rate of the allowance; to a woman where she and a man to whom she was not married were living together as husband and wife.

Ms Drake, married and living with her husband, gave up her work to look after her severely disabled mother who came to live with her. On 5 February 1985 Ms Drake applied for the invalid care allowance, but the adjudication officer refused her the award of the benefit since she was a married woman residing with her husband. The Social Security Tribunal who dealt with the claim next ruled in favour of Ms Drake: the Tribunal held that the rule of Section 37(3) excluding married women constituted discrimination on grounds of sex contrary to the Social Security Directive. The adjudication officer appealed against that decision to the Chief Social Security Commissioner. The Commissioner stayed proceedings and referred two questions of interpretation to the Court of Justice. The first question sought to establish whether the invalid care allowance constituted part of a statutory scheme providing protection against invalidity to which Article 3(1) (a) of the Social Security Directive applied. The second question sought confirmation that the rule excluding married women constituted discrimination contrary to Article 4(1) of the Directive.

Before the Court, the adjudication officer observed that the invalid care allowance cannot in itself be regarded as providing protection against the risk of invalidity within the meaning of the Directive. He pointed out that Article 3 of the Directive is directed at schemes providing persons with protection against risk to them, not, as in the case of the invalid care allowance, against risks to third parties. He argued that Article 2, which defines the personal scope of the Directive, is concerned only with persons who are directly affected by one of the risks listed in Article 3 and thus excludes from the scope of the Directive benefits made available to other persons. Moreover, he observed that the benefits to which the Directive refers are all work-related. Since the invalid care allowance was intended for persons who did not work and therefore did not belong to the working population, it could not be regarded as one of those benefits.

The Court was apparently not very impressed by those arguments. First, it stated that in order to fall within the scope of the Directive, according to Article 3(1) a benefit must constitute the whole or part of a statutory scheme providing protection against one of the specified risks or a form of social assistance having the same objective. Second, the Court referred to the broad definition of the term 'working population' in Article 2. According to the Court

> [that] provision is based on the idea that a person whose work has been interrupted by one of the risks referred to in Article 3 belongs to the working population. That is the case of Ms Drake, who has given up work solely because of the risks listed in Article 3, namely the invalidity of her mother. She must therefore be regarded as a member of the working population for the purposes of the Directive.

Third, the Court considered that it is possible for the Member States to provide protection against the consequences of the risk of invalidity in various ways. For example, like in the UK, a Member State may provide for two separate allowances, one for the disabled person and one for the carer, while another Member State may arrive at the same result by paying at a rate equivalent to the sum of those two benefits. Therefore, in order to ensure the implementation of the principle of equal treatment in a harmonious manner throughout the Community, Article 3(1) must be interpreted as including any benefit which in a broad sense forms part of one of the statutory schemes referred to or a social assistance provision intended to supplement or replace such a scheme.

Finally, the Court emphasized that a situation of invalidity is a *conditio sine qua non* for the payment of the invalid care allowance and that there is a clear economic link between the benefit and the disabled person, since the disabled person derives an advantage from the fact that an allowance is paid to the person caring for him or her. According to the Court it follows for all those reasons that the fact that a benefit which forms part of a statutory invalidity scheme is paid to a third party and not directly to the disabled person does not place it outside the scope of the Directive. Otherwise it would be possible, by making formal changes to existing benefits covered by the Directive, to remove them from its scope.[55]

The answer to the second question was much easier. Even the adjudication officer suggested in his observations that the exclusion of married women from obtaining the benefit is contrary to the Directive. The Court held that discrimination on grounds of sex contrary to Article 4(1) of the Social Security Directive arises where legislation provides that a benefit which forms part of one of the statutory schemes referred to in Article 3(1) of that Directive is not payable to a married woman who lives or is maintained by her husband, although it is paid in corresponding circumstances to a married man. The Court considered in particular that such a national provision is contrary to the aim of the Directive which under Article 189 of the Treaty is binding on the Member States as to the result to be achieved.

The *Drake* case concerned a quite peculiar UK social security provision and from this point of view it seems of limited importance only. Nevertheless the judgement is interesting since it shows the Court is willing to construe the provisions of the Social Security Directive broadly. In the first place it did not accept that the Directive only applies to persons who are themselves *directly* affected by one of the risks listed in Article 3, even if the risk in question happened to a third person.

More generally it seems that the Court will not allow the complexity, diversity and peculiarity of the national social security legislation to narrow both the personal and substantive scope of the Directive.

To a certain extent the judgement of the Court is a bit surprising. The invalid care allowance is not an employment-related benefit but rather a benefit for caring, since the Social Security Act did not provide for testing for previous employment in this respect. The Social Security Directive, on the other hand, aims merely at equal treatment of men and women in social security in so far as their employment is concerned: it applies to the 'working population' and the risks listed in the Directive are employment-related. 'Caring' is not mentioned amongst the contingencies. Consequently, if the invalid care allowance had been treated by the Court as a benefit for caring, the Directive would not apply. However, the Court ignored this possibility. It focused rather on the situation of invalidity and on the more general problems of 'harmonious' implementation of the Directive in the Member States.[56]

The next four cases to be discussed here concerned the direct effect of the Directive's provisions.

In the Dutch *FNV* case[57] the Court ruled that Article 4(1) of the Social Security Directive has direct effect since 23 December 1984. The provision at issue in the main proceedings was Article 13(1) (point 1) of the Wet Werkloosheidsvoorziening (Law on Unemployment Benefit, hereafter the WWV). This provision excluded from the right to benefit workers who, having the status of married women, may not be described as wage-earners[58] under rules adopted by the competent minister after consulting the central commission, or who do not live permanently separated from their husbands.

The Netherlands government initially intended, as a part of a wide-ranging reform of the social security system, simultaneously to transpose the Directive into national law and to merge the WWV and the Werkloosheidswet (Law on Unemployment). That reform was to include the abolition of the wage-earner requirement. However, it appeared impossible to implement the reform in the six years stipulated in the Directive. A draft of a provisional bill amending Article 13(1) (point 1) of the WWV and designed to extend the wage-earner requirement to unemployed males was submitted to the Second Chamber of the State General.[59] However, this Chamber rejected the draft on 13 December 1984. By letter of 18 December 1984 the State Secretary for Social Affairs and Employment informed the President of the Second Chamber that the government intended to draw up a new bill with retroactive effect to 23 December 1984 in order to implement the Directive. The Parliament was urged to approve the bill by 1 March 1985. Furthermore, by circular of 21 December 1984, the State Secretary notified the competent authorities, that the contested provision of the WWV had to continue to be applied pending the retroactive amending law. Several months later, by the law of 24 April 1985, which entered into force on 1 May 1985, Article 13(1) (point 1) of the WWV has been abolished with retroactive effect from 23 December 1984. That law provides that the abolition of the wage-earner requirement is not to apply to workers whose unemployment commenced before 23 December 1984. Moreover, the law reduces the duration of the benefits in the case of unemployed persons of under 35 years of age. The Court of Justice summarized the new situation as follows:

> ...since the entry into force of the law of 24 April 1985 male and female unemployed persons are subject to the same system, also as regards the period between 23 December 1984 and the date of entry into force of the new law; however, differences based on the status of wage-earner continue to affect the entitlement to benefit of unemployed persons whose unemployment commenced before 23 December 1984.[60]

This consideration from the judgement is rather important since the transitional measures it aims at gave rise to a new preliminary procedure.[61] In the meantime, the Federatie Nederlandse Vakbeweging (Netherlands Trades Union Federation) summoned the State in interlocutory proceedings before the President of the Arrondissementsrechtbank (District Court) in The Hague. The FNV sought an order requiring the State to suspend, or at least not to give effect to Article 13(1) (point 1) of the WWV until new legislation entered into force. The FNV maintained that the wage-earners' rule was contrary to the principle of equal treatment as defined in the Social Security Directive, since married women were disqualified from receiving unemployment benefit. On 17 January 1985 the President ordered the State to amend the article in question before 1 March 1985.[62] The State appealed against that decision and the FNV brought counter-proceedings.

The Gerechtshof (Regional Court of Appeal), on appeal, suspended the proceedings and referred three questions to the Court. To put it briefly, the Court wanted to know whether or not Article 4 of the Social Security Directive had direct effect. Neither in the main proceedings nor before the Court was it contested that Article 13(1) (point 1) of the WWV was contrary to the principle of equal treatment.

Before the Court the Dutch government unfolded a curious theory on direct effect. It argued that no direct effect may be attributed to Article 4 of the Directive because that provision does not lay down for the Member States the methods whereby the system of social security must be set up. That circumstance should leave the Member State a large measure of discretion when implementing the Directive. The government went on by giving some examples of solutions which might be taken into consideration when amending the WWV. As the Advocate General has rightly pointed out,[63] this argument confuses the issue of direct effect with that of the discretion available to Member States under Article 189 of the Treaty in transposing the Directive into national law.

The Court of Justice reiterated its established case law according to which

> wherever the provisions of a Directive appear, as far as their subject-matter is concerned, to be unconditional and sufficiently precise, individuals may rely on those provisions in the absence of implementing measures adopted

within the prescribed period as against any national provision which is incompatible with the Directive or in so far as the provisions define rights which individuals are able to assert against the State.[64]

The Court considered that standing by itself, and in the light of the objective and contents of the Social Security Directive, Article 4(1) precludes, generally and unequivocally, all discrimination on grounds of sex. Therefore, it concluded that the provision is sufficiently precise to be relied on in legal proceedings by an individual and applied by the courts. The Court went on to examine whether the prohibition of discrimination may be regarded as unconditional as well. In this respect the Court held that Article 7 of the Directive is not relevant. It lays down no condition with regard to the application of the principle of equal treatment as regards Article 4 of the Directive. As to Article 5, the Court considered that this provision leaves the Member States only a discretion with regard to methods. The *result* which those methods must achieve is prescribed in unequivocal terms: the abolition of any provisions contrary to the principle of equal treatment. Furthermore, the Court gave some guidance on the criteria to be used for determining which rules should apply to women.It held:

...that until such time as the national government adopts the necessary implementing measures women are entitled to be treated in the same manner, and to have the same rules applied to them, as men who are in the same situation, since, where the Directive has not been implemented, those rules remain the only valid point of reference.[65]

As to the argument of the Dutch government that Article 4 has no direct effect since the Member States have several possibilities to bring their legislation in line with the Directive, the Court replied briefly:

...that the fact that a Directive leaves choice of the form and methods for achieving the desired result to the Member States may not be relied upon in order to deny all effect to those provisions of the directive which may be invoked in legal proceedings even though the said Directive has not been implemented in its entirety.[66]

In *McDermott and Cotter*[67] the following facts gave rise to the preliminary ruling of the Court: under the Irish Social Welfare (Consolidation) Act 1981 the unemployment benefit received by married women was less than that paid to married men and single persons and it was paid for a shorter period. It was explained in the order of reference that the law on social security in Ireland is based on the principle that a married woman is deemed to be the dependant of her husband if she is living with him or is wholly or mainly maintained by him. The husband, on the other hand, is only a dependant of his wife if he is incapable of self-support by means of some physical or mental infirmity and is being wholly or mainly maintained by her. In order to implement the Social Security Directive, the Social Welfare Act 1985 was passed by the Oireachtas (Irish Parliament) on 16 July 1985. However, the relevant sections of the 1985 Act did not come into force until 15 May 1986.

The provision of the 1981 Act concerning the duration of benefits was repealed by Section 6 of the new Act which provided that married women are entitled to unemployment benefits[68] for the same period as other claimants. Moreover, this section gave limited retroactive effect to the repeal inasmuch as only married women who had received unemployment benefits within the period of 78 days ending on the date on which the section came into force were entitled to take advantage of it. Furthermore, Section 2 of the 1985 Act provided that the rate of unemployment benefits was to be the same for men and women.

Ms McDermott and Ms Cotter ceased to receive unemployment benefits in January 1985. They brought two actions against the Minister for Social Welfare and the Attorney General. They asked to quash decisions made by or on behalf of the Minister of Social Welfare terminating the payment of unemployment benefits to the claimants after a period of 312 days and, in the case of Ms Cotter, to restore the pay-related benefits automatically withdrawn. In the main proceedings they argued that if they had been men or single women they would have been entitled to unemployment benefits for a further period of 78 days, that, as married women, they received lower unemployment benefits than men and that the decisions infringed their rights under Article 4(1) of the Social Security Directive.

The High Court in Dublin entertained doubts as to the effect of the Directive. Consequently it stayed the proceedings and submitted two questions to the Court of Justice for a preliminary ruling. In essence, it wanted to know whether Article 4(1) of the Social Security Directive had direct effect from 23 December 1984.

The Irish government and the Netherlands government, who both submitted observations to the Court, invoked more or less the same arguments as in the FNV case: the Directive accords a wide degree of discretion to Member States and does not give rise to sufficiently clear obligations to confer rights which could be invoked before national courts.

However, after the FNV judgement it was clear what the answer of the Court would be. Indeed, the Court referred to the FNV case and it held that:

...Article 4(1) is sufficiently precise and unconditional to allow individuals, in absence of implementing measures, to rely upon it before the national courts as from 23 December 1984, in order to preclude the application of any national provision inconsistent with that Article [and that] until such time as the national government adopts the necessary implementing measures women are entitled to have the same rules applied to them as are applied to men who are in the same situation, since in such circumstances those rules remain the only valid point of reference.[69]

A highly complex and obscure transitional provision came up in *Borrie Clarke*.[70] The legislation concerned can be summarized as follows: from 29 November 1984 the UK non-contributory invalidity pension was abolished. It was replaced by a new benefit, the severe disablement allowance, which is available to claimants of either sex on the same conditions. In particular they have to comply with the 80 per cent severe disablement test. However, to ensure that those previously entitled to the non-contributory invalidity pension would not lose the benefit, the transitional provision allowed persons who were entitled to the non-contributory invalidity pension formerly available to qualify automatically for the new severe disablement allowance without having to show that they satisfied all the new conditions. Thus, the automatic entitlement to the payment of the new allowance was subject to the same criteria as those which determined entitlement to the old non-contributory invalidity pensions. Under those latter criteria a married woman, residing with her husband, was not entitled to the pension, except where she was incapable of performing normal household duties. A comparable condition was not imposed on men. For a man it was enough that he was incapable of work. Due to the transitional provision, the old discriminatory condition was transported on to the new benefit.

In April 1983 Ms Clarke was refused a non-contributory invalidity pension because she could perform normal household duties. During the subsequent proceedings brought by Ms Clarke the new law on severe disablement allowance came into force. Before the Social Security Commissioner it was then contended on her behalf, that after 23 December 1984 she could claim severe disablement allowance by relying on Article 4 of the Social Security Directive without proof of the additional conditions (for the non-contributory invalidity pension) applicable only to married women. In particular, she reasoned that if she were a man she would have been entitled to the non-contributory invalidity pension since she met the conditions applicable to men, and consequently she would automatically qualify for the severe disablement allowance.

In the main proceedings (and subsequently before the Court) it was not really disputed that the provisions at issue, including the transitional provision, were contrary to the principle of equal treatment laid down in Article 4 of the Directive. However, the Social Security Commissioner took the view that the *effect* of Article 4 was not clear. He stayed the proceedings and referred to the Court the following question:

Does Article 4 (1) of Council Directive 79/7/EEC have a direct effect such that a woman can from 22 December 1984 qualify for an invalidity benefit by reason of her having before that date satisfied conditions sufficient to enable a man to qualify for that benefit notwithstanding that she did not also before that date satisfy a further condition applicable under domestic law only to a class of women of whom she was one?

The Court considered that the question seeks essentially to ascertain whether Article 4 of the Directive may be relied upon by individuals in a Member State to prevent the extension beyond 22 December 1984 of the effects of an earlier national provision inconsistent with Article 4 and, if so, whether the women concerned acquired entitlement to benefits as from that date on the same conditions as men.

The Court answered those questions in the affirmative. After having recalled that, according to FNV and McDermott and Cotter, Article 4 has direct effect, the Court considered that the Directive does not provide for any derogation from the principle of equal treatment in order to authorize the extension of the discriminatory effects of earlier provisions of national law. Thus, beyond 22 December 1984, a Member State may not maintain any inequalities of treatment which have their origin in the fact that the conditions for entitlement to benefit are those which applied before that date. The fact that those inequalities are the result of transitional provisions adopted at the time of the introduction of a new benefit does not influence this conclusion. This implies that individuals may rely Article 4 as from 23 December 1984 in order to prevent the extension beyond that date of the old discriminatory provisions. Furthermore, the Court recalled that, from 23 December 1984, women are entitled to be treated in the same manner, and to have the same rules applied to them, as men who are in the same situation since, where the Directive has not been implemented correctly, those rules remain the only valid point of reference. The Court considered that in the particular case of Ms Clarke it meant that if, as from 23 December 1984, a man in the same position as a woman was automatically entitled to the new severe disablement allowance under the transitional provision without having to re-establish his rights, a woman was also entitled to that allowance without having to satisfy an additional condition applicable before that date exclusively to married women.

The last case concerning direct effect of Article 4 of the Directive decided by the Court until now is Dik.[71] The provision at issue was Article II of the Dutch law of 24 April 1985, which had been at issue in FNV: the discriminatory wage-earner provision (Article 13, paragraph 1, point1) of the Wet Werkloosheidsvoorziening (Law on Unemployment Benefit; hereafter WWV) was repealed with retroactive effect from 23 December 1984, but the abolition of the wage-earner requirement was not to apply to workers whose unemployment commenced before 23 December 1984. Consequently, married women who lost their employment before that date had to comply with the wage-earner requirement to obtain the WWV benefit even after 23 December 1984.

The plaintiffs in the main proceedings, Ms Dik, Ms Menkutos-Demirici and Ms Laar-Vreeman, all married women, became unemployed before 23 December 1984. Their respective applications for benefit under the WWV were rejected on, respectively, 5 February 1985, 30 May 1985 and 17 June 1986, since they were not wage-earners. Thereupon the plaintiffs brought actions against the decisions before the Raad van Beroep in Arnhem (Social Security Court), which referred the following questions to the Court of Justice:

1. Does Directive 79/7/EEC confer on the Member States a discretionary power to include in the law implementing the Directive a transitional provision on the basis of which a 'wage-earner' requirement applies even after 23 December 1984 to a married woman who became unemployed before 23 December 1984?

2. Is it compatible with the Directive for a transitional provision such as that referred to in question 1 to be given retroactive effect from the date at which the period prescribed in Article 8 (1) of the directive expired?

Before the Court the plaintiffs maintained that the application of the Dutch transitional provision had the effect that men who lost their employment before 24 December 1984 were entitled to the benefit under the WWV before, on and after 23 December 1984 whereas married women who were in the same situation did not receive the benefit in respect of 23 December 1984 and subsequent periods, unless they met the wage-earner criterion, a condition which does not apply to men. They claimed that according to the judgement of the Court in *FNV*, since 23 December 1984 women are entitled to be treated in the same manner and to have the same rules applied to them as men who are in the same situation.

The Dutch government considered that there was no obligation in the Directive for the Member States to adopt legislative provisions to terminate inequalities of treatment resulting from the legislation in force before 23 December 1984. Furthermore, it observed that the interpretation proposed by the plaintiffs would cause considerable problems of interpretation and implementation. It explained that application for benefits under the WWV might be made in respect of unemployment beginning in the distant past and that claims made under the WWV have to be considered in the light of the legal provisions as were applicable at the date on which unemployment began. Thus the question would arise as to the date to which the effect of the Directive should go back.

The Court ignored the arguments of the Dutch government and answered the first question with a clear 'no' perfectly in line with its – recent – case-law on the direct effect of Article 4 of the Directive. The Court recalled that Article 4 is sufficiently precise and unconditional to be relied upon in legal proceedings and applied by a court; the Directive does not provide for any derogation from the principle of equal treatment in order to authorize the extension of national law; Member States may not maintain any inequalities of treatment which have their origin in the fact that the conditions for entitlement to benefit are those which applied before that date, the fact that the inequalities are the result of a transitional provision is irrelevant; and, finally, that where the Directive has not been implemented correctly, women are entitled to be treated in the same way as men and to have the same rules applied to them, since those rules remain the only valid point of reference. The Court explained that in the case of Ms Dik, Ms Menkutos-Demirici and Ms Laar-Vreeman it means that if a man who has lost his employment before 23 December 1984 was entitled after that date to the benefit under the WWV, a woman who is in the same position is also entitled to that benefit without having to satisfy an additional condition applicable before that date exclusively to married women.

As far as the second question is concerned, the Court considered that if the national implementation measures are adopted belatedly, the simultaneous entry into force of the Directive in all Member States is ensured by giving the measures retroactive effect to 23 December 1984. However, the Court stressed that when adopting such measures, the Member States must observe the rights which individuals had acquired under Article 4 of the Directive after the expiry of the period provided for implementation.

It follows from these four cases that the Court's clear approach as to the direct effect of Article 4 of the Directive made this Article a relatively easily applicable instrument to tackle discriminatory provisions in social security legislation. The direct effect of Article 4 implies that if the Directive has not been implemented correctly or not in time, from 23 December 1984 women are entitled to have applied to them the same rules as men who are in the same situation. Moreover, the clear obligation of Article 4 (together with Article 8) means that discriminatory treatment resulting from legislation in force before 23 December 1984 must be terminated. If a Member State fails in this respect, e.g. by introducing none or incorrect transitional measures, an individual may rely on Article 4 to prevent such effects.

On 4 February 1985 the Raad van Beroep in Amsterdam, referred to the Court a case of alleged indirect discrimination under the Social Security Directive. The facts of this *Teuling* case[72] are, to put it simply, the following: in 1967, in the Netherlands the Wet op de Arbeidsongeschiktheid (Law on Insurance against Incapacity for Work, hereafter: WAO) came into force. This law governs the compulsory insurance of workers against loss of salary arising from incapacity to work for periods of more than one year. The benefits are earnings-related and payable to both men and women with no account being taken of personal circumstances. Furthermore, the law provided for a minimum level of benefit which was equal to the statutory minimum wage. On 1 October 1976 another law providing for insurance against the same risk came into force, the Algemene Arbeidsongeschiktheidwet (General Law on Incapacity for Work, hereafter: AAW). Contrary to the WAO, the AAW applies in principle to all Dutch residents. The benefit is calculated by reference to a minimum subsistence level and takes account of the personal and family circumstances of the person entitled. Moreover, until 1979 married women were not eligible for the AAW benefit. The relationship between the two laws is rather complicated, but in very general and simple terms it may be said that the main benefit is awarded under the AAW and an additional benefit, if certain conditions are met, is payable under the WAO. In 1979, the AAW was amended. On the one hand, the amendments abolished the exclusion of married women from the scheme. On the other hand they laid down stricter requirements governing eligibility for the benefit and reduced the amount of the benefit to 70 per cent of the statutory minimum wage. However, Article 10, paragraph 4 of the AAW was amended in such a way that persons having dependent spouses or children received a supplement to the benefit. In such circumstances the benefit amounted to 100 per cent of the minimum wage.

In 1982, in order to reduce social security expenditure and as a part of a general reform of the social security system, the link between the minimum benefit under the WAO and the minimum wage was repealed by the Dutch legislature. A new formula for calculating the benefit was introduced which in general produced an amount lower than the minimum wage. The benefit could drop to 70 per cent of the minimum wage, the 'standard' level of an AAW allowance. Only persons who satisfied the conditions laid down in Article 10, paragraph 4 of the AAW, had their benefit supplemented up to 100 per cent of the minimum wage. The whole reform was accompanied by several transitional measures. Those measures made, among others, the repeal of the (100 per cent) minimum wage guarantee effective only from 1 January 1984.

Ms Teuling had worked for various undertakings till 1971 when she became unable to work. From September 1972 she obtained an allowance under the WAO which was initially calculated on the basis of her last wage. From 1975 the benefit equalled the statutory minimum wage. This benefit was not influenced by the fact that she was married and by the income earned by her husband. However, from 1 January 1984, her benefit was reduced to 70 per cent of the minimum wage, in accordance with the reform of 1982. Since her spouse had an income, she did not meet the conditions of Article 10, paragraph 4 of the AAW and consequently she did not qualify for any increases. Before the national court she submitted that a social security system which is essentially based on the existence of a dependent family constitutes indirect discrimination against women and is therefore incompatible with the Community rules and in particular with the principle of equal treatment laid down in Article 4, paragraph 1 of the Social Security Directive.

The Raad van Beroep stayed the proceedings and referred five questions to the Court of Justice.

With the first question the Raad van Beroep sought to establish whether a system of benefits in respect of incapacity for work under which the amount of the benefit is calculated taking into account either the civil status and any remuneration or other income of the spouse of the person entitled, or the existence of dependent children, constitutes indirect discrimination contrary to the principle of equal treatment laid down in Article 4, paragraph 1 of the Directive.

The Court established first that according to Article 4, paragraph 1 of the Directive increases are prohibited if they are directly or indirectly based on the sex of the beneficiary. A system of benefits operates in which supplements are provided for on the basis of the marital status or family situation of the beneficiary and when it emerges that a considerably smaller proportion of women than of men are entitled to such supplements, such a system is contrary to Article 4, paragraph 1 of the Directive, unless it can be justified by reasons which exclude discrimination on grounds of sex. Because it appeared from the documents before the Court that in the Netherlands many more married men have a dependent spouse than married women, and consequently many more married men qualify for the supplements, the Court continued with considering the possible justifications. The Dutch government explained before the Court that the AAW seeks to provide a minimum subsistence income to persons with no income from work. The Court considered in this respect that such a guarantee by Member States to persons who would otherwise be destitute is an integral part of the social policy of the Member States. Thus, if supplements to a minimum social security benefit are intended to prevent the benefit from falling below the minimum subsistence level for persons who bear heavier burdens than single persons because they have a dependent spouse or children, the supplements may be justified under the Directive. However, this was not the end of the story, because

> if a national court, which has sole jurisdiction to assess the facts and interpret the national legislation, finds that supplements such as those in this case correspond to the greater burdens which beneficiaries having a dependent spouse or children must bear in comparison with persons living alone, serve to ensure an adequate minimum subsistence income for those beneficiaries and are necessary for that purpose, the fact that the supplements are paid to a significantly higher number of married men than married women is not sufficient to support the conclusion that the grant of such supplement is contrary to the Directive.[73]

The next question to be answered was whether a law is compatible with Article 4, paragraph 1 of the Directive when it guaranteed first to all workers suffering from an incapacity for work that their (net) benefits would be at least equal to the (net) statutory minimum wage and which was later amended to the effect that the guarantee applied only to persons with a dependent spouse or child, or whose spouse has a very small income. The Court recognized that this amendment disadvantaged mainly women, since a much greater number of women than men could not claim having a dependent spouse and their benefits were consequently reduced to 70 per cent of the statutory minimum wage. However, the Court held that it must be recognized that Community law does not prevent a Member State, in controlling its social expenditure, from taking into account the fact that the needs of beneficiaries who have a dependent child or spouse or whose spouse has a very small income are greater than those of single persons.

In the first place it appears from this judgement, especially from the answer to the second question, that the Court is willing to accept level-down operations, even when this means that in particular the position of women deteriorates, as long as the new system is not discriminatory.

In the second place, the Court's approach to the concept of indirect discrimination in social security seems to have considerable merit. The Court applied the same test as already developed under Article 119, in particular in *Bilka*, which is a clear and practicable method of dealing with indirect discrimination: the apparently neutral conditions of Article 10, paragraph 4 of the AAW affect in reality predominantly women. Such a rule gives rise to discrimination unless it can be objectively justified. In this case the Court accepted that the guarantee of a minimum level of subsistence for persons with family charges may be such a ground for justification.[74] However, the national court must assess whether the increases at issue correspond with the expenditure incurred by a dependent family and whether these increases are appropriate and necessary to achieve the objective, i.e. the minimum level of subsistence. This latter is obviously the minimum level of subsistence recognized as such in the Member States concerned (at least as long as there is no official EEC minimum subsistence level).

On the other hand, the Court's judgement raises several questions. The judgement seems to aim at a situation where the beneficiary has no other occupational income. Although the Court did not consider it explicitly, it follows from the context of the case that it is not only the absence of any occupational income of the person concerned that matters, but the absence of income within the family as a whole. Further, the Court mentions an *occupational* income only. Does it mean that any other income, for example an occupational pension, another social security allowance, a benefit paid under a private insurance, interest or dividend, may not be taken into consideration? The Court's judgement obviously focused on the specific facts of the *Teuling-Worms* case and consequently it gives hardly any indication what the answer should be. It may be argued that the objective justification test, being a sort of derogation from the principle of equal treatment, must be interpreted as strictly as possible and that increases are only permitted in order to guarantee a social minimum for a person with a dependent spouse or child. If the person entitled has another non-occupational income, he or she does not need an increase of his or her benefit to guarantee the social minimum. Nor does this person need any increases if the spouse or child has a non-occupational income of his or her own, since then they should not be considered as dependent. In both situations the increases do not seem necessary.[75]

However, in several cases such a rigorous interpretation of the Court's criteria may cause considerable hardship. It would mean that as soon as there is any income, occupational or not, within the family, increases for a dependent spouse or child are no longer justified, since they are then indirectly discriminatory and consequently not allowed under the Directive. In all probability the result will be a levelling-down solution, the increase will be withdrawn and the family will have to get by on a minimum standard of subsistence. Moreover, it must be borne in mind that if such a levelling-down solution may still be acceptable in the Netherlands, when the Dutch social security system is known as a relatively generous one, a very strict interpretation of the justification test may lead to unacceptable results in some other Member States where the general level of social security is considerably lower. In other words, a high price – in social terms – will be paid for equality and it may be asked whether the Court will accept such a solution under any circumstances.

Another but closely related problem occurs under social security systems which provide exemptions of the occupational income of a spouse (up to a certain level) from the family-based means test.[76] Under such provisions the calculation of a social security benefit, which depends on the family-based means test in general, will not be influenced by an occupational income of the spouse. These exemptions may result in increases of benefits due in respect of a dependent spouse, even when the spouse has his or her own (low) income, since the income is not taken into consideration. The reasons behind such exemptions is usually to allow the spouse to pursue some (minimal) occupational activities.[77] However, if the 'standard benefit' (i.e. without increases) plus the exempted income of the spouse produce a sum higher than the minimum level of subsistence, it may be argued that in such a case increases of the benefit are no longer necessary and consequently not allowed. This position seems to fit within the line of reasoning of the Court when dealing with the first question in the *Teuling* case. However, when answering the second question, the Court held that a Member State may take into consideration the fact that the need of a person who has a dependent child or spouse or whose spouse has a very small income is greater than that of a single person. Should this imply that the 'social minimum justification' may apply not only in cases where there is no income in the family at all, but in cases where a very low income of the spouse exists as well?

From the point of view of equal treatment in social security the exemptions of a spouse's income seem undesirable, since they undermine the strict social minimum test. On the other hand it has been submitted that the Equal Treatment Directive, or at least its purposes, militate in favour of these exemptions. One of the purposes is equal opportunities as regards access to employment.[78] This should mean, among other things, that women should not be discouraged from entering employment. However, if their income results in a reduction of their husband's benefit, since he loses the increases he was entitled to previously, the absence of exemptions may have such a discouraging effect.[79]

For all those reasons it seems that, although in *Teuling* the Court gives some indications how to deal with indirect discrimination under the Social Security Directive, the judgement does not permit more general conclusions to be drawn yet.

Conclusions

Notwithstanding all its shortcomings, it is clear that the Social Security Directive is an important instrument for women to exercise their rights, in particular when one considers the Court's case-law on direct effects of Article 4. The Directive certainly lacks clarity on several points and the list of matters excluded from its scope allows existing inequalities to continue in many areas without challenge. However, it may be asked what would be the situation if this Directive did not exist. Considering the sad record of implementation in the UK, Ireland and the Netherlands (the three Member States which insisted on the long implementation period of 6 years!),[80] it is not difficult to guess the answer.

Furthermore, it has been submitted that the majority of the exclusions in the Directive are or may be interpreted as 'women-friendly' but since they are based on the traditional family model, in the long term they may operate to women's disadvantage. However, as long as large numbers of men and women live according to this traditional model and the Member States are not willing or cannot be obliged to accept 'levelling-up' solutions to these factually discriminatory situations, to abolish these exclusions will probably do more harm than good. Consequently, a phased 'step-by-step' reform seems to be preferable.

For the time being, the practical significance of the Directive in the short term seems to depend on the further interpretation of the indirect discrimination concept. In several social security schemes the family is used as a benefit assessment unit. The family for these purposes was presumed, until recently (and to a certain extent still is), to include an economically active male 'breadwinner' and a dependent female, who was at home, caring for the family and having no paid employment. From this point of view it was not necessary to provide social security for women. However, even when women started to enter employment, the breadwinner/dependent model continued to be the basis of social security: wives were still presumed to be dependent; even if they received – often limited – benefits, it was the men who automatically or even exclusively qualified for certain higher and longer benefits or for dependents' allowances. No doubt it is under the influence of the Directive that these kinds of provisions, which are directly discriminatory, are disappearing from the social security legislation of the Member States. However, although they are replaced by sex-neutral ones, the breadwinner/dependent model continues to structure the social security systems. Dependency is maybe no longer regarded as gender-specific. However in practice even women who have had an income, worked for years and paid contributions, are still not treated in the same way as men. Moreover, those neutrally drafted provisions continue to reinforce the gender division of roles and discourage women to take up employment.

The concept of indirect discrimination can be used to a certain extent to help to dismantle this breadwinner/dependent model: if it appears that the concrete application of this model affects persons of one sex mainly, for example in the form of supplements to or reductions of a (means-tested) benefits, only an objective justification may warrant its existence. It appears from the Court's case-law that sex-neutral social security provisions operating to the detriment of women may be permitted if their purpose is to guarantee a minimum level of subsistence. However, it is not clear under what circumstances this social minimum justification applies. The second test of correspondence and proportionality seems even more intangible. At this very moment, the concept of indirect discrimination has an uncertain and probably quite limited value as an instrument to challenge the dependency principle in social security. If a provision does not affect especially women (or men) or if it is justified, the fact remains that individuals who are in most respects independent members of society are not treated as such in social security. To dismantle totally the breadwinner/dependent model would mean that each individual is treated alike for the purposes of social security, regardless of gender, marital status and the unit in which he or she lives.[81] However, this is clearly a more far-reaching concept than the plain prohibition of (indirect) discrimination.

Finally, it cannot be denied that, although the situation may vary from one Member State to another, considerable numbers of both men and women still live according to the breadwinner/dependent model. For those categories it seems justified and equitable to take their factual situation into account when assessing the benefit. As long as the above-mentioned individualization of social security rights stays a remote goal (and it will, since an individualization implies considerable public expenditure), the adverse effects of the breadwinner/dependent model should be limited in other ways. The indirect discrimination concept may help in such situations but it should be combined with appropriate transitional measures to prevent serious financial trouble of the persons entitled. A differentiation could be made for example between older and younger persons, or between women with and without an employment record to prevent an indiscriminate application of the dependency principle. Last but not least, measures facilitating employment for women, such as more and better child-care facilities and more flexible working hours, may help considerably as well. It must be borne in mind that the so-called indirectly discriminatory measures in social security affect predominantly women simply because many more women than men *are* dependent. A remedy may be to diminish this dependency, rather than abolish for example increases for dependent spouses.[82]

Notes

1   Leenen, in Fase (ed.) (1986) p. 38.
2   Laurent, in Verwilghen (ed.) (1986) pp. 149–150.
3   Social security provisions of the Member States do not 'directly affect the establishment or functioning of the common market'. See further Chapter 2, p. 43.
4   A good example of programme – or policy – provisions are Articles 117 and 118 of the Treaty. Those provisions are not sufficiently precise and unconditional to be relied upon by individuals in national courts.
5   O.J. C309/10, 19 November 1987. See Chapter 7, p. 293.
6   See Zorbas (1986) pp. 142–148. However, as appears from the Report on the application of Directive 79/7/ECC of 19 December 1978 on the progressive implementation of the principle of equal treatment for men and women in matters of social security, COM (88) 769 final, the settlement was not definite. See pp. 16–18 and p. 119. More recently the Commission has brought an action before the Court against Belgium concerning this problem. See case 229/89 *Commission* v. *Belgium* O.J. C217/5, 23 August 1989.
7   See Leenen, *loc. cit.* note 1, p. 41, and case 30/85 *Teuling* v. *Bedrijfsvereniging voor de Chemische Industrie,* (1988) 3 CMLR 789, discussed below, p. 192.
8   Compare case 77/82 *Peskeloglou* v. *Bundesanstalt für Arbeit* (1983) E.C.R. 1094. This case concerned the Act of Accession of Greece. However, there are no reasons why the principle should not apply to Directives. See as well the opinion of Advocate General Mancini in case 30/85 (Teuling) *loc. cit.* note 7, and the case-law he refers to. The Advocate General mentions two (very closely related) arguments in this respect: Article 5 of the Treaty and the so-called 'blocking effect' of Directives. This latter means that once notified to the Member States, the Directive prohibits the adoption of measures contrary to its provisions during the implementation period. See on the effect of Directives e.g. Timmermans, 1980, p. 411 *et seq.*
9   e.g. case 148/78 *Publico ministero* v. *Ratti* (1979) E.C.R. 1629.
10   See for example the reduction of the duration of certain benefits in the case of unemployed persons under 35 years mentioned in case 71/85 *State of the Netherlands* v. *Federatie Nederlandse Vakbeweging,* (1986) E.C.R. 3855, discussed below, p. 185. Another example is the abolition in the UK of Non-Contributory Invalidity Pension by the Health and Social Security Act 1984, which was replaced by Severe Disablement Allowance: the gender-based discrimination disappeared, but the test to qualify for the allowance was made harder for both men and women. It has

even been argued that a directly discriminatory social security scheme has been replaced by an indirectly discriminatory one. See Luckhaus (1986) p. 153. See also Commission document 'Implementation of the equality directives', Luxembourg 1987, p. 53.

11 See case 126/86 *Zaera* v. *Instituto National de la Seguridad Social*, judgement of 29 September 1987, not yet reported. The Court considered that neither Article 2 nor Article 117 impose an obligation upon Member States. Consequently, they have no direct effect. Nevertheless, the Court added that Article 117 is important for the interpretation of other Articles of the Treaty and of secondary legislation.

12 Compare the case-law of the Court of Justice concerning the social security for migrant workers (e.g. case 75/63 *Unger* v. *Bestuur van de Bedrijfsvereniging voor detailhandel en ambachten* (1964) E.C.R. 177). In this case-law the term 'worker' has a community meaning. In case 48/88 *Achterberg* v. *Sociale Verzekeringsbank* O.J. C 72/7, 18 March 1988, the Dutch Social Security Court wondered whether the term 'worker' in the Social Security Directive should be interpreted as the term 'worker' in Article 1(a) and Article 2, paragraph 1 of the regulation no. 1408/71. Two other cases, also concerning the personal scope of the Directive are case 106/88 *Bersen* v. *Sociale Verzekeringsbank* and 107/88 *Egbers* v. *Sociale Verzekeringsbank*, O.J. C 132/6, 21 May 1988. The Court joined the cases of Achterberg, Bersen and Egbers; the cases were decided on 27 June 1989, too late to be discussed in the text.

13 Compare Bates, in McLean and Burrows (eds.) p. 126. The problem of exclusion of part-time workers from social security benefits is factually at issue in case 102/88 *Ruzius* v. *Bestuur van de Bedrijfsvereniging voor Overheidsdiensten* (pending); the Dutch social security court asked the following question in this respect: Is a system of allowances for (not unemployed) workers in the event of incapacity for work which provides for allowances at the level of the minimum subsistence income except in cases where the wage previously earned by the person entitled to the allowance was, in part because he or she was working part-time, below that level in accordance with Article 4(1) of Directive no. 79/7? See O.J. C 124/8, 11 May 1988.

14 Case 80/70 *Defrenne* v. *Belgium* (1971) E.C.R. 445. See for a more detailed description Chapter 3, p. 55.

15 The Court did not mention this last point explicitly. However, it was discussed by Advocate General Dutheillet de Lamothe in his opinion in this case. It may be assumed the Court accepted implicitly this argument.

16 Advocate General Warner in his opinion in case 69/80 *Worringham and Humphreys* v. *Lloyds Bank* (1981) E.C.R. 806.

17 Opinion in case 80/70 (Defrenne II), *loc. cit.* note 14, pp. 459–460.

18 Compare the opinion of Advocate General Slynn in case 23/83 *Liefting* v. *Academisch Ziekenhuis bij de Universiteit van Amsterdam* (1984) E.C.R. 3244.

19 See Chapter 3 and Chapter 7, p. 57 and p. 285 respectively.

20 Compare consideration 23 in case 150/85 *Drake* v. *Chief Adjudication Officer* (1986) E.C.R. 1995. See for a detailed discussion of this case below p. 182.

21 Although there are apparently several reasons why not to equate those two systems, it seems that the Commission considers the special schemes as falling within the material scope of the Directive. See Frenkel and Betten in Fase (ed.) (1986) p. 126.

22 See for a more detailed description of the contracted-out system Chapter 3, p. 58.

23 Case 192/85 *Newstead* v. *Department of Transport* (1988) 1 CMLRep 219. See for discussion of this case partly Chapter 3 and partly Chapter 4, p. 64 and p. 126 respectively.

24 See also Chapter 7, p. 285. As far as benefits under a contracted-out scheme are concerned, a recent case has been referred to the Court from the UK. See case 233/89 *Cray Precision Engineers* v. *David William Clarke* (not yet decided) O.J. C219/10, 25 August 1989.

25 Note that the same dilemma was at the origin of the Occupational Schemes Directive. See above, p. 165.

26   Convention of 28 June 1952, UNTS vol. 210, p. 131 and EEC regulation no. 1408/71, Article 4, O.J. Special Edition 1971 (II), p. 416 *et seq.*

27   See Report on the equal treatment of widows and widowers as regards social security, EP document 1-1506/83.

28   For example, by relating 'survivors'' benefits to income levels.

29   Leenen, *loc. cit.* note 1, p. 40.

30   e.g. under the 'old' Dutch AAW (General Law on Incapacity to Work) married women were excluded. In 1979 this directly discriminating provision was abolished. Both men as well as women are since then entitled to a benefit of 70 per cent of the social minimum. This minimum may be supplied up to 100 per cent if the person entitled is a 'breadwinner'. As the majority of breadwinners are men, such systems may be indirect discriminatory. See case 30/85 (Teuling) *loc. cit.* note 8. See also Luckhaus (1986) p. 153.

31   Chapters 3 and 4.

32   This peculiar idea, that as long as the concepts are neutrally defined there will be neither direct nor indirect discrimination, was defended by the Dutch government. See Sjerps (1984) pp. 87–88.

33   Compare for example the invalid care allowance at stake in case 150/85 (Drake) *loc. cit.* note 20.

34   Interim report on the application of Directive 79/7/EEC of 19 December 1978 on the progressive implementation of the principle of equal treatment for men and women in matters of social security, COM(83)793 final, p. 9. See also the final report on the application of the Directive, *loc. cit.* note 6, pp. 117–119.

35   *Ibid.* However, if those benefits fall under the social minimum, an increase in those cases will be justified again.

36   Compare Chapter 4, p. 109.

37   See for example the judgement of the Hoge Raad (Dutch Supreme Court) of 9 January 1987, NJ 1987, no. 927.

38   The so-called 'birth premiums' existing in different forms in several Member States must probably be regarded as family benefits excluded from the scope of the Directive by Article 3, paragraph 2.

39   It must be noted that for example in the Netherlands, the benefits received during pregnancy and maternity leave are governed by Article 29 of the Health Insurance Law. However, this does not imply that pregnancy and maternity should be regarded as sickness in the terms of the Directive. In other Member States special legislation has been enacted to deal with those matters, such as the 'Mutterschutzgesetz' in West Germany.

40   It should be noted that Article 6 of the Social Security Draft Directive provided that the Member States may exclude from its field of application the determination of periods of employment for pension purposes, in particular as regards the reckoning for pensions purposes or time spent out of employment for reasons of pregnancy or childbirth. O.J. C 34/3, 11 February 1977.

41   The argument that women and men cannot be compared in this respect because there is no equivalent leave for men should be ignored. See Chapter 4, p. 108.

42   This recital was inserted at the demand of France. Why it appears in the preamble and not in the Directive itself, is not clear. It must be mentioned here, that the French legislation contains several special rights for women in the field of social security. See Report on the application of Directive 79/7, *loc. cit.* note 6, pp. 54–63. It may be asked whether all those provisions are compatible with the Directive.

43   See below p. 180. Moreover, if national social security legislation provides for certain benefits during such a leave, the Directive does not apply, since the leave is not listed amongst the contingencies of Article 3. Those benefits should be considered as falling within the scope of the Equal Treatment Directive.

44   Compare as well the Occupational Schemes Directive, Article 7.

45   However, problems may arise if the statutory scheme is not administered or operated

directly by the state, but by a semi-public or even private body. Such a body administering or operating the scheme must be considered as an extension of the state and consequently as a public authority. Another difficulty is the contributions. For example, if a woman wants her employer to pay (higher) contribution to a state scheme, though he is not obliged to do so, an action against the employer seems to be the proper way to follow. Unless there is a possibility to start proceedings directly against the State, claiming that the State did not ensure equality in a certain scheme.

46   Case 222/84, *Johnston* v. *Royal Ulster Constabulary* (1986) E.C.R. 1651, discussed in Chapter 4, p. 130.
47   Judgement of 29 May 1986, Series A, no. 99.
48   Compared to the draft directive (O.J. C 34/3, 11 February 1977) the list of exceptions has been considerably extended.
49   See the opinion of the Economic and Social Committee on the draft directive, O.J. C 180/36, 2 August 1977, under point 2.6.
50   However, one never knows. In *Burton* voluntary redundancy has been qualified as dismissal to which the Second Directive applies and nevertheless an exclusion of the *Third* Directive was declared 'relevant' to the case. See Chapter 4, p. 121.
51   Report on the application of Directive 79/7, *loc. cit.* note 6.
52   See, in particular, pp. 114–123 of the above-mentioned report.
53   See the proposal for a Council Directive completing the implementation of the principle of equal treatment for men and women in statutory and occupational social security schemes, O.J. C 309/10, 19 November 1987, discussed below in Chapter 7, p. 293.
54   Case 150/85, *loc. cit.* note 20.
55   The Commission put it maybe even more clearly by arguing 'that the effectiveness of the Directive might be seriously compromised if it were to be held that the way in which the benefit is paid could determine whether or not the benefit was covered by the Directive'.
56   See on this case, more generally Luckhaus, in McLaughlin (1987) p. 39 *et seq.*
57   Case 71/85, *loc. cit.* note 10.
58   The Dutch term is 'kostwinner' which may be better translated by 'breadwinner'. The Advocate General used the term 'head of household' which is not a proper translation either.
59   One of the two chambers of the Dutch Parliament.
60   Case 71/85 (FNV), *loc. cit.* note 10, p. 3874.
61   Case 80/87 *Dik et al.* v. *College van Burgemeester en Wethouders te Arnhem et al.*, judgement of 8 March 1988 (not yet reported), discussed below, p. 120.
62   The President did not found his order on Community law provisions but rather on the general principle of non-discrimination.
63   Opinion of Advocate General Mancini in case 71/85 (FNV), *loc. cit.* note 10.
64   Case 71/85 (FNV), *loc. cit.* note 10, p. 3874.
65   *Ibid.* p. 3877.
66   *Ibid.*
67   Case 286/85 *McDermott and Cotter* v. *The Minister for Social Welfare and the Attorney General*, (1987) ECR 1453.
68   In fact, the national law concerned two kinds of benefits: unemployment benefits and pay-related benefits. The entitlement to pay-related benefits ceased automatically at the date of the cessation of the payment of unemployment benefits.
69   Case 286/85 (McDermott), *loc. cit.* note 67, pp. 1467 and 1468.
70   Case 384/85 *Borrie Clarke* v. *The Chief Adjudication Officer*, (1987) E.C.R 2865.
71   Case 80/87 *loc. cit.* note 61. A question on the Directive's scope *ratione temporis* has been submitted again to the Court in joint cases 48, 106 and 107/88, *loc. cit.* note 12. The Court, however, did not need to address the problem.
72   Case 30/85, *loc. cit.* note 7.

73   *Ibid.* p. 806.
74   This justification has been already put forward by the Commission. See above, p.
      175.
75   For example under the Dutch AAW for the calculation of the benefit allowances
      paid under private health and accident insurances and certain allowances under the
      Health Insurance Act are not taken into account at all. Unfortunately, no attention
      was paid to this problem in *Teuling*.
76   Cornelissen, in Franssen *et al.* (eds) (1987), pp. 59–61.
77   The exemptions will generally apply with respect to the income of the person entitled
      as well, in order not to 'punish' him or her for some – often marginal – activities.
78   Compare case 14/83 *Von Colson and Kamann* v. *Land Nordrhein-Westfalen* (1984) E.C.R.
      1891, at p. 1908 (real equality of opportunity).
79   Cornelissen, *loc. cit.* note 76, p. 61.
80   Laurent (1982) p. 379.
81   This applies as far as adults are concerned. Another problem seems to be the
      children. However, their existence within the 'unit' should not affect the principle
      of individual rights. They may be treated as joint dependants of their parents.
82   Another possible solution that has been put forward is to accord economic value
      to domestic work and provide wages for housework which may consequently
      make women (more) independent. Strictly economically speaking this may be a
      good solution for *financial* dependency. However, it does in no way mean that
      women's subordinate position in general will change. On the contrary, such pay will
      encourage them to stay home and will perpetuate their inequality in other spheres.

6 European Law before the National Courts

At this point the reader will have realized that the role of the Court of Justice in the area of sex discrimination is important in two respects. First, the Court is asked to give authoritative interpretations of Community legislation in order to assist a domestic court or tribunal to apply either the provisions of Community law or the provisions of domestic law in so far as their scope may have been affected by Community provisions. Where this happens, the domestic court will have stayed proceedings in order to await the decision of the European Court and, after this decision is given, proceedings are resumed. At this stage it is the job of the domestic court or tribunal to apply the law in the light of the interpretation given by the Court of Justice. It is important, therefore, to see how the domestic courts have dealt with the interpretations given by the Court to see whether European law has had a real impact on municipal law. Second, the Court is asked to rule on the alleged failure of Member States to fulfil an obligation arising out of their membership of the European Community. Following a finding of non-compliance, the Member State concerned is obliged to put its house in order or, more precisely:

> If the Court of Justice finds that a Member State has failed to fulfil an obligation under this Treaty, the State shall be required to take the necessary measures to comply with the judgement of the Court of Justice.[1]

In order to assess whether the judgements of the Court have had any effect it is, therefore, important to examine subsequent state practice to see whether or not the offending state has complied with the judgement of the Court.

The aim of this chapter is to follow up the decisions of the Court of Justice which have been discussed in the previous chapters. As will be evident, a substantial number of the preliminary references have come from UK courts or tribunals and the UK has been a party to two enforcement actions. For this reason it is proposed to examine the British situation first.

UK

On the issue of equal pay there have been, to date, six preliminary references from British courts or tribunals. These will be discussed in the chronological order of the judgements delivered by the Court of Justice.

The case of *Macarthys* v. *Smith* was a preliminary reference from the Court of Appeal and concerned the issue of 'contemporaneity'.[2] Ms Smith was unable, under the terms of the relevant UK statute, to compare her pay with that of a man who had previously been engaged in 'like work'. In its interpretation of Article 119, the Court of Justice stated that:

> the principle that men and women should receive equal pay for equal work, enshrined in Article 119 of the EEC Treaty, is not confined to situations in which men and women are contemporaneously doing equal work for the same employer.[3]

Accordingly, when proceedings were resumed in the Court of Appeal, the employer's appeal was dismissed and 'the employers conceded that they had no alternative but to submit to judgement in the appeal'. On the issue of the costs of the litigation the Court of Appeal held that:

> Since the 1972 Act has made EEC law part of United Kingdom law, and since EEC law takes priority over inconsistent United Kingdom law, a litigant is obliged to look at both EEC law and United Kingdom law, and if he loses his case he should pay the costs of the litigation in the normal way.[4]

In this case, therefore, Ms Smith was spared the heavy costs of litigation but it does raise the question of the expense which is necessarily incurred when individuals resort to the courts to resolve their difficulties. From the point of view of *Macarthys*, their decision to appeal made the whole process extremely costly and they were not, in fact, represented before the Court of Justice. It may be that the imposition of costs in this way will provide a healthy incentive to employers to comply with the legal requirements of sex discrimination legislation. Ms Smith was supported by the Equal Opportunities Commission, a factor which explains why so many cases have gone on to be argued before the Court of Justice from the UK.

The next judgement to be delivered by the Court of Justice was in the case of *Worringham and Humphreys* v. *Lloyds Bank*.[5] Like *Macarthys* this case came to the Court of Justice from the Appeal Court and it concerned the question of whether certain contributions to a retirement benefits scheme were pay within the meaning of Article 119. The European Court had decided that such contributions did fall within the scope of Article 119 and on receipt of this interpretation the parties had agreed to a settlement.

This settlement took the form of a declaration issued by the Court in the following terms:

> A declaration that, pursuant to the equality clause included in the applicants' contracts of employment by reason of s.1 (1) of the Equal Pay Act 1970, as amended, and pursuant to art. 119 of the EEC Treaty, on terminating their employment with the respondents, the applicants were entitled to be paid a sum of money equal in amount to the refund of pension contributions in respect of the period referred to in s.2(5) of the 1970 Act which they would have received if they had been male employees employed on like work in whose name contributions had been paid to a retirement benefits scheme by the respondents (subject in each case to statutory and other lawful deductions).[6]

In this case, therefore, the complainants received monetary compensation to the extent to which they had suffered such loss. More importantly, perhaps, was the issue of the system itself. The Advocate General pointed out that negotiations had been carried out between the bank, the staff association and the relevant union with a view to improving the pension scheme. These negotiations were suspended during the litigation itself and thereafter were resumed. The men's and women's pension schemes were amalgamated and all employees now receive the same gross pay.[7] The case of *Worringham and Humphreys* could, therefore, be seen as a very successful test case strategy with far-reaching implications for all employees of Lloyds Bank.

The case of *Jenkins* concerned the issue of differential rates of pay for men and women workers, and came to the Court of Justice from the Employment Appeal Tribunal. The Court of Justice ruled that:

> A difference in pay between full-time workers and part-time workers does not amount to discrimination prohibited by Article 119 of the Treaty unless it is in reality merely an indirect way of reducing the pay of part-time workers on the ground that the group of workers is composed exclusively or predominantly of women.[8]

Thereafter the case was returned to the Employment Appeal Tribunal for consideration.[9]

Given the complexity of this case, and of the issues raised by it, and in particular the relationship between Article 119 and the relevant UK legislation, it is worth going back over the history of the case in the context of British law. Ms Jenkins had originally brought a claim against her employer in an industrial tribunal. She claimed that the fact that she was paid at a lower hourly rate than a man doing the same work was a breach of the 1970 Equal Pay Act. The employers argued that she was paid at a lower rate, not on the ground of her sex, but because she was a part-time worker and they wished to encourage full-time employment so as to maximize the utilization of plant. They pointed out that the rates of pay had been negotiated between themselves and the relevant trade union. Following an earlier decision of the Employment Appeal Tribunal,[10] the Industrial Tribunal held that the fact that Ms Jenkins worked only 75 per cent of a 40-hour week was a substantial difference justifying a lower rate of pay.

Ms Jenkins appealed to the Employment Appeal Tribunal arguing that the difference in the number of hours worked was not a 'material difference' in terms of the 1970 Act.[11] In the course of argument before the Employment Appeal Tribunal, she argued that the case raised issues of European Community law and, in order to clarify the issues, the Employment Appeal Tribunal referred certain questions to the Court of Justice.[12]

When the case was referred back to the Employment Appeal Tribunal, Justice Browne-Wilkinson identified four questions which fell to be decided in the light of the judgement of the European Court:

(1) Is the fact that the woman is a part-time worker and the comparable man a full-time worker by itself, and without more, 'a material difference' within section 1(3) of the Act of 1970 such as to prevent the equality clause from operating? (2) Is the fact that the woman is a part-time worker and the comparable man a full-time worker an irrelevant factor in considering whether there is a material difference for the purposes of section 1(3)? (3) is the fact (if it be a fact) that the differential in pay between part-time workers and full-time workers encourages greater utilisation of the employers' plant and discourages absenteeism a relevant or sufficient material difference for the purposes of section 1(3)? (4) Is it sufficient for the purposes of section 1(3) of the Act of 1970 and article 119 for the employers to show only that they had no intention of discriminating or must they also show that the differential in pay is objectively justified for some other reason?[13]

Before answering these questions, Justice Browne-Wilkinson examined the relationship between Community and domestic law. He accepted that Article 119 now applies internally within the UK and that although difficulties might arise for the domestic judge where there was a contradiction between a clear construction of a UK statute and Article 119, where there was ambiguity in the UK provision then such a provision ought to be construed so as to accord with Article 119. In the present case there was ambiguity in the wording of section 1(3) of the 1970 Act 'genuinely due to a material difference (other than the difference of sex) between her case and his'. Therefore section 1(3) should be construed in the light of the judgement of the European Court. However, he went on to explain, although Article 119 does confer rights on individuals, this does not mean that they might not have more extensive rights under British law. In the light of the above considerations the judge proceeded to answer the four questions.

On the first question, it was clear that under previous UK law the difference between part-time and full-time work by itself was a material difference under section 1(3). However, the ruling of the Court of Justice showed that 'a differential in pay cannot be justified simply by showing that the women are part-time workers'.[14] Previous UK decisions on this point, and in particular *Kearns*,[15] could no longer be regarded as good law.

On the second question, Justice Browne-Wilkinson pointed out that in certain circumstances the difference between part-time and full-time work may be a relevant consideration which can in some circumstances justify a differential in pay.

The third question was rather more difficult. The judge pointed out that this question would only arise if the employer could prove that the differential in pay produces the results claimed for it, that is, if it achieves a greater utilization of plant or reduces absenteeism. If the employer could prove this to be the case, and not merely that these were the intentions behind the differentials, then that would constitute a material difference. Counsel for Ms Jenkins had quoted the *Clay Cross* case in support of their argument that such economic factors were extrinsic to the question of equal pay.[16] Quoting the Court of Appeal, Counsel argued that:

> to constitute a material difference one had to look at the personal equations of the woman and the man (i.e. matters personal to them and to their work) and that reasons 'personal to the employer' or 'economic factors' were irrelevant. By analogy, Mr. Lester argued that considerations such as increasing the utilisation of plant were economic factors personal to the employers which could not constitute a 'material difference'.[17]

On this point Ms Jenkins had to accept defeat. Her counsel conceded that the judgement of the European Court had concluded the point against him since the Court had given an example of where pay differentials might be justified where 'an employer is endeavouring on economic grounds which may be objectively justified, to encourage full-time work irrespective of the sex of the worker'.[18] Therefore, differentials are justifiable if they can be proved to achieve economic advantages for the employer.

On this particular point must be noted the detrimental effect which the ruling from the European Court had on UK law. The Clay Cross case had been an important development in British sex discrimination law and now the British courts were allowed to bypass that judgement and to reintroduce the concept of economic advantage to the employer. Following Justice Browne-Wilkinson's judgement, an employer could claim economic advantages for paying lower wages to part-time employees and get away with it.[19]

The fourth question raised by the British court related to the intentions of the alleged discriminator and asked whether, to satisfy section 1(3) of the Equal Pay Act employers only had to show that they had no intention to discriminate to justify a differential in pay. It should first be pointed out that under existing British sex discrimination law the intention of the alleged discriminator is irrelevant. The Sex Discrimination Act 1975 defines both direct and indirect discrimination without reference to the question of intention.[20] Section 1 provides that:

> A person discriminates against a woman in any circumstances relevant for the purposes of any provision of this Act, if:
> (a)   on the ground of her sex he treats her less favourably than he treats or would treat a man, or
> (b)   he applies to her a requirement or condition which he applies or would apply equally to a man, but –
> (i)   which is such that the proportion of women who can comply with it is considerably smaller than the proportion of men who can comply with it, and
> (ii)   which he cannot show to be justifiable irrespective of the sex of the person to whom it is applied, and
> (iii)   which is to her detriment because she cannot comply with it.

The definition of direct discrimination therefore rests on the conditions of less favourable treatment meted out to a person because of their sex. Justice Browne-Wilkinson used a slightly different definition of direct discrimination:

> We use the phrase 'direct discrimination' to mean cases where a distinction is drawn between the rights of men and the rights of women *overtly* on the ground of their sex.[21] (Emphasis added.)

It is likely that Justice Browne-Wilkinson introduced this idea of 'overt' discrimination from his knowledge of the judgements of the European Court of Justice. As was pointed out in Chapter 1, the European Court had caused a great deal of confusion with its muddled presentation of the differences between direct and indirect discrimination. It appears that this confusion had now been transferred to the British courts. *Macarthys* had certainly been cited before the Employment Appeal Tribunal and in that judgement the European Court stated that Article 119 applied to 'all forms of direct and overt discrimination', apparently equating one form of discrimination with another. Overt discrimination is not defined in British law. It would seem that it would consist of open and obvious discriminatory behaviour which is not the typical form of behaviour. Overt discrimination may be direct discrimination but by no means is all direct discrimination overt. If it were, then more women would be successful in their claims under the anti-discrimination laws.

This confusion on the part of the judge was perhaps not too problematic. What did cause difficulties was his confusion in relation to indirect discrimination. Here the judge stated:

'Indirect discrimination' covers cases where, because a class of persons consists wholly or mainly of women, a difference drawn between that class and other persons operates in fact in a manner which is discriminatory against women, e.g. the present case. Indirect discrimination may itself be either intentional or unintentional. It is intentional if the employer (although not overtly discriminating) treats the class differently because he intends to differentiate on grounds of sex, i.e. he is dissimulating his real intentions. Indirect discrimination is unintentional where the employer has no intention of discriminating against women on the ground of sex but intends to achieve some different purpose, such as the greater utilisation of his machinery.[22]

In fact, in British law, indirect discrimination is something else. The Equal Opportunities Commission has explained it thus:

The concept of indirect discrimination is less obvious and concerns the application of a practice that is fair in form but is unfair in its impact. There are four elements of indirect discrimination. The first is that the defendant applies a requirement or condition to men and women equally. Secondly, the complainant, if a woman, has to show that the proportion of women who can comply with it is considerably smaller than the proportion of men who can do so. Thirdly, the requirement or condition must not be justifiable irrespective of the sex of the person to whom it is applied, though the burden of proof in this instance is on the respondent. The fourth and final element is that the complainant must show that the requirement or condition leads to a detriment to her because she cannot comply with it.[23]

There is no mention of intention here and it would seem that the issue of intention was introduced solely because of the judgement of the European Court which Justice Browne-Wilkinson had to apply in the case before him. In its decision, the European Court had stated that:

Where the hourly rate of pay differs according to whether the work is part-time or full-time it is for the national courts to decide in each case whether, regard being had to the facts of the case, its history and *the employer's intention*, a pay policy such as that which is at issue in the main proceedings although represented as a difference based on weekly working hours is or is not in reality discrimination based on the sex of the worker.[24] (Emphasis added.)

This passage led the judge to introduce a discussion of whether a defence could be argued on the part of the employer that he or she did not intend to discriminate in the operation of company policy. In British law, the question of intention might be discussed as evidence as to the existence of discrimination, but it is not a defence to show lack of intention. As Justice Browne-Wilkinson explained:

Were it not for the judgement of the European Court of Justice, we would have held that section 1(3) requires an employer to do more than disprove an intention to discriminate. In our view, for the variation in pay to be 'due to' a material difference it would have to be shown that there was some other matter which in fact justified the variation.[25]

In the context of discrimination in working conditions, the Employment Appeal Tribunal had in 1978 shown how to apply the justifiability test. In *Steel* the Employment Appeal Tribunal stated that:

> It may be helpful if we add a word of detail about what we consider to be the right approach to this question. First, the onus of proof was upon the party asserting this proposition, in this case the [respondent] Post Office. Secondly, it is a heavy onus in the sense that at the end of the day the Industrial Tribunal must be satisfied that the case is a genuine one where it can be said that the requirement or condition is necessary. Thirdly, in deciding whether the employer has discharged the onus, the Industrial Tribunal should take into account all the circumstances including the discriminatory effect of the requirement or condition if it is permitted to continue. Fourthly, it is necessary to weigh the need for the requirement or condition against that effect. Fifthly, it is right to distinguish between a requirement or condition which is necessary and one which is merely convenient and for this purpose it is relevant to consider whether the employer can find some other and non-discriminatory method of achieving his object.[26]

Justice Browne-Wilkinson did not refer to this decision and adopted a less stringent test, but before developing his own test he assumed that Article 119 'does not apply to cases of unintentional indirect discrimination'. This is not an accurate summary of European law. The question of intention had been discussed by the Court in only two of its discrimination cases, *Jenkins* and *Prais*.[27] There is nothing in the wording of Article 119 which suggests that it does not apply to unintentional indirect discrimination[28] and only *Jenkins* itself seems to suggest that intention was a component part of the definition of discrimination. However, the judgement in *Jenkins* is so muddled that it is understandable that Justice Browne-Wilkinson came to this conclusion. He was then in the difficult situation of trying to reconcile British law, which is silent on the question of intention as relating to indirect discrimination, with perceived (albeit falsely) European principles. In effect what the British judge did, therefore, was to ignore the decision of the European Court.

In order to do this Justice Browne-Wilkinson argued that there was nothing in European law or in UK law to prevent domestic legislation conferring greater rights than those conferred by Community law. Therefore, even if Article 119 did not prohibit what he termed 'unintentional indirect discrimination', British legislation did. He therefore held:

> that in order to show a 'material difference' within section 1(3) of the Act of

1970 an employer must show that the lower pay for part-time workers is in fact reasonably necessary in order to achieve some objective other than an objective related to the sex of the part-time worker.[29]

The Employment Appeal Tribunal therefore remitted the case to the Industrial Tribunal to determine whether the policy of paying lower wages to part-time workers was reasonably necessary to achieve the stated objectives of the employer – a reduction in absenteeism and a maximum utilization of plant. In fact this case did not reappear before the Industrial Tribunal. The firm in question went into receivership and, in these circumstances, Ms Jenkins decided to withdraw her case.[30]

A great deal of confusion was created by the decision of the European Court in *Jenkins* and, in particular, for the Employment Appeal Tribunal. To some extent the confusion created by the European Court was clarified in its later decision in *Bilka*.[31] In *Bilka* the Court made no reference to intention in its judgement, despite the fact that the respondents in that case had based their defence to a charge of discrimination on the fact that they did not intend to discriminate against women in the operation of their pension scheme. In *Bilka* the Court decided that an indirectly discriminatory provision, that is one which has detrimental effects on a much greater number of women than men, is contrary to Article 119 unless it is based on 'objectively justified factors which are unrelated to any discrimination based on sex.'[32] The Court went on to offer guidelines for the national courts to decide whether a provision is objectively justified. The employer must prove that the policy in question was chosen to meet a genuine need of the enterprise, was suitable for attaining the objective set and was necessary for the purpose. Thus the European Court adopted the proportionality test (like *Steel*) and it required a more stringent test than the 'reasonably necessary' test advocated by Justice Browne-Wilkinson in *Jenkins*.

The case of *Garland* was a reference to the European Court from the House of Lords[33] and concerned special travel facilities provided for former male employees by British Rail which were not provided for females. The European Court held that such travel facilities constituted pay within the meaning of Article 119. Accordingly, when the case returned to the House of Lords, it held that the provisions of the 1975 Sex Discrimination Act were to be construed, if they were reasonably capable of bearing such a meaning, as being intended to carry out the obligations contained in Article 119 and not be inconsistent with it. In this case section 6(4) of the Act was to be given a narrow interpretation. This section excluded provisions in relation to retirement for the ambit of the Act. It did not exclude all provisions *about* retirement from the ambit of the Equal Pay Act and particularly those which arose from a privilege granted during employment and continued thereafter. British Rail, therefore, were forced to concede Ms Garland's claim.[34]

The case of *Burton* was as easily disposed of when it was returned to the Employment Appeal Tribunal.[35] The European Court had in that case delivered a judgement in favour of British Railways. Following this decision, Mr Burton withdrew his action for unfair dismissal and accepted the ruling of the European Court. Mr Newstead too lost his argument before the European Court and was obliged to accept defeat.

How far the British Courts have learned the lesson of marrying European and British standards relating to discrimination in the field of equal pay was seen in the case of *Rainey* v. *Greater Glasgow Health Board*.[36] Unfortunately, what happened here was that the House of Lords relied on the judgements of the European Court so as to justify its own conservative approach to the equal pay legislation.

The issue in *Rainey* concerned prosthetists (fitters of artificial limbs) working for the National Health Service in Scotland. In 1979, the government wished to establish a public prosthetics service as part of the National Health Service. Previously all prosthetic work was contracted out to prosthetists working in the private sector. In order to recruit qualified personnel into the National Health Service, higher rates of pay were offered than were normally available for comparably qualified employees, and the National Health Service was successful in recruiting 20 male prosthetists. It was decided, however, following this exceptional *en bloc* recruitment that, in future, prosthetists employed by the National Health Service would be paid at the same rates as medical physics technicians whose pay was considerably less than that of the 20 original recruits. Ms Rainey was subsequently engaged as a prosthetist and paid as a medical physics technician. She subsequently brought an action in an industrial tribunal comparing her wages to those of one of the original recruits (Mr Crumlin). The Health Board did not dispute the fact that Ms Rainey was employed on like work with Mr Crumlin, nor that she received less remuneration than him. They relied for their defence on the material difference clause (section 1(3) of the Equal Pay Act). The Tribunal dismissed the appeal stating that it was satisfied that the reason for the difference was the different method of entry and had nothing to do with sex. This view was upheld by the Employment Appeal Tribunal and the Court of Session.

The crucial question in this case was whether there was a material difference between the case of Ms Rainey and that of Mr Crumlin. The Court of Session was divided two to one on the central definition in British law of section 1(3) of the Equal Pay Act.[37] At this stage there was no mention of Community law. All three judges quoted, and approved, the English Court of Appeal judgement in *Fletcher*[38] but it was apparent that they each took a different view as to the meaning of the Court of Appeal in that case. In the context of this book it is unnecessary to go into the details of *Fletcher* except to state that the Court of Appeal had found it extremely difficult to give precise meaning to the broad words of section 1 (3) as to what exactly is 'a material difference between her case and his'. In *Fletcher*, Lord Denning Master of the Rolls had talked of the personal equation of the man and the woman and directed the tribunal to ignore extrinsic forces which led to a man being paid more. In that case, Lord Justice Lawton had been even more forceful in directing the tribunal to ignore extrinsic forces. He said:

> The variation must have been genuinely due to (that is, caused by) a material difference (that is, one which was relevant and real) between – and now come the important words – her case and his. What is her case? And what is his? In my judgement, her case embraces what appertains to her *in* her job, such as the qualifications she brought to it, the length of time she has been in it, the skill she has acquired, the responsibilities she has undertaken and where and under what conditions she has to do it. It is on this kind of basis that her case is to be compared with that of the man's. What does not appertain to her job or to his are the circumstances in which they came to be employed.[39]

However, what was to defeat Ms Rainey in the Court of Session was the so-called 'red-circling' exception which Lord Denning had suggested might be the kind of material difference foreseen by section 1(3). Lord Emslie explained that exception thus:

> Where it may reasonably be said in any case that the more favourable salary position of a man or a woman has been attained to protect his or her pay level, then whether or not market forces have played their part in the matter it may well be open to a tribunal to hold, if the circumstances in which that protection has been accorded are sufficiently curious and exceptional, and permit the inference that the higher rate of wages are attained on personal basis because of the special position of the person who enjoys that higher rate, that the necessary 'material difference' for the purposes of s.1(3) has been demonstrated.[40]

Both Lord Emslie and Lord Cameron agreed that the special circumstances surrounding the recruitment of prosthetists fell under this type of exception.[41]

The issue was finally decided by the House of Lords who dismissed Ms Rainey's appeal.[42] In doing so the House of Lords placed a much more illiberal definition of section 1(3) than that given by the Court of Appeal in *Fletcher*. Lord Keith expressed the view that the statements of Lord Denning and Lord Justice Lawton, cited in *Rainey*, 'are unduly restrictive of the proper interpretation of section 1(3)'. He continued:

> The difference must be 'material' which I would construe as meaning 'significant and relevant,' and it must be between 'her case and his'. Consideration of a person's case must necessarily involve consideration of all the circumstances of that case. These may well go beyond what is not very happily described as the 'personal equation', i.e. the personal qualities

by way of skill, experience or training which the individual brings to the job. Some circumstances may on examination prove to be not significant or not relevant, but others may do so, though not relating to the personal qualities of the employee. *In particular, where there is no question of intentional sex discrimination whether direct or indirect (and there is none here) a difference which is connected with economic factors affecting the efficient carrying on of the employer's business or other activity may well be relevant.*[43] (Emphasis added.)

The tests put forward in *Fletcher* were, therefore, overturned.

It is interesting to speculate on what was in the minds of the judges in the House of Lords when they examined the section 1(3) exception and decided to widen its scope. Certainly the passage quoted above reflects a great deal of current government thinking about the need to free business from what are seen as undue restrictions so as to allow them to operate more freely. It is also certainly the case that workers' rights in the UK have been sacrificed for this same goal of business efficiency. However Lord Keith did not rely on political arguments. He was able to quote the authority of the European Court of Justice in favour of his interpretation. Lord Keith quoted both *Jenkins* and *Bilka* to conclude that:

There is now no reason to construe section 1(3) as conferring greater rights on a worker in this context than does Article 119 of the Treaty. It follows that a relevant difference for the purpose of section 1(3) may relate to circumstances other than the personal qualifications or merits of the male and female workers who are the subject of comparison.[44]

Lord Keith then went on to find that the circumstances surrounding the recruitment of prosthetists was such as to constitute a material difference for, as he said, 'it was not a question of the appellant being paid less than the norm but of Mr. Crumlin being paid more'.[45]

The effect of the European Court's ruling in *Jenkins* has, therefore, had very far-reaching implications in British law, and it must be said that from a point of view of British women it has had the effect of weakening the anti-discrimination legislation which was introduced to protect their interests. Of course it could not be foreseen that *Jenkins* would provide the lever for the House of Lords to oust the very liberal-minded interpretation of section 1(3) of the Equal Pay Act. However the Jenkins and Rainey cases point to the salutary lesson that not all references to the European Court will lead to an extension of women's rights, and that a judiciary which is not altogether noted for its support of the women's movement will use whatever weapons it has to hand to restrict the scope of women's rights. In this instance the House of Lords seized on the muddled and confusing judgement in *Jenkins* to tighten the web around the Equal Pay Act.

Furthermore, in doing so, the House of Lords have given the impression that Community law can provide a basis for the *restriction* of rights formerly granted under domestic legislation. The statement by Lord Keith that 'there is now no reason to construe section 1(3) as conferring greater rights on a worker in this context than does Article 119 of the Treaty' is not an accurate description of the relationship between Community and domestic law. Whilst it is true that Community law has precedence over conflicting legislation, and that Community law can create enforceable Community rights, there is nothing to suggest that a Member State of the Community must limit its own code of rights to fit into the minimal standards of Community law. The Court of Justice has never suggested that Community law obliges Member States to limit their own bills of rights or legislative provisions but merely that such provisions at least meet the Community standard. It was, therefore, a rather disingenuous argument on behalf of Lord Keith to rely for his authority on the decisions of the European Court in *Jenkins* and *Bilka*.

The European Court was also asked to rule on the failure of the UK to fully implement the Equal Pay Directive.[46] In 1982 the Court ruled that the UK had failed to fulfil its obligations in that the equal pay legislation in force did not create the right for an individual to make a claim on the basis of the equal worth of his or her employment. The UK reluctantly accepted the decision of the Court and the Equal Pay Act was amended by statutory instrument.[47] Both the way in which these amendments were introduced and their content has given rise to critical comment by several authors.[48] Furthermore, in *Pickstone*,[49] in the Court of Appeal, Lord Justice Nicholls criticized the amendments as still failing to implement the Directive and falling short of Community requirements. Three important cases illustrate some of the difficulties created by the amended legislation.

The first case relates to Ms Hayward who was a cook employed by a large shipbuilders in Liverpool. She brought an action in an industrial tribunal claiming that she was employed on work of equal value to other (male) skilled shipyard workers who had trained for the same length of time as herself and who had the same degree of industrial experience.[50] She based her claim on section 1(2)(c) of the Equal Pay Act, a section which had been introduced as a result of an action brought by the Commission against the UK for failure to implement the Equal Pay Directive. The Industrial Tribunal appointed an independent expert to evaluate whether Ms Hayward was engaged in work of equal value to the men and he found in her favour. The Industrial Tribunal, accepting the report, directed the parties to settle the dispute between themselves, and failing such a settlement to bring the matter back to it.

The parties could not agree on an interpretation of section 1(2)(c) of the Act which reads:

> where a woman is employed on work which...is, in terms of the demands made on her (for instance under such headings as effort, skill and decision), of equal value to that of a man in the same employment – (i) if...any term

of the woman's contract is or becomes less favourable to the woman than a term of a similar kind in the contract under which that man is employed, that term of the woman's contract shall be treated as so modified as not to be less favourable, and, (ii) if...at any time the woman's contract does not include a term corresponding to a term benefiting that man included in the contract under which he is employed, the woman's contract shall be treated as including such a term.

Two alternative interpretations were presented to the Tribunal. Ms Hayward argued that *any* less favourable term in her contract should be improved so as to bring it up to the level of the men's. In particular, Ms Hayward argued that overtime rates of pay should be the same, as differences in these rates led to a difference in the weekly rate of pay. The employers argued that in construing the Equal Pay Act regard must be had to the overall package rather than to individual items in the contract. Using this approach, they argued, account should be taken of the shorter working hours of the appellant, her free meals and additional sickness benefit. Using this approach Ms Hayward, they argued, was the more favourably treated.

No definition of pay is given in the Equal Pay Act; the Industrial Tribunal therefore imported the definition of pay contained in Article 119. On this basis, the Tribunal held that considerations other than rates of pay should be taken into consideration when evaluating equal pay claims. The Employment Appeal Tribunal upheld this decision stating that Article 119 should be applied and that the Tribunal must look at the overall package, and the Court of Appeal agreed.[51]

The effect of this judgement would be to require industrial tribunals to take into consideration all aspects of the employee's contract of employment when deciding on equal pay. This avoids so-called 'leap-frogging' which was frowned upon by both the Employment Appeal Tribunal and the Court of Appeal. Leap-frogging essentially means that a man and a woman could examine each other's contract so that both would receive the more favourable benefits in either contract. Applying industrial common sense, it was held that the legislation could not allow employees to do this. However, it is submitted, this is exactly what equal pay legislation is meant to do. It is to provide equality of treatment, and may mean that employers should be forced to consider very carefully each aspect of pay and afford equal treatment. This may mean considerable renegotiation but that is, nonetheless, the obligation imposed by equality legislation. A true reading of Article 119 requires equality in respect of all aspects; it does not require equality as an aggregate of all aspects. This must be the interpretation behind such cases as *MacCarthys*, *Worringham* and *Garland*. There is certainly nothing in the case-law of the European Court to suggest the interpretation given to it by the British Court in this instance.

This case was appealed to the House of Lords which overturned the decision of the Court of Appeal.[52] The House of Lords held that each term in a woman's contract may be compared to a corresponding term in a man's contract to see whether she is more unfavourably treated. In reaching this view the judges in the House of Lords relied on the British legislation but Lord Mackay also examined the relevant provisions of Community law and found that he would have reached the same result on the basis of it. This case was then remitted to the Industrial Tribunal so that it could make the appropriate award of arrears of pay.

Another important case has reached the House of Lords relating to the application of Article 119. In *Pickstone* v. *Freemans PLC*[53] the judges were again asked to give a judgement relating to section 1(2)(c) of the Equal Pay Act. The text of this section is quoted earlier in the context of the discussion of *Hayward*. *Pickstone* concerned the very important point as to whether that section of the Act met the standards required by Community law in the area of equal value claims.

Ms Pickstone was employed as a 'warehouse operative' and she wished to argue that her work was equal in value to a male 'checker warehouse operative' who was paid more than she. At the time she made her complaint, a man was also employed as a warehouse operative and he received the same wages as Ms Pickstone. The employer argued that she was precluded from bringing such a claim since, in terms of the Equal Pay Act, she could only bring an equal value claim under section 1(2)(c) if she was unable to bring a claim under the previous two sections. In other words the equal value claim could only be pursued if, and only if she was not employed on 'like work' with a man or if her job had not been evaluated (by the employer) as being equivalent with that of a man in the same employment.

By the time the case reached the Court of Appeal, the arguments of the parties had been rehearsed both in the Industrial Tribunal and the Employment Appeal Tribunal, both of which had decided in favour of the employers. When the case came before the Court of Appeal, counsel for Ms Pickstone argued that section 1(2)(c) did not have the meaning argued for by the employers and, furthermore, the appellants had a directly enforceable Community right to equal pay for work of equal value arising from Article 119.

In a very closely reasoned judgement, Lord Justice Nicholls accepted the construction of the Equal Pay Act put forward by the employers that paragraph (c) applies only where the woman is employed on work 'not being work in relation to which para (a) or (b) above applies' (the wording of the Act). Ms Pickstone could have no remedy, therefore, under the British Equal Pay Act. The judge then turned his attention to European Community law and, in particular, to the relationship between Article 119 and Directive 75/117. He said:

As authoritatively decided by the European Court of Justice, the first sentence of Article 1 of the equal pay Directive re-states the principle of equal pay set out in Article 119 of the Treaty, but Article 1 'in no way alters the content or scope of the principle as defined in the Treaty'. The main purpose of Article 1 of the Directive was to facilitate the practical application of that principle: see Jenkins.[54]

After reviewing the arguments of the parties he went on to state:

Article 119 enshrines a broad, general principle: equal pay for equal work. The equal pay Directive makes clear that in this context equal work embraces work of equal value as well as work which is the same. I can see no justification for implying into this general principle, whereunder equal pay includes both these categories, a rigid and inflexible limitation, to the effect that, although a woman is entitled to compare herself with a man doing work of equal value, she is only so entitled if and so long as no man is doing the same work as herself, and that whenever and for so long as there is a man doing the same work the woman cannot make that comparison, even if the difference in pay is attributable solely to grounds of sex.[55]

He then went on to hold that Article 119 as defined by the equal pay Directive applied directly in the UK 'and that it is the duty of this Court to give effect' to the decisions of the European Court to that effect. The judge was then led to the inescapable conclusion that the British Act did not provide a remedy in all cases of work of equal value and that the UK had not fulfilled its obligations under the Treaty. As a result he held that:

I would allow the appeal and direct that these applications proceed in front of the Industrial Tribunal on the footing that under Article 119 (although not under s.1(2)(c) of the Equal Pay Act 1970) a woman employed on work which is the same as that of one man but which is also of equal value with the work of another man is not debarred from claiming equal pay with that other man by reason of the fact that she is already being paid as much as the man engaged in the same work as herself.[56]

The judgement of the House of Lords in this case provides a very interesting example of the difficulties faced by judges when legislation which purports to incorporate Community rights into domestic law fails to do so in clear terms. The House of Lords, taking a different approach, treated the issue as a matter of construction of the Statutory Instrument which amended the 1970 Sex Discrimination Act. In his judgement, Lord Keith stated that it was plain that the British government could not have intended to fail to bring its legislation into line with Community law and that accordingly it was necessary to imply some additional words into section 1(2)(c) which would allow a woman to compare the value of her work to that of a man working for the same employer, notwithstanding the fact that there was another man doing the same work as her for the same pay. He suggested that the words of the Statutory Instrument be construed purposively rather than literally.

Lord Templeman was of the same opinion. He examined the interaction of Community and domestic law and reviewed the history of section 1(2)(c) and sought an interpretation of the section consistent with Community law. In order to do this he implied an additional phrase into the section so as to avoid such an inconsistency and to deter the creation of a new form of discrimination. He quoted the principle enunciated by the European Court in *Von Colson*[57] to the effect that the national court should interpret and apply the legislation adopted for the implementation of a directive in conformity with the requirements of Community law in so far as it is given discretion so to do. In the present case Lord Templeman could see no difficulty in construing the 1983 Regulations in such a way as to give effect to the intention of the government and to be consistent with the provisions of Directive 75/117, Article 119 and the rulings of the European Court.

Lord Oliver was persuaded by Lord Templeman's argument and agreed that the Regulations were reasonably capable of bearing a meaning consistent with the obligations imposed by Community law. His initial reaction had inclined to the opposite view and he had felt that the Regulations were in fact in breach of the obligations imposed by Article 119. Having come to a common viewpoint, the House of Lords dismissed the appeal by the employers. The case reverted to the Industrial Tribunal which was then responsible for evaluating the work of Ms Pickstone as against the male warehouse checker.

The third case which should be mentioned in this context is one which is still in the process of decision. It relates to the pay of three women speech therapists who wish to compare the value of their work with clinical psychologists and pharmacists employed by regional health authorities in England and Wales. This case reached the English High Court for a judicial review of decisions of the Secretary of State for Social Services who was the Minister responsible for promulgating and enforcing the pay of the women at levels negotiated in the Whitley Council.[58] The Whitley Council is composed of representatives of employers and employees within the National Health Service and within which there are separate sub-councils for various groups of workers. The wages of all workers are fixed within this system and enforced by the Secretary of State for Social Services. Therefore individual health authorities have no powers to fix or negotiate salaries outside this system. Within the Whitley Council, speech therapists, 90 per cent of whom are women, have traditionally been paid much less than clinical psychologists. Before the Industrial Tribunal the Health Authorities argued that the variation in the women's contracts and those of their chosen male counterparts was due to a material factor other than sex, since they, the Health Authorities, were bound to comply with the Regulations laid down by the Secretary of State. The applicant argued that Article 119 and Directive 75/117 had overriding force over the

Regulations and the rates set by the Secretary of State. The Industrial Tribunal accepted the view of the Health Authorities and then said that the remedy for the applicants was a judicial review of the decisions of the Secretary of State.

Lord Justice Croom-Johnson, in the proceedings for judicial review, accepted that if there is a conflict between Community law and domestic law then Community law prevails. Furthermore he said that if the Community law principle of equal pay had been breached, then the applicants must have a remedy. The problem was in deciding what the relevant procedure was. The judge stated that it was for the Industrial Tribunal to examine first whether a woman speech therapist's work is equal in value to a man's and, if so, then to decide whether the difference is genuinely due to a material factor. He then cited the case of *Rainey* v. *Greater Glasgow Health Board* to define the meaning of material difference showing that it was for the Tribunal to investigate all the relevant facts and circumstances. Therefore, he remitted the case to the Industrial Tribunal to continue the hearing, with a declaration that the mere fact that the pay of the applicants had been approved by the Secretary of State pursuant to the relevant Regulations did not provide a defence to the employers against the claims under the 1970 Act (as amended) and Community law. The Industrial Tribunal found against the women who have now appealed the case to the Employment Appeal Tribunal.[59]

The cases of *Hayward, Pickstone* and *Clarke* demonstrate the obvious impact which Community law has had on British equal pay legislation. From these cases it is apparent that British judges are both familiar with the relevant Community law and the interpretation placed on the law by the European Court. *Hayward* shows an understanding by the House of Lords of the philosophy underlying equality legislation (although are there indications in Lord Goff's judgement that he does not like it?), and *Pickstone* shows a readiness on the part of the House of Lords to accept a Community obligation in the spirit and the letter of the law, and to accept the so-called indirect effect of the Equal Treatment Directive.[60] The case of *Clarke*, however, demonstrates the enormous difficulties still faced by women to demonstrate the equal value of their work, despite the existence of Community law.

On the issue of equal treatment there have been four requests for preliminary rulings from British Courts, as well as one infringement action brought against the UK. Of these cases *Burton* has already been discussed. In that case the European Court found that there had been no discrimination and Mr Burton, accepting this view, withdrew his action for unfair dismissal. In the case of *Roberts* v. *Tate and Lyle Industries*,[61] the European Court had held that a private contractual provision which lays down a single age for dismissal in the case of redundancies, which includes the grant of a retirement pension when the normal retirement age for men and women is different, did not infringe the Equal Treatment

Directive. Ms Roberts, therefore, was also forced to withdraw her action. Other cases before the Court have, however, had more far-reaching effects on British legislation and practice.

In 1984 the Court ruled that the UK had failed to implement the Equal Treatment Directive 76/207 in that British legislation failed to ensure that clauses in collective agreements which are incompatible with the obligations imposed by the Directive are rendered inoperative, eliminated or amended. In the same case, the Court held that the exclusion of the prohibition of discrimination between the sexes in private households or small undertakings was a further failure on the part of the UK to implement the Equal Treatment Directive.

Following this case the UK undertook to amend its legislation in order to conform to the judgement of the European Court. The Sex Discrimination Act 1986[62] was the British response to the ruling of the European Court. Section 6 of the 1986 Act extends the scope of the 1975 Sex Discrimination Act to cover clauses contained in collective agreements. Such terms are void. However, it has been argued by Fredman that section 6 adds nothing to existing legislation. She argues:

> The Government chose to implement the Directive by declaring discriminatory terms void, rather than amending them. No new remedies are established. The impact is therefore minimal...The only remedies are at individual level, (as was already the case prior to the present Act), in the form of an application to an industrial tribunal under the Equal Pay Act 1970 or Sex Discrimination Act 1975, or to a County Court.

Fredman then goes on to show that the changes made by the 1986 Act are in reality merely cosmetic and intended to comply with the letter of the Court's judgement whilst flouting its spirit. She says:

> The decision to rely on individual remedies does not, however, take into account the severe limitations to which individuals are subject. As the European Court recognised in the non-compliance case, the main function of a collective agreement is to lay down a code of terms and conditions for a whole sector or area of employment. A discriminatory collective agreement could therefore give rise to thousands of individual claims, an expensive and slow process, potentially leading to different conclusions by different tribunals. A more effective amendment would be to create a mechanism for remedying the collective agreement itself; for example, by extending the limited jurisdiction of the Central Arbitration Committee (CAC) under s. 3 Eq.PA, as suggested by the Advocate General in the European Court and strenuously urged by the opposition in Parliament. However, the Government regarded the European Court judgement as requiring changes which were "merely presentational", arguing that individual remedies were adequate and that the main effect of the section was to act as an incentive

to unions and employers to renegotiate agreements. Indeed, it used the occasion of the Act to repeal s.3 EqPA rather than extending it. Voluntary references to the CAC do remain possible, and the EOC has the power to undertake a formal investigation in the case of a discriminatory collective agreement.[63]

It remains to be seen whether the Commission will be satisfied that the changes made by section 6 meet the requirements of the Equal Treatment Directive.

The 1986 Act also deals with the objection raised by the Commission, and sustained by the Court of Justice, relating to employment in small undertakings. Section 1 of the 1986 Act repeals the offending provision of the Sex Discrimination Act 1975, which exempted private households and undertakings of five employees or less from the operation of that Act. However, a new exception is included in the Act in the section dealing with 'genuine occupational qualification'. This new exception relates to employment where the holder of the job or the person living in a private home has a degree of 'physical or social contact with a person living in the home' or has 'knowledge of intimate details of such a person's life'. In these circumstances a particular post might be reserved to a person of one sex rather than another. This amendment certainly satisfies the objections raised in *Commission* v. *United Kingdom* and it seems that the exception contained in the 1986 Act is sufficiently narrow to make it acceptable to the Commission.

Sections 1 and 6 of the 1986 Act deal with the issues raised in the infringement proceedings brought against the UK. However, the 1986 Act is a 'tidying up' Act which also deals with several other issues. One of these is the problem which was raised in the *Marshall* case.[64] In that case the European Court had ruled that it was contrary to the Equal Treatment Directive to dismiss a female employee at the age of 60 when men were dismissed at the age of 65. The Court also ruled that the Directive had a vertical direct effect in so far as any worker employed by the state could rely on the Directive in the national courts. This left private employees in an inferior position in terms of their rights since they were not able to rely on the Directive against their own employer. Accordingly section 2 of the Act provides that it is unlawful for a person to discriminate against a woman:

> in such of the terms on which he offers her employment...in relation to the way in which he will afford her access to opportunities for promotion, transfer or training or as provide for her dismissal or demotion.

Thus all employees, whether in the private or public sector, have equal rights in respect of retirement age. This does not necessarily mean an end to discrimination in the area of retirement benefits since the UK has not yet equalized the pensionable age itself. However, in this respect UK practice is in line with existing Community law.

Marshall, therefore, led to an amendment of existing British legislation. It also has two further implications, one for Ms Marshall herself and one on a question of principle. The question of principle relates to the crucial point as to who may rely on the Directive in the absence of implementing legislation. *Marshall* had decided that directives have only vertical direct effects and, accordingly, individuals could rely on a directive only against the state. The European Court did not, however, define what was meant by the term 'the state'. It did reiterate the fact that Member States should be prevented from taking advantage of their own failure to comply with Community law and that it is for the national court to apply these considerations to the circumstances of each case. These comments in *Marshall* have led British courts to the view that it is for them to give a definition of 'the state' in the cases before them, and the definition given has been an extremely restricted one. In *Turpie* v. *University of Glasgow*,[65] the Industrial Tribunal refused to define a Scottish university as being part of the state, despite the fact that, in Scotland, the universities receive the bulk of their funding from the central government and that the terms and conditions of staff are, to a large extent, negotiated nationally through government-appointed quangos. In *Rolls Royce plc* v. *Doughty* the Employment Appeal Tribunal held that Rolls Royce, which at the time of the original application, was 100 per cent owned by the state, was not to be equated with the state since to do so would require the court to lift the corporate veil.[66] Then in *Foster*, the English Court of Appeal refused to define British Gas, at that time a nationalized industry, as being part of the state. *Foster* was appealed to the House of Lords which stayed proceedings and requested a preliminary ruling from the Court of Justice as to whether the British Gas Corporation was a body of such a type that the appellants were entitled to rely directly on the Equal Treatment Directive in their claim for damages.[67] This case has not been resolved by the Court of Justice but its resolution may solve the dilemma of who exactly can rely on the direct effects of a directive.

To some extent, these cases have an historical interest only, since the 1986 Act did bring Britain (excepting Northern Ireland) into line with the Equal Treatment Directive. However, they do have major implications. It should be stressed that the European Court in *Marshall* did not declare that it was for the national courts to define under national law what is meant by the state. The European Court accepted the view of the national court that an Area Health Authority is an emanation of the state, but the considerations which the national court must take into account are laid down in *Marshall*. These considerations are essentially that the Member States bear the burden of responsibility for implementing their Community obligations and they should not be allowed to take advantage of their own failure in order to benefit. These considerations are hardly mentioned in the three examples cited above where the judges relied on national considerations to reach their conclusions. This leads to very serious anomalies. Employees of Dutch universities, for instance, may derive rights from the Directive, whereas Ms Turpie could not in a Scottish university. Within the University of Glasgow, lecturers in clinical medicine (who are simultaneously employed by the National Health Service) may derive rights from the Directive, whereas lecturers in law may not, and so on.

In another context, the European Court has stated that the term 'employment in the public service' must be given a Community meaning,[68] and the European Court has always interpreted this phrase to give the widest possible rights to individuals and restricted the Member States' use of the criterion to exclude individuals from applying for particular posts. By analogy, the domestic courts should restrict the scope for avoidance of Community obligations by States and give a wide meaning to terms like 'the state'. If they are unable to find a Community definition, they are, of course, free to apply to the European Court for a definition of the term in any particular circumstance. However, as things stand within the UK at the moment, the definition given in *Foster* v. *British Gas plc* will govern the question of what constitutes the state for the purposes of the Equal Treatment Directive.[69]

As has already been stated, the Marshall case also had implications for the original applicant. The ruling given by the European Court was given in response to a question from the English Court of Appeal. On its receipt of the European Court's judgement, the Court of Appeal allowed Ms Marshall's appeal and remitted her case to the Industrial Tribunal to consider the question of the appropriate remedy.

The Industrial Tribunal decided[70] that the appropriate remedy was to award Ms Marshall monetary compensation. She was at this time 70 years of age and no other remedy would have been appropriate.

The Tribunal awarded a total sum of £19 405 which included compensation for loss of earnings, loss of pension benefits and of income loss from private practice work, 10 per cent interest thereon and £1000 for the hurt done to Ms Marshall's feelings. Of this sum £6250 was deducted since the Health Authority had already paid this sum to the applicant. What is interesting about the level of compensation set is that it far exceeds the limits for compensation set down in the Sex Discrimination Act. The Tribunal took the view that this Act did not provide an adequate remedy as required under Article 6 of Directive 76/207 since the limits set by the 1975 Act do not act as a deterrent. Taking into consideration the judgements of the European Court in *Von Colson* and *Johnston*, the Tribunal concluded:

the arguments as to whether there is a separate right under Article 6, or whether one has to construe the 1975 Act in the light of that, do not need to be considered. Or, if they are to be considered, then clearly Article 6 of Directive 76/207 has primacy. It laid on obligation upon the United Kingdom Government to adopt all necessary measures 'to ensure that the Directive is fully effective in accordance with the objective which it pursues'. The last phrase is to us telling. We all know the object which is pursued. The duty is laid upon the national court to deal with that situation. Put another way, the United Kingdom government has, in accordance with Article 189 of the Treaty, chosen the form and method, but has gone on to provide an obstacle. Just as it did on the first question in Miss Marshall's case and in Johnston. The Community law permits of no obstacle.[71]

Ms Marshall was, therefore, given a somewhat belated but adequate remedy – eight years after her original dismissal. It remains to be seen whether the Health Authority will appeal against this decision and whether the European Commission will take the open invitation from the Tribunal to take further infringement proceedings against the British government for their failure to provide an adequate remedy.[72]

The final case to be discussed in respect of the Equal Treatment Directive in the UK is the case of *Johnston* v. *RUC*.[73] This case came to the European Court on a reference from the Industrial Tribunal of Northern Ireland and concerned the refusal of the Chief Constable to renew the contract of a female full-time RUC reservist.[74] The Court of Justice decided that section 53(2) of the 1976 Sex Discrimination Order (Northern Ireland) infringed the Equal Treatment Directive in so far as it allows the competent authority to deprive individuals of the possibility of asserting by judicial process their rights under the Directive.

The Court also held that the national court was the proper authority for determining whether the Chief Constable was correct in restricting certain tasks, and the training leading thereto, to men in the light of the context of policing in Northern Ireland. In so deciding, the national court was to ensure that the principle of proportionality is observed.

When this case came back to the Industrial Tribunal, and after some argument and adjournment, the parties agreed to a settlement rather than carry on with the case. However, the Tribunal had to decide on costs and awarded costs against the Chief Constable on the basis that he had acted 'unreasonably in failing to appreciate his obligations under the sex discrimination laws'. Under the terms of the settlement Ms Johnston and 30 others in similar situations received compensation totalling £250 000. Perhaps more importantly than this, the Chief Constable certainly began to appreciate his obligations more fully since:

> In addition to compensation, the Chief Constable agreed to reduce the height requirement for women applicants to the RUC from 5 foot 6 inches to 5 foot 4 inches. Moreover, the Chief Constable agreed to access for women to all training and also to the establishment of an Advisory Committee on Equal Opportunities in the Police Service. This

Committee will have representatives from the RUC, the Northern Ireland Policy Authority, the Police Association, and from the Equal Opportunities Commission for Northern Ireland. Its remit is to examine and keep under review the principle of equal treatment of men and women in respect of matters such as recruitment, training, promotion, conditions of service and any other matters covered by the principle of equal treatment in the regular RUC and the RUC Reserve and to advise and make recommendations to the Chief Constable having regard to the exigencies of the unusual situation prevailing in Northern Ireland.[75]

In the discussion of the second Marshall case above it is clear that *Johnston* has had an impact on the Industrial Tribunal in England since it was quoted as authority for the proposition that Article 6 has primacy over existing UK law and gives individuals a right, enforceable in British courts, to an appropriate remedy for breach of the Directive. In Northern Ireland it may prove to have even more far-reaching effects. As is obvious from the discussion of the impact of the decisions of the European Court in the UK so far, one of the major problems faced by UK courts is to reconcile existing British legislation with an expanding body of Community law and with the interpretations placed on Community legislation by the European Court. It is now clearly established that British courts will seek to construe British law so as not to conflict with Community obligations. *Garland* established that the House of Lords was willing to construe the 1975 Equal Pay Act in such a way as to be consistent with Article 119 of the Treaty, which became law for the UK in 1972. *Pickstone* established further that the House of Lords accepted their obligation to give a purposive interpretation to a British legislation the stated aim of which was to implement a Community obligation, even though the actual wording of the legislation led to another conclusion.

However, one problem remains for the UK and that is where the courts are faced with a clear conflict between a UK statute and a Community Directive. This situation can be illustrated by reference to the case of *Duke* v. *GEC Reliance Ltd*[76] in which Ms Duke sought damages from her employers when she was dismissed at the age of 60, whereas men were not dismissed until the age of 65. Ms Duke's dismissal took place before the coming into force of the 1986 Sex Discrimination Act. As has already been seen, the 1975 Act permitted employers to apply discriminatory working conditions in relation to retirement, whereas Directive 76/207 outlaws such discrimination. The UK brought its legislation into line with the Directive in 1986 following the Marshall case.

In *Duke*, Lord Templeman reviewed the relationship between national and Community law and the duty of the national courts in cases where conflict arose. He argued that the construction of a British Act of Parliament was a matter to be determined by the British courts and to be derived from the language of the legislation considered in the light of circumstances prevailing at the date of enactment. Since the 1970 and 1975 Acts were not passed to give effect to the Equal Treatment Directive, but were intended to preserve discriminatory retirement ages, it followed that Ms Duke's claim could not succeed under British law. Furthermore, since the Equal Treatment Directive did not have horizontal direct effect, Ms Duke could not rely on Community law. He then argued that there was nothing in Community law to demand that a national court distort the meaning of a domestic statute so as to conform with Community law which is not directly applicable. He then went on to state that it would be unfair to the employer in this case to distort the construction of the 1977 Act in order to accommodate the 1976 Directive.

It is useful at this point to reiterate what the European Court has said in relation to the obligations of the national court in these circumstances.[77] From *Von Colson and Kamann* and *Johnston*,[78] it is clear that the national court is under a duty to interpret and apply national legislation, in particular that which is adopted for the implementation of a directive, in conformity with the requirements of Community law, in so far as it is given discretion to do so under national law. *Kolpinghuis*[79] confirms that the national court must take the Directive into consideration when it is interpreting implementing legislation or any other rule of national law, within the limits of its discretion. Moreover, it follows from this judgement that this obligation exists as soon as the Directive has been adopted and is published. It is also clear that the duty of the national court is limited by the general principle of legal certainty and the prohibition of retroactivity. The problem faced by the House of Lords, as perceived by Lord Templeman, was the extent to which that court had a discretion to interpret the 1975 Act to be in conformity with the 1976 Directive against the wishes of Parliament. This is, indeed, a problem for the British courts and the House of Lords in particular. It is not one, however, which it need, or should, solve alone. The House of Lords should have referred the issue to the Court of Justice for its guidance: after all, their Lordships were faced with a question of Community law. The problem can be summed up as follows: Community law requires the national courts to interpret purposively national legislation to try to ensure that it does not conflict with a directive. In the UK, existing legislation was deemed to be adequate to meet the requirements of the Directive and no new legislation was adopted – until this point was disproved by *Marshall*. The national court was, therefore, faced with conflicting obligations arising out of its duty to Community law on the one hand and its duty to construe national legislation in accordance with the express will of Parliament on the other (i.e. a constitutional requirement). In *Duke*, Lord Templeman did not accept that the 1975 Act could be seen to be the implementing legislation for the Directive. There is an argument, based on the failure of the British government to amend its legislation within the limits laid down in the Directive, to say that at the time of Ms Duke's dismissal the implementing legislation of the Directive must be deemed to be the 1975

Act. If Lord Templeman had started from this point of view, he might have taken a more positive view of his construction of the British statute to achieve the result requested by Ms Duke.

Finally, it must be said that from a reading of Lord Templeman's judgement it appears that his main reason for dismissing Ms Duke's arguments was his sense of fairness towards the employer. Employers in the UK had been led to believe that the maintenance of different retirement ages for men and women was legitimate. The relevant statute appeared to expressly permit them to act in this way and the Court of Appeal had interpreted the statute so as to allow the discrimination to continue.[80] In these circumstances, Lord Templeman was reluctant to allow any effect to the Directive which would have imposed an obligation on the employer. In effect, he was applying the principle of legal certainty and, as the Court of Justice had pointed out in *Kolpinghuis*, the national court is limited, in interpreting Community law, by the principle of legal certainty. However, in this respect, Lord Templeman again may be criticized for failing to involve the European Court in the matter since the balancing of the general principle of certainty against the rights deriving from Community sex discrimination legislation is a question of Community, not national, law.[81]

Following this case the Commission may wish to pursue an action against the UK for improperly implementing the Directive. The 1986 Act provides that in future all women in England, Wales and Scotland have the right to be retired at the same age as men but it does not provide compensation or any remedy for women in Ms Duke's situation. Whether the Commission will take such action has yet to be seen.

As has been stated already, there is no equivalent legislation in Northern Ireland to the 1986 Act. How then will the Irish tribunals deal with the situation where a woman is retired before a comparable male? The answer to this question may lie in the unreported case of *Finnegan*.[82] In this case the Industrial Tribunal in Northern Ireland took the view that the 1976 Sex Discrimination (NI) Order was intended to implement the principle of equal treatment and, following *Von Colson* and *Johnston*, it was under an obligation to interpret the 1976 Order in such a way as to coincide with the Equal Treatment Directive. Thus, the Tribunal held that an employer had discriminated against a woman dismissed at the age of 60 where men continued in employment until the age of 65. It can be seen that in construing the same words, the Industrial Tribunal in Northern Ireland reached the opposite conclusion to the House of Lords in *Duke*.

At the time of writing, it is unclear how this case will go. It may be that on appeal the courts will apply the House of Lords ruling in *Duke*. In that situation, the way must clearly be open to the Commission to bring an action against the UK since women in Northern Ireland will have no remedy at all against dismissal at the age of 60.

As regards the Social Security Directive, there have been two cases referred from the British courts. The first was a reference from the Social Security Commissioner relating to the payment of an invalid care allowance to be paid to persons caring for a severely disabled relative except where the claimant is a married or cohabiting woman. In the case of *Drake*,[83] the Court of Justice held that the Directive covers benefits payable to third parties, i.e. not to the disabled person self, as long as they form part of a scheme covering a risk listed in the Directive. The invalid care allowance was one such scheme and, because it was denied to married women but not to married men, the refusal to pay the benefit was a contravention of the Social Security Directive. Following the decision of the European Court, the Social Security Commissioner awarded Ms Drake the allowance she sought. The day before the judgement the British government announced its intention of repealing the exclusionary rules.[84] Thereafter married and cohabiting women became entitled to an allowance of £23 per week at a cost of some £55 million per year.[85]

The second case to come to the European Court on the Social Security Directive related to a transitional provision adopted when the British government attempted to bring the rules relating to non-contributory invalidity pension in line with the Social Security Directive. The complaint of Ms Borrie Clarke related to the discriminatory effects of this transitional provision, and her complaint was upheld by the European Court.[86] Therefore, when the case was returned to the Social Security Commissioner she was awarded payment of a severe disablement allowance from the period 23 December 1984 to 17 August 1985 (the period of her claim).[87] The severe disablement allowance was the new provision which was designed to replace non-contributory invalidity pension. This case has had an obvious impact on the claimant herself and others in the same position, but it is of limited interest in terms of principles. What is more interesting is that the severe disablement allowance itself may, in fact, contravene the Directive. Luckhaus argues that the introduction of an age bar into the new tests for the benefit merely replaces overtly discriminatory provisions with indirectly discriminatory ones.[88] The question has not yet been taken up either by claimants or by the Commission.

Republic of Ireland

Only one case has come to the European Court on the issue of equal pay from the Republic of Ireland: *Murphy* v. *An Bord Telecom Eireann*. This case had come to the European Court for an interpretation of Article 119 from the Irish High Court.[89] In its preliminary ruling, the European Court had stated that Article 119 must be interpreted as covering the case where a worker who relies on that provision to obtain equal pay is engaged in work of *higher* value than that of a person with whom a comparison is to be made. When the case returned to the Irish High Court, Justice Keane indicated two possible courses of action which might be appropriate in the light of this ruling.[90] The first course of action was to remit the case back to the Labour Court with a direction that the appellants' claim be determined on the basis that they and the male employee were engaged in like work within the meaning of the 1974 Act. The second course was for the High Court itself to resolve the question as to whether the inequality of pay complained of was due to sex discrimination. Justice Keane chose the former approach on the basis that Article 119 forms part of Irish law and that Community law takes precedence over any conflicting provision of domestic legislation. According to the normal canons of construction normally applied in Irish courts, a conflict had arisen between the 1974 Act and Article 119 and it was for the relevant national court to apply Community law. In this case it was for the Labour Court to apply the relevant provision of Community law rather than the literal interpretation of the 1974 Act. A further consideration of Justice Keane related to the constitutionality of the 1974 Act. This Act, unless the contrary is shown, is presumed to be constitutional and it is further presumed that the Oireachtas would not legislate in a manner which is in breach of rights protected under Community law. Rights arising from Article 119 already existed when the 1974 Act was passed; therefore that Act should be construed not in a literal way but by adopting a teleological approach. This course of action (implying the words 'at least' before the words 'equal in value' in the 1974 Act) had been urged by counsel on behalf of the appellants at the original hearing and Justice Keane now accepted this view in the light of the interpretation given by the Court of Justice. He therefore remitted the case to the Labour Court with the appropriate direction.

This case can quite usefully be compared to the case of *Pickstone* before the House of Lords. Indeed *Murphy* was quoted by Lord Templeman in his judgement in that case. In both situations the judges were faced with a conflict of a literal interpretation of their domestic legislation with the more expansive approach of the European Court. In both cases they wished to avoid a constitutional conflict – in the Irish case this was specifically left unanswered and in the English case the judges refused to follow normal interpretative techniques so as to achieve an answer which was consistent both with Community law and domestic constitutional requirements. In both cases, the judges had to write something in, or to imply a meaning which was absent from the original legislation. It is perhaps surprising that the same result was achieved given the divergence between constitutional theory in those two jurisdictions and, in particular, that the House of Lords should be prepared to bend the principle of legislative supremacy of Parliament. The Irish approach to Community law is historically more sympathetic; it is the more remarkable therefore that the courts arrived at similar conclusions to the same problem.

In relation to the Social Security Directive, one case has been referred to the European Court for a preliminary ruling from the Irish High Court. In *McDermott and Cotter*[91] the European Court declared Article 4(1) of the Social Security Directive to have direct effects with the result that it could be relied on to preclude the application of Irish social welfare legislation which accorded married women unemployment benefits at a lower rate, and for a shorter period of time, than married men and single persons. The European Court further stated that individuals could rely on Article 4(1) as from 23 December 1984 where the Directive has not been implemented by national legislation. The Court went on to say that in the absence of adequate implementing legislation, women are entitled to have the same rules applied to them as men in the same situation since these rules are, for those women, the only valid point of reference.

The Irish High Court was then faced with the difficult problem of reconciling the rather recondite system of Irish social welfare legislation with the very basic principle of non-discrimination.[92] Ms Cotter, a married woman living with her husband and two small children, was in continuous insurable employment until January 1984, when she was made redundant. Thereafter she applied for unemployment benefit and pay-related benefit. At the time of her application the relevant national legislation was governed by the Social Welfare (Consolidation) Act 1981 which was subsequently amended by the Social Welfare (No. 2) Act 1985. This latter Act was passed by the Irish Parliament in July 1985 but, at the time of the case coming before the European Court, the Minister had not fixed the day on which it would come into operation. The 1985 Act was designed to rectify the following discriminatory provisions contained within the earlier legislation:

1. The period for which unemployment benefit was paid to a married woman was 312 days as compared to 390 days for men and single women.
2. The rate of unemployment benefit payable to a married woman was lower than that paid to men and single women.
3. Since pay-related benefits were paid only to those persons in receipt of unemployment benefits, this meant that the period for which married women received pay-related benefits was shorter than the equivalent period for men and single women.

The rationale for these anomalies lay in the fact that in Ireland married women were deemed to be dependent on their husbands if they were living with them or were supported by them, whereas husbands were deemed to be dependent only if they were incapable of self-support by virtue of some physical or mental disability. The 1985 Act was designed to remove married women from the categorization of automatic dependency.

Ms Cotter asked the Irish High Court for a judicial review of the decisions of the relevant officials in the Ministry of Social Welfare who had applied the Irish rules to her circumstances. In respect of unemployment benefit she asked that arrears be paid to her to entitle her to be paid at the same rate as a married man for three periods:

- from 23 December 1984 to 18 April 1985;
- from 21 January 1986 to 20 November 1986; and
- from 20 November 1986 to 22 April 1987 or at such other time that she take up employment.

The Irish judge had no difficulty in determining that for the first of these periods she was entitled to be paid at the same rate as a married man. This, he said, was on the basis of the ruling given by the European Court of Justice. As regards the second period the judge accepted the decision of the Ministry that Ms Cotter had been unavailable for work for the period 21 January to 7 April 1986 but stated that from the period 7 April 1986 to 14 May 1986 she should have been paid at the same rate as a married man. However, the judge went on to say that as from 15 May, Ms Cotter had been paid at the same rate as a married man since, as from that date, the Irish amending legislation had come into effect, thereby equalizing both the period for which and the rate at which unemployment benefit is paid to men and women.

A rather more difficult question arose in respect of additional payments made to unemployed persons by virtue of their having dependants. Ms Cotter claimed such additional payments in respect of her husband and two children.

The 1981 Act defined 'adult dependant' as being a wife who is living with or who is wholly maintained by her husband, or a husband who is incapable of self-support by reason of physical or mental disability and who is wholly or mainly supported by his wife. Unemployment benefits are increased where a beneficiary has such an adult dependant.[93] The Irish judge held this provision to be inconsistent with the Directive, and stated that Ms Cotter was entitled to rely on the provisions of the Directive to preclude the application of the 1981 Act to her application to entitlement to the increases both for the period 23 December 1984 to 18 April 1985 and for 7 April 1986 to 20 November 1986. He then went on to examine the provisions of the 1985 Act and concluded that under the new law Ms Cotter had suffered no discrimination.

The third head of claim by Ms Cotter related to unemployment assistance from 18 April until 20 June 1985. Unemployment assistance is a means-tested benefit which is paid after the expiry of unemployment benefit proper. Ms Cotter had not previously applied for unemployment assistance since she was unable to obtain the necessary 'qualification certificate'. The law governing the payment of unemployment assistance sets out the relevant conditions which govern the grant of this certificate, and in the case of a married woman, but not a married man, the applicant must prove either that her husband is dependent on her or that neither she nor her husband is a dependant of the other and she has one or more dependants. A husband does not have to satisfy these conditions which, as the judge recognized, are clearly discriminatory.

Given that the Irish judge had recognized the inherently discriminatory nature of the law relating to dependants' allowances and unemployment assistance, his final declaration seems all the more surprising. The Court held, as regards unemployment assistance, that Ms Cotter had not proved that she would have been entitled to unemployment assistance and consequently he refused to make any declaration in respect of this claim.[94]

In respect of the dependants' allowance, where the judge had recognized the inconsistency of the Irish position with the Directive, the judge denied any claim for relief under this heading. In a rather astonishing passage, he claimed to base his judgement on the equity of the case. Citing an earlier Irish case[95] which itself cited *Defrenne* v. *Sabena*, the judge in Ms Cotter's case felt it would be unjust and inequitable to pay the applicant a dependants' allowance since her husband was at all relevant periods not dependent on her and was engaged in full-time employment. The injustice would be on the people of Ireland. In the court's view the injustice to be suffered by the Irish state outweighed the injustice suffered by Irish women in the operation of the social welfare system. Undoubtedly it is possible to sympathize with the view that it is unreasonable to pay dependants' allowances to persons who are capable of earning their own living, and who do in fact do so. The Irish solution does not solve this problem since men may claim an allowance for a working wife, but a wife may not claim such an allowance for a working husband. Equal treatment demands that either all spouses receive the allowance or none. Furthermore, it is difficult to sympathize with the Irish government since they had plenty of time and opportunity to bring their legislation into line with their Community obligations.

The High Court went further in its decision and added that although the Directive had direct effects in Ireland as from 23 December 1984, it cannot be relied on to support claims for social security concerning periods prior to the judgement of the European Court (24 March 1987) except for those people who have brought proceedings or made an equivalent claim before that date. No doubt the Court was influenced in this respect by the arguments of the Ministry for Social Welfare which stated that the sum required to meet all possible retrospective demands would be in the region of £200 million.

This latter point is worthy of note since it concerns some very basic principles of European Community law and its interpretation. One of the most important features of Community law is that it is to be applied uniformly throughout the territory of the Community. One way of ensuring such a uniform application has been to entrust the European Court of

Justice to *interpret* the provisions of Community law, leaving the courts of the Member States to *apply* the law in the cases which have come to it. The system of preliminary references exists to ensure this uniformity and it is not up to the national courts to impose domestic limitation on rights arising under Community provisions. In the Cotter case, the Irish Court seemed to have adopted a limitation principle which the European Court had itself applied in *Defrenne* v. *Sabena*. Here, it may be recalled, the European Court had declared that Article 119 had direct effects but had decided that its direct effects could only be relied on as from the date of its own judgement except in proceedings which had already been initiated. The European Court examined the particular circumstances and, in view of the high costs involved, plus the uncertainty created for employers both by the governments and by the Commission in relation to the effect of Article 119, decided to impose a temporal limit on the effects of its own judgement. In this respect, the European Court was acting as the interpreter of the Community provision, and no other court would have been capable of reaching this conclusion.

This view of its own function as sole interpreter of Community law has been emphasized in the recent case of *Barra*,[96] a request for a preliminary ruling from the Tribunal de Première Instance, Liège. Monsieur Barra, a French national, had been a student at a Belgian technical college and had been obliged to pay a 'minerval' (a supplementary fee) to the college, although Belgian students were not thus obliged. In February 1985, in the case of *Gravier*,[97] the European Court had declared that the imposition of the minerval was contrary to the principle of non-discrimination contained in Article 7 of the EEC Treaty. When this case returned to the Belgian Court, the judge took the view that the plaintiffs had paid fees which were not due. However, in June 1985 a Belgian education law was adopted which prohibited the refund of fees charged between 1 November 1976 and 31 December 1984, apart from fees charged to nationals of Member States of the Community. The latter were to be refunded in accordance with judicial decisions on actions for repayment commenced before Belgian Courts before 13 February 1985. Barra's case arose out of this legislative problem.

The European Court was quite clear on this matter, stating that it was only the Court itself, in the context of a preliminary ruling, which could impose temporal limitations on a provision of Community law. In relation to its own judgement in the case of *Defrenne* v. *Sabena*, the Court pointed to the exceptional circumstances of that case.[98] In the case of *Gravier*, the Court had not imposed any limitation, and in *Barra* they declined to impose any such limitations, reiterating the fact that the judgement in *Gravier* was not limited to applications made for admission to vocational training courses made after the date of the judgement and, accordingly, it applied to the period before that date. Furthermore, the Court held that national legislation may not deprive individuals of their right to repayment if they did not bring their applications before the date of the Gravier judgement.

Applying these principles to the Cotter case it can be seen that the Irish Court was wrong to impose, on its own motive, a temporal limitation on the direct effects of Article 4 of the Social Security Directive. The European Court had explicitly stated that the direct effects of that Article took effect on the 23 December 1984 and did not make any reference in its preliminary ruling to a temporal limitation. In the Cotter case, the Irish Court usurped the function of the European Court and, in doing so, placed Ireland in the position of Belgium in the situation described above. If national legislation may not be permitted to deprive individuals of their rights granted under Community law, neither can judgements given by national courts. The High Court could, of course, have requested a further preliminary ruling on this question and, thereby, invited the European Court to impose a temporal limitation. It is interesting to speculate as to whether the European Court would have done so. In *Barra* the European Court reiterated the exceptional circumstances which obtained in the Defrenne case. These exceptional circumstances do not apply in *Cotter*. True, the financial considerations are on the same scale; however there is here no problem of infringing the general principle of legal certainty. The Irish government, who will after all be the affected party, was well aware of its obligations to implement the Social Security Directive by December 1984. They had, indeed, been given six years in which to comply. In these circumstances it is difficult to see why the European Court should allow a temporal restriction to be placed on the direct effects of the Directive, and it is also difficult to see why the Irish High Court deemed the solution which it adopted to be 'equitable'. The Irish High Court has, in fact, facilitated the Irish government along its path of illegality. Moreover, the Court not having restricted the interpretation as to the direct effect of Article 4 in his first judgement on the matter, a restriction in a later judgement is, according to *Barra*, not conceivable.

It now remains to be seen what will happen. Other litigants may well raise the issue again in further proceedings and the Commission may wish to initiate an action against Ireland for the failure of its courts to uphold Community law. It is too early to see how this situation will develop.

The Netherlands

The majority of questions referred to the Court of Justice by the Dutch courts concerned social security schemes. The first case that came to the Court of Justice was *Liefting*.[99] It concerned the question whether certain social security contributions paid by public authorities on behalf of civil servants and included in the calculation of the gross salary of the latter should be considered as pay within the meaning of Article 119. The Court of Justice, focusing on the peculiarities of the Dutch scheme at issue, held that:

a social security scheme under which:

1. the contributions are calculated on the basis of the employee's salary but may not exceed a certain limit,

2. a husband and wife are treated as one person, the contributions being calculated on the basis of their combined salaries, subject once again to the upper limit,

3. the state is bound to pay on behalf of its employee the contributions owed by him, and

4. where husband and wife are both civil servants, the authority employing the husband is primarily responsible for paying the contributions and the authority employing the wife is required to pay the contributions only in so far as the upper limit is not reached by the contributions paid on behalf of the husband, is compatible with the principle laid down in article 119 of the EEC Treaty that men and women should receive equal pay for equal work, in so far as the resultant differences between the gross salary of a female civil servant whose husband is also a civil servant directly affect the calculation of other benefits dependent on salary, such as severance pay, unemployment benefit, family allowances and loan facilities.[100]

The case was returned to the Centrale Raad van Beroep (court of last instance in social security matters) in September 1984. However, it took nearly another two years before this Court decided the case. In a number of judgements delivered in June 1986[101] the Centrale Raad declared null and void the initial refusal of the public authorities employing a number of applicants to pay the AOW/AWW contribution on their behalf to the collector of direct taxes. The whole case had started by a request by Ms Liefting asking the employing authorities to pay the contributions. Under the 'old system'[102] these contributions would have been returned by the tax authorities to the civil servant concerned, in so far as they exceeded the maximum limit for contributions due for a married couple who were both civil servants. However, under the new legislation,[103] attacked in fact in the Liefting case, the employing authorities should no longer contribute for female civil servants when it appeared that the maximum contribution had been already paid by another employing authority on behalf of the civil servant's husband.

The reasoning of the Centrale Raad van Beroep was quite simple: it established that the differences between the gross salary of a female civil servant married to another civil servant and the gross salary of a male civil servant may directly determine the allowance on the calculation of benefits provided for under the Algemene Arbeidsongeschiktheidswet

(General Law on Incapacity for Work) and, since 1983, also for the calculation of benefits payable under the Wet Werkloosheidsvoorziening (Law on Unemployment Benefit). Thus, reasoned the Centrale Raad, the differences between the gross salaries do affect the calculation of other benefits; therefore the new legislation is incompatible with Article 119 of the Treaty and, consequently, individual decisions based on this legislation must be declared null and void.

The judgement of the Centrale Raad van Beroep caused considerable confusion, especially on the side of employing public authorities who faced thousands of requests from female civil servants to pay the AOW/AWW contributions to the tax collector. On 22 August 1986, the Minister of the Interior sent a circular to all the employing authorities, stressing that they could not be obliged to comply with such requests, since the judgement of the Centrale Raad was binding only for the nine cases decided. He added that he found it even undesirable. In other terms, he asked the authorities to refuse. However, soon it appeared that something must be done: several new proceedings before the courts were expected, in the Parliament questions had been posed concerning the issue and the civil servants' unions insisted on a general solution. Finally, in December 1986, the unions and the Minister reached an agreement: a limited number of test cases will be brought before the courts; the judgements rendered will be accepted as decisive for the claims introduced and only those introduced before 15 of January 1987 may be possibly honoured; requests presented at a later date will be rejected.[104] Both this agreement and the cases brought in the courts subsequently upon the judgement of the Centrale Raad van Beroep raised several problems.

Some employing authorities refused, for instance, to decide upon the requests presented by female civil servants to either pay the AOW/AWW contribution directly to them or to pay the contributions to the tax collector. The employer found that they could not take a decision as long as the test cases were pending. The Civil Service Tribunals in the Hague and in Utrecht came, when dealing with this issue, to contradictory judgements.[105] The Hague Tribunal found that the employer was obliged to take *a* (positive or negative) decision: the interest of the applicant, the civil servant, to handle independently from others her own affairs and to bring, where necessary, her case before the courts is much more important than the interest the employer may have in awaiting the results of the test cases. The Tribunal in Utrecht decided, on the contrary, that the refusal of the employer could be considered as reasonable because a decision would thwart the agreement between the Minister and the civil servants' unions.

Another problem was the *de facto* deadline of 15 January 1987. In this respect the President of the Civil Service Tribunal in Groningen[106] considered that under Dutch law a civil servant may at any time request his or her employer to reconsider a decision, even when the latter became final, i.e. could not be challenged in a court. The President found that the date of 15 January 1987 agreed upon by the Minister and the unions was irrelevant to the case before him and, more generally that such an agreement was no obstacle to introducing new requests which must be dealt with by the employing authority. Then he declared null and void the employer's refusal to examine the appellant's request on the ground that it was introduced too late.

Two other judgements[107] illustrate a problem which is in a sense more fundamental. As already mentioned, a civil servant may at any time ask his or her employer to reconsider a former decision. The employing authority has discretionary power to do so and to decide otherwise. The new decision may be reviewed by a court, though only 'marginally', i.e. the court will examine whether the employing authority, given its discretionary power, could reasonably arrive at the decision. Often this review consists of an arbitrariness test. In the two cases under discussion, both applicants requested their employers to reconsider former decisions in the light of the judgement of the Centrale Raad van Beroep. For one applicant the request concerned the implicit decision of the employer no longer to pay any AOW/AWW contributions to the tax collector on her behalf. The second case was more complicated: in March 1980 the employer refused to pay the AOW/AWW contributions on her behalf as the applicant requested. She brought a claim against this refusal before a Civil Service Tribunal, but her claim was dismissed, in particular because at that time the Centrale Raad van Beroep found that the applicable legislation was not incompatible with Article 119 of the EEC Treaty.[108] After the new judgement of the Centrale Raad in *Liefting*, the applicant again requested her employer to pay the AOW/AWW contributions to the tax collector. In May 1987 the employer refused to do so. However, both cases were dismissed. In the first case, the Civil Service Tribunal in The Hague remembered the case-law of the Court of Justice according to which:

> In the present state of Community law there is nothing to prevent a citizen who contests before a national court a decision of a national authority on the ground that it is incompatible with Community law from being confronted with the defence that limitation periods laid down by national law have expired, it being understood that the procedural conditions governing the action may not be less favourable than those relating to the similar actions of a domestic nature.[109]

The Tribunal deduced from this case-law that there exists no obligation under Community law as it stands now for the employing authorities to reconsider a former decision that became final. Moreover, there existed no such obligation under national law either. Finally, the Tribunal found that, having regard to all the interests concerned, the employer could reasonably come to the contested decision, i.e. the refusal to pay the AOW/AWW contributions to the tax collector on the applicant's behalf or, instead, to pay her damages.

In the second case, the Civil Service Tribunal in Den Bosch reached the same result but on slightly different grounds. It considered that the judgement of the Centrale Raad of 24 June 1986 implies an apparent derogation from its former case-law. However, such a derogation cannot result in an administrative body being obliged to reconsider its former decisions. Seen in the light of the gradual development of legal conceptions, the decision taken by the employer in the past cannot be considered as obviously erroneous. Consequently, the Tribunal found that the decision challenged in the case before it may also be said to be taken reasonably.

These judgements are illustrative of, in a sense, a paradoxical situation: a Member State introduces legislation that is equivocal from the Community law point of view, but it is sanctioned by the highest Court competent in the field concerned, which refuses to refer a case concerning the above-mentioned legislation to the Court of Justice. Five years later, just *because* this same Court did ask some preliminary questions, it decides more or less the opposite. The Minister anxious to limit the financial consequences for the state (or to structure the procedural chaos?) agrees with trade unions on a number of test cases that will be decisive for all other claims, and on a deadline before which all the claims must be brought. It may be clear that such an agreement may be useful to keep the litigation within certain limits, but it can never be an argument to refuse to examine a request of an applicant or to refuse to decide upon such a request: the national authorities may not adopt any rule which reduces or makes impossible for the individual concerned to bring proceedings when his or her rights derived from Community law are at stake.[110]

However, even if one ignores the agreement, what happened? Generally speaking there are three categories of women concerned:

- those who just accepted the new legislation,
- those who submitted a request to the employer but who resigned themselves to the refusal,
- those who brought their case in a court but lost it.

In all the three situations the decisions became final (under the Dutch law on the Civil Service, the time limit for an action before the courts is 30 days) and consequently they may only ask for reconsideration. Here the employing authority concerned enjoys large discretionary powers and the judge will review the decision marginally, i.e. on its 'reasonableness'. As long as the courts find that, given the interests concerned and the former case-law of the Centrale Raad, the employees may reasonably refuse to comply with the requests, the judgement of the Court of Justice in *Liefting* does not receive its due. It may also be clear that this problem is a more general one: the sanctioning of negligence of the Member States to comply with their EEC obligations. The principle of legal certainty, which is after all the rationale behind time limits, turns out unfavourably for the individuals concerned.

However, this is not yet the end of the Liefting story. Other civil servants started proceedings before the Kantonrechter (cantonal judge; the first instance court dealing with labour law conflicts), in order to obtain supplements to their gross salary which was lower due to the contested legislation.[111] The approach of the civil courts was different from that of the administrative courts.

The former focused much more on the judgement of the Court of Justice and especially on the question whether the person concerned suffered some concrete damage due to the differences in gross salary. The Kantonrechter in the Hague,[112] for instance, found that in the case before him the applicant's lower rate of gross salary did not affect the calculation of other benefits and could not do so in the future either. The applicant brought her case one year after the abolition of the contested legislation and it appeared that in the past she did not apply for an AAW or WWV benefit. Further, according to the Kantonrechter, the fact that the applicant no longer received the contributions from the tax authorities, after the introduction of the new legislation, was not relevant because the loss of this advantage as such was not discriminatory: men did not get it either. Therefore the Kantonrechter found against the applicant.

The Rechtbank Utrecht (District Court), dealing with a case in appeal, followed a similar approach.[113] According to this court, the termination of the reimbursement of the superfluous AOW/AWW contributions did not place, under any circumstances, a female civil servant in a worse position than that of a male civil servant. Nevertheless, in some cases, the legislation at issue has as its effect that a female civil servant might be put at a disadvantage, in particular when she applies for certain social security benefits which are calculated on the basis of the lower gross salary level. In the case before the Rechtbank it did not however appear that the applicant suffered a concrete loss due to the legislation concerned and the Rechtbank therefore dismissed the case.

These two judgements are apparently based on a slightly different interpretation of *Liefting* than the one of the Centrale Raad van Beroep. The latter was satisfied with the fact that the differences in gross salary *may* affect the calculation of benefits and that the conditions laid down by the Court of Justice for the applicability of Article 119 were therefore met. The civil courts required, however, that the applicants suffered (or will in all probability suffer) a concrete loss. There is some force in this reasoning.[114] The Court of Justice held that the amounts which the public authorities are obliged to pay in respect of contributions owed to the social security scheme by persons working for the state and which are included in the calculation of the gross salary payable to civil servants must be regarded as pay within the meaning of Article 119 in so far as they directly determine the calculation of other advantages linked to the salary. Further, the Court considered that:

> The principle that men and women should receive equal pay for equal work, as laid down in Article 119, has not therefore been complied with in so far as those other advantages linked to the salary and determined by the gross salary are not the same for male civil servants and for female civil servants whose husbands are also civil servants.[115]

These considerations suggest that what counts is rather the inequality in the 'advantages' than in the gross salary. The limitation of the applicability of Article 119 to gross salary only in cases where this latter affects other advantages must have some specific meaning. After all, it was also possible for the Court to decide that Article 119 applies to gross salary just like that. Therefore it may be argued that only when it happens that a female civil servant, in a concrete case, is put at a disadvantage with respect to some benefits or other advantages, Article 119 should apply.[116] However this may be, it seems that the dispute is far from being settled since several judgements have been appealed and are pending before the Centrale Raad van Beroep. Ironically, the legislation concerned has been abolished.[117] Since 1 January 1985 men and women are bound to pay contributions only on their own behalf. Moreover, since 1 June 1985 the civil servants pay the contributions themselves.

Much less problematical was the national follow-up in *Beets-Proper*.[118] In this case the Court of Justice held that it was contrary to the Equal Treatment Directive to dismiss a female employee at the age of 60 when men were dismissed at the age of 65. The fact that under the employer's pension scheme women became entitled to a retirement pension at 60 and men at 65 was irrelevant. More in particular, the Court held, in order to answer the question of the Hoge Raad (Dutch Supreme Court):

> Article 5(1) of Directive n° 76/207 must be interpreted as meaning that it does not allow the Member States the freedom to exempt from the application of the principle of equality of treatment an express or implied condition in a contract of employment concluded on the basis of a collective wage agreement, if that condition has the effect of terminating the contract of employment on the ground of the age attained by the employee and the relevant age is determined by the age – which is different for men and women – at which the employee becomes entitled to a retirement pension.[119]

For a better understanding of the national judgement, it is worthwhile to remember briefly the facts of the case. The relationship between Ms Beets-Proper and the bank was governed by the collective labour agreement for the banking sector for the years 1980 and 1981 and the pension scheme of the bank's pension fund. Article 3 of that scheme provided that the persons affiliated to it were entitled to an old age pension 'from the date of retirement'. That date was defined in Article 1 as 'the first day of the month following the month in which a person affiliated to the scheme attains the age of 65 in the case of a man and 60 in the case of a woman'. When Ms Beets-Proper reached the aged of 60 in August 1982, the bank took the view that the employment relationship automatically ended on 1 September 1982 by virtue of an implied condition to that effect in the contract of employment, without the need for any notice of dismissal. In the subsequent national proceedings Ms Beets-Proper submitted that her employment was not terminated in a legally valid manner. She relied in this respect on Article 1637ij of the Dutch Civil Code. The first two paragraphs of this Article read as follows:

> As regards the conclusion of a contract of employment, staff training, the terms of employment, promotion and the termination of the contract of employment, an employer may not make any distinction between men and women, either directly or indirectly, for example by reference to marital status or family circumstances. The terms of employment do not include benefits or entitlements under pension schemes. The first sentence of this paragraph shall not apply in those cases in which an employee's sex is a decisive factor.
> Any clause which is contrary to the first sentence of paragraph 1 shall be void.

The Rechtbank Amsterdam (District Court) dismissed Ms Beets-Proper's application and this judgement has been confirmed by the Gerechtshof Amsterdam (Regional Court of Appeal). The Gerechtshof found that the exception referred to in the second sentence of paragraph 1 of Article 1637ij was applicable. In particular, it based its judgement on the existence of a 'close connexion between the termination of the contract of employment and the commencement of the pension' and on the fact that the bank's female employees, who retire at the age of 60, acquired pension rights, on a non-contributory basis, at a rate of 2 per cent of the basic salary for each year of service, whereas male employees, whose retirement age is fixed at 65, acquired such rights at the rate of 1.75 per cent. Thus, the Hoge Raad had to decide whether the derogation of the second sentence of Article 1637ij, paragraph 1, was applicable or not.

When the case was returned by the Court of Justice to the Hoge Raad, the latter considered[120] that Article 1637ij of the Civil Code, which implements the Equal Treatment Directive, must be construed in such a manner that a condition in a contract of employment which makes this contract terminate on the date when the employee attains pensionable age, is covered by the first sentence of the first paragraph, which prohibits different treatment of men and women. The condition does not fall within the scope of the second sentence. Consequently, the disputed condition is, by virtue of the second paragraph of Article 1637ij, null and void. Further, the Hoge Raad considered the consequences of the invalidity of the condition. It found that, in order to fill the legal vacuum, the rules applied to male employees must also be applied to women, unless the parties decide otherwise, which probably means that women may still retire at 60, if they want to. According to the Hoge Raad, it would not be fair to require male employees to retire at the age provided for female employees since first when they have reached the age of 65 they are entitled to a retirement pension. Then it referred the case to the Gerechtshof in The Hague for final settlement, concerning, in particular, wage arrears Ms Beets-Proper should receive from the bank, while taking into account that she was also entitled to a retirement pension from the bank's fund. The Hoge Raad added that the pension rights of Ms Beets-Proper were in no sense affected by the invalidity of the contested condition which, after all, concerned only dismissal.

In *Teuling*[121] the breadwinner's increases to AAW benefits (benefits paid under the General Law on Incapacity for Work) were under discussion. The Court of Justice considered in this respect that, to put it shortly, the increases were indirectly discriminatory since many more men qualified for them than women, unless the increases could be justified. The Court found that the supplements may be justified if they guarantee a minimum level of subsistence. However, the national court must find out whether the breadwinner's increases at issue correspond with the expenditure incurred by a dependent family, serve to ensure an adequate minimum subsistence income for the breadwinner and are also necessary for that purpose.

The Raad van Beroep in Amsterdam (Social Security Court) gave a fairly surprising judgement in favour of Ms Teuling.[122] In the first place the Court considered the assumption by the Court of Justice, based on information of the Dutch government, that the AAW provides a minimum subsistence income to persons with no income from or in relation with work, is an incorrect one. The AAW provides for benefits at the level of minimum subsistence. However, it was possible, within the period relevant for the dispute, that a person entitled under the AAW also received a WAO benefit (Wet op de Arbeidsongeschiktheidverzekering – Law on Insurance against Incapacity for Work). Another example is that of a partially incapacitated person who is still employed and who receives only a certain percentage of the AAW benefit. Thus the AAW does not function in all cases as a guarantee for a minimum subsistence level.

Then the Raad van Beroep turned to the specific problem of breadwinner increases. It assumed first that, according to the Court of Justice, the existence of a very small income should not be an obstacle to the allowance of an increase up to the social minimum. However, under the AAW system, several types of income either of the beneficiary or his or her spouse are left outside the consideration for the assessment of whether the person concerned should receive increases or not. For instance, if the beneficiary enjoys a WAO benefit, or allowances paid under a private health and accident insurance, or certain benefits under the Health Insurance Act, or an invalidity pension by virtue of any other scheme, this 'income' has no consequences for the breadwinner's increases. Therefore, the Raad van Beroep had serious doubts as to the necessity of the AAW increases in order to guarantee a minimum level of subsistence. Moreover, these doubts were further strengthened by the fact that the appropriate law to provide for the minimum level of subsistence is the Algemene Bijstandswet (General Law on Social Assistance) which is the general system to preserve people from destitution. Furthermore, the Raad van Beroep also doubted whether the increases in the AAW are appropriate to reach the objective, since under certain circumstances a beneficiary with dependent family will get an AAW allowance which is under the social minimum level.

Thus, it being established that the AAW increases do not seem to be appropriate and necessary to achieve the objective of guaranteeing a minimum subsistence, the Raad van Beroep continued by considering that the justification functions as an exception to the principle of equal treatment and, consequently, must be interpreted strictly. Further, according to Community law, the author of the allegedly discriminatory measure must prove that the measure pursues an objective which has nothing to do with sex-based discrimination whatsoever. In this respect, according to the Raad van Beroep, it was important to note that the legislator, by the law of 29 December 1982, had abolished a system which was perfectly compatible with the principle of equal treatment and had replaced this system by a new one which in its effects gives rise to a presumption of discrimination.

In the light of all those considerations, the Raad van Beroep found that the breadwinner's increases system of the AAW and the law of 29 December 1982 are incompatible with the Third Directive and it declared null and void the decision that reduced Ms Teuling's benefit from 100 per cent to 70 per cent of the statutory minimum wage.

This judgement is interesting from at least two points of view. In the first place, it shows how important the role of the national judge may be when he or she applies the criteria developed by the Court of Justice to assess whether a *prima facie* discriminatory treatment is justified. Probably due to a misunderstanding before the Court of Justice as to the character of the AAW, the preliminary ruling in *Teuling* did not seem very promising for the applicant. However, the Raad van Beroep discharged the task appointed to it by the Court of Justice in a very careful manner, fully within the spirit of the fundamental principle of equal treatment of men and women.

In the second place, the judgement may have far-reaching implications. If the Centrale Raad van Beroep, which deals with the case in appeal, confirms this judgement, the Dutch social security legislation has to be reviewed on several points. As has already been said, the Dutch government intended to transpose the Social Security Directive into national law together with a wide-ranging reform of the social security system and thus make its implementation a part of the operation.[123] One of the results of the reform is that the system of breadwinner increases became more important. Some newly introduced social security schemes and a number of already existing but by now amended schemes follow basically the same pattern as the one at issue in *Teuling*:[124] minimum level of benefit for a single person may be supplemented when the beneficiary has dependent spouse and children, while certain forms of income of the persons concerned or his or her spouse are not taken into account when assessing the entitlement to the increases. Consequently, it may happen that a person will receive a supplement which is said to function as a guarantee for a minimum subsistence level, while the beneficiary or his or her spouse enjoys, beside the benefit, another form of income. On the one hand, it may be clear that under such circumstances the increase can hardly be considered as necessary. On the other hand, differences exist between the social security schemes on this point. A general conclusion that *all* the increases cannot be objectively justified will be too hasty.[125] For the moment it is unclear what income of the beneficiary or his or her spouse does not jeopardize, according to the Court of Justice, the entitlement to increases. In *Teuling* the Court accepted only a *very small income of the spouse*, which may be a helpful indication for other cases concerning the question under what circumstances a breadwinner increase can be considered as necessary for the maintenance of minimum level of subsistence.[126]

The *FNV* and *Dik*[127] cases are two highlights in a long and sad story concerning the adaptation of the Dutch Wet Werkloosheidsvoorziening (Law on Unemployment Benefit, the so-called WWV) to the equal treatment standards of the Third Directive. As this story is illustrative of the unwillingness and the short-sighted approach of, in particular, the Dutch government that accompanied the implementation of equal treatment in social security, it seems appropriate to discuss the national follow-up of the two above-mentioned judgements within a wider framework.

On very rough lines, the Dutch legislation on unemployment benefits was, before 1987,[128] the following: the Werkloosheidswet (Law on Unemployment) provided for benefits, based on the level of the last pay received, during the six months following the commencement of unemployment. After that period of six months, the WWV usually took over.[129] Under this law the worker was entitled to receive a benefit for the two next years and the benefit was also based on the last pay received. Finally, there was the Algemene Bijstandswet (General Law on Assistance) under which unemployed persons not entitled to benefit under the first two laws any more received social assistance benefits. The amount of the latter was determined solely by the needs of the worker's family unit.

Article 13, paragraph 1 of the WWV provided that

The following shall be excluded from the right to benefit: workers...who, having the status of married women, may not be described wage-earners under the rules adopted by the competent minister after consulting the central commission, and who do not live permanently separated from their husbands...

This wage-earner[130] requirement applied to women only and, actually, it has never been disputed that this provision was discriminatory. Some cases were brought on this issue in the courts before the expiry date for the implementation of the Third Directive, but without success.[131]

Initially, the Dutch government intended to abolish the wage-earner requirement within the framework of an extensive reform of the social security system. However, it appeared impossible to implement the reform in the six-year period prescribed by the Directive. A provisional solution was needed. In this respect, the government submitted a draft of a law to Parliament which extended the wage-earner requirement to cover men. The government probably did not realize that this so-called sex-neutral solution would give rise to indirect discrimination. However this may be, the Second Chamber of the States General rejected the draft on 13 December 1984. Five days later, the State Secretary for Social Affairs and Employment informed the President of the Second Chamber that the government intended to draw up a new bill with retroactive effect to 23 December 1984 in order to implement the Third Directive. Parliament was urged to approve the bill by 1 March 1985. Furthermore, the State Secretary notified the competent (i.e. local) authorities, by circular of 21 December 1984, that the wage-earner provision of the WWV had to continue to be applied pending the retroactive amending law. It was under these circumstances that the FNV summoned the state in interlocutory proceedings, seeking an order requiring the state to suspend, or at least not to give effect until the new bill entered into force, to the wage-earner rule of the WWV. The Gerechtshof (Regional Court of Appeal) of The Hague, dealing with the case in appeal, suspended the proceedings and, by order of 13 March 1985, it referred to the Court of Justice three questions. While the case was pending in Luxembourg, by a law of 24 April 1985, the wage-earner provision was repealed with retroactive effect from 23 December 1984. The law entered into force on 1 May 1985. However, Article II of this law contained a transitional provision according to which the abolition of the wage-earner requirement was not to apply to workers whose unemployment commenced before 23 December 1984 unless he or she was in receipt at that date of a benefit under the WWV.

When the Court of Justice held that Article 4, paragraph 1 of the Third Directive has direct effect and that, in the absence of measures implementing that Article, women are entitled to be treated in the same manner, and to have the same rules applied to them, as men who are in the same situation, it did so with respect to the period between 23 December 1984 and 1 May 1985 since that situation, no implementation at all, was the object of the proceedings brought by the FNV. However, with respect to the new legislation the Court observed that differences based on the status of wage-earner continue to affect the entitlement to benefit of unemployed persons whose unemployment commenced before 23 December 1984.

When the *FNV* case came back to the Gerechtshof Den Haag (Regional Court of Appeal) there was more or less nothing left to be decided:[132] the state and the FNV agreed that the Law of 24 April 1985 brought about what the FNV was initially seeking, and thus the only matter to be decided were the costs of the procedure. In this respect the Gerechtshof had to verify in favour of which party it would have probably found on the merits. The Gerechtshof considered that from the judgement of the Court of Justice it followed that Article 13, paragraph 1, point one, could no longer be applied from 23 December 1984. In the light of the uncertainty, existing at the time when the proceedings were brought, about the moment the WWV would be amended in order to comply with the Directive, the FNV had an urgent interest in bringing the case. Moreover, according to the Gerechtshof, the state could easily conform itself to the requirements of the Directive by issuing a circular asking the competent authorities not to apply the wage-earner provision any more. For those reasons, the Gerechtshof condemned the state in the costs, at least as far as the counter-proceedings of the FNV was concerned. With respect to the appeal brought by the state against the decision in favour of the FNV of the President of the Arrondissementsrechtbank (District Court), the Gerechtshof found that both parties failed partly in their arguments and it compensated the costs.[133]

In the meantime, the law of 24 April 1985 became the new WWV issue, especially the transitional provision, Article II, which extended the discriminatory wage-earner provision beyond 23 December 1984. Cases challenging this provision had been brought in the courts and they have been decided with varying degrees of success for the claimants.

In June 1986, that is before the judgement of the Court of Justice in *FNV*, the President of the Raad van Beroep (Social Security Court) in Den Bosch found that the disputed Article II cannot have for effect that the wage-earner provision abolished as from 23 December 1984 should be maintained for a certain category of persons.[134] In order to come to this decision, the President followed rather curious reasoning based mainly on the interpretation of the law of 24 April 1985. Nevertheless, he also considered that the interpretation is in conformity with the Third Directive. In particular, it would be incompatible with the latter to reintroduce, after the implementation deadline, discriminatory provisions.

The State Secretary who – indeed – disagreed with this judgement wrote a letter to the local authorities explaining that he considered the law of

24 April 1985, Article II included, to be a correct implementation of the Directive. The judgement of the President being appealed, he asked the local authorities to continue to apply the wage-earner provision in those cases where the woman concerned became unemployed before 23 December 1984 and was at that date not in receipt of a WW benefit.[135]

The Court's judgement in *FNV* was of no avail, in spite of the clear hint stating that 'differences based on the status of wage-earner continue to affect the entitlement to benefit of unemployed persons whose unemployment commenced before 23 December 1984'.[136] The State Secretary held his own interpretation of the FNV judgement. In Parliament he explained[137] that the Court's judgement concerns only a situation where the Directive is not yet implemented. The Court says clearly that in the absence of measures implementing Article 4 of the Directive women are entitled to be treated in the same manner as men who are in the same situation, since the rules applicable to men remain the only valid point of reference where the Directive has not been implemented. However, in the meantime the Directive had been transposed into national law by the law of 24 April 1985. Consequently, it was this law that governed the demands for WWV benefits. The State Secretary did not see any reason to change the law in consequence of the FNV judgement. He found that the Court of Justice leaves the legislator the discretion as to the way the latter wants to implement the principle of equal treatment in social security.

Apparently, the State Secretary confused again[138] the issue of direct effect with that of the discretion available to Member States under Article 189 of the Treaty in transposing directives into national law. He did not, or rather did not want to, understand that the discretion under Article 189 is no licence to implement the Directive incorrectly and that, at least from Community law point of view there is no real difference between non-implementation and an incorrect implementation.

Be this as it may, the litigation in the courts went on. The Raad van Beroep in Den Bosch confirmed in two judgements the interpretation of the law of 24 April 1985 given by its President.[139] Moreover, the Raad was found to be confirmed in its views by the judgement in *FNV*. The Raad van Beroep in Rotterdam also refused to apply Article II, but it based the decision directly on the FNV judgement.[140] In particular, the Raad considered that, according to the Court, Article 4, paragraph 1 of the Directive does not confer on Member States the power to make conditional or to limit the application of the principle of equal treatment. Since Article II still continued unequal treatment of a certain category of women after 23 December 1984, the provision being thus incompatible with Article 4, paragraph 1 of the Directive, cannot be applied. A similar approach has been also followed by the Raad van Beroep in Groningen.[141] On the other hand, the Centrale Raad van Beroep continued to apply the disputed provision and the Raad van Beroep in Amsterdam did not find untenable the argument that the Directive concerns only situations of unemployment commenced after 23 December 1984.[142] Finally, it was *Dik*[143] that cleared the air.

In *Dik* the Court of Justice found, to put it shortly, that, when the Directive has not been implemented correctly, by virtue of its Article 4 women are entitled to be treated in the same way as men. In the case of the claimants it meant that if a man who had lost his employment before 23 December 1984 was entitled after that date to the benefit under the WWV, a woman who is in the same position is also entitled to that benefit without having to satisfy the wage-earner condition. Thus the transitional provision extending the discriminatory condition beyond 23 December 1984 was incompatible with the Directive. Moreover, the Court held that when a Member State adopts measures with retroactive effect in order to comply with the Directive, it must observe the rights which individuals had acquired under Article 4 of the Directive after the expiry of the period provided for implementation.

On 5 May 1988, the State Secretary issued a circular dealing with the consequences he intended to tag on to the Court's judgement[144] The circular was later completed by a letter of 27 June 1988.[145] In outline the contents were the following: the Court of Justice judgement concerns married women who would be entitled on 23 December 1984 to WWV benefits if the wage-earner provision did not exist. Where the period provided by the WWV would have – theoretically – expired before 23 December 1984, Community law obviously does not apply to such a situation. Consequently, only those married women may be eligible for a WWV benefit whose unemployment commenced on 23 June 1982, or later, assuming that they would then qualify for a six-month WW benefit first and, subsequently, for two years' WWV benefit. In situations where a woman would not qualify for a WW benefit but only for a WWV benefit, the category concerned are those women who lost their employment on 23 December 1982 or on a later date. It follows that married women who until 23 December 1984 were debarred from entitlement under the WWV by virtue of the wage-earner provision, may nevertheless be entitled to benefit under the WWV for the period for which they would still have been entitled after 23 December 1984 if the wage-earner provision had never existed and they would have applied for a WWV benefit immediately after the termination of the WW benefit or the commencement of unemployment. When assessing the individual applications for benefit under the WWV, the competent authorities must, as strictly as possible, hold to the remaining conditions applicable, for example that the person concerned did not, in the meantime, accept employment but remained available for the labour market during the unemployment and was registered with the Regional Labour Exchange.[146]

Furthermore, the State Secretary rendered inoperative Article 18 of the WWV according to which, in principle, the benefit begins to run from the date of the application, unless there are reasons to make it run from an earlier date. The State Secretary decided, namely, that the day from which the *remaining* benefit will run, is 23 December 1984.

Finally, the State Secretary warned the competent (local) authorities that any allowance of WWV benefit which goes further than the circular prescribes will not be refunded by the state.[147]

This solution to the problems concerning the WWV transitional provision can hardly be considered in conformity with Court's judgement in *Dik*. The State Secretary makes the assumption that the women concerned applied for a WWV benefit immediately after the termination of the WW benefit or after the commencement of unemployment. Then he starts counting days and only in those cases in which a woman would be still entitled to benefits at 23 December 1984 is he prepared to pay the remaining benefit, which may vary from one day to two years. Moreover, every case where a married woman became unemployed before 23 June 1982 is automatically excluded. However, under the WWV there was no time limit for the application for WWV benefit, nor did the right to the benefit expire, nor was it barred by prescription. It was very well possible that a – male – person had for whatever reason postponed his application for WWV benefit until a later date than the termination of his WW benefit or the commencement of unemployment. In this respect it is exactly the above-mentioned Article 18 of the WWV that leaves the competent authorities a margin of appreciation as to the commencing date of the benefit when the application has been made in respect of unemployment beginning in the relatively distant past. Consequently, when the State Secretary will prescribe that a category of women (unemployed before 23 June 1982) is not entitled at all to WWV benefit and another category will only receive the *remaining* benefit, he violates Community law. The Court of Justice held in *Dik* that when a Member State adopts retroactive measures, it must observe the rights which individuals had acquired under Article 4 of the Third Directive after the expiry of the period provided for implementation. The rights acquired by Dutch married women in the period 23 December 1984-1 May 1985 were to be treated in the same manner as men, i.e. when it was possible for men to apply and qualify for a WWV benefit after 23 December 1984 when they became unemployed or lost their WW-benefit before that date, the same must be possible for women. This right may not be limited retroactively by legislation or circulars. Moreover, if Article 18 was applicable to a man's case, it cannot be set aside in the case of a married woman.

The judgement of the Raad van Beroep Arnhem[148] in *Dik* of 20 July 1988 may then only be applauded. The Raad considered that, according to the case-law of the Centrale Raad van Beroep, the claims for WWV benefit have to be considered in principle in the light of the legal provisions applicable at the date on which unemployment began. The claimant's unemployment commenced before 23 December 1984, thus at a time when the disputed wage-earner provision was not yet prohibited by Community law. However, according to the Raad van Beroep, this circumstance did not necessarily mean that the wage-earner provision may affect the position of the claimant after 23 December 1984. It followed from the case-law of the Court of Justice, and in particular from the judgement in *Dik*, that a married woman who was unemployed on 23 December 1984 is entitled to a WWV benefit irrespective of the date on which her unemployment has commenced. The Raad van Beroep stressed in this respect that under the WWV an application can be made at a much later date than the beginning of unemployment. Further, the postponement of the application cannot lead to a limitation of the statutory determined maximum period of the benefit. Then the Raad considered that a married man will in principle see his postponed or renewed application accepted, when new facts and circumstances occur, and will receive benefits from the date of application and for the full statutory period of two years. The Raad found that in the case before it the expiration of the implementation deadline is to be considered as a new circumstance in the above-mentioned sense. Consequently, the Raad held that the claimant was entitled from 23 December 1984 to a WWV benefit for a period of two years and added that the view of the State Secretary must be considered as an incorrect one.[149]

Despite its obvious shortcomings the Dutch cabinet transformed the State Secretary's circular into a bill and sent it for consideration to certain advisory bodies.[150] In the meantime, by a letter of 3 November 1988, the Commission informed the Dutch government that by failing to adopt, with respect to the WWV, the measures necessary to secure the full implementation of the Third Directive and, in particular, of the Court's judgement in *Dik*, the Dutch government did not fulfil its obligations under the Treaty. However, it seems that Commission's letter concerns only the fact that there is no new legislation and not the contents of the circular or the bill.[151]

It will be clear from the foregoing that, in particular, the Third Directive gave rise to very lively litigation in the Dutch courts. However, it was not only the Directive. It is worth mentioning here, though very briefly, another (parallel) development in the field of equal treatment in social security.

According to Article 94 of the Dutch Basic Law, provisions of international law may have direct effect within the national legal order, just like Community law. If the national judge finds that a provision of international law is directly effective, then this provision will render inapplicable any national law or provision thereof that is incompatible with the international provision concerned. Early in the 1980s a number of actions were started in Dutch social security courts, where the claimants submitted that the wage-earner provision of the WWV, thus the one also at issue in *FNV*, was incompatible with certain provisions of international law, in particular, Article 26 of the International Covenant on Civil and Political Rights.[152] This Article provides

All persons are equal before the law and are entitled without any discrimination to the equal protection of the law. In this respect, the law shall prohibit any discrimination and guarantee to all persons equal and effective protection against discrimination on any ground such as race, colour, sex, language, religion, political or other opinion, national or social origin, property, birth or other status.

Initially, the actions were not successful. In November 1983, the Centrale Raad van Beroep[153] found that Article 26 has no direct effect in the field of social security, mainly because social security is covered by the International Covenant on Economic, Social and Cultural Rights.[154] The objectives of this Covenant can only be realized in gradual stages by appropriate legislation and other implementing measures. According to the Centrale Raad this was also more or less the approach of the Community legislation which gave the Member States a period of six years for the implementation of the Third Directive.

One of the claimants, Ms Broeks, did not reconcile herself to the judgement and submitted a complaint against the State of Netherlands with the Human Rights Committee.[155] The Committee gave its decision on 9 April 1987. It found that due to the wage-earner provision Ms Broeks was a victim of a violation, based on sex, of Article 26 of the International Convenant on Civil and Political Rights, because she was denied a social security benefit on an equal footing with men, and that the state should offer Ms Broeks an appropriate remedy.[156] Although this decision as such could not directly influence the question of the direct effect of Article 26 within the Dutch legal order as that is a matter of constitutional law,[157] it is clear that the decision is of considerable importance and it had probably contributed to a change of view of the Dutch courts as far as the direct effect of Article 26 is concerned.

On 14 May 1984 the Centrale Raad van Beroep gave a judgement concerning the entitlement to a special pension provided for victims from World War II by the Wet Uitkering Vervolgingsslachtoffers (Law on the Benefit for Victims of Persecution, the WUV),[158] This law contained a wage-earner provision that had to be complied with by married women. The Centrale Raad van Beroep found that this provision was incompatible with Article 26 of the Covenant on Civil and Political Rights and that this Article had direct effect in the Dutch legal order as from 23 December 1984. The Centrale Raad thus linked the direct effect of Article 26 to the implementation deadline of the Third Directive. Theoretically, this is a curious approach. The International Covenant on Civil and Political Rights entered into force for the Netherlands on 11 March 1979; if a provision of this Covenant is capable of having direct effect,[159] then it will do so in principle from 11 March 1979. The approach of the Centrale Raad seems to be a more practical one. As it held in the past, equal treatment in social security can be only realized by a step-by-step process; as appears, in particular, from the Third Directive, the legislator needs some time.

However, at a certain moment the implementation period comes to an end. The Centrale Raad found apparently that this moment was 23 December 1986, *also* with respect of Article 26 of the Covenant.

The next case concerned transitional provisions in the Algemene Arbeidsongeschiktheidswet (General Law on Incapacity for Work, the AAW). As has been already mentioned when discussing *Teuling*,[160] until 1979 married women were not eligible for an AAW benefit. By a law of 20 December 1979, which entered into force on 1 January 1980, the AAW has been drastically changed (with retroactive effect from 1 January 1978). The main objective of the whole operation was to introduce equal treatment into the AAW. However, the transitional provisions of this law of 1979 had for effect that the persons entitled under the 'old' AAW – men and unmarried women – were automatically passed through into the system, while married women had to satisfy the new conditions which were much harder than the old ones. In fact, the transitional provisions resembled very closely those at issue in *Borrie Clarke*:[161] an extension of old discriminatory provisions into the new law that is adopted in order to comply with the principle of equal treatment. On 5 January 1988 the Centrale Raad van Beroep gave a number of judgements[162] in which it held the transitional provisions of the AAW incompatible with Article 26 in that married women must satisfy certain conditions that are not required from married men. Furthermore, the Centrale Raad held that Article 26 of the International Covenant has, in this field, direct effect as from 1 January 1980 since it was apparently the intention of the legislator to realize, from this date, equal treatment of men and women in the AAW.

Other social security courts also accepted the direct effect of Article 26 of the International Covenant, for instance with respect to the wage-earner provision of the WWV,[163] or with respect to widows' benefit.[164] If this line is continued by the Dutch courts it may result in a more encompassing protection of equal rights than the Third Directive provides. Article 26 covers, for instance, not only the working population, it may cover the fields that are excluded under the Third Directive and it may apply from an earlier date than 23 December 1984. On the other hand, it is not clear what the consequences are to be drawn from linking Article 26 and the Third Directive. In a more recent judgement the Centrale Raad van Beroep held, for instance, that Article 26 of the Covenant and the Third Directive are not interdependent, although a synchronization of their application is desirable.[165] Moreover, much will depend on the interpretation by the courts of Article 26. Unlike the Directive, this Article allows justification for both *direct* and *indirect* discrimination.[166]

The reactions by the authorities to these developments are symptomatic of the way the Dutch government deals with equal treatment of men and women in social security. The very first reaction was to denounce the International Covenant, but when it appeared that such an action would not really be of much help, the idea was abolished. Nevertheless,

Ms Broeks was denied an appropriate remedy;[167] the WUV will be changed in such a way that the consequences of the judgement will be minimized[168] and the solution for equal treatment in the AAW seems to be to deprive men and unmarried women of their rights, rather to expand the rights to married women.[169] Moreover, the government still disagrees with the direct effect of Article 26 of the International Covenant in the field of social security. According to the government, this direct effect could, among others, thwart the implementation of the principle of equal treatment within the framework of the EEC![170] More generally, it must be observed that the Dutch legislator has been warned in time and by various professionals or advisory bodies that the legislation in the field of social security is on several points incompatible with, or at least questionable from the point of view of the principle of equal treatment. In spite of that, the government continued its own way and the Parliament, in particular the two government parties, accepted almost everything. The social security claims brought by women within the Dutch courts are the result of the arrogance and incompetence of the government who, in order to save money, continue to treat women as second-rank citizens.[171]

Germany

The judgements of the Court of Justice in *Von Colson and Kamann* and *Harz*[172] gave rise to much speculation in German legal writing.[173] To summarize, the problem was as follows.

Article 611a of the Bürgerliches Gesetzbuch (Civil Code), adopted to implement the Equal Treatment Directive, provides that

1. An employer must not discriminate against a worker on grounds of sex, in connection with an agreement or a measure, in particular in the course of the establishment of an employment relationship...
2. If an employment relationship has not been established because of a breach of the prohibition of discrimination in subparagraph 1 attributable to the employer, he is liable to pay damages in respect of the loss incurred by the worker as a result of his reliance on the expectation that the relationship would not be precluded by such a breach...

According to the Arbeitsgericht (Labour Court) Hamm and Arbeitsgericht Hamburg the only sanction applicable for discrimination in respect of access to employment was the compensation for 'Vertrauensschaden', that is for expenses actually incurred by the employee as a result of his or her other reliance on the fact that he or she would not be refused a post as a result of a breach of the prohibition of discrimination. In practice the damages under Article 611a amounted to indemnification of the costs incurred in relation to the application for a job, like stamps. Soon the provision was named the 'postage-Article'.[174] Further, it was exactly the intention of the legislator to limit the right to compensation of women who have been discriminated against in the course of a job application procedure solely to the amount payable in respect of 'Vertrauensschaden'.[175] Because both courts had doubts as to the compatibility of such minimal compensation with the Equal Treatment Directive, they referred a few questions to the Court of Justice. They wanted to know whether the Directive implied that discrimination must be sanctioned by requiring the employer in question to conclude a contract of employment with the candidate who was discriminated against and, if not, what sanction would then apply.

The Court of Justice replied that a Member State may choose the sanction and that the Directive does not require an employment of the person discriminated against. However, if a Member State opts for reparation of damages as sanction, then the reparation must be effective and must have a deterrent effect; it must stand in adequate relation to the damage suffered, and must go beyond the purely symbolic compensation which the indemnification of job application costs amounts to.

Before the Court, the German government argued that it is possible for German courts to elaborate adequate solutions from the general context of private law. The general provisions of the Civil Code governing compensation were not limited or excluded by Article 611a. These provisions could provide for an effective sanction.

It was in all probability on the basis of this information that the Court of Justice held the national courts under the obligation to interpret, within the limits of their discretion, the national law in conformity with the requirements of Community law.

However, in practice such an interpretation appeared much less simple than the German government suggested. In the literature, several possibilities and impossibilities were reviewed.[176] It has been even suggested that the German explanation of the possible solutions for adequate damages under the Civil Code was a – successful – attempt to prevent the Court of Justice ruling that Article 611a violated the Equal Treatment Directive.[177]

Despite all the alleged or real problems, the Arbeitsgericht Hamm[178] awarded Ms Von Kolson and Ms Kamann compensation amounting to DM 21 000 each, which corresponded with a sum of six gross monthly salaries. The Arbeitsgericht considered first that according to the case-law of the Bundesverfassungsgericht (Federal Constitutional Court) interpretation by the Courts would exceed their judicial function if it contradicts the wording of the provision at issue, the spirit of the measure and the intention of the legislator. According to the intention of the legislator and the general rules of 'systematische Auslegung' (systematic interpretation) Article 611a of the Civil Code had to be interpreted as limiting the right to compensation to the amount payable in respect of 'Vertrauensschaden' and as excluding the application of the general provisions governing compensation. In other words, the Arbeitsgericht would exceed its competence under national law if it interpreted the law in the manner suggested by the German government before the Court of Justice. However, the Arbeitsgericht went on to consider that the interpretation required by the Court of Justice is limited solely by the actual wording of the provision. The systematic and historical interpretation methods do not apply. Seen in this light, the compensation for 'Vertrauensschaden' must then be interpreted as dealing with a specific ground for obtaining compensation without excluding the applications of Article 823 of the Civil Code, the general provision governing compensation. More particularly, the compensation awarded was based on Article 823, paragraph 2 of the Civil Code, which reads as follows:

> The same obligation (i.e. compensation for damages[179]) attaches to a person who infringes a statutory provision intended for the protection of others. If according to the purview of the statute infringement is possible even without fault, the duty to make compensation arises only if some fault can be imputed to the wrongdoer.

The Arbeitsgericht found that Article 611a, paragraph 1 (the prohibition of discrimination) was such a statutory provision intended for the protection of individuals which was, in the case before it, broken by a fault of the employer.

Further, the Court explained how it arrived at the figure of DM 21 000: according to the Law on Protection against Dismissal, an employee may be dismissed during the first six months of employment. It is only after the expiry of six months that the employment contract becomes definitive. The Arbeitsgericht chose this maximum compensation possible because of the serious discrimination of the applicants by the public authority which is, in particular, bound to consider only the candidates' abilities, qualifications and professional capacities.[180]

Finally, the Arbeitsgericht explained why it could not sustain the applicant's claim to be employed: the Court of Justice left the Member States a margin of discretion to choose between the different sanctions suitable for achieving the objective of the Equal Treatment Directive. If a Member State decides to sanction the violation of the equal treatment principle by the award of compensation, thereby expressly excluding the right of engagement, like the German authorities did, this choice lies within its legislative competence and must be respected by the courts.

The Arbeitsgericht Hamburg[181] arrived at the same solution in *Harz*, compensation amounting to a sum of six monthly salaries, though it did so on slightly different grounds. In the first place, the national court considered that it is impossible to construe Article 611a, paragraph 2 of the Civil Code in such a way that the applicant will get other damages than the compensation for 'Vertrauensschaden'. In the case of Ms Harz the damage to be repaired under Article 611a, paragraph 2 would be 1,80 DM for postage, 0,47 DM for the envelope and 0,04 DM for the letter paper. The Arbeitsgericht found that this legal provision was not appropriate to deter the employer from discrimination. As the Court of Justice had already established, Article 611a, paragraph 2 was not in conformity with the Equal Treatment Directive. Consequently, the national court had to decide about the consequences of the violation of the principle of non-discrimination without taking this provision into account. According to the Arbeitsgericht, the right to compensation could be based on Article 823, paragraph 2 of the Civil Code, together with Article 611a, paragraph 1.[182] However, another basis could also be Article 823, paragraph 1 of the Civil Code which provides:

> A person who wilfully or negligently injures the life, body, health, freedom, property, or other right of another contrary to law is bound to compensate him for any damage arising therefrom.

The court found that the discrimination against Ms Harz amounted to a violation of the 'Persönlichkeitsrecht', the right to personality, which includes the respect for human dignity of an individual and the development of his or her personality.[183] The 'Persönlichkeitsrecht' was an 'other right' in the sense of Article 823, paragraph 1. Article 611a, paragraph 1 of the Civil Code is, according to the Arbeitsgericht, a specific realization of the right to personality in the field of access to employment. The violation of this provision brings about a violation of personal development and the possibility of participation in society. Consequently, the applicant had the right to the indemnification of moral damage.[184] Finally, the Arbeitsgericht considered the sum of 15 000 DM,[185] accorded to Ms Harz, necessary in order to make the sanction effective.

The interpretation of German law by the national courts in *Von Colson and Kamann* and *Harz* was, however, not an unqualified success. Although some courts agreed with the approach,[186] others voiced sharp criticism. The Landesarbeitsgericht Niedersachsen,[187] for instance, expressed serious doubts based on the assumption that it was in principle a task for the legislator to bring national law into conformity with Community law. In particular, it referred to the limitation acknowledged by the Court of Justice, namely that the national courts must stay within the limits of their discretion. The Landesarbeitsgericht Köln[188] went even further, refusing to construe national provisions in conformity with Community Law. It referred in particular to two initiatives taken by the Land Hessen and by the socialist party to amend the law. In such circumstances there was no place for judicial intervention.[189]

The judgement of the Landessozialgericht Hamburg (Higher Social Court) in *Hofmann* was not surprising.[190] The case concerned the problem of maternity leave and a corresponding maternity benefit which was, as an option, accorded to physical mothers only and which started to run after the expiry of the compulsory eight-week protective leave for working women following childbirth. Neither fathers nor adoptive mothers could qualify for the leave.[191] As far as the Equal Treatment Directive was concerned, the Landessozialgericht referred to the judgement of the Court of Justice:[192] the maternity leave was compatible with the Directive and, in particular, the Directive does not impose on Member States a requirement that they shall, after the compulsory protective period has expired, allow a leave to be granted alternatively to mother or father. Further, Hofmann's arguments based on national, in particular constitutional, law were of no help either. The Landessozialgericht hold that both from the wording and the *travaux préparatoires* of the Mutterschutzgesetz (Law for the Protection of Working Mothers) it appeared that the legislature deliberately reserved maternity leave for physical mothers. The Court found that the law was in conformity with Article 3 of the German Basic Law, which provides for equal treatment of men and women. According to the Court, Article 3 allowed special legislation that could be justified by objective biological and functional differences, such as childbirth, breastfeeding and motherhood in general. Further, the Court did not agree with the argument of Hofmann that the main object of maternity leave is to protect the child. The Landessozialgericht held that the essential ground of the legislature for the introduction of maternity leave was the protection of the mother's health, in particular with respect to the physical and psychological changes due to pregnancy and childbirth. The withdrawal of the leave in the event of the child's death is to be explained by the fact that at that moment of the double burden borne by a woman, i.e. the caring of the child and the consequences of pregnancy and childbirth, comes to an end. Since a man can never be subject to such a double burden, the Landessozialgericht found the unequal treatment justified. Consequently Hofmann's appeal against the judgement of the Sozialgericht Hamburg (Social Court), which also found that only mothers can claim maternity leave, was dismissed by the Landessozialgericht. Apparently the latter court made the same mistake as the Court of Justice by not considering that another effective and less discriminatory way to relieve the mother of her double burden is to allow a 'child care leave' for the father.[193]

Further litigation in the German courts concerning the issue of maternity leave does not seem to have been successful either. For instance, in 1985 the Bundesarbeitsgericht (Federal Labour Court) found that the maternity leave for the physical mother only was neither unconstitutional nor – according to the Court of Justice's *Hofmann* judgement – incompatible with Article 5 of the Equal Treatment Directive.[194] In August 1986 the Bundesverfassungsgericht (Federal Constitutional Court) did not admit for judgement three 'Verfassungsbeschwerde', objections on a point of constitutional law,[195] because they did not have sufficient chance of success.[196] In fact, it meant that maternity leave was constitutional. The constitutional objections came from a physician who wanted to care for his child, from a worker who asked to be awarded maternity leave by way of parental leave since the mother had died shortly after the birth, and from Mr Hofmann.

In the meantime the 'Bundeserziehungsgesetz' (Law on Rearing Benefit and Leave) came into force on 1 Janary 1986.[197] This law, which replaces the maternity leave and benefit, provides for a gender-neutral twelve-month leave (plus benefit) which can be allowed to mothers,[198] fathers, adoptive and step-parents included, to guardians and other caretakers.

In *Bilka*,[199] the Bundesarbeitsgericht (Federal Labour Court) found, in an extensively reasoned judgement, in favour of Ms Weber, a former sales assistant in one of Bilka's department stores, who claimed to be a victim of indirect discrimination. The test the Bundesarbeitsgericht had to apply according to the judgement of the Court of Justice[200] was whether Bilka's staff policy excluding certain category of part-time employees from an occupational pensions scheme affects a far greater number of women than men and, if so, whether this policy pursues a real need on the part of the undertaking and, eventually, whether that policy is an appropriate and necessary means to achieve the objective.

As to the first point, the Bundesarbeitsgericht found, on the basis of figures submitted by Bilka, that the requirement of at least fifteen years' full-time employment in order to qualify for the old age pension scheme affected merely women. The finding that 'part-time work is female work' was also confirmed by figures of the Statistisches Bundesamt (Federal Office for Statistics). The Court added that this phenomenon should be sought in social relations and, in particular, in the division of roles between men and women. Further, the Court considered that it was necessary to prevent women, because of their harmful position on the labour market, being paid less than men in comparable situations.

The next point the Bundesarbeitsgericht turned to was the justification of Bilka's policy. It was up to the employer to establish that the objective sought by the policy corresponded to a real need on the part of the undertaking and that it was an appropriate and necessary means. According to the Court, the employer's arguments were unsuccessful. Bilka argued that the policy was intended to encourage full-time work. Part-time workers cause organizational problems, like refusing to work on Saturdays, and involve higher staff costs. The Bundesarbeitsgericht was not convinced that the employment of full-time workers was a real need for the department store. It held that according to literature on staff management and labour law the employment of part-time workers caused hardly any extra costs and organizational problems, and that these minor disadvantages are compensated by much more important advantages, which is particularly the case with respect to the opening hours of department stores.

Further, the Bundesarbeitsgericht considered that even if it was necessary to encourage work on Saturday, it was unclear how Bilka's pension policy could serve this purpose. The pension scheme does not differentiate between Saturday workers and part-time workers, nor does it make it possible for part-time workers to qualify for the pension by accepting work on Saturday. Thus, because Bilka did not succeed in justifying the pension policy, a case of indirect discrimination contrary to Article 119 of the EEC Treaty was established.[201] The Bundesarbeitsgericht declared the fifteen years of employment requirement for part-time workers null and void and it held that Ms Weber was entitled to an old age pension under Bilka's scheme. Bilka's argument, based on the higher and unexpected cost of the pensions scheme when part-timers have to be included with retroactive effect, was dismissed by the Bundesarbeitsgericht. The Court considered, in particular, that the interest of Ms Weber of not being discriminated against and getting the pension must have precedence over the financial interest of the employer concerning the size of the pension reserve. The organization of the pension scheme was primarily the responsibility of the employer who was also in a better position to judge the uncertainty of the law as it stands. The Bundesarbeitsgericht found that as far as the past is concerned, Article 119 can be only complied with by including part-timers in the scheme and to increase the assessment of the pension reserve accordingly. Changes in the scheme itself were possible for the future only.

Finally, the Bundesarbeitsgericht made some interesting remarks on the relationship of Article 119 and the Occupational Schemes Directive.[202] The employer argued that this Directive, which deals specifically with pension schemes like the one at issue in *Bilka*, requires the implementation of the principle of equal treatment by 1 January 1993 and does not provide for any retroactive measures. The Bundesarbeitsgericht found that the employer could not rely on the Directive. Directives as secondary legislation cannot amend the provisions of the Treaty or limit their effects in the time. The Occupational Schemes Directive was designed for situations in which the implementation of the equal pay principle implies the adoption of additional measures; thus it applies only where the direct effect of Article 119 is insufficient. However, in the case before the Bundesarbeitsgericht, Article 119 was as such applicable. The Court of Justice gave the national judge criteria which made the application of Article 119 possible, without resort to additional measures being necessary.[203]

The national judgement in *Rummler*[204] was to a certain extent disappointing, in particular because the Arbeitsgericht (Labour Court) Oldenburg did not really deal with the answers it got from the Court of Justice.[205] The Court first quoted the questions it referred to Luxembourg and then the operative part of the Court of Justice's judgement, which was, briefly the following: so long as a job classification system as a whole precludes any discrimination on grounds of sex, it is not incompatible with the Equal Pay Directive to use the criterion of muscle demand or muscular effort or that of the heaviness of the work if the work to be performed requires the use of a certain degree of physical strength. Further, according to the Court, it follows from the Directive that work which is objectively the same must attract the same rate of pay whether it is performed by a man or a woman, and that the use of values reflecting the average performance of workers of one sex as a basis for determining the extent to which work requires effort or is heavy, constitutes a form of discrimination on grounds of sex.

Apparently, the Arbeitsgericht must have found that the job classification scheme at issue in *Rummler* was compatible with the requirements of the Directive as formulated by the Court because it did not evaluate the scheme explicitly, but turned directly to the examination of the work performed by Ms Rummler. The Court found that her activities corresponded with wage group III and not with wage group IV as she claimed. Consequently, the case was dismissed as ill-founded.

However, it seems that *Rummler* is, as interpretation of Article 1 of the Equal Pay Directive, of particular importance in Germany. During the Weimar Republic and the postwar years it was common practice to provide in wage-rate agreements that women will receive lower pay than men for equal work. In 1955 the Bundesarbeitsgericht held such provisions incompatible with Article 3 of the Basic Law, the prohibition of discrimination on grounds of sex. However, in the same judgement the Court suggested the creation, in wage-rate agreements, of different wage groups corresponding to the heaviness of the work. So it happened that the so-called 'Leichtlohngruppen' (light wage groups) were established with, as their main criterion, 'physically light work' or 'minor physical effort'. The discrimination of women continued however in another way: the activities that fell within the light wage groups were those mainly performed by female workers.[206] *Rummler* means for wage-rate agreements which contain 'Leichtlohngruppen', that they must include such criteria in relation to which women have greater ability in order to balance the system.[207]

Another, closely related problem is the question which criterion must be used to determine whether certain types of work are physically light or not. For a long time, the point of departure has been the male physical strength standard. In 1980, the Arbeitsgericht Bochum decided that the female standard was more in conformity with the principle of equal treatment and that men should be treated in this respect as women.[208] The Bundesarbeitsgericht was in 1985 of the opinion that a differentiation is necessary: the point of reference for the assessment of the degree of physical effort required should be for women the female values and for men the male ones.[209] Although *Rummler* seems to require that the standard to be used should be the average of the male and female values taken together,[210] it appears from a more recent judgement that the Bundesarbeitsgericht did not change its mind.[211] However, in the same judgement this court resorted to *Rummler* in support of an interesting thesis: in the case before it, the Bundesarbeitsgericht had to decide how to evaluate whether an activity requires a 'minor physical effort'. The Court considered this had to be done in accordance with the 'Verkehrsanschauung', i.e. by applying generally accepted standards, which no longer focused on muscular effort only, but also on all other circumstances which affect the human body, such as standing work, inconvenient position, noise, stress and repetitive work. The Bundesarbeitsgericht found that this broader interpretation of 'Verkehrsanschauung' was more in conformity with *Rummler* than the old one, which referred only to muscular effort, since 'the other circumstances' seem to affect men and women (more) equally.

Finally, it should be mentioned here briefly what measures Germany took to comply with the judgement of the Court in case 248/83.[212] The court held in this case that Germany failed to fulfil its obligations under the Treaty by not having compiled a complete and verifiable list of occupations and activities excluded from the application of the principle of equal treatment because, by reason of their nature or the context in which they are carried out, the sex of the worker constitutes a determining factor. The German government notified the Commission of a catalogue of the excluded occupations in 1987.[213] It includes, for instance, actors, mannequins, occupations outside the EC countries in which for religious or cultural reasons only men are accepted, religious functions, functions within the military, police or in prisons etc. It seems that when compiling this catalogue, the German authorities examined a considerable number of legal provisions excluding women; several of them were amended next because they could not be justified. Further, those occupations which may sometimes require activities to be performed by a person of a certain sex only, like body-search, have not been excluded. On the other hand, the government refers to the fact that it is solely up to the courts to interpret the laws and thus also to determine the scope of the general exclusion of Article 611a. In other words, the value of the catalogue is, as a non-binding document, limited.

Belgium

In the first *Defrenne* judgement[214] the Court of Justice held that a retirement pension established within the framework of a social security scheme laid down by legislation does not constitute consideration which the worker receives indirectly in respect of his employment from his employer within the meaning of the second paragraph of Article 119 of the EEC Treaty. In its follow-up judgement[215] the Conseil d'Etat recalled first that the applicant demanded annulment of the Royal Decree of 3 November 1969 laying down rules for civil aviation crews on entitlement to pension and that she claimed the infringement of Article 119 of the EEC Treaty; she argued that her pension and, in particular, the employer's contributions had to be considered as pay within its meaning. The Conseil d'Etat then just simply quoted the answer of the Court of Justice and it held that Ms Defrenne's claim was directed against a provision with legislative character concerning a retirement pension established within the framework of a social security scheme. Therefore her case was dismissed.

While the second *Defrenne* case[216] was of eminent importance on the European level, the judgement of the Cour du Travail[217] (Labour Court) in Brussels delivered pursuant to the Court of Justice's preliminary ruling was less spectacular. Ms Defrenne claimed before the Cour du Travail three things:

1. arrears of remuneration, namely 12 716 Belgian francs representing the difference between the remuneration received by her from 15 February 1963 to 1 February 1966 and the remuneration which a cabin steward with the same seniority would have received;
2. additional severance pay; and
3. damages for loss of pension rights.

By judgement of 23 April 1975, the Cour du Travail[218] dismissed the last two claims. Both claims were mainly based on the difference of age limits between male and female members of the cabin crew: the contract of employment of an air hostess included a clause bringing the contract to an end when she reached the age of 40 years, while no such limit was attached to the contract of male cabin attendants. The court held that the problem of different age limits does not fall within the scope of Article 119 of the EEC Treaty. According to the Cour du Travail, this Article relates only to pay and not to other conditions like the termination of a contract. However, with respect to the first claim, the Cour du Travail referred two questions to the Court of Justice. After the Court's famous judgement as to the direct effect of Article 119, the Cour du Travail, in a very short judgement, simply recalled Ms Defrenne's claim, quoted the Court's preliminary ruling and awarded her the sum of 12 716 Belgian francs by way of arrears of salary.

Ms Defrenne lodged an appeal before the Cour de Cassation against the judgement of the Cour du Travail of 23 April 1975 in so far as that judgement dismissed her second and third claim. To the subsequent questions of the Cour de Cassation the Court of Justice replied[219] that Article 119 does not prescribe equality in respect of other working conditions, in addition to equal pay, and that at the time of the events which formed the basis of the main action there was no other rule of Community law prohibiting discrimination between men and women in the matter of working conditions other than the requirements as to pay referred to in

Article 119 of the Treaty. It may be clear that on this basis the Cour de Cassation dismissed the appeal.[220]

Denmark

The first Danish preliminary cases have yet to be decided,[221] so the only case to be discussed here in case 143/83, *Commission* v. *Denmark*.[222] In this case the Court of Justice found that Denmark did not fulfil its obligation under the Treaty, because the law no. 32 of 4 February 1976 on equal pay for men and women provided only for equal pay for the same work and not also for equal pay for work of equal value, as required by the Equal Pay Directive.[223] The national measures taken by Denmark were very simple indeed. Law no. 32 has been amended by law no. 65.[224] The present version of the law on equal pay refers to both, same work and work to which equal value is attributed.

Conclusions

It is difficult to draw general conclusions from this survey of how the national courts and legislators have reacted to the judgements of the European Court. Each individual case is quite specific and the facts unique. However, it is possible to see certain patterns arising in the Member States. First it is possible to state that even in those countries with a clear constitutional commitment to the principle of equality, as well as those such as the UK without such a provision, the legislator remains equivocal about the equal rights of men and women. This is clearly the case in matters of social security where the legislators in several states have not fully implemented the directive.

However, in other areas, such as equal treatment and pensions, this is also the case. Thus, the national courts find themselves in a dilemma when they are confronted with a conflict between Community principles and national legislation. Some courts have accepted the principle of supremacy of Community law and resolved the conflict in this way. Others have been more reluctant to adopt what they perceive to be a too activist judicial stance. For them the solution to the conflict lies with the legislator and, of course, it is true to say that the primary obligation to implement Community directives lies with the legislator. The best solution is the full and proper transposition of Community law into national legislation. Second, the national courts are faced with the genuinely difficult problem of knowing exactly what the directives mean and to what extent they create rights for individuals. They may, of course, request preliminary rulings on both these questions and have done so. The process is a long and complicated one. The rulings of the Court of

Justice are not always clear and, almost inevitably seem to raise further questions. *Marshall*, for example, cleared up the horizontal/vertical direct effects of directives problem, but *Foster* demonstrates that the answer is not so simple. Third, it is clear that not only is the approach of the courts of the several member states different, but also that *within* the member states different courts adopt divergent approaches. This is not helpful for individuals who may fail in their case if they happen to approach the wrong court for a resolution of their claim. Fourth, individuals may have a long and difficult struggle in their own particular case and, although they may eventually win, their success may lead to a deterioration in the overall position of others in similar circumstances.

As long as states are free to accept 'equal but worse' solutions, it must be questioned whether the struggle for equality is worth it. These solutions have been adopted by states in the area of social security, thus, by definition, adversely affecting the poorest sections of society. However, as a final and more positive note, it is apparent that there have been some notable and worthwhile successes for Community law. Despite all these difficulties, Community law has provided a positive input in several important areas. National law has been improved, refined and developed at a time when equal rights for men and women seemed almost unfashionable in some states of the Community. The directives have provided another source of argumentation; hence they have highlighted specific problems and have continued to provide an inspiration to find an equitable solution.

Notes

1   Article 171 EEC.
2   Case 127/79 *Macarthys Ltd* v. *Wendy Smith* (1980) E.C.R. 1275.
3   p.120.
4   Macarthys Ltd v. Smith (1981) 1 All E.R. 111, p. 120.
5   Case 69/80 *Worringham and Humphreys* v. *Lloyds Bank* 1981 (ECR) 767.
6   *Worringham* v. *Lloyds Bank* (1982) 3 All E.R. 373, p.375.
7   Information provided by BIFU.
8   Case 96/80 *Jenkins* v. *Kingsgate (Clothing Productions) Ltd* (1981) E.C.R. 911, p. 928.
9   *Jenkins* v. *Kingsgate (Clothing Productions) Ltd* (1981) I.R.L.R. 388; (1981) I.C.R. 715.
10   *Handley* v. *H. Mono Ltd.* (1978) I.R.L.R. 534.
11   Equal Pay Act 1970, s 1(3) reads: 'An equality clause shall not operate in relation to a variation between the woman's contract and the man's contract if the employer proves that the variation is genuinely due to a material difference (other than the difference of sex) between her case and his.'
12   See Chapter 3 for a discussion of the case, pp. 71-4.
13   (1981) I.C.R. p. 721.
14   Case 96/80 *loc. cit.* note 8, p. 722.
15   *Kearns* v. *Trust House Forte Catering Ltd* (unreported) 15 June 1978.
16   *Clay Cross (Quarry Service) Ltd* v. *Fletcher* (1979) I.C.R. 1.
17   (1981) I.C.R. p. 723.
18   *Ibid.* p. 925.

19 See the discussion of the *Rainey* case below.
20 No distinction between direct and indirect discrimination is given in the Equal Pay Act although British judges have tended to read the Equal Pay Act and the Sex Discrimination Act as a code.
21 (1981) I.C.R. p. 723.
22 *Ibid.*
23 *Legislating for Change* (Manchester; EOC, 1987) p. 9.
24 Case 96/80 *loc. cit.* note 8 p. 926.
25 (1981) I.C.R. p. 721.
26 *Steel* v. *The Post Office* (1978) I.L.R. 198. In fact the EAT applied the proportionality test.
27 Both discussed in Chapter 1, p 16.
28 In a later case the European Court did in fact hold that Article 119 applies to cases of unintentional indirect discrimination. See case 170/84 *Bilka Kaufhaus GmbH* v. *Karin Weber Von Hartz* (1986) 2 C.M.L.R. 701.
29 (1981) I.C.R. 726.
30 Information provided by the EOC.
31 Case 170/84 *loc. cit.* note 28. This case is discussed in Chapter 3, p. 64 and pp. 74-6.
32 Case 170/84 p. 716.
33 Case 12/81 *Garland* v. *British Rail Engineering Ltd* (1982) E.C.R. 359.
34 *Garland* v. *British Rail Engineering Ltd* (1982) 2 All E.R. 402.
35 *Burton* v. *British Railways Board* (1983) I.C.R. 544.
36 *Rainey* v. *Greater Glasgow Health Board* (1987) 2 C.M.L.R. 11.
37 *Rainey* v. *Greater Glasgow Health Board* (1985) S.L.T. 518. The Lord President (Lord Emslie) and Lord Cameron agreed with the findings of the industrial tribunal. Lord Grieve dissented.
38 *Clay Cross (Quarry Services) Ltd* v. *Fletcher* (1979) I.C.R. 1.
39 *Ibid* p. 9.
40 (1985) S.L.T. 523.
41 Lord Grieve disagreed on this issue. See his views on p. 532.
42 *Rainey* v. *Greater Glasgow Health Board* (1987) 2 C.M.L.R. 11.
43 *Ibid.* p. 17.
44 *Ibid.* p. 20.
45 *Ibid.* p. 22.
46 For a discussion of the case see Chapter 4, pp. 130-4.
47 The Equal Pay (Amendment) Regulations 1983 (S.1 1794/1983); The Industrial Tribunals (Rules of Procedure) (Equal Value Amendment) Regulations 1983 (S. 1. 1807/1983).
48 See, for example, Szyszcak (1985) Atkins and Hoggett (1984) Chapter 2.
49 *Pickstone and Others* v. *Freemans PLC* (1987) I.C.L.R. 218. His views were based on a literal interpretation of the UK Act. The House of Lords did not accept his arguments.
50 *Hayward* v. *Cammell Laird Shipbuilders Ltd* (1987) All E.R. 344.
51 The Court of Appeal refused leave to appeal to the House of Lords on this issue, but on 7 May 1987 the Appeal Committee of the House of Lords gave leave to Ms Hayward to appeal.
52 *Hayward* v. *Cammell Laird Shipbuilders* (1982) 2 All E.R. 257.
53 (1987) I.C.L.R. 218, (Court of Appeal); (1988) 2 All E.R. 803 (House of Lords).
54 (1987) I.C.L.R. p. 222.
55 *Ibid.* p. 223.
56 *Ibid.* p. 224.
57 Case 14/83 *von Colson and Kamann* v. *Land Nordrhein-Westfalen* (1984) E.C.R. 1891.
58 *Regina* v. *Secretary of State for Social Services and others ex parte Elizabeth Ann Clarke and others* [1988] 1 C.M.L.R. 279.

59   The Industrial Tribunal found against the appellants in December 1988. At the time of writing, the case had been appealed to the Employment Appeal Tribunal, although ro date had been set for the hearing (information supplied by the Equal Opportunities Commission). In the proceedings in the High Court, the defendants had argued for the adoption of alternative procedures, *loc. cit.* p. 286. Compare also *Reed Packaging Ltd* v. *Boozer and Others* (1988) I.R.L.R. 333 on similar issues.

60   For a discussion of the indirect effects of a directive see Chapter 2 above and Fitzpatrick (1987).

61   Case 151/84 *Joan Roberts* v. *Tate & Lyle Industries Ltd* (1986) 1 C.M.L.R. 714.

62   1986 C. 59.

63   Freedman (1986) p. 59.

64   Case 152/84 *Marshall* v. *Southampton and South West Hampshire Area Health Authority* (1986) 1 C.M.L.R. 688.

65   (Unreported.)

66   *Rolls Royce PLC* v. *Mrs D. Doughty* (1988) 1 C.M.L.R. 569.

67   *Foster* v. *British Gas* (1988) 2 C.M.L.R. 697. There is no report of the House of Lords proceedings. The case was referred to the European Court on 29 May 1989. See O.J. C 160/11, 27 June 1989.

68   See, for example, case 149/79 *Commission* v. *Belgium* (1980) E.C.R. 3881.

69   Lord Donaldson's definition is as follows 'An emanation of the State being understood to include an independent public authority charged by the State with the performance of any of the classic duties of the state, such as the defence of the realm or the maintenance of law and order within the realm' *Foster* v. *British Gas loc. cit.* note 67, p. 701. It may be questioned whether an Area Health Authority would fall into this definition. Are the duties of such authorities part of the classic duties of the state? On the continent 'health rights' are not considered to be classical. In Britain where constitutional lawyers have not come to grips with a theory of the state, the question remains moot.

70   *Marshall* v. *Southampton and S.W. Hants A.H.A.* (No. 2) (1988) I.R.L.R. 325.

71   *Ibid.* p. 330.

72   See the editor's comments in (1988) I.R.L.R. 324.

73   Case 222/84 *Marguerite Johnston* v. *Chief Constable of the Royal Ulster Constabulary* (1986) 3 C.M.L.R. 240. This case is discussed in Chapter 4 above.

74   A discussion of this case, including its history and settlement appears in Paisley (1987).

75   *Ibid.* p. 364.

76   *Duke* v. *GEC Reliance Ltd* (1988) 2 All E.R. 626. This case is also discussed in Chapter 2 above.

77   This is explained fully in Chapter 2 above, pp. 33–9.

78   Case 14/83 *Von Colson and Kamann* v. *Land Nordrein-Westfalen* (1984) E.C.R. 1891 and case 224/84 *loc. cit.* note 73.

79   Case 80/86 *Kolpinghuis* [1989] 2 CMLR 18.

80   *Roberts* v. *Cleveland Area Health Authority sub nom Garland* v. *British Rail Engineering Limited* 2 All E.R. 1163.

81   Nigel Foster, in commenting on this case, has argued that Lord Templeman's conclusions on the British European Communities Act 1972, lacks sufficient reason or argument. The relevant provisions of this Act are sections 2 (1) which provides that 'All such...obligations...from time to time created or arising by or under the Treaties...are without further enactment to be given legal effect or used in the United Kingdom shall be recognised and available in Law, and be enforced, allowed and followed accordingly'. Section 2(4) then provides that Acts of Parliament or enactments passed or to be passed 'shall be construed and have effect subject to the foregoing provisions of this section'. Foster argues that section 2(4) is not limited to 'where possible' or 'without distortion' or to directly applicable Community law. He suggests the section 2(4) 'may have been intended and should certainly be used

to overcome the difficulties faced with non-directly applicable Community law to interpret inconsistent national law. The logic for this is that directly applicable Community law does not require the aid of section 2(4), whereas non-directly applicable Community law concerns exactly the situation which requires the use of section 2(4) as an aid to construction.' This argument is appealing but may not convince the House of Lords in the future, Foster (1988).

82   *Finnegan* v. *Clowney YTP Ltd* (unreported).
83   Case 150/85 *Jacqueline Drake* v. *Chief Adjudication Officer* (1986) 3 C.M.L.R. 43.
84   For a discussion of the outcome see Luckhaus (1987). Luckhaus questions whether the Drake case was a complete success, given the fact that the system itself is grounded in discrimination.
85   *Aberdeen Press and Journal*, 23 May 1988.
86   For a discussion of the case see Chapter 5, pp. 189-90.
87   Information provided by the Office of the Chief Adjudicating Officer. The decision is not yet reported but was given on 10 August 1987 and amended 19 February 1988.
88   Luckhaus *op. cit.* note 84. pp. 38–39.
89   Case 157/86 *Murphy* v. *An Bord Telecom Eireann* (1987) 1 C.M.L.R. 879. The case is discussed in Chapter 3, pp. 79-80.
90   *Murphy* v. *An. Bord Telecom Eireann* (1988) 2 C.M.L.R. 753.
91   Case 286/85 *McDermott and Cotter* v. *The Minister for Social Welfare and the Attorney General*. This case is discussed Chapter 5, pp. 187-8.
92   *Ann Cotter* v. *The Minister for Social Welfare and the Attorney General* (1987) (unreported). This case is being appealed. The case of McDermott was decided on the same basis as Cotter and, therefore, will not be discussed separately.
93   Ms. Cotter had applied for an increase both in respect of her husband and her two children. The Irish judge examined the provisions relating to dependent children and concluded that they were not discriminatory. In this respect his decision may be questioned since it appears that there is a presumption in favour of the father as being the person responsible for the maintenance of the child. Only in cases where the child's father or stepfather is incapable of self-support by reason of some physical or mental infirmity is the mother or stepmother seen as being responsible for the child.
94   Although presumably Ms Cotter would agree to attempt to obtain a qualification certificate and the Irish government will, in this respect, be under an obligation to rectify this situation so as to comply with the Directive.
95   *Murphy* v. *The Attorney General* (1982) I.R. p. 241.
96   Case 309/85 *Barra* v. *Belgium and City of Liège* (1988) 2 C.M.L. Rep. 409.
97   Case 293/83 *Gravier* v. *City of Liège* (1985) E.C.R. 593.
98   'As it has acknowledged in its judgement of 8th April 1976 (*Defrenne* v. *Sabena*), it is only in exceptional cases that the Court may, in pursuance of the general principle of legal certainty inherent in the Community's legal system and in view of the risk of serious disturbances to legal arrangements already made in good faith to which its judgement might give rise retroactively, be induced to restrict the possibilities for any interested party to rely on the provision as interpreted so as to challenge those legal arrangements.'
99   Case 23/83 *Liefting* v. *Academisch Ziekenhuis bij de Universiteit van Amsterdam* (1984) E.C.R. 3244. See for discussion Chapter 3, p. 62.
100   *Ibid.* p. 3241.
101   For instance, CRvB 26 June 1986, RSV 1987, no. 91.
102   See for a description Chapter 3, p. 62.
103   Wet Gemeenschappelijke Bepalingen Overheidspensioenwetten (Law laying down common provisions with regard to laws governing the pensions of civil servants) of 9 November 1972, Uitvoeringsbesluit Beperking Meervoudige Overneming AOW/AWW-Premie (Order restricting the assumption of payment of contributions due under the Old-Age Pensions Law and the Widows' and Orphans' Benefits Law by

more than one institution) of 21 February 1973, and various implementing provisions. The new system was usually called the 'BOPA-regulation'.

104 SR 1987, p. 17.
105 Judgements of 9 March 1988, respectively 29 March 1988, TAR 1988, nos 127 and 128.
106 Decision of 8 May 1987, TAR 1987, no. 179.
107 Judgement of 18 May 1987 of the Civil Service Tribunal in The Hague, TAR 1987, no. 136 and judgement of 21 June 1988 of the Civil Service Tribunal in 's-Hertogenbosch, TAR 1988, no. 177.
108 Judgement of 16 April 1981, AB 1981, no. 408.
109 Case 45/76 *Commet BV* v. *Produktschap voor Siergewassen* (1976) E.C.R. 2043.
110 See Chapter 2, p. 41.
111 The choice of the forum depended namely on the nature of the employment relationship, i.e. whether a person was appointed as a civil servant or whether he or she was working with the public authority on the basis of an employment contract.
112 Judgement of 5 March 1987, TAR 1987, no. 116.
113 Judgement of 25 May 1988, TAR 1988, no. 159.
114 This interpretation has been argued by Prechal and was basically founded on the idea that Article 119 concerns neither gross pay nor net pay but that it should apply in those situations where a concrete damage has been suffered. See Prechal (1987). This approach has been sharply criticized by Andringa (1987).
115 Case 23/83, *loc. cit.* note 99, p. 3240.
116 Compare Chapter 3, pp. 58–67. In particular the 'effect-approach' of the Court of Justice seems to militate in favour of this interpretation.
117 This happened, among other things, in order to comply with the Social Security Directive. It may be clear that the problems raised in *Liefting* were in reality rooted in a discriminatory social security scheme rather than in unequal pay.
118 Case 262/84, *Beets-Proper* v. *van Landschot Bankiers* (1986) E.C.R. 773, discussed in Chapter 4, p. 123.
119 *Ibid.* p. 793.
120 Judgement of 21 November 1986, N.J. 1987, no. 351.
121 Case 30/85, *Teuling* v. *Bedrijfsvereniging voor de Chemische Industrie*, (1988) 3 CMLR 789, discussed in Chapter 5, p. 192.
122 Judgement of 29 December 1987, NJCM Bulletin 1988, p. 104.
123 See Chapter 5, p. 185.
124 In particular the newly introduced Toeslagenwet (Law on increases) that should guarantee a minimum income level for persons entitled to benefits under the law on unemployment (WW), Health Insurance Act (ZW), Law on Insurance against Incapacity for Work (WAO) and General Law on Incapacity for Work (AAW); further the profoundly changed General Law on Old Age (AOW), two new laws providing an income guarantee for older and partially incapacitated employees or former self-employed (IOAW and IOAZ) and the General Law on Social Assistance (ABW).
125 Compare Levelt–Overmars (1988) (I), pp. 598–599, in particular with respect to the old age pension which is in its present form probably untenable, Levelt–Overmars (1988) (II).
126 See also Chapter 5, pp. 195–7.
127 Case 71/85 *State of the Netherlands* v. *Federatie Nederlandse Vakbeweging*, (1986) E.C.R. 3855 and case 80/87 *Dik et al.* v. *College van Burgemeester en Wethouders to Arnhem et al.*, judgement of 8 March 1988 (not yet reported), both discussed in Chapter 5, p. 185 and 190 respectively.
128 Within the framework of the reform of the social security system, the WWV has been abolished as from 1 January 1987.
129 However, under certain circumstances, it was also possible that a person qualified immediately for a WWV benefit.

130   Or, in a more literal translation, the breadwinner.
131   For instance CRvB 24 April 1985, R.S.V. 1985, no. 174.
132   Judgement of 23 June 1988, NJCM Bulletin 1988, p. 635.
133   The President's decision was based on arguments of national law; it has been quashed by the Court of Appeal.
134   Decision of 11 June 1986, Nemesis 1986, p. 215.
135   Nemesis 1986, p. 217.
136   Case 71/85 (FNV), loc. cit. note 127, p. 3874.
137   Proceedings of the Second Chamber, TK 18 December 1986, 38–2185.
138   Compare Chapter 5, p. 186.
139   Judgements of 25 February 1987, Nemesis 1987, p. 311, and 29 April 1987, PS 1987, no. 426.
140   Judgement of 9 January 1987, Jurisprudentie WWV/WSW 1987, no. 46.
141   Judgement of 3 June 1987, NJCM Bulletin 1987, p. 399.
142   Judgements of 16 April 1986 and 3 July 1987, Nemesis 1987, pp. 312–313.
143   Case 80/87, loc. cit. note 127.
144   PS 1988, no. 440.
145   PS 1988, no. 551.
146   Though this latter condition was not 100 per cent hard since even the State Secretary realized that if a woman in the past knew she was not eligible for a WWV benefit anyhow, it can be hardly expected from her to be registered as a person in search of employment.
147   Which meant that the municipalities have to pay it from their own funds.
148   SR 1988, p. 270.
149   On the other hand, the Raad van Beroep Roermond rendered a judgement in conformity with the circular; 8 July 1988, PS 1988, no. 794. Moreover, it is understood that the judgement of the Raad van Beroep Arnhem is appealed directly by the government on the basis of a special and rarely used provision of the 'Beroepswet'.
150   PS 1988 no. 611, no. 781 and no. 783. For a clear and critical comment see Bout (1988).
151   NJB (1989), p. 172.
152   Brownlie (ed.) (1983), p. 270.
153   Judgements of 1 November 1983, R.S.V. 1984, no. 147–150.
154   Brownlie (ed.) (1983), p. 258.
155   This is possible under the Optional Protocol to the International Covenant on Civil and Political Right of 16 December 1966, which entered into force on 23 March 1976. See Brownlie (ed.) (1983), p. 292.
156   NJCM Bulletin 1987, p. 377.
157   See Chapter 2, p. 25.
158   CRvB 14 May 1987, R.S.V. 1987, no. 246. The ground for the pension was the loss of earning capacity due to the prosecution during the war.
159   This depends for instance on the nature and wording of the provision, on its context etc., and is decided by the national judge.
160   Case 30/85, loc. cit. note 121. However, the problem discussed here is another one than that before the Court of Justice.
161   Case 384/85 Borrie Clarke v. The Chief Adjudication Officer, (1987) 3 CMLR 277, discussed in Chapter 5, p. 189.
162   CrvB 5 January 1988, R.S.V. 1988, nos 104, 198, 199, 200.
163   Nemesis 1988, p. 73. The Raad van Beroep in Utrecht even held that Article 26 has direct effect as from 11 March 1979.
164   NJCM Bulletin 1987, p. 470.
165   Judgement of 7 December 1988, N.J.B. 1988, p. 1688.
166   Under the Directive justification is allowed only with respect to indirect discrimination. Compare Chapter 4, p. 108.

167   Nemesis 1988, p. 70.
168   Levelt–Overmars (1988) (I), p. 593.
169   Levelt–Overmars (1988) (III), pp. 642–644, who rightly observes that this legislation
       is incompatible with Community law, especially in the light of the judgement in *Dik*.
       The AAW provisions at issue were namely not only incompatible with Article 26 of
       the Covenant but they violated, from 23 December 1984, the Third Directive as well.
       In fact, under the bill that tries to cope with the consequences of the judgements of
       Centrale Raad, the rights from married women that came into being through the
       application of the principle of equal treatment will be cancelled with retroactive
       effect.
170   N.J.B. 1988, p. 179.
171   Compare S.M.A. 1988, p. 82 *et seq.* and p. 268 *et seq.*
172   Case 14/83 *loc. cit.* note 78 and case 79/83 *Harz* v. *Deutsche Tradax* (1984) E.C.R. 1921,
       discussed in Chapter 4, p. 135.
173   See, for instance Nicolaysen (1984), Zuleeg (1984), Bleckmann (1984), Bertelsmann
       and Pfarr (1984).
174   Colneric (1988) p. 973.
175   See Bertelsmann and Pfarr (1984) p. 1297; see also below, the judgement of the
       Arbeitsgericht Hamm.
176   See above, note 173.
177   Bertelsmann and Pfarr (1984) p. 1298.
178   Judgement of 6 September 1984, DB (1984) p. 2700.
179   'The same obligation' refers to paragraph 1 of Article 823 quoted below.
180   See in particular Article 33, paragraph 2 of the Basic Law that provides: 'Every
       German shall be eligible for any public office according to his aptitude, qualifications
       and professional achievements'.
181   Judgement of 7 March 1985, DB (1985) p. 1402.
182   Thus the national solution in *Von Colson and Kamann*.
183   The right is protected under the Basic Law. Article 1, paragraph 1 provides: 'the
       dignity of man shall be inviolable' and Article 2, paragraph 1 provides 'everyone
       shall have the right to the free development of his personality, in so far as he
       does not infringe the rights of others or offend against the constitutional order or
       the moral code'.
184   Article 823 is then read together with Article 847, which provides, among other
       things, 'in the case of injury to body or health, or in the case of deprivation of
       liberty, the injured party may also demand an equitable compensation in money for
       the damage which is not a pecuniary loss'.
185   Plus 2,31 DM on the basis of Article 611a, paragraph 2.
186   Landesarbeitsgericht Hamburg in its judgement of 11 February 1987, DB (1988) p.
       131 and, implicitly, Landesarbeitsgericht Frankfurt, judgement of 11 March 1988, DB
       (1988) p. 1754.
187   Judgement of 23 November 1984, DB (1985) p. 1401.
188   Judgement of 26 May 1986, Colneric (1988) p. 973.
189   It is understood that the Federal Ministry for Labour is preparing a new law to settle
       the problems. See Colneric (1988) p. 973.
190   Judgement of 22 November 1984 (mimeographed version).
191   See for adoptive mothers for instance Bundesarbeitsgericht, judgement of 27 July
       1983, BB (1984) p. 535. Further the law discriminated also between women
       themselves. For instance, a self-employed woman or a housewife had no right
       to maternity benefit. See Schleicher (1985).
192   Case 184/83 *Hofmann* v. *Barmer Ersatzkasse* (1984) E.C.R. 3047, discussed in Chapter
       4, p. 127.
193   See Chapter 4, p. 130.
194   Judgement of 31 January 1985, DB (1986) p. 179.
195   See Chapter 4, p. 164, note 125.

196 DB (1986) p. 2286.
197 BB, supplement 1/1986.
198 All categories of mothers: studying, self-employed, housewives etc.
199 Judgement of 14 October 1986 (mimeographed version); a very short summary in DB (1987) p. 994, a more extensive version in BB 1987 p. 829.
200 Case 170/84 *loc. cit.* note 28.
201 However, in a judgement of 11 November 1986, the Bundesarbeitsgericht found that a pension scheme that provides for retirement pension for staff members in executive functions only was not indirectly discriminatory even if the number of women who qualified for this pension was very small. The Court found this policy justified: it was important for an enterprise to hold on to its qualified and valuable staff members, by providing, among other things, only for them a retirement pension. See DB (1987) p. 995.
202 Directive 86/378 of 24 July 1986 on the implementation of the principle of equal treatment for men and women in occupational social security schemes, OJ L 255/40, 12 August 1986, discussed in Chapter 7, p. 276.
203 See on the relationship between this Directive and Article 119 Chapter 7, p. 285.
204 Judgement of 30 September 1986 (mimeographed version).
205 Case 237/85 *Rummler* v. *Dato-Druck* (1987) E.C.R. 2101, discussed in chapter 3, p. 86.
206 Colneric (1988) p. 971.
207 *Ibid.*
208 *Ibid.* p. 970.
209 *Ibid.*
210 See in particular consideration 13 of the judgement of the Court of Justice: '...where a job classification system is used in determining remuneration, that system must be based on criteria which does not differ according to whether the work is carried out by a man or by a woman...' and consideration 23: '...any criterion based on values appropriate only to workers of one sex carries with it a risk of discrimination and may jeopardize the main objective of the directive, equal treatment for the same work. That is true even of a criterion based on values corresponding to the average performance of workers of sex considered to have less natural ability for the purposes of that criterion...'. See also Colneric (1988) p. 970.
211 Judgement of 27 April 1988, BB (1988) p. 1606.
212 Case 248/83 *Commission* v. *FRG* (1985) E.C.R. 1459, discussed in Chapter 4, p. 145.
213 Bundesarbeitsblatt 11/1987, p. 40. The catalogue is in fact a survey of existing legal provisions excluding women from certain occupational activities.
214 Case 80/70 *Defrenne* v. *Belgium* (1971) E.C.R. 445, discussed in Chapter 3, p. 55.
215 Judgement of 10 December 1971, Recueil des Arrêts et Avis du Conseil d'Etat (1971) p. 1149.
216 Case 43/75 *Defrenne* v. *Sabena* (1976) E.C.R. 455, discussed in Chapter 3, p. 49.
217 Judgement of 24 December 1976 (mimeographed version).
218 CMLR (1975) 101. It should be noted that the action before the Cour du Travail was an appeal against a judgement of 17 December 1970 of the Tribunal du Travail in Brussels which dismissed all Ms Defrenne's claims as unfounded. Thus, formally speaking, whether the Cour du Travail could uphold (for a part, where appropriate) the judgement of the Tribunal or declare the appeal well founded.
219 Case 149/77 *Defrenne* v. *Sabena* (1978) E.C.R. 1365, discussed in Chapter 3, p. 68. Ms Defrenne's arguments before the Cour de Cassation were similar to those before the Court of Justice.
220 Although there have been no other cases referred to the Court of Justice by the Belgian courts until now, it certainly does not mean that the Belgian courts do not apply European law and jurisprudence on equal treatment. See, for instance, judgement of 25 April 1977 of the Cour du Travail in Mons (application of Defrenne II), JTT (1977) p. 252; judgement of 27 March 1984 of the Tribunal du Travail in

Antwerpen (comparability of work under Article 119), RDS (1984) p. 406; judgement of 23 December 1986 of Tribunal du Travail in Brussels (age limit for dismissal linked to different pensionable ages), JTT (1987) p. 209; judgement of 12 November 1984 of the Tribunal du Travail in Charleroi (collective agreement providing for compulsory part-time work for women who are non-breadwinners in order to save other jobs within the enterprise) R.D.S. (1984) p. 420.

221 Case 109/88 *Handels-Og Kantorfunktionaerernes Forbund i Danmark* v. *Dansk Arbeidsgiverforening for Danfoss A/S*, O.J. C124/8, 11 May 1988, and case 179/88 *Hertz* v. *Aldi Marked*, O.J. C205/6, 6 August 1988, are pending.

222 (1985) E.C.R. 427, discussed in Chapter 3, p. 95.

223 Directive 75/117 of 10 February 1975 on the approximation of the laws of the Member States relating to the application of the principle of equal pay for men and women, O.J. L 45/19, 19 February 1975.

224 Karnovs Lovsamling, 11th ed. (1987) p. 1059.

7 New Proposals and Legislation

The Community step-by-step approach in the area of equal treatment may seem to be long winded but, nevertheless, it has until now been a relatively effective method of combatting sex-based discrimination in a more and more extended field. It is clear that Article 119 and the three Directives now in force and implemented have had considerable impact on the legislation of the Member States and it is to be expected that they will remain an important touchstone in the future. However, new areas must be covered by further Community legislation in order to establish a coherent body of sex-discrimination law, filling the gaps that remain. After all, decisions of the Court of Justice stating that Community law as it stands does not prohibit the discrimination at issue are unsatisfactory.[1] Moreover, the promotion of equal opportunities for women, and that is where everything started, may require other legislation than equality safeguards only.

After the adoption of the Social Security Directive in 1978, the Commission did not stand still in so far as proposals for further legislation are concerned. However, it was not until 1986 that the Council adopted two new directives. Both are disappointing when compared to the original proposals. One of them, on self-employed women, is a peculiar mixture of hard and soft obligations for the Member States, some essential issues being set out in the form of recommendations. The other proposals, on occupational schemes, may be considered on certain points to be, in fact, a step back. Further, two draft directives on vital issues have been blocked within the Council since the mid-1980s. These relate to parental leave and part-time work.

In 1987 and 1988, the Commission submitted to the Council draft directives on two new subjects. One proposal attempts to deal with issues excluded until now under the Social Security Directives. Unfortunately, it is very badly drafted and to a certain extent disappointing as well. It does not cover all the remaining problems and it is weak on the point of individualization of rights, an issue emphasized in the Medium-term Programme.[2] The second draft directive concerns the burden of proof. Although it seems to be a useful instrument which, rather than giving new rules, brings some more clarity in the field concerned, its practical value remains to be seen, as does the possibility of its adoption by the Council in the near future.

Finally, it appears from the Medium-term Programme that the Commission is considering proposing the adoption of Community legal instruments in several other areas. Legislation on protection of women during pregnancy and maternity is a possible candidate, protection against sexual harassment at the workplace, further individualization of entitlements in social security, and last but not least, income taxation, as certain income tax systems have an adverse effect on women's employment.[3]

Equal treatment in occupational social security

As has already been said,[4] the adoption of the Occupational Schemes Directive was certainly not devoid of difficulties. While drafting the Equal Pay Directive, it appeared to the Commission that, according to *Defrenne I*, occupational pensions and perhaps even contributions to occupational schemes are capable of constituting 'pay' for the purposes of Article 119. Nevertheless, provisions covering these areas were finally omitted since the Commission took the view that a prior removal of differences in treatment in statutory schemes was necessary first.[5]

The Commission's proposal for the third Directive covered both statutory and occupational schemes. However, the Council did not follow this proposal in its entirety and postponed the implementation of the principle of equal treatment in occupational schemes until later.[6] It was not until 1986 that the Council adopted the Occupational Schemes Directive.[7]

From an international law point of view the Directive is not something new. Early in the 1950s the idea had been put forward within the ILO that occupational pensions must be considered as 'pay' and according to Convention no.100,[8] that these pensions should be equal for male and female workers. However, this idea had never been elaborated in an international instrument.[9]

Occupational schemes existing in the Member States are manifold [10] and of various types. They fall into a category of schemes situated between statutory social security schemes on the one hand and purely individual insurance contracts on the other. Affiliation to occupational schemes derives, directly or indirectly, from the contract of employment or from the exercise of a certain occupational activity. Their content is not, unlike statutory schemes, defined by law.[11] Neither is their substance determined by free negotiations between individuals and insurance companies. Usually the aim of the schemes is to supplement the benefits of the statutory ones, often in regard to retirement, but sometimes also in the field of sickness, unemployment, invalidity or death. Occupational schemes may be based on collective agreement between employers' and workers' representatives and may apply not only to an undertaking, but even to a whole occupational sector or several such sectors. They may be set up by the representatives of a self-employed occupation such as lawyers or doctors.[12]

The schemes may be financed by employers' contributions only[13] or by contributions of both employers and employees[14] and they can be administered in dozens of different ways: by an insurance company, as an independent fund, as staff expenditure etc. Also the calculation of benefits to be paid may differ considerably. They may be earnings-related or flat-rate benefits. In the first case, for example, every insured period (year) corresponds with a percentage of the salary, the last earned or the average; in the second case every insured period may correspond with a fixed sum of money. Another possibility is that a capital sum is built up by the accumulation of contributions and then transformed into a pension. Under some schemes a pension is paid in order to fill the gap between the statutory pension and a certain percentage, for example 75 per cent of the last earned salary of the person concerned. There are certainly many more differences between the various schemes that could be pointed out, but within the context of this chapter these differences do not need to be detailed since the main problem here is inequality between men and women within occupational schemes.[15]

Like statutory social security schemes,[16] occupational schemes reflect traditional assumptions made about men's and women's role in society, and more particularly in employment: women should enter employment – if at all – only for a short period, since they marry and become dependent on men. Moreover, inasmuch as occupational schemes have been established to supplement statutory ones, they often include the same inequalities. It will be no surprise that many occupational schemes have different pension ages or do not provide for survivors' benefits at all, or not without proof of dependency if the person deceased is a woman. However, there are also other differences which can be explained on the basis of the traditional role pattern assumption: under some schemes married women are systematically excluded; under others they may join on a voluntary basis while for men membership is compulsory; some of the schemes lay down higher age or seniority conditions for women to enter the scheme in order to dissuade them from joining; and several undertakings employing mainly women often do not operate an occupational scheme at all.

Another, but closely related, problem is that women have an employment pattern of their own: they often work on a part-time basis, interrupt their employment for a period to bring up children or to meet other family responsibilities; they earn on average less than men and they tend to change their employment more frequently. It is clear that under these circumstances women are adversely affected by the exclusion of part-time workers from a scheme, by salary level conditions for entry into the scheme, by earnings-related benefits and by the fact that it is often impossible or, at least, very inequitable to transfer acquired rights from one scheme to another. Finally, the calculation of the level of benefits[17] is often based on different sex-related actuarial data, in particular different mortality rates. The average life expectancy of the female population being higher than that of men, women will receive a lower pension for the same capital input. Thus, interruption of employment, higher age, seniority or salary conditions, relatively low salary, lower pension age and the use of actuarial data: all these factors, in combination or individually, may result in a woman being left with a very small or even an absolutely inadequate pension if she has joined an occupational scheme at all.[18] The next question is, therefore, to what extent the Fourth Directive remedies these inequalities.

According to its first Article, the aim of the Directive is the implementation in occupational social security schemes of the principle of equal treatment for men and women.

Article 2, paragraph 1 defines occupational social security schemes as schemes which are not governed by Directive 79/7, and whose purpose is to provide workers, whether employees or self-employed, in an undertaking or group of such sectors, with benefits intended to supplement the benefits provided by statutory social security schemes or to replace them.[19] Whether membership of the schemes is compulsory or optional is irrelevant.

Paragraph 2 excludes from the scope of application of the Directive individual contracts, schemes having only one member and, in the case of salaried workers, insurance contracts to which the employer is not a party. These three exclusions seem quite logical: individual insurance contracts can hardly be considered as social security.[20] Moreover, as has already been stated above, occupational schemes normally fall between statutory social security schemes and private insurance contracts. Unfortunately, the Council succeeded[21] in including a fourth exclusion, namely the optional provisions of occupational schemes offered to participants individually to guarantee them either additional benefits, or a choice of date on which the normal benefits will start, or a choice between several benefits. It is hard to understand why these provisions have been excluded. The fact that they are optional and are offered on an individual basis certainly does not mean that they are no longer part of the occupational scheme. Moreover, the latter exclusion is the more deplorable since it is often under these optional provisions that women have the possibility of balancing, to a certain extent, the inequalities arising from the scheme. For instance, under the option a woman may provide some pension for her husband, or she may pay additional contributions to ensure herself of a more adequate pension after retirement.[22]

Article 3 indicates that the Directive shall apply to members of the working population including self-employed persons, persons whose activity is interrupted by illness, maternity, accident or involuntary unemployment and persons seeking employment, and retired and disabled workers. The Fourth Directive seems to cover the same persons as the Third. Thus, what has been said in relation to the personal scope of the Social Security Directive applies here as well.[23] Nevertheless, three additional remarks must be made. In the first place, the Directive covers persons whose activity is interrupted by maternity. Such a reference to maternity is missing in the Third Directive. This certainly does not mean that women on pregnancy or maternity leave are not covered by the Social Security Directive.[24] Maternity was probably included because, under several schemes, the period spent on maternity leave or *mutatis mutandis* on family leave[25] may interrupt the retention or acquisition of rights under the occupational scheme.[26] However, an interruption as such seems to be allowed under the Directive, provided that there is no discrimination.[27]

In the second place, it is not very clear how the provisions of the Directive can be applied to the unemployed and those seeking employment. Both categories can probably only be covered by the Directive if the persons concerned have some employment record, have joined an occupational scheme and were, for instance, insured against unemployment.[28]

Finally, it had been suggested that part-time workers, temporary workers and those working at home should be explicitly included in Article 3.[29] Although such an addition would certainly be in favour of women, since large numbers of them are part-time, temporary or home workers, it does not seem to be strictly necessary. The whole matter depends on the interpretation of the term 'working population' and there is no reason why those categories of workers should not be considered as such. Of course, it should be remembered that 'working population' must have a Community meaning.[30]

The substantive scope of the Directive is defined in Article 4. In the first place the Directive applies to occupational schemes which provide protection against sickness, invalidity, old age, including early retirement, industrial accidents and occupational diseases and unemployment. The risks covered are the same as those listed in Article 3 of the Social Security Directive.[31] However, in the second place, the Directive also applies to occupational schemes which provide for other social benefits, in cash or in kind, and in particular survivors' benefits and family allowances, if such benefits are accorded to employed persons and thus constitute a consideration paid by the employer to the worker by reason of the latter's employment.

The scope of the Directive is, therefore, as far as the self-employed are concerned, the same as that of the Social Security Directive. For employees, however, it covers a much wider area since it includes all the benefits which may be considered as 'pay' within the meaning of Article 119.[32]

According to Article 5, the principle of equal treatment implies that there shall be no discrimination on the basis of sex, either directly or indirectly, by reference in particular to marital or family status. Discrimination is prohibited especially as regards the scope of the schemes and the conditions of access to them, the obligation to contribute and the calculation of contributions, the calculation of benefits, including supplementary benefits due in respect of a spouse or dependants, and the conditions governing the duration and retention of entitlement to benefits. This definition of the principle of equal treatment corresponds literally with that in Article 4 of the Social Security Directive. Therefore, remarks made in respect of the latter Article apply *mutatis mutandis* to Article 5 of the Fourth Directive, as well.[33] Furthermore, the second paragraph provides, just like the Third Directive, that the principle of equal treatment shall not prejudice provisions relating to the protection of women by reasons of maternity. First, in this respect, it must be recalled that very often *prima facie* protective or even affirmative measures in this field have, in fact, an adverse impact as far as the position of women within society in general and in the long term is concerned.[34] Second, this provision in the Fourth Directive seems to make more sense than in the Third. It has been argued with respect to the latter that the 'protection on grounds of maternity clause' seems superfluous as far as benefits during maternity leave are concerned.[35] After all, maternity is not included in the list of risks under the Social Security Directive. However, under the Fourth Directive it is conceivable that an occupational scheme may, among others, provide for a benefit during maternity leave. Under Article 4(b) it will fall within the scope of the Directive. Thus Article 5 paragraph 2 seems significant.

Article 6 specifies some provisions which will – if based on sex – be regarded as contrary to the principle of equal treatment. The list, which is not exhaustive, reflects the main instances of discrimination in occupational schemes.[36] Some of the examples relate to access to the schemes. Equal treatment is required when determining the persons who may participate, when fixing the compulsory or optional nature of participation in a scheme and when laying down different rules as regards the age of entry into the scheme. Other provisions concentrate on so called benefit-related aspects: there shall be no discrimination when setting different conditions for the granting of benefits or restricting such benefits to certain categories of workers, when fixing different retirement ages or when fixing the minimum period of employment or membership of the scheme required to obtain the benefit. Under another provision the rules applicable to the guarantee or retention of entitlement to deferred benefits when a worker leaves a scheme may not differentiate according to the sex of the worker. Further, there is the aforementioned protection of rights during maternity leave or leave for family reasons and a provision concerning the reimbursement of contributions where a worker leaves a scheme without having fulfilled the conditions guaranteeing him or her a deferred right to long-term benefits. Finally, Article 6 includes a number of provisions which are very disappointing. Initially, the Commission's draft contained a provision according to which it was contrary to the principle of equal treatment to provide for different levels or amounts of benefits by taking into account different sex-based factors of calculation, actuarial or otherwise, with regard to the phenomena of ill health, mortality or life expectancy. In other words, the use of separate actuarial data for men and women for the calculation of benefits was not allowed. The final version of the Directive reflects the opposite: the use of separate actuarial data for men and women is permitted in fixing levels of benefits which are contribution-defined.[37] On the other hand, the employer is allowed, under the same Article 6, to pay different contributions for a worker of a given sex in order to approximate the amount of the contribution-defined benefits. It may be questioned whether employers are ready to pay higher contributions when they are not obliged to guarantee equal benefits in the sense of, for example, equal monthly pensions for former male and female workers. Moreover, although Article 6 provides that there must be no discrimination based on sex in fixing levels of workers' contributions, under Article 9(c) the use of different actuarial data for men and women is allowed in this respect up to thirteen years after the notification of the Directive.

It may be clear that these provisions and the use of actuarial data considerably reduce the impact of the Directive on occupational schemes. Moreover, as will be pointed out later, this leads to anomalies in respect of, in particular, Article 119. The use of sex-based actuarial data is at first sight incompatible with the principle of equal treatment since the sex of the person concerned becomes a criterion for the calculation of benefits. The next question is, however, whether such unequal treatment cannot be justified on the ground that there is a difference in, for example, life expectancy between the statistically average man and woman. And that is exactly what the Directive accepts. The consequence is that certain characteristics of a whole group become a factor, often the sole one, in determining the individual case: a female worker receives a lower pension than a male even if she dies much earlier, because women as a category seem to live longer. It is hard to accept this justification. Several strong arguments have been put forward against the use of sex-related actuarial data.[38] First, actuarial data, in particular on longevity, used nowadays, are calculated on the basis of the total female population. Female employees are only a part of this whole group and there are strong indications that their life expectancy does not correspond with the statistical expectancy of the group. Second, there exist considerable differences in life expectancy between different occupational groups of male employees, but such differences are not taken into account. The same applies to other risk factors like the use of alcohol and tobacco, obesity and hereditary predisposition. Life expectancy is, after all, determined by many more factors than sex alone. Third, it has been pointed out that the objective of the Directive is to achieve equality in respect of individual rights, and that the life expectancy of an individual may differ considerably from the average for a group. Finally, it is clear that use of different actuarial data for men and women is not indispensable for a sound administration of a scheme. They are not used under statutory schemes; in some Member States they are more common than in others, and several occupational schemes themselves calculate the contributions and the benefits on a more 'neutral' basis, the general average of *all* employees.

In the light of these arguments it comes as no surprise that the Commission proposed to allow only the use of unisex actuarial data. Its approach was supported by the European Parliament and the Economic and Social Committee.[39] Moreover, it found an unusual ally, the Supreme Court of the United States.[40] The proposal of the Commission was not accepted by the Council, probably due to an effective lobby of various interest groups[41] and the unsympathetic attitude of the UK and the Netherlands.[42]

Paragraph 2 of Article 6 provides that where the granting of benefits within the scope of the Directive is left to the discretion of management bodies, the latter must take account of the principle of equal treatment.

As has already been said, under Article 9 Member States may defer the application of the principle of equal treatment with regard to the use of sex-based actuarial data for fixing the levels of employees' contributions. However, Article 9 makes a deferral possible in respect of two other issues as well.

In the first place, no equal treatment is required with regard to the determination of pensionable age for the purpose of granting old age or retirement pensions, and the possible implications for other benefits. The deadline is in this case either the date on which equality is achieved in statutory schemes or, at the latest, until equality is required by a directive.

In the second place, sex-based discrimination is allowed as far as survivors' pensions are concerned, until a directive requires the principle of equal treatment in statutory social security schemes in that regard. The Commission's proposal contained a much more feasible provision in this respect: the right of deferral existed only when equality on those two points has not yet been implemented in the statutory schemes. The moment, however, equality was achieved in statutory schemes, the right to deferral ceased to exist.

As far as pension ages are concerned, the Commission's draft was logical. Since there is a close link on this point between statutory schemes and occupational schemes, a simultaneous implementation of the equal treatment principle is highly desirable. Otherwise there will be, for instance, a chance that a worker receives for several years only a part of his or her 'total pension' (i.e. statutory and occupational together). The Council's solution, however, lacks any logic. It means, for instance, that in the Netherlands where the statutory age is 65, occupational schemes may continue to operate two different pensionable ages, usually 60 for women and 65 for men,[43] unless a directive to that effect is adopted quickly, which is not realistic.[44] Moreover, it is not clear what is the scope of 'the possible implication (of different pension ages) for other benefits'. Probably this provision aims at possibilities for early or late retirement.

What the Directive has done with survivors' pensions is an even sadder story. First, the list of risks in Article 4(a) does not include the death of a spouse as was proposed by the European Parliament.[45] This means, as far as the self-employed are concerned, that pensions for surviving spouses or a wider arrangement of survivors' pensions are not covered by the Directive. Under Article 4(b) the principle of equal treatment applies to survivors' benefits. However, they are simultaneously excluded under Article 9, even where similar benefits are provided for under statutory schemes. Moreover, while the Commission's draft concerned only pensions awarded to the surviving spouse, the Council excluded all survivors' benefits. Finally, the cherished argument that as long as there is no equal treatment required for survivors' benefits under statutory schemes no such demands in this respect can be made *vis-à-vis* occupational schemes is a false one. The close link with the statutory schemes such as exists in the case of pension ages does not hold true here. Once there is a survivors' pension under the occupational scheme, it must be equal for men and women. The consequence may certainly be that the widowers' pension is inadequate when the widows' pension is organized as a supplement to the statutory one, but should this be a valuable argument to provide for no widowers' pension at all or under very limited circumstances? Is some pension not better than no pension?

The remaining Articles of the Directive provide for similar obligations for the Member States as the other three directives on equal treatment: discriminatory provisions must be declared null and void or amended, schemes containing such provisions may not be approved or extended by administrative measures, a person must have the possibility to pursue his or her claim in law, workers must be protected against dismissal subsequent to a complaint or legal proceedings etc. It is noteworthy that, according to Article 7, the Member States must ensure that discriminatory provisions in *legally compulsory* collective agreements, staff rules of undertakings or any other agreements are null and void or may be declared null and void or amended. Certainly, this provision makes sense in so far as provisions which are not binding can hardly be sanctioned by nullity. On the other hand, the Court had considered in the case *Commission* v. *UK* that even when collective agreements are not legally binding they have important *de facto* consequences and that, therefore, discriminatory clauses in such agreements must be rendered inoperative, eliminated or amended by appropriate means.[46] Thus, although occupational schemes are normally governed by legally binding provisions, nevertheless Article 7 seems to be unnecessarily restrictive. Further, that Article is certainly not a carte blanche for discriminatory provisions in those rules and arrangements which are not legally binding.

Finally, the implementation of the Directive: within three years after its notification (i.e. three years after 30 July 1986) the Member States must bring into force the legislation necessary to comply with the Directive. The deadline for the revision of the schemes themselves is 1 January 1993. Article 8, paragraph 2 provides in this respect that rights and obligations relating to a period of membership of a scheme prior to its revision may remain subject to the 'earlier' provisions. Thus, for instance, benefits in the process of being paid will not be affected by the Directive.

It follows from the description just given that the Directive does not solve all problems relating to equal treatment of men and women in occupational social security schemes. Certainly on some points it is a change for the better. As to the conditions of access to the schemes are concerned, the Directive seems quite effective: different entry ages or seniority requirements for men and women have to disappear, married women may not be excluded any more. Since indirect discrimination is prohibited as well, there is a fair possibility that exclusion, or worse treatment, of part-time, temporary or home workers can be attacked under the Directive. However, eventual success will depend on the objective justification test.[47] Alternatively, the special problems of this category of workers can be solved by special social protection measures.[48] On the other hand, there are problems for which the Directive *and* the whole principle of equal treatment it enshrines is useless. As long as occupational schemes are offered by employers on a discretionary basis, nothing can be done about those undertakings employing mainly female workers and which – often for that reason – do not operate a scheme. When a woman's pension is earnings-related, and for that reason relatively low, the remedy must be looked for in the sphere of pay. The same may be often true of salary level conditions for entry to the scheme, although the indirect discrimination test may here be helpful as well. If there are no equitable rules for transfer of acquired rights, nothing can be done under the Directive: only when existing rules are discriminatory does the Directive apply.[49]

Furthermore, the Directive has introduced an anomaly in relation to interruption of employment in respect of childbirth and family responsibilities. Retention and acquisition of rights during periods of maternity leave or leave for family reasons may be suspended as long as there is no discrimination between male and female workers. It is submitted, however, that such a suspension may be tantamount to discrimination and, consequently, contrary to the Directive in the case of maternity leave. When employment is continued during this leave[50] suspension would mean that the sex of the employee (maternity leave is after all available to women only) becomes a criterion for, for example, the calculation of benefits.[51] It may be clear that problems relating to interruption of employment are of a more general character and should be solved elsewhere, for example, by a better division of labour within the family, better child-care facilities, more suitable working hours.

The last category of problems concerns exceptions to the principle of equal treatment, which reduce the importance of the Directive considerably, and they do so on scarcely convincing grounds. Survivors' benefits and optional provisions have already been discussed above. The continuation of different pensionable ages under the Fourth Directive may be understandable regarding the Third Directive because of the relationship between the two. This does not alter the fact that the matter could have been settled under the Social Security Directive[52] and that the Council made the exception in the Fourth Directive unnecessarily broad and uncertain. It has also been explained already that the use of sex-based actuarial data is not indispensable under occupational schemes and that there is a fair alternative: to calculate an average contribution for all men and women on the basis of life expectancy (or frequency of illness[53] etc.) and subsequently to transpose this capital to equal benefits. Now the permitted use of separate actuarial data for men and women in contribution-defined schemes, reinforced by the difference in pensionable ages, results in or, more exactly, perpetuates an ambivalent situation: equal contributions mean lower benefits for women; equal benefits require higher contributions from or for women.

The Directive being highly unsatisfactory on several issues, the question arises as to what can be done about it. Unlike the shortcomings of the Social Security Directive, which can probably be remedied by further Community instruments only,[54] occupational pension schemes may be covered by Article 119 of the Treaty. One has only to remember the judgements in *Defrenne I, Garland* and *Bilka*.[55] Also, the Commission and the Council apparently departed from the idea that the Directive must implement Article 119. The first recital of the Directive recalls the principle of equal pay; the second adds that although this principle does indeed apply directly in the cases of 'overt'[56] discrimination, there are also situations in which implementation of the principle of equal pay implies the adoption of additional measures which more clearly define its scope. Further, Article 4(b) elaborating the substantive scope of the Directive as far as employees are concerned is nearly literally phrased as the second paragraph of Article 119 defining 'pay'. However, the Council did not follow the Commission's proposal to mention Article 119 explicitly in the preamble. Moreover, it added Article 235 of the Treaty as the legal basis of the Directive, while the Commission's version referred to Article 100 only. The reference to Article 235 is understandable as Article 119 does not cover self-employed persons. However, the omission of Article 119 does not make any difference as to the 'implementing nature' of the Directive, at least with respect to workers.

This conclusion, i.e. that the Directive implements in part Article 119, does not mean that Article 119 did not meet the requirements of precision and clarity necessary to give rise to rights and obligations in national courts in the field of occupational schemes, nor that it was ineffective in this respect. Similar arguments have been invoked before the Court of Justice with regard to the Equal Pay Directive. However, the Court clearly did not accept them when it held that the Equal Pay Directive does not prejudice the direct effect of Article 119, and that the period fixed by that Directive for compliance therewith does not affect the time limits laid down by Article 119.[57] The 'status' of the Fourth Directive is in fact very similar to that of the First: it can be considered as a measure 'designed to facilitate the practical application of the principle of equal pay outlined in Article 119', and – and this is extremely important – 'it can in no way alter the content or scope of that principle as defined in the Treaty'.[58] Further, it is noteworthy that in *Bilka* the UK government argued that the fact that the Commission considered it necessary to submit a draft directive for occupational schemes shows that those schemes are not covered by Article 119 but by Articles 117 and 118, so that the application of the principle of equal treatment for men and women in that area requires the adoption of special provisions by the Community institutions. Obviously, the Court did not take on board this argument when it decided that benefits paid under Bilka's pension scheme constituted consideration within the meaning of Article 119.

Although the Directive has been presented as an additional measure defining more clearly the scope of Article 119, there are strong indications that the Directive is on several points *contrary* to Article 119.[60] However Article 119, being a primary source of Community law, takes precedence over any contrary provision of secondary legislation.[61] Therefore it is very important to know when or, to be more precise, what aspects of occupational schemes may be covered by Article 119. Focusing on this particular question, the following points are worthy of consideration: according to the Court's case-law benefits and contributions paid under a statutory scheme of social security are not covered by Article 119. Exception is made for contributions which are *included in the gross salary* payable to employees and which have repercussions for the calculation of other benefits linked to salaries.[62] Thus, in general the logical first step seems to be to determine the nature of the scheme; the criteria can be found in *Defrenne I* and in *Bilka*.[63] The rule of thumb seems to be that Article 119 is applicable to any scheme of contractual or consensual origin.

The specific problems relating to special and contracted-out schemes have already been discussed when dealing with the *Defrenne* test for the determination of the statutory nature of a social security scheme.[64]

However, it is worth repeating that the Fourth Directive is clearly envisaged to apply to contracted-out schemes.[65] It follows that this type of scheme cannot be considered statutory and, consequently, that they can enter the scope of Article 119. The system of the two Directives seems to be a balanced one: what is not covered by the Third Directive is covered by the Fourth and thus as far as employees are concerned, by Article 119 as well, the Fourth Directive being in this respect an implementing measure. Any other conclusion would mean that there exists a category of social security schemes that do not fall within Article 119 but are not covered by the Third Directive either.[66] Such an assumption, however, does not seem to be in conformity with the basic demarcation between Articles 117 and 118 on the one hand and 119 on the other as established by the Court in, in particular, *Defrenne I* and *III*.

Once it is established that a scheme is of contractual or consensual origin there is still no guarantee that Article 119 will remedy any sex-based discrimination under the scheme. At least three different aspects have to be considered in this respect: benefits, contributions and other conditions.

The issue of benefits paid under such a scheme does not seem to be very problematic. Such benefits will easily enter the definition of pay in Article 119. In particular, old age pension benefits can be considered as remuneration, although deferred. In *Garland* it became clear that Article 119 applies to any consideration which the worker receives from his or her employer even after retirement.[67] Further, since *Bilka*,[68] there should be no doubts on the remunerative character of benefits paid under an occupational scheme and the consequent applicability of Article 119. Thus, for instance, different benefits because of the use of sex-related actuarial data are not allowed under Article 119. The same applies to survivors' benefits even if the eventual pension is not paid directly to the employee. It is an important advantage for him or her to provide for a pension in case of his or her death.

The question whether contributions to an occupational scheme can be considered as 'pay' within the meaning of Article 119 is much more difficult to answer. As far as contributions paid by the employer are concerned, *Worringham* and *Liefting*[69] suggest that they constitute remuneration. However, it must be borne in mind that those two cases concerned a specific situation where the respective contributions supplemented the gross salary. Moreover, it was in the Court's eyes apparently important that the difference in gross salary affected other advantages. Those two judgements do not really lend themselves to generalization. Thus, in principle, employers' contributions do not seem to be covered by Article 119. They reflect in fact the costs for the employer. But Article 119 does not deal in the first place with such costs. It provides for equality in respect of pay.[70] The employee is probably not interested in what the contributions are, as long as there is no difference in the remuneration sphere. What matters to him or her is the weekly or monthly amount of pension or salary and it is the primary concern of Article 119 that there is no sex-based discrimination in this respect. Where unequal contributions result in different benefits or in different gross pay, Article 119 does indeed apply. But it does so with respect to the benefits or gross pay and not directly with respect to the contributions. Nevertheless, it is clear that if the different contributions are the cause of inequalities in the 'remuneration sphere', they have to be adjusted. From this standpoint it is thus possible to argue that to secure for male and female workers equal benefits, even when different pension ages still exist and the use of separate actuarial data is allowed, the employer may pay different contributions. Unfortunately, this solution does not seem a very satisfactory one since it makes women more expensive and, consequently, less attractive to the employer. Another possibility would be to ask female workers to pay higher contributions. It has been suggested that unequal contributions by men and women would themselves be a breach of the principle of equal pay.[71] This would not be so much the case because employees' contributions should be considered as pay[72] – they are not a consideration paid by the employer – but because the result would be contrary to Article 119: unequal 'take-home pay' for men and women. However, after *Newstead*,[73] this argument seems invalid. Finally, it is possible that the employer assumes the employee's contribution and pays it on his or her behalf.[74] Such a payment falls within the scope of Article 119 since it is a clear advantage for the employee: the employer pays his or her contribution in the same way as it is an advantage when the employer decides to pay off a part of the employee's mortgage.

The third issue, the 'conditions' of an occupational scheme, is even more complex. Does Article 119 cover terms of access to occupational schemes such as entry ages, employment records, salary thresholds? Or to different standards for male and female workers with regard to the possibility of transferring acquired pension rights? Can it apply to the obligation to contribute or to different conditions of entitlement to benefit, such as pension ages? The best point of departure when dealing with this question seems to be *Defrenne III*.[75] In this judgement the Court drew a distinction between equal pay, to which Article 119 applies, and equal treatment of men and women in other respects which is to be achieved pursuant to Articles 117 and 118 of the Treaty.

Ms Defrenne argued in this case that the termination of employment at 40 was, *inter alia*, prejudicial to her allowance on termination of service and her pension. The Court held, however, that the fact that the fixing of certain conditions of employment, such as a special age limit, may have pecuniary consequences is not sufficient to bring such conditions within the field of application of Article 119. The same line of reasoning seems to fit *Burton*.[76] Article 119 did not apply since the case was not concerned with the benefit itself but with conditions of access to the benefit. On the other hand, when one considers *Worringham*,[77] it was in fact the age limit of 25 years which conditioned the access to the scheme which was the very root of the discrimination. However, the decisive factor in this case was probably that the payment of contributions was organized in a way which resulted in unequal gross salaries which made the whole problem fall within the scope of Article 119. In *Bilka*,[78] the UK government argued that the conditions placed by an employer on the admission of its employees to an occupational pension scheme do not fall within the scope of Article 119 since they must be considered as elements of employment having financial consequences in the meaning of *Defrenne III*. The scheme at issue provided that part-time workers may obtain a pension only if they had worked full time for at least fifteen years over a total period of twenty years. This is indeed a condition of entitlement. Nevertheless, the Court held Article 119 applicable.

It may be clear that the distinction between conditions of work or conditions of an occupational scheme on the one hand and remuneration on the other is a vague one. Probably none of the conditions are without monetary implications, either direct or indirect. However, at this very moment it is not clear when a condition is capable of entering the field of Article 119. It has been suggested that Article 119 prohibits discrimination on the basis of sex in the granting or the calculation of benefits. Discrimination in the provisions on the duration of, or access to, the benefit should not be covered by Article 119.[79] However, the case-law is too vague and no valid conclusions can yet be drawn. Once it is established that a condition falls within the scope of Articles 117 and 118, a new problem may arise: which one of the Directives applies? It seems sufficient to refer here to *Newstead*[80] and more particularly to *Marshall* and *Beets-Proper*[81] where the Court dealt in a more imaginative way with problems resulting from inequalities in occupational pension schemes.

In this respect it should be reiterated that according to the Court, Article 1, paragraph 2, which excludes social security matters from the scope of the Equal Treatment Directive, must be interpreted strictly. Apparently, the mutual relationship between the Treaty provisions (Articles 117, 118 and 119), and between the secondary legislation, in particular the Second Directive on the one hand and the Third and Fourth on the other, is very complex.[82] Nevertheless, it is clear that on several points the Occupational Schemes Directive seems to be incompatible with Article 119. The Directive is useful as an instrument intended to secure the principle of equal treatment in occupational schemes for the self-employed and to encourage the implementation of this principle as far as employees are concerned. The mere existence of Article 119 did not suffice in this respect. Moreover, the Directive has probably a much wider range than the case-by-case approach of the Court of Justice. But as far as the Directive's scope is concerned, continuous attention must be paid to ensure that the Directive is not used to restrict the substantive and temporal scope of the principle of equal pay laid down in the Treaty. The danger is not imaginary.

Equal treatment of self-employed women

The Council's Directive 86/613 relating to the equal treatment of self-employed women was adopted on 11 December 1986.[83] The explanatory memorandum of the Commission submitted to the Council setting out the proposal explains the background to this Directive.[84] The Commission points out that the Equal Pay Directive applies only to *employees*, whether in the public or private sector, whereas the Equal Treatment and Social Security Directives are more general in their coverage and apply to the entire working population. However, there still exist specific problems of those women in self-employment (broadly defined) whose occupational status is unclear. The spouse of a person in a family business may, for example, be neither employee nor business partner. Problems of wives working in agriculture had been taken up by the Community where it was difficult to determine their contribution to the family income, i.e. their wages, and hence their entitlement to social security.[85] Family rather than labour law might determine their status and if they are not clearly employees then they might also be denied access to technical and vocational training. Furthermore, women working in family businesses are not always able to take part, because of their unclear employment status, in bodies representing their occupations. Finally, women engaged in running family businesses, self-employed women or farmers are not always able to claim any maternity benefits for the weeks before or after their confinement and hence they are disadvantaged as compared to other working women. Directive 86/613 is aimed at resolving this wide range of specific problems by setting broad objectives for the Member States.

The legal bases for the Directive are Articles 100 and 235 of the Treaty. Resort was had to Article 235 since the categories of persons covered by the proposal was so diverse and, hence, existing Treaty provisions did not entirely confer the necessary powers. The aims and scope of the Directive are set out in Articles 1 to 3. Its purpose is to ensure the application of the principle of equal treatment of men and women to self-employed persons. These are defined in two ways: self-employed *workers*, who are persons pursuing a gainful activity for their own account under conditions laid down by national law, including farmers and the liberal professions; the spouses of the above category, not being either employees or partners, where they participate in the activities of the self-employed worker and perform the same or ancillary tasks. Thus the Directive covers, for example, farmers and farmers' spouses where the latter work on the farm, shopkeepers and their spouses who help to run the shop, lawyers and other members of the liberal professions. The by now familiar standard of equal treatment is to be accorded to such workers. In this respect, Directive 86/613 uses the same wording as that found in Directives 76/207 and 79/7; however a word must be said about the meaning of the equal treatment standard as it appears in the self-employed Directive. As will be apparent from the discussion which follows on the substantive provisions, this Directive does not only aim to provide for the same treatment to be accorded to persons in comparable situations regardless of sex; what it also does is to provide a framework of legislation which creates newly defined legal statuses for persons whose exact status was previously unclear, thereby allowing them to benefit from the same treatment as other workers. This Directive, therefore, goes beyond the scope of the previous three adopted by the Community.

Article 4 provides that men and women shall be accorded the same treatment in respect of the establishment, equipment or extension of a business or other self-employed activity, including access to finance. This Article is aimed at according, particularly, married women the same rights to obtain credit on the same terms as men. In several countries access to credit for married women is more difficult than for any other group since the laws relating to matrimonial property are quite restrictive. Sometimes, for example, women may only borrow money with their husband's consent or are not free to use their own property as collateral for a loan. Member States are obliged to eliminate all provisions which conflict with the principle of equal treatment in this respect. They may thus be forced to re-evaluate their family and property laws to see whether they do in fact discriminate directly or, more importantly, indirectly against women.

Article 5 relates to the formation of companies. In several Member States spouses are prohibited from both being partners in the same company. The Directive obliges Member States to ensure that the conditions for the formation of a company shall not be more restrictive for married persons than for unmarried persons. The aim of this Article is to encourage family businesses to be run as partnerships in the hope that this will lead to a recognition of the worth of the work of the spouse. Furthermore, as the Commission's explanatory memorandum states, both spouses would then hold shares and become entitled to a consideration in the form of assets for their contribution to the operation of the company. This Article, of course, has further far-reaching effects, particularly in relation to the dissolution of marriage. Women who work for family businesses during the course of their married lives often find themselves in serious hardship if they become divorced. As neither employees nor partners they may find themselves without redundancy or social security payments or any form of income from the business. Article 5 is obviously aimed at alleviating this situation.

Article 6 entitles the spouses of self-employed workers to join a contributory social security scheme if they are not protected under the schemes of their spouses. This provision again seeks to remedy the occupational status of the spouses of self-employed workers.

Article 7 is couched in very general terms and obliges States to examine how the worth of the work of the spouses of self-employed workers may be recognized, and in the light of such an examination, to take steps to encourage such recognition. The original draft of the Commission had been much more specific, laying down four areas in which action should be taken. The first of these was in the consideration to be received in respect of work performed; the second related to the right to build up entitlements in respect to social security, including pregnancy and maternity benefits; the third was of a qualitative kind, giving the right to be enrolled in associations of an organization connected to the relevant occupation; the fourth related to the right to vote in and stand for elections to such associations or organizations. To some extent these provisions are covered by other Articles in the Directive, although the first has been omitted. Presumably it was considered that this would encroach too much on the organization of small businesses particularly since, in the original proposal, there were fairly detailed rules as to how to work out the amount of consideration concerned. At this point it may be worth noting that a further provision has also been omitted from the original draft. Article 6 of that draft obliged Member States to abolish fiscal provisions and practices which constitute discrimination in that they prejudice the status of the spouse as an employee. The specific problem here which the Commission wished to eradicate was the situation which exists in most Member States where wages paid to a spouse are generally tax-deductible from the taxable income of the head of the business. National ceilings are generally imposed which tend to limit the amount which the worker received. The Commission wished to see such ceilings abolished or separate assessments to be made for spouses working in the same business. Once again this proposal would clarify the occupational status of the spouse of the self-employed worker, but it proved too contentious for the Member States and it was dropped. However, the new Article 7 may cover fiscal provisions since the latter Article is couched in such general terms.

Article 8 relates to provisions concerning pregnancy and maternity benefits. Both the Economic and Social Committee and the European Parliament had stressed the importance of replacement services for women who require leave before and after their confinement. Both institutions were agreed that the major problem was not so much the financial one as in the woman obtaining time off work and interrupting her work to have her children. Both financial awards and replacement services are covered by Article 8 which obliges States to examine the possibility (and the conditions) of providing access to self-employed women and the wives of self-employed workers to services supplying temporary replacements or existing national social services; and to cash benefits provided under a social security or public protection system.

The final provisions of the Directive specify the nature of the obligations assumed by the States. First, States must ensure that persons who consider themselves wronged by failure to apply the Directive have recourse to a form of judicial process, possibly after recourse to other competent authorities. Second, States must bring the measures which they adopt pursuant to the Directive to the attention of bodies representing self-employed workers and vocational training centres. Third, the Council must review the Directive before 1 July 1993. Fourth, the Member States must bring into force the measures necessary to comply with the Directive by 30 June 1989 or, in the case of Article 5, by 30 June 1991 where the State has to amend its legislation on matrimonial rights and obligations. Fifth, States must inform the Commission of the measures which they have taken to comply with the Directive. Finally, they must report to the Commission by 30 June 1991 all the information necessary to enable it to draw up a report for the Council on the implementation of the Directive.

This Directive is much less specific in the nature of the obligations which are imposed on the Member States who will presumably react in different ways to the Directive. However, the impact of this Directive, if it is implemented in the spirit which is intended, should be enormous. First of all the Directive tackles the problem of the marginal status of the many millions of women who effectively work for their husbands in agriculture and in small businesses but who have not, in the past, been viewed by the law as workers. It therefore goes to the very heart of the problem faced by women (there are very few men in this situation) that their working status is defined by matrimonial rather than labour law. These women are in a sense doubly dependent on their husbands who are seen both as primary breadwinners and employers. Such women often find themselves in practice as employees but lack any associated employment rights and without any recognition of their labour. It can be argued, therefore, that this Directive, although couched in the same language as other directives in the equal treatment area, is not about equal treatment at all, but it is about placing women who were previously outside the scope of the earlier directives firmly within them. Its real aim is to provide a legally defined occupational status.

How far the Directive will be implemented in the Member States remains to be seen. In the British government's view, small businesses should be freed from regulatory controls to make them economically efficient.[86] This attitude may be shared by other Member States who will then view the Directive as coming in between their plans for economic recovery and, therefore, try to limit its impact. It seems fairly predictable that this will be the response at least of the UK.

Completion of equal treatment in social security

In October 1987, the Commission submitted to the Council a proposal for a Directive completing the implementation of the principle of equal treatment for men and women in statutory and occupational security schemes.[87] This proposal is the third, and it is said final,[88] step towards equal treatment in social security. It attempts to cover all the problems not settled by the Social Security Directive[89] and the Occupational Schemes Directive,[90] i.e. the exemptions and deferrals. Thus, in the first place, the draft Directive aims at extending the principle of equal treatment to social security areas previously excluded, but it does so while respecting the right of the Member States to choose their own solutions.[91] In the second place, although equal treatment does not necessarily imply individual entitlement, the draft Directive attempts to promote such individualization of entitlements as an alternative to the extension of derived rights.[92] Unfortunately, in this respect the draft is in fact rather limited. Finally, the proposal should guarantee that no harm accrues to the entitlement of persons concerned, either directly or indirectly. Where the principle of equality will be disadvantageous for them it should be excluded. Moreover, adequate transitional measures should be provided for.[93] It is deplorable that the Commission did not also consider the problem of level-down solutions. Only in the preamble of the draft Directive is it said that equal treatment of male and female workers necessitates, in particular, the achievement of equality as regards the conditions of coverage by statutory and occupational social security schemes whilst maintaining the improvement of such conditions.[94]

The personal scope of the draft Directive is wider than that of the previous two social security Directives. It covers the whole working population: *inter alia*, employees, the self-employed, sick workers, unemployed workers, retired workers etc.[95] However, because of the type of benefits the Directive covers, the personal scope has been extended to members of the family, survivors of and dependent persons on the members of the working population. Who is to be considered as a member of the family, survivor or dependent person is determined by national law.

The substantive scope covers in the first place provisions of statutory schemes concerning survivors' benefits and family benefits and social assistance where this latter supplements or replaces the said benefits. In the second place the Directive applies to corresponding provisions of occupational schemes, i.e. in particular provisions on survivors' and family benefits for the self-employed, since this category was not covered in this respect by the Fourth Directive. The next areas included are those of Article 7, paragraph 1 (a–d) of the Third Directive and social assistance where supplementing or replacing these benefits, and the area of Article 9 (a) of the Fourth Directive. Obviously, the most important issue here is equal pensionable age for men and women.

The proposal does not cover the use of sex-related actuarial data. In this respect it can thus hardly be regarded as the 'finishing touch' of equal treatment in social security. A considerable loophole remains.[96]

For surviving spouses' benefits two alternatives are put forward. Either widowers must have the same rights to a pension and other benefits as widows, or a system of individual entitlements to all surviving spouses must be introduced replacing a system of widows' benefits, i.e. of derived rights.[97] The Articles concerning orphans' benefits and other survivors' benefits prohibit discrimination on grounds of sex of the deceased parent or the orphan, respectively the deceased person or the survivor.

The next category covered by the draft Directive is family benefits. Sex-based discrimination is prohibited with respect to child benefit and benefits introduced to assist parents to assume their parental responsibilities. Benefits for the maintenance of children and benefits for the parents themselves, for instance, birth and adoption grants, allowances intended to top up wages, allowances paid during parental leave and allowances for single-parent families are thus covered. The principle of equal treatment applies to both parents and other persons responsible for a child (not necessarily adoptive parents). Where the parents live together and there is no statutory provision to share entitlement, they should have the possibility of choosing which of them will receive the benefit. If they have not exercised this option, the benefit shall be paid to the mother. The Commission presumes that this will be in the interest of the child.[98] In the case of divorce or separation, benefits shall be paid to the parent who is actually taking care of the child. Further, with regard to benefits for dependent adults, there shall be no discrimination based on sex of the dependent adult or the person caring for the dependent adult.[99]

According to the next provision of the draft Directive, Article 9, when a pensionable age is determined for the purpose of granting old age and retirement pensions it shall be identical for both sexes. If the fixing of an equal pensionable age results in reduction or increase of that age for workers of a given sex, adequate transitional measures must be provided for. These latter should include gradual implementation and temporary safeguards maintaining the status quo for workers who have reached a certain age. Another alternative provided for in order to achieve equal treatment with respect to pensionable age is flexible retirement, which should mean that the choice of age is left to the beneficiaries who meet certain prescribed conditions, identical for both sexes, or the so-called seniority pension. Under this type the entitlement depends solely on the completion of a given number of contribution years, which must be identical for both men and women.

Article 10 of the proposal attempts to deal with the exemptions of Article 7, paragraph 1 (b, c and d) of the Social Security Directive.[100] First, advantages in respect of old age pension granted to persons who have brought up children and the acquisition of benefit entitlement following periods of interruption of employment due to the bringing up of children must be available to both men and women. Further, it appears from this Article or, at least, it may be understood since this Article is very vague in its drafting, that derived old age and invalidity benefits and increases of certain long-term benefits for a dependent wife must be extended to husbands as well.[101] Moreover, these benefits and increases will be authorized only where the spouse concerned was not able to establish her or his own right to benefits. This limitation has been introduced to prevent direct discrimination being replaced by indirect discrimination by reference to a dependent spouse.[102]

Article 11 contains another encouragement to replacing derived rights by a system of individual entitlements.[103] This Article is formulated as an option for the Member States and concerns health service care, appropriate old age pension, and entitlement to financial assistance for reasons of health or social situation and, when appropriate, temporary benefits for dependent children, in the event of a death of a spouse. The Commission explains that in particular in the case of a breach of the marital relationship the existence of derived rights may be endangered (i.e. rights to social security benefits extended to the spouse of the insured person by virtue of their legal ties). The system of personal rights may better guarantee the protection of spouses.[104]

Finally, it is worth mentioning that the proposal provides that the Articles from other Directives on, for instance, effective judicial protection, protection against dismissal, the declaration of nullity, the avoidance of discriminatory provisions in collective agreements shall apply to the matters covered by the present Directive as well.[105] With respect to benefits of the surviving spouse, or the pensionable age, the proposal contains a transitional measure: the Directive may not be relied upon in respect of applications submitted before the date of its implementation.[106] The period for implementing the Directive seems over-optimistic: three years.

Burden of proof

Discrimination, even when clearly defined in abstract terms, which is not the case under present Community law,[107] presents serious difficulties in practice, in particular as far as the obtaining of evidence and the distribution of the burden of proof is concerned. The initial burden is generally on the complainant. This implies that the applicant must collect evidence to establish her or his case. In this respect two major problems exist:[108] knowing what evidence will be necessary to prove discrimination and actually obtaining it. The relevant information is often in the hands of the employer, who may be reluctant to place it at the disposal of the complainant or the employer might not have kept the necessary records at all. Moreover, it may be necessary for an expert to give evidence, for example, in claims for equal pay for work of equal value, or that witnesses are heard. Therefore it is very important that a court, or another authority[109] has the power either on its own initiative, or on the applicant's request, to order the production of documents, even confidential ones when it seems necessary,[110] to order expert reports and to call witnesses. With respect to expert evidence, however, the problem of costs may cause serious difficulties. Further, witnesses will often be unwilling to give evidence since it may put their jobs in jeopardy.

In civil cases, most national legal systems have a general rule that complainants must prove their case on a balance of probabilities. If the respondent can provide an explanation which raises a doubt as to the validity of the complaint, the case falls because the persuasive burden remains on the complainant. In the area of equal treatment it appears that this burden of proof is difficult and sometimes even impossible for the complainant to establish.[111] Apart from the already mentioned problem of collecting evidence, some particular problems may arise because of the widespread prejudices with regard to women and their role within the society which may, sometimes even unconsciously, influence acts and decisions. Further, problems exist concerning the willingness of courts to draw inferences from the evidence presented and in respect of the application of unfamiliar concepts like indirect discrimination.[112]

In the legislation of several Member States, there already exists a certain modification of the burden of proof which should make it easier for persons who consider themselves discriminated against to prove their case. However, this modification varies from Member State to Member State and it applies often to certain types of litigation only, like in the area of maternity protection or unfair dismissal.[113] At a Community level, until now, some guidance was provided with regard to indirect discrimination only: if the applicant has established a *prima facie* case of indirect discrimination, it is for the respondent to prove that an act, decision or practice is objectively justified.[114] Illustrative of the existing uncertainties may be the following questions submitted to the Court in a Danish reference for a preliminary ruling:[115]

> where it is established that a male and a female do the same work or work of equal value, who in the view of the Court of Justice, is the person (employer or employee) on whom the burden lies of proving that a differentiation in pay between the two employees is attributable/not attributable to a circumstance determined by sex?

In the New Community Action Programme[116] the problem of assembling evidence and of distribution of the burden of proof has been considered as one of the causes responsible for the scanty use by women of arrangements for redress. Therefore, the Commission recommended to bring to the attention of some Member States the experience of other Member States with respect to the reversal of the burden of proof, i.e. the onus is placed on the employer or whoever has acted in an allegedly discriminatory way.

Moreover the Commission committed itself to conducting a comparative analysis of national procedures with a view to proposing Community action with respect to legal redress. This comparative analysis was completed in 1984.[117] With respect to the burden of proof, this study recommended that it should be formally altered. The complainant should have only to show that she or he has been less favourably treated than a person of the opposite sex. The burden would then shift to the alleged discriminator to show that his or her reasons for the treatment were not the complainant's sex.[118]

In the Medium-term Community Programme[119] the Member States were asked to review the provisions relating to the burden of proof to ensure that persons subject to discrimination will not be required to undertake a task that is often impossible. Furthermore, the Commission announced that it would put forward a Community legal instrument on the principle of the reversal of the burden of proof applying to all equal opportunities measures. In May 1988, the proposal for a Council Directive on the burden of proof in the area of equal pay and equal treatment for women was presented by the Commission.[120] In December 1988, the Directive was blocked within the Council and there are no prospects for its early adoption.

The proposal comprises three sections: general provisions, substantive provision and provisions regarding implementation. The general provisions, Articles 1 and 2, concern the purpose and the scope of the Directive. The purpose is to ensure that measures taken by Member States to enable individuals to pursue their equality claims are made more effective. The Directive is intended to apply to all Community law concerning equal treatment between men and women, existing[121] and future, unless these future instruments expressly exclude its application. Moreover, the Directive will apply to national procedures, civil or administrative, in both the public and private sector. An exception is made for criminal procedures. A change in the burden of proof in criminal procedure would too easily impose criminal liability on individuals which would be incompatible with the principle that a person is held innocent until his or her guilt is proved.[122] The provisions dealing with implementation, Articles 6 to 9, specify the usual obligations of the Member States, that they must put into force the necessary laws and regulations, to forward all necessary information to the Commission and so on.

Of most importance and interest are the substantive provisions. Article 3 concerns the modification of the burden of proof: where persons establish, before a court or other competent authority, a presumption of discrimination, it shall be for the respondent to prove that there has been no contravention of the principle of equality. The complainant shall have the benefit of any doubt that remains. According to paragraph 2, a presumption of discrimination is established where a complainant shows a fact or a series of facts which would, if not rebutted, amount to direct or indirect discrimination. Thus, the complainant is required to establish a rebuttable presumption of discrimination, or must show that less favourable treatment has occurred on grounds of sex. The elements put forward must be sufficient for a court or other competent authority to hold that there has been unlawful discrimination. However, he or she has not to prove it conclusively.[123] Once the complainant has established a *prima facie* case, the evidential burden shifts to the respondent. He or she must rebut the presumption by proving that the sex of the complainant was not the reason for the unequal treatment, or by showing that the principle of equality did not apply, because, for instance, the matter was covered by one of the exceptions contained in Community sex discrimination law. By giving the benefit of any doubt to the complainant, the Member States are required, once a presumption of discrimination has been established, to place the burden on the respondent of providing the ultimate evidence that there was no unlawful discrimination.[124]

The choice made by the Commission is thus a modification of the burden of proof rather than a reversal. The legal burden of persuasion remains with the complainant, but the evidential burden shifts to the respondent. The latter must prove that no discrimination has occurred. Nevertheless under paragraph 3 of Article 3, the Member States may reverse the burden of proof completely by imposing the legal burden of persuasion upon the respondent. In such a situation it will suffice for the complainant to show that less favourable treatment has occurred. The respondent must prove positively and objectively that there was no discrimination based on sex. The Commission's approach seems to be inspired by the already existing distribution of the burden of proof in some Member States[125] and by the case-law of the Court of Justice in indirect discrimination cases.[126] Although this initiative must be welcomed as providing some more and clearer guidance for the problem of proof in sex discrimination cases, on the other hand much depends on the attitudes of national courts which may not be changed by a Community Directive.

Article 4 concerns the problem of obtaining evidence. First, the courts or other competent authorities must have the power to order any measure to ensure the effective examination of any complaint of discrimination. Second, all relevant information may be obtained from the party who possesses it or who may reasonably be required to obtain it. An exception is made for confidential information, disclosure of which would cause substantial damage to the party concerned, other than the litigation. This provision aims at matters such as business secrets and sensitive information.[127]

Article 5 defines the concept of indirect discrimination. It does so as follows:

Indirect discrimination exists where an apparently neutral provision, criterion or practice disproportionately disadvantages the members of one sex, by reference in particular to marital or family status, and is not objectively justified by any necessary reason or condition unrelated to the sex of the person concerned.

Paragraph 2 provides that the intention of the respondent may not be taken into account. The definition is said to be based on the case-law of the Court of Justice and national courts, national legislation and guidelines and certain statements of the Commission.[128] It contains in fact nothing new and seems to be in conformity with the Court's judgements.[129] The real value of the definition will depend on the interpretation of the terms 'disproportionately' and, in particular, 'necessary'. It should be reiterated here that the objective justification test means two steps: is the objective to be reached important enough to prevail over the principle of equal treatment and is the provision, criterion or practice really necessary to reach the objective?[130] It is regrettable that the Commission did not draft the definition in such a way that these two touchstones showed up well; the more precise the test, the less room is left for vague justifications. Finally it may be asked whether the phrase 'unrelated to the sex of the person concerned' is not incorrect, or at least puzzling. First, a 'reason unrelated to the sex of the person concerned' may suggest that the element of intention is important, which is, according to paragraph 2, apparently not the purpose. Second, even if the reason has nothing to do with sex of the person concerned, the fact remains that a criterion, provision or practice affects women or men. If such disadvantageous treatment is not necessary, the criterion, provision or practice should disappear. It is irrelevant to ask whether the reason for maintaining it is related to sex or not.

Parental leave and part-time work

The Commission has also made proposals for the adoption of two Directives on the issues of parental leave and voluntary part-time work. Neither of these specifically relate to sex discrimination but they quite obviously have a relationship with the problems which have been discussed within this book. It is for this reason that they are discussed here.

The Commission's draft Directive on parental leave or leave for family reasons[131] is contentious and, given the strong opposition to it from the UK and employers' organizations throughout the Community, is unlikely to be adopted in the near future. The nature of this opposition stems from the reluctance, particularly on the part of the British government, to impose what are seen as additional costs on employers, and more specifically on small businesses which are seen to be the generators of wealth within the British economy. Entitlement to maternity benefits has already recently been restricted within the UK and it is unlikely that any change of heart will persuade the British government to place the welfare of workers over the pursuit of short-term profit. Similar fears were expressed by the Employers' Group of the Economic and Social Committee which issued a statement rejecting the Commission's proposal which was appended to the Opinion of the Economic and Social Committee.[132] This statement talks of harmful consequences for business, increased labour costs and reduced flexibility which would lead to a loss of international competitiveness and to increase in financial burdens both on employers and on national budgets and social security schemes.

On the other hand, supporters of the measure see in it an improvement in working conditions for both men and women, but particularly for the latter since one of the aims of the proposal is to encourage a rethinking of the distribution of responsibilities within the family. At present the double burdens of work outside and inside the home are largely carried by women with the consequent toll both on their health and on their prospects for well paid and continuous employment. These are the underlying considerations why the Commission announced its intention to take action to promote parental leave and leave for family reasons.[133] In this the Commission is supported by the European Parliament which, in February 1981, adopted a resolution on the situation of women in the European Community which emphasized the need for harmonization of the Member States' laws and practices concerning parental leave and, in June 1983, adopted a resolution on family policy where the priority for the need for parental leave was stressed.

The Commission's proposal, as it stands, is for a Directive adopted on the basis of Article 100 EEC. As has already been stated, Article 100 allows the Community to harmonize domestic laws where this is necessary for the effective functioning of the common market. On its own, Article 100 may be a questionable basis for action in this area since it may be doubted whether the provision or absence of provision of parental leave does directly affect the functioning of the common market. This is the thrust behind the proposed amendments within the Economic and Social Committee which regarded parental leave as 'an unwarranted luxury' and not as a harmonization of existing conditions but the introduction of new ones. The proposed Directive states that existing disparities between national provisions are great enough to affect the functioning of the common market and the remedy is to approximate laws towards the most advanced provisions in the terms of Article 117 of the Treaty. The proposals are seen as an improvement of standards of living and working conditions of the labour force.

The final recital of the Directive refers to Council Directive 76/207/EEC, the Equal Treatment Directive and the principles of equal treatment contained therein. Of course it must be remembered that the draft was prepared *before* the judgement of the European Court in *Hoffmann*[134] where the Court held that the extension of an additional period of maternity leave beyond that needed for the physical recovery of the mother granted to women by German law was not contrary to the Equal Treatment Directive since its purpose is to nurture the bond between mother and child. That case has been criticized elsewhere in this book and there is no need here to rehearse those arguments.[135] *Hoffmann* demonstrated that existing Community law, in particular the Equal Treatment Directive, did not cover the type of leave granted by German law. However, it is doubtful if the present proposal will cover the gap left by *Hoffmann*, for reasons discussed below. However, the inclusion of a reference to the Equal Treatment Directive does indicate that parental leave is viewed very much as a working condition to which men and women are equally entitled.

In its first Article, the draft Directive defines parental leave, and the persons entitled thereto, and leave for family reasons. Parental leave is an entitlement to leave for wage-earners, including staff in the public sector, consequential upon the birth of a child, during the period following, but not necessarily consecutive with maternity leave. In the case of an adoption, it is a period of leave following the reception of the child into the home of the would-be adoptive parents or upon adoption of a child. In both cases the beneficiary must take responsibility for the actual care of the child.

Several problems raised by this definition are clarified in later Articles of the draft. The first is whether such periods of leave are available to all wage-earners or only those in full-time employment. Article 3 makes it clear that all wage-earners are so entitled, including part-time workers. Allowances granted or periods of insurance credited to part-timers must be calculated in the same way for full- and part-time workers on a proportionate basis. This situation compares favourably with that relating to maternity leave where there are quite wide disparities in entitlement. In some States, maternity leave is available only to those women who work a certain number of hours, this number differing between different States.[136] However, within the draft Directive itself there is no definition of part-time workers and until there is a Community definition it will be the Member States who define the workers who are entitled to leave. The Directive does allow for parental leave to be made subject to a requirement regarding length of service or employment, which may not exceed one year (Article 5(3)). Some groups of workers are excluded from this definition, for example, the self-employed. It may be argued that such workers are free to determine their own entitlements, and this is true. However, where a State provides a benefit for persons taking parental leave then the self-employed would be disadvantaged.

A further question arises from the definition given in Article 1 which is not solved in the Directive itself. This relates to when the period of leave is deemed to commence. Leave may, but does not necessarily have, to follow upon the expiry of maternity leave. It may be asked at this stage why the Commission did not first turn its attention to the issue of maternity leave itself since there is diversity both in the range of entitlement to maternity leave and to types of maternity leave. Without harmonization in this area it may be difficult for employers to accept the need for harmonization in what might be seen as a second stage. As the report on the protection of working women during pregnancy and motherhood shows,[137] the duration of post-natal maternity leave varies in the Member States, from six weeks in the Netherlands (where a proposed extension to eight weeks is currently opposed by employers) to three months in Italy. Examples given in the Commission's report show that extensions of maternity leave are possible in France and the UK where the mother is ill, or in France where there has been a multiple birth. In this case, French maternity leave can be extended by various periods, depending on the circumstances, up to 30 weeks. Furthermore, in Ireland and Germany, as was demonstrated in *Hoffmann*, maternity leave is divided between a type of maternity leave which allows for the physical recovery of the mother and one which allows for the psychological bonding of mother and child. In these cases, when does maternity leave expire? The answer to these questions must, in so far as maternity leave provisions are not harmonized, be dependent on national law. However, without this prior harmonization, the aim of the Directive which is, according to the Commission, to reduce disparities, will remain unmet since parental leave is additional on existing provisions. The question becomes important if the mother opts to take parental leave consequent upon maternity leave. It is not so problematic where it is someone other than the mother who is the beneficiary. The wording of Article 1 would allow a father to take parental leave concurrent with the mother's maternity leave providing that he does so in order to take responsibility for the care of the child. Article 4(2) of the draft does, however, preclude two persons from simultaneously taking parental leave in respect of one child (but not twins?) since the beneficiary is to be solely or principally responsible for the child. Therefore, two parents could not be absent from work for the same period taking parental leave.

This latter phrase raised further problems. Presumably wage-earners may take their entitlement to parental leave on the basis of their statement that they will be responsible for caring for the child without having to furnish evidence that they are in fact doing so.

Parental leave is to be granted to the following categories of workers: fathers and mothers, adoptive fathers and mothers, stepfathers and mothers, or any person acting in the place of such persons in circumstances such as death or serious illness of the latter.

Article 1 defines leave for family reasons as being an entitlement to short periods of leave granted for pressing family reasons to workers with family responsibilities.

Article 2 states that the purpose of the Directive is to entitle workers, that is, to grant them a right to such periods of leave under harmonized conditions in the Member States. Further Articles of the Directive lay down guidelines for these conditions. Furthermore, the principle of non-discrimination is to apply to such entitlements to leave, irrespective of the family or marital status of the worker. This provision would prohibit the employer from differentiating between single or married persons (except for the length of leave, see below), although it may mean that the father of an illegitimate child may have to show his right to leave, i.e. prove that he is in fact the father of the child. Furthermore, Article 2 states that the periods of leave foreseen in the draft Directive do not affect provision relating to paternity leave. Hence the father of a child may be eligible for both paternity leave and parental leave where national law allows him the former.

Certain minimal procedures are laid down in Article 4 before workers may exercise their rights to parental leave. They are required to give adequate notice to the employer of their intention both to take leave and to return to work after their period of leave. In no case shall the period of notice be more than two months. Member States are, therefore, free to determine both the form such notice shall take, for example that it be in writing, and the period of notice, providing this does not exceed two months. These procedures are reasonable and give the employer an opportunity to make suitable arrangements for the replacement of workers who have opted to take leave. It is not explicitly stated, but it may be assumed, that the wage-earner's contract of employment is not interrupted by periods of leave. Again this compares favourably with the situation relating to maternity leave since, in at least one Member State, the UK, the contract of employment is terminated where a woman takes maternity leave and recommences on her return to work. Parental leave may be granted on more than one occasion – since workers are entitled to it after each birth or adoption. The duration of each period of leave is three months, although this may be extended in the case of single parents or for parents with handicapped children living at home. Leave must be taken before a child reaches the age of two years except in the case of adoption of a child under five, when the entitlement to leave expires two years after the adoption, or in the case of a disabled child, when the entitlement to leave expires when the child reaches five years.

The period of leave may be taken as continuous full-time leave, or with the agreement of employer and employee as a period of extended part-time leave. It is not clear whether one parent can take part-time leave at the same time as the other parent, for example mother is at home in the morning and father in the afternoon. If the employee does not use up the full entitlement, then the entitlement to the remaining part ceases. Where the parent becomes ill during the period of leave, parental leave is suspended within the age limits of the child set out above.

Article 5 provides that the taking of parental leave does not prejudice any entitlement acquired or in the process of being acquired. Such entitlements are not defined within the draft Directive but the term must be taken to mean entitlements to such things as holidays, seniority, pensions, and further periods of parental leave. Perhaps the most crucial part of the draft is slipped into Article 5(6), which provides that parental leave is assimilated with periods of maternity leave for the purpose of insurance as regards sickness, unemployment and invalidity benefit and old age pension. Parental and maternity leave are therefore in a comparable situation. Thus they are internally, but not externally, harmonized in the sense that Member States do differ as to how they credit maternity leave for the purposes set out above.[139] On termination of leave the worker is entitled to return to the same or an equivalent job. This latter provision will give employers practical difficulties, particularly in relation to highly qualified, well trained staff where temporary replacements are difficult to find.

Article 6 states that Member States may provide, from public funds including social security, a parental leave allowance. This provision is permissive and not mandatory and lays any obligation as to pay on the State rather than on the employer. There is no obligation in the draft on employers to pay the wages of employees taking parental leave and, without an allowance, it may be questioned how many parents will be able to avail themselves of the opportunities granted under the Directive. Depending on the social security systems in force, such persons may of course be eligible for other benefits, but again the range of available benefits is not yet harmonized as between the Member States.

Leave for family reasons shall be provided, according to Article 8 of the draft, for a minimum number of days (to be laid down by the Member States) for pressing family reasons. This level of discretion does not, again, meet the problem of disparities within the Community since, inevitably, some Member States will be more generous than others. The Directive lists some of the pressing family reasons, but the list is not exhaustive. These include: illness of a spouse, child or person caring for a child; the death of a near relative or the wedding of a child. No doubt enlightened employers already make provision for some of these contingencies but the Directive makes it clear that leave for these purposes is a right of a worker (albeit for a limited number of days) rather than a benefit granted by an employer. The number of days of leave may be extended in the case of heads of single-parent families or where the beneficiary has three or more children living at home, under an age limit determined by the Member States or where the beneficiary is responsible for the care of a disabled person living in the same household. For the purposes of remuneration, social security contributions and allowances and pension entitlements, periods of leave for family purposes are to be assimilated to paid holidays. Thus, for these purposes, it is the employer who must pay for the benefits provided.

The final provisions of the draft are similar to those in previous Directives, giving the right to pursue their claims by judicial process to persons considering themselves wronged by failure to apply the Directive;

workers are protected against dismissal when they seek to enforce their rights and the Directive must be brought to the attention of employers and workers. Member States must introduce the necessary provisions and make the necessary amendments to enforce the Directive and inform the Commission of any action in this field. These measures must be taken within two years of notification of the Directive and Member States must report to the Commission within three years of its notification of progress made in this field.

It is very unlikely that further progress in the area of parental leave will be made in the near future. The Single European Act which, in some ways, sets outs a guideline for progress in the coming years, provides in Article 118A that Member States shall encourage improvements in matters relating to health and safety at work and it may be argued that parental leave might come under this heading. However, the same Article also provides that developments in this area shall avoid administrative, financial and legal constraints which would hold back the creation and development of small and medium-sized undertakings. The parental leave Directive is viewed in just such a light by the British government. Its adoption would, however, ease the burden for working parents either by giving them the chance to have additional time with their children and without losing their place in the work-force, or by allowing parents to take more responsibility for family matters.

The second proposed Directive which appears to be stuck in the Council's decision-making process relates to voluntary part-time work. Like parental leave, this proposal does not directly relate to the principle of equal treatment of men and women, but the impact of any legislation relating to part-time work will of course be felt first by women who constitute some 90 per cent of the part-time work-force. The origins of the draft Directive lie in two distinct, although related issues. The first of these is the question of the adaptation of working time within the Community, an issue which has been under discussion since 1979 in the Economic and Social Committee, the Commission and the Council.[140] Discussions on this topic arose partly out of a desire to find a solution to the growing problem of unemployment in the Member States and partly out of a perceived demand on the part of workers for a more flexible working week and a desire to extend leisure time. The second source lies in the debates within the European Parliament on the situation of working women in the Community. As has been noted, the bulk of the part-time working population is female and, therefore, the disadvantages associated with part-time work fall more heavily on women. These advantages have been described as being low status, low pay, discrimination in access to social benefits including pensions, denial of access to promotion and training and unequal working conditions.

Part-time work, as has been seen, has given rise to cases before the European Court where women have alleged that they have received disadvantageous treatment which amounts to sex-based discrimination since the burden falls more heavily on women than on men.[141] The European Court has accepted that according less favourable treatment to part-time workers may amount to indirect discrimination and the employer must, therefore, show an objective justification for the difference in treatment. However, differences in treatment do not necessarily amount to sex discrimination since there may be objective justifications for treating full-time workers better than part-timers.

The draft Directive recognizes those special features of part-time work but demands for part-time workers the same rights as full-timers.[142] The Directive is based on Article 100 of the Treaty and, like parental leave, makes reference to Article 117. It must be seen then as a harmonization of working conditions necessary to ensure the effective functioning of the common market. The Council, in its Resolution on the Adaptation of Working Time, had laid down four guiding principles to govern voluntary part-time work.[143] The first principle stressed that part-time work should be voluntary, that is, agreed between the employer and the employee; it should be based on the equal treatment of men and women and it should not be limited to unskilled work. The second principle is that part-time work should be made available to groups of workers, such as parents of young children or older workers. In itself this principle is laudable in that it seeks to fit patterns of employment to patterns in lifestyle of particular groups. However, these very groups of people are the ones who already opt for part-time work and who suffer from its disadvantages. The third principle determines that part-time workers should have the same social rights and obligations as full-time workers. As the Commission noted in its report, in this respect a vast array of discriminatory practices will need to be eliminated in particular in the areas of pay, social security schemes, pensions (statutory or occupational, job security and tax provisions). The Commission recommended in this respect that part-time workers should be treated in the same way as other workers, whose rights and obligations should be based on the principle of proportionality. This principle must be qualified, however, by both practical and theoretical considerations, particularly in regard to rights which are qualitative as compared to quantitative. The fourth principle enumerated by the Council provides that part-time work could be defined on a variety of bases, daily, weekly or monthly, according to the needs of workers and undertakings.

These principles have all been translated into the draft Directive which defines part-time work as work performed on a regular basis where an employer and employee agree to shorter working hours. Article 2 applies the classic principle of non-discrimination to part-time workers. They are to receive the same treatment as full-time workers in the same situation except where the difference in hours of work objectively justifies these differences in treatment. Article 2 then defines areas where differences in treatment cannot be justified. These include health and safety at work conditions, rules relating to redundancy and dismissal, trade union representation, and access to training, promotion and social facilities. Certain aspects of the part-time worker's contract, remuneration, holiday, redundancy and retirement pay are to be calculated on the same basis as full-time workers in proportion to those of the latter. Remuneration is given the meaning contained in Article 119 of the Treaty.

Article 3 gives part-time workers the right to be covered by both statutory and occupational social security schemes. Their contributions to and benefits from those schemes are to be determined on the same basis as full-time employees, taking into account the remuneration received and/or hours worked. Eligibility thresholds are, however, permitted.

The possibility of changing from a full-time to a part-time post and vice versa is covered by Article 6. Workers within an establishment are said to have priority over outside recruitment when such changes in posts are to be made. The 'one-way ticket problem' outlined by the Commission whereby a worker finds it difficult to move from part-time to full-time status should thereby be alleviated. Article 6 accords with the Belgian Employers' Federation's proposal that part-time workers should have priority for vacancies in the same establishment.

Article 7 requires that part-time workers are taken into the total count of the work-force for the purpose of defining the employer's social obligations which are linked to the numbers employed. Article 8 provides for consultation and participation of workers' representatives before part-time working is introduced. This Article has been introduced to allay fears that employers will force part-time work on unwilling employees in an effort to reduce costs and improve productivity at the expense of the existing work-force.

The remaining Articles oblige the Member States to introduce the necessary measures to comply with the Directive and to inform the Commission of measures which they have taken in this respect. In the draft as it stands there is no time limit for implementation.

If this draft is adopted, which is unlikely in the near future, it will go some way to improving the situation of women in the working population. Part-time employees do suffer enormous disadvantages as compared to full-time employees and the Directive is a definite step forward in helping to eliminate some of the disadvantages. However, the draft may be seen to limit the flexibility of employers who have traditionally used the pool of part-time labour as an expendable and cheap source. It is the view of certain governments that employers should not be deprived of their flexibility and it may be, therefore, that there will be little future development in this area.

Notes

1   This was exactly the situation in cases 149/77 *Defrenne* v. *Sabena* (1978) E.C.R. 1365

discussed in Chapter 3 above, 19/81 *Burton* v. *British Railways Board* (1982) E.C.R. 555 discussed in Chapters 3 and 4 above, and 192/85 *Newstead* v. *Department of Transport and H. M. Treasury* (1988) 1 C.M.L. Rep 219 discussed in Chapters 3 and 4 above.

2   The Medium-term Community Programme on the promotion of equal opportunities for women (1986–1990), COM(85)801 final.

3   See 'The dignity of women at work: a report on the problem of sexual harassment in the Member States of the EC' V/412/1/87–EN. As far as taxation is concerned in December 1984 the Commission submitted a Memorandum to the Council. COM(84)695 final, recommending a system of totally independent taxation for all or, at least, an option of separate taxation available to couples. The European Parliament and the Economic and Social Committee take the view that a Directive is necessary in this field. See O.J. C 229/128, 9 September 1985, and O.J. C 218/23, 29 August 1985.

4   See Chapter 5 above p. 165.

5   Knopper suggests that the UK took the position that if the First Directive were to include occupational schemes they would veto it. (Knopper, in Fase (ed.) (1986) p. 142.)

6   Article 3, paragraph 3 of the Social Security Directive.

7   Council Directive 86/378 of 24 July 1986 on the implementation of the principle of equal treatment for men and women in occupational social security schemes, O.J. L 225/40, 12 August 1986. This Directive is usually referred to as the Fourth Directive.

8   Convention no. 100 Concerning Equal Remuneration for Men and Women Workers for Work of Equal Value, 1951 UNTS Treaty no. 2181, vol. 165, p. 303.

9   See Laurent (1986) pp. 754 and 758.

10   About 80 000 in the UK. See 'European Parliament Report on the Commission's proposal for a Council Directive on the implementation of the principle of equal treatment for men and women in occupational social security schemes', Document 1–1502/83, p. 17. In the Netherlands there were, in 1982, about 21 000 occupational pension schemes (80 pension funds covering several industrial sectors, 1000 company pension funds and 18 000 to 20 000 collective pension arrangements placed with insurance companies); see Madlener (1984) pp. 18–19.

11   Of course, they have to meet certain legal requirements. The element of state control and intervention may differ considerably. However, in our view, even an extensive statutory regulation does not make them statutory in the sense of the Third Directive. See on diverse categories of occupational schemes Plender (1982), pp. 639–643.

12   See 'Explanatory Memorandum on the Commission Proposal for a Directive on the implementation of the principle of equal treatment for men and women in occupational social security schemes', COM (83) 217 final, pp. 1–2, and the European Parliament Report, *loc. cit.* in note 10, p. 20.

13   Compare the scheme in case 170/84 *Bilka – Kaufhaus GmbH* v. *Karin Weber Von Hartz* (1986) E.C.R. 1067, discussed in Chapter 3, p. 64.

14   It is even possible that only employees contribute.

15   See 'Discriminatie tussen mannen en vrouwen in de bedrijfspensioenregelingen', Working Document of the Commission, V/148/80–NL.

16   See Chapter 5 above p. 197.

17   Or contributions, where appropriate.

18   Compare 'Explanatory Memorandum of the Commission', *loc. cit.* note 12, p. 3 and pp. 6–10, 'European Parliament Report', *loc. cit.* note 10, pp. 23–25, Laurent (1982) pp. 380–381, Curtin (1987) pp. 216–217.

19   Thus, this provision aims clearly at contracted-out schemes.

20   See Laurent (1986) p. 757.

21   The Commission's proposal did not include any exclusions at all. The first three exclusions in the final version of Article 2 can be however considered as immanent to occupational schemes.

22   See in more detail Curtin (1987) pp. 220–221.
23   See Chapter 5 above p. 168.
24   *Ibid.*, in particular p. 177.
25   In the case of family leave the principle of equal treatment implies, of course, that either there is for both men and women an interruption or for nobody.
26   See 'Explanatory Memorandum' p. 8, *loc. cit.* note 12.
27   Compare in particular Article 6, paragraph 1(g) of the Directive. See however on an anomaly in this Article below, p. 284.
28   See the opinion on the Directive of the Economic and Social Committee, O.J. C 35/9, 9 February 1984.
29   European Parliament Report *loc. cit.* note 10, p. 9.
30   See Chapter 5 above p. 168.
31   The Fourth Directive refers however, unlike the Third, explicitly to 'early retirement' as well.
32   Second paragraph of Article 119 states: 'For the purpose of this Article, "pay" means the ordinary basis or minimum wage or salary and any other consideration, whether in cash or in kind, which the worker receives, directly or indirectly, in respect of his employment from his employer'. The resemblance is striking.
33   See Chapter 5 above pp. 173-7.
34   *Ibid.* p. 178. Note that unlike the Social Security Directive, the preamble of the Fourth Directive no longer mentions 'specific provisions for women to remove instances of unequal treatment'.
35   See Chapter 5 above p. 177.
36   Compare Laurent (1986) p. 755.
37   The most common form is the money purchase system (accumulated contributions are transformed into a pension).
38   See, for instance, Laurent (1982) p. 383, and Laurent (1986) p. 760, European Parliament Report, *loc. cit.* note 10 p. 17 and pp. 26–27, Explanatory Memorandum of the Commission, *loc. cit.* note 12, pp. 8–9.
39   See Resolution of the European Parliament on the proposal for the Occupational Schemes Directive, O.J. C 117/171, 30 April 1984, and the 'Opinion of the Economic and Social Committee', *loc. cit.* note 28. However, the Committee was quite critical of Commission's proposal, in particular, it argued that the Commission should submit more and stronger arguments to defend this point.
40   See *City of Los Angeles* v. *Manhart*, 435 US 702 and *Arizona Governing Committee* v. *Norris,* 463 US 1073.
41   See Curtin (1987) p. 228.
42   See Laurent (1986) p. 761.
43   See, for instance, case 262/84 *Beets-Proper* v. *van Landschot Bankiers* (1986) E.C.R. 773, discussed in Chapter 4 above, p. 123.
44   A Commission proposal for a Council Directive completing the implementation of the principle of equal treatment for men and women in statutory and occupational social security schemes has been published in O.J. C 309/10, 19 November 1987. See below p. 293.
45   See European Parliament Report *loc. cit.* note 10, p. 10. See also the Parliament's Resolution on widows' and widowers' pensions, O.J. C 117/173, 30 April 1984.
46   Case 165/82 *Commission* v. *UK* (1983) E.C.R. 3431. See for discussion Chapter 4 above p. 143.
47   See Chapters 1, 4, and 5 especially pp. 19, 107 and 176.
48   The Commission's proposal for a Council Directive on voluntary part-time work, O.J. C62/7, 12 March 1982 (amended version in O.J. 1983, C 18/5, 22 January 1983), is however not likely to be adopted, at least not soon. See below pp. 306-8.
49   The draft Directive included in Article 6(j) 'transfer of entitlement to another scheme'. The Council did not follow this proposed text. The list of Article 6 being enumerative only, this omission does not mean that transfer is not covered.

50 In legal terms, of course.
51 Compare Chapter 5 above, p. 177. In the event of dismissal when taking maternity leave Article 6(j) will apply.
52 Moreover, since 152/84 *Marshall* v. *Southampton and South West Hampshire Area Health Authority* (1986) E.C.R. 723 and *Beets-Proper* (case 262/84 *loc. cit.* note 43) there are additional reasons to solve the problem of unequal pension ages.
53 There is something very ironic in paying women lower benefits in case of illness or asking them to contribute more because women in general are more often ill than men. It may be asked whether the possible cause is not the double 'workload' a woman has to deal with: her job and her unpaid work at home.
54 In exceptional cases 'something' can also be done under Article 119. See case 23/83 *Liefting* v. *Academisch Ziekenhuis bij de Universiteit van Amsterdam* (1984) E.C.R. 3225 discussed in Chapter 3 above, p. 62.
55 Cases 80/70 *Defrenne* v. *Belgium* (Defrenne I) (1971) E.C.R. 445; 12/81 *Garland* v. *British Rail Engineering Ltd*, (1952) E.C.R. 359; 170/84 (*Bilka*) *loc. cit.* note 13. See for discussion Chapter 3 pp. 55, 70 and 64 respectively.
56 See Chapter 1 and 3 above p. 15 and p. 53.
57 Consideration 67 in Case 43/75 *Defrenne* v. *Sabena* (Defrenne II) (1976) E.C.R. 455 discussed in Chapter 3 above p. 85.
58 Consideration 22 in case 96/80 *Jenkins* v. *Kingsgate (Clothing Productions) Ltd* (1981) E.C.R. 911 discussed in Chapter 3 above p. 86.
59 Case 170/84 (*Bilka*) *loc. cit.* note 13.
60 Compare Laurent (1986) p. 758 and Curtin (1987) p. 218.
61 Compare the decision of the President of the Court on 13 March 1987 in case 45/87, *Commission* v. *Ireland* (1989) 1 CMLR 225.
62 See case 80/70 (Defrenne I) *loc. cit.* note 55 on the one hand, and cases 23/83 (*Liefting*) *loc. cit.* note 54 and 69/80 *Worringham and Humphreys* v. *Lloyds Bank Limited* (1981) E.C.R. 767 discussed in Chapter 3 p. 58 on the other.
63 See Chapters 3 and 5 above pp. 57, 64 and 69.
64 See Chapter 5, p. 170 and p. 171.
65 See Article 2.
66 See Plender (1982) p. 643.
67 Case 12/81 *loc. cit.* note 55.
68 Case 170/84 *loc. cit.* note 13.
69 Case 69/80 *loc. cit.* note 62 and case 23/83 *loc. cit.* note 54.
70 See in this sense Advocate General Warner in his opinion in 69/80 (*Worringham*), *loc. cit.* note 62, p. 806. See also Plender (1982) p. 645, who observes that if Article 119 did concern equality in costs, the employer could differentiate in the wages of male and female employees to the average additional costs of employing women, which can, for example, arise from statutory requirements with respect to pregnancy leave.
71 Advocate General Warner, *loc. cit.* note 70. See also Imbrechts (1986) pp. 236–237.
72 However, see the opinion of Advocate General Dutheillet de Lamothe in case 80/87 (Defrenne I), *loc. cit.* note 55. He held that 'the deduction for the pension which as a rule the employed person suffers during his active period is in fact only a reduction of salary which he accepts in consideration for the promise of a retirement pension'. From this point of view a pension is clearly deferred pay the employee would have otherwise enjoyed during his or her active employment and the contributions should be covered by Article 119 as well.
73 Case 192/85 *loc. cit.* note 1.
74 This was in fact the case in 23/83 (*Liefting*) *loc. cit.* note 54. The public authority with which a civil servant was employed paid the contributions on his or her behalf. Those who were not civil servants had to pay the contributions themselves.
75 Case 149/77 *loc. cit.* note 1, discussed in Chapter 3 above p. 68.
76 Case 19/81 *loc. cit.* note 1, discussed in Chapter 3 and 4 above p. 69 and p. 121.

77   Case 69/80 *loc. cit.* note 62.
78   Case 170/84 *loc. cit.* note 13.
79   See the opinion of Advocate General VerLoren van Themaat in case 19/81 (*Burton*) p. 589 *loc. cit.* note 1. It is possible that the decisive test is a benefit or no benefit at all. This was for example the case in *Bilka*, while in *Defrenne*, *Burton* and *Newstead* the claimants 'got their money' in one way or another. But this is of course pure speculation without any plausible explanation.
80   Case 192/85 *loc. cit.* note 1.
81   Cases 152/84 and 262/84 respectively *loc. cit.* notes 52 and 43.
82   This relationship between Article 119 and the Directives is, again, the 'heart' of case 262/88 *Douglas Harvey Barber* v. *Guardian Royal Exchange Assurance Group* referred to the Court of Justice by the Court of Appeal in London. See O.J. C279/14, 29 October 1988. See also case 233/89 *Gray Precision Engineers* v. *David William Clarke* (not yet decided) O.J. C219/10, 25 August 1989.
83   Council Directive 86/613 of 11 December 1986 on the application of the principle of equal treatment between men and women engaged in an activity, including agriculture, in a self-employed capacity, and on the protection of self-employed women during pregnancy and motherhood. OJ L 395/56, 19 December 1986.
84   COM. (84) 57 final.
85   COM. (81) 758 final.
86   See Cmnd. 9794 'Building Businesses...Not Barriers' (HMSO 1986)
87   O.J. C 309/10, 19 November 1987.
88   See 'Explanatory Memorandum of a Commission Proposal for a Directive completing the implementation of the principle of equal treatment for men and women in statutory and occupational social security schemes', COM. (87) 494 final, p. 2.
89   Directive 79/77, OJ L 6/24, 10 January 1979. See Chapter 5.
90   Directive 86/378, OJ L 225/40, 12 August 1986. See above, p. 276.
91   Explanatory Memorandum, *loc. cit.* note 88 p. 3.
92   *Ibid.*
93   *Ibid.*
94   In a report on the Commission's proposal the Commission for Women's Rights of the European Parliament suggested an explicit provision forbidding deterioration during the implementation period; Document A2–159188, p. 11.
95   Compare Article 2 of the Social Security Directive; see also Chapter 5, p. 168, and Article 3 of the Occupational Schemes Directive, discussed above, p. 279.
96   See on actuarial data above, in particular p. 281.
97   The first alternative has been introduced in Germany, the second in Denmark. See Cornelissen, in Franssen *et al.* (1987) pp. 61–62.
98   Explanatory Memorandum, *loc. cit.* note 88 p. 5.
99   Note that this resembles the situation in case 150/85 *Drake* v. *Chief Adjudication Officer* (1986) E.C.R. 1995 discussed in Chapter 5 p. 182.
100   See for discussion Chapter 5, p. 180.
101   Article 7, paragraph 1 (c and d) refer only to 'wife'.
102   Explanatory Memorandum, *loc. cit.* note 88 p. 6.
103   The first in Article 4, and perhaps, to a certain extent, Article 10, paragraph 2.
104   Explanatory Memorandum, *loc. cit.* note 88 p. 7.
105   More specifically, Articles 5 and 6 of the Social Security Directive and Articles 7, 10, 11 of the Occupational Schemes Directive.
106   Persons concerned may, however, rely on Article 119 or another Directive when appropriate. See above pp. 285–9.
107   The Directives give no definition of both direct and indirect discrimination. See for further discussion of those concepts Chapters 1, 3, 4 and 5 above.
108   Compare Report of a comparative analysis of the provisions for legal redress in Member States of the European Economic Community in respect of Article 119 of the

Treaty of Rome and the Equal Pay, Equal Treatment and Social Security Directives. V/564/84-EN pp. 45–50.

109 For instance an officer of the national court especially appointed to examine the available information and to order the production of documents which he or she claims necessary before the court itself considers the matter. The Report on legal redress, *loc. cit.* note 108 p. 78, considers a system of such 'rapporteurs' highly desirable. Another possibility is, for example, to give more powers to Labour Inspectorates or to Equality Officers, and to appoint them in those Member States where they do not exist.

110 Compare *Nasse* v. *Science Research Council* (1979) I.R.L.R. 465.

111 See 'Explanatory Memorandum of Commission Proposal for a Directive on the burden of proof in the area of equal pay and equal treatment of women and men', COM (88) 269 final, p. 2.

112 *Ibid.*; see also Report on legal redress, *loc. cit.* note 108 pp. 55–56.

113 Report on legal redress, *loc. cit.* note 108 pp. 53–55.

114 Cases 170/84 (*Bilka*) *loc. cit.* note 13 and 30/85 *Teuling* v. *Bedrijfsvereniging voor de Chemische Industrie* (1988) 3 CMLR 789.

115 Case 109/88 *Handels-Og Kantorfunctionaernes Forbund I Danmark* v. *Dansk Arbeijdsgiverforening for Danfoss A/S* O.J. C124/8, 11 May 1988 (not yet decided).

116 The New Community Action Programme on the Promotion of Equal Opportunities for Women (1982–1985), COM. (81) 758 final.

117 This is the Report on legal redress, *loc. cit.* note 108.

118 *Ibid.* p. 80.

119 See above, note 2.

120 O.J. C176/5, 5 July 1988.

121 Thus Article 119, and Directives 75/117, 76/207, 79/7, 86/378 and 86/613.

122 This 'presumption of innocence' is included in Article 6, paragraph 2 of the European Convention on Human Rights. However, its scope is unclear. Compare, for example, Commission decision of 19 July 1972 (*X* v. *UK*), Collection of Decisions of the E.C.H.R, 42 (1973), p. 135, Commission decision of 11 December 1981 (Lingens and Leitgeb), Decisions and Reports 26 (1982), p. 171, and judgement of the European Court for Human Rights of 25 March 1983 (Minelli), Series A, no. 62.

123 See Explanatory Memorandum, *loc. cit.* note 111, pp. 6–7.

124 *Ibid.* p. 6.

125 Compare Report on legal redress, *loc. cit.* note 108, p. 53.

126 In particular case 170/84 (*Bilka*) and case 30/85 (*Teuling*), *loc. cit.* notes 13 and 114.

127 Explanatory Memorandum, *loc. cit.* note 111 p. 7.

128 *Ibid.* p. 8.

129 Case 170/84 (*Bilka*), case 30/85 (*Teuling*), *loc. cit.* notes 13 and 114.

130 See Chapters 4 and 5 p. 107 and p. 174.

131 Amended proposal for a Council Directive on parental leave and leave for family reasons. O.J. C 316/7, 27 November 1984.

132 See O.J. C 206/47, 6 August 1984. The measure of opposition is seen in the vote within ECOSOC on its opinion which was adopted by 87 votes to 53, with 8 abstentions.

133 In the New Community Action Programme on the promotion of equal opportunities for women 1982–1985. COM. (81) 758 final.

134 Case 184/83 *Hofmann* v. *Barmer Ersatzkasse* (1984) E.C.R. 3047.

135 See Chapter 4 above pp. 127–30.

136 See generally the Report on the Protection of Working Women During Pregnancy and Motherhood in the Member States of the European Communities V/1829/84 – EN.

137 *Ibid.*

138 See EIRR 174, July 1988, p. 7.

139 See Report on the Protection of Working Women *loc. cit.* in note 136, *passim*.

140   For a discussion of the issues see Commission Report on Voluntary Part-time Work, COM.(80)405 final.
141   See Chapters 1 and 3 above pp. 16–19 and 71–7.
142   O.J. C62/7, 12 March 1982.
143   O.J. C2/1, 4 January 1980. These principles are discussed in the Commission's Report on Voluntary Part-time Work *loc. cit.* note 140 pp. 6–12.
144   See Annexe to the Commission's Report on Voluntary Part-time Work, p. 19.

8 Successes and Shortcomings of the Community Approach

The history of the European Community involvement in the area of sex discrimination is impressive. The sole Treaty reference to the equal treatment of men and women in Article 119 seems an inauspicious beginning to what has come to be a crucial aspect of European social policy. Several important factors have led the Member States to the situation where sex equality now plays a fundamental part in the Community. The first point relates to the inclusion of Article 119 in the Treaty itself. As has already been stated in this book, the issue of equal pay has both an economic and social aspect as does the whole issue of working conditions and social security. The Community aims at a progressive development and an improvement of living standards within the Community. This improvement requires to be balanced to ensure that one Member State will not rely on the maintenance of minimal standards in order to gain or retain a comparative advantage. The raising of standards is, therefore, a Community issue in the purest economic sense. However, and this is the second point, 'Social Europe' was given an additional dimension in 1972 when the Council of Ministers agreed that the Community was in need of developing and enhancing its image as being of concern to the citizens within its boundaries and not merely interested in tariff rates and the elimination of quantitative restrictions. The post-1972 commitment to Social Europe gave added impetus to the sex equality issue since the aspirations of Community citizens in this area had been enlarged with the growing consciousness of the sex discrimination issue from the 1960s onwards. A third factor lies in the existing legal dimension. The Court of Justice, particularly in some early staff cases, brought the whole issue of sex equality into the legal arena with its statements that the principle of non-discrimination based on sex is a part of the fundamental human rights which go to make up the Community legal order. The Court could not, however, go beyond the limits laid down in the Treaty and was initially confined in its preliminary references to interpretation of Article 119. Here the application by the Court of the concept of direct effects to Article 119 breathed life into it and demonstrated to individuals the potential of Community law as a generator of personal rights.

These three factors are specific to the European Community although there were other, external, influences such as the lessons to be drawn from American experience, the development of international law in the area, the changing working patterns of men and women and the liberalization of social roles between men and women in the 1960s and 1970s.

The result has been the development of a body of Community legislation in the areas discussed in this book. It is not worthwhile recapitulating what has been said already, but it must be said that what has been achieved to date has been impressive given the limitations inherent in the decision making process of the Community and given the opposition of certain Member States to legislation which is seen to fetter the right of management to manage their own affairs and/or which will impose costs on the State itself or on the employer. The steady and progressive development of law relating to equality is a tribute to the European institutions and to certain other Member States with a somewhat more lofty view of the dignity and worth of, in particular, women.

Furthermore, the existence of Community legislation has had a positive influence on some of the Member States whose own existing legislation and practice was far from ideal. The Directives which have been adopted and the judgements of the Court of Justice have had to be given effect at the national level and have kept the issue of discrimination in both the public and the governments' eye. In addition, women's lobby groups and trade unions have been able to use the Community weapon in their struggle to enhance the status of women and will be able to do so in the future. As Chapter 7 demonstrates, the Commission has further proposals for legislation and whereas certain Member States may feel that they have already done enough the Commission is prepared to demonstrate that much more could be done.

This then is the plus side of Community involvement. The reader will by now also be ready to point to the minus side. First the legislation itself is the result of compromise between the Member States' views in the Council as compared to the desires of the Commission. It has been noted several times that the initial proposals for directives were considerably weakened by the addition of exceptions which are in reality special pleading by the Member States.

Furthermore, the compromise character of the Community legislation is mirrored in the vagueness of certain provisions and, in particular, the fact that the Member States have procrastinated on several important points and still continue to do so. The history of the pension issue demonstrates the reluctance on the part of some Member States to eliminate discrimination in certain areas. Thus an important and sometimes very difficult task has been left to the courts and, in particular, the Court of Justice who have to determine the scope of the exceptions, the meaning of imprecise provisions and the mutual relationship of the different legislative instruments. This perhaps may be the essence of all judicial activity. However, it must be noted that in order to have bad and vague legislation further clarified, it is indispensable to have, as a rule, cases brought by private individuals. The costs of the compromise are shifted to the courts and, indirectly, to the individual. Furthermore, it is apparent that the quality of the new generation of directives adopted or proposed after 1978 leaves much to be desired, more than the Equal Pay, Equal Treatment and Social Security Directives. Finally, three vital proposals are blocked within the Council, two already for years. What are then the prospects for the near future? The commitment of the Delors Commission to the social issue is as such a positive factor. However, it may be expected that until 1992, and probably even beyond, the great majority of Community legislative activities will concern the realization of the internal market. The question is, therefore, what will this mean for the Community labour and social policy in general and for equality legislation and related issues in particular? The concern that the social dimension accompany the internal market is from a relatively recent date;[1] it is still unclear what – if any – priority the sex discrimination problem will get within the entirety of actions just developing which are deemed necessary to implement the social dimension of the internal market. However, if one of the main concerns is the prevention of 'social dumping' in the sense of achievement of profits by beating down pay and working conditions, the protection of 'peripheral' workers such as part-timers, workers on fixed-term contracts and home workers, is one of the priorities from which mainly women may benefit.

Furthermore, it must be mentioned that the Single European Act, with which the whole 1992 euphoria started, introduced some changes to the European Community legislative procedures. It added, among other things, to the EEC Treaty an Article 100a. This Article has introduced qualified majority voting within the Council for the adoption of approximation measures necessary for the establishment and functioning of the internal market. The 'old' bases for equality legislation, Article 100 and Article 235 of the EEC Treaty require unanimity. Unfortunately, Article 100a is not a step forward in the field of social legislation decision making. Its paragraph 2 specifically excluded from the qualified majority rule the approximation of provisions relating to the rights and interests of employed persons. The only possibility for improvement of social legislation decision making seems to be then the likewise new Article 118a. This Article requires member States to pay particular attention to encouraging improvements, especially in the working environment, as regards the health and safety of workers. Directives in this field should also be adopted by qualified majority. Thus whether the Community social and labour legislation will be affected and eventually accelerated by the qualified majority voting depends entirely on the interpretation of Article 118a. A broad interpretation of 'working environment' may after all cover working conditions which touch the problems of gender-based discrimination and other measures necessary to make women's opportunity in the labour market a real one. Finally it should be noted that sex discrimination and equal opportunities may also be included in the European 'social dialogue' between management and labour to be launched under Article 118b of the Treaty.

The second demerit to be pointed out relates to the inherent problems with a system of law making which relies on the national authorities for its implementation. Within the Community legal order the directive has its limitations. Member States, in the course of implementation, may deliberately or otherwise fail to give full effect to the spirit behind the directive. Alternatively they may fail to implement part or whole of the directive and the Commission's powers to bring a recalcitrant State before the Court are a fairly weak method of enforcing the State to act. Moreover, the 35 years old practice of jurisdiction by the Court of Justice has revealed that the most important or 'hot' issues have been brought before the Court by individuals. This is certainly also true in the field of equal treatment with pioneers like Ms Defrenne. Further, given the somewhat ambiguous position of the Commission in some of the references in which it has submitted observations, it may be clear that the Commission's discretion to start an infringement proceeding is no guarantee for a sanctioning of incorrect or non-implementation of EEC law. However, as Chapter 6 demonstrates, where an individual does attempt to claim Community-based rights, in the Courts, there is an element of chance, even after the European Court has declared the direct effects of a provision, in that one national judge may reach an entirely different decision from another judge given similar facts and the same law. Uniformity in implementation and application is far from achievement in the sex equality area.

Thirdly, the Court of Justice too may be criticized. It has, on occasion, chosen to interpret Community provisions rather too narrowly and/or, to a certain extent, inconsistently with its own previous decisions. Sometimes a lack of clarity in the wording of the Court's decision has led to a diminution rather than an expansion of the principle of equal treatment, as, for instance, in the *Jenkins* case. Again it may seem to a lay person that the arguments within the Court are simply academic and bear little relation to the everyday problems which initially give rise to the case. So too, that person may think that the legal procedures, and in particular the preliminary reference, is too lengthy and expensive a procedure to give an answer to a relatively straightforward question of industrial relations.

These criticisms are all justifiable but they are unavoidable given the nature of the Community system on top of the already cumbersome procedures which exist in some of the Member States.

As the amount of (unclearly drafted) equality legislation increases, it is obvious that the Court will be confronted with new and more questions in this field. When the manuscript of this book was finished, there were already ten new cases pending. However, it is also to be expected that some 'old' problems will come back for further clarification: the demarcation of wage discrimination and the Equal Treatment Directive, of the Equal Treatment Directive and the Social Security and Occupational Schemes Directives as individuals will try to minimize the effects of exceptions; the question of pensions and Article 119 will probably return to the Court, perhaps together with the problem of compatibility of the Occupational Schemes Directive and Article 119; more guidance from the Court will be necessary on the issue of non-discriminatory job-evaluation schemes; national judges will probably make an appeal to the Court when dealing with alleged indirect discrimination, in particular as regards the question of how vast the affected group of persons must be to establish a *prima facie* case and on the issue of balancing the principle of non-discrimination against other interests. Although the pattern of the Court's equality jurisprudence seems to be firmly set down, its embroidery may bring both pleasant and unpleasant surprises.

A more fundamental question than any of these should, however, be addressed and this relates to the issue of what the Member States of the Community are seeking to achieve when they adopt legislation to provide for equality of treatment. It should be borne in mind that the rationale behind the Community is to provide for a better standard of living for everyone within the Community, in particular, in order to contribute to the optimal development of individuals' personality and abilities. As part of this aim there is the desire to enhance working and living conditions for the benefit of individuals and for the benefit of the society to which they belong. The abolition of discrimination and the achievement of equality in treatment is to serve this end; these are not goals in themselves. It must, therefore, be questioned whether, within the legal activities outlined in this book, the ultimate goal of an overall improvement is being achieved, or is likely to be achieved by equality legislation, and whether the attainment of equal treatment in some areas has been a positive step forward.

At this point it may be worth recalling that the right to equal treatment which forms part of Community law has been described as derivative from the right to equality. In Dworkin's analysis of the right to equality, he distinguishes two important concepts: the right to equal treatment and the right to treatment as an equal. The former, he states, 'is the right to an equal distribution of some opportunity or resource or burden'. The latter is 'the right, not to receive the same distribution of some burden or benefit, but to be treated with the same respect and concern, as anyone else'. He goes on '[I]n some circumstances the right to treatment as an equal will entail a right to equal treatment, but not, by any means, in all circumstances'.[2] The distinction is important as it predicates the standard of behaviour which will be expected in a particular instance.

The standard which has been adopted in the Directives and in Article

119 is the equal treatment standard. Consequently, it is not surprising that this is also the standard applied by the Court of Justice. Moreover, the cases before the Court did not really give rise to a necessity to distinguish between the right to equal treatment and the right to be treated as an equal. It may be objected that the distinction between the two aspects of the right to equality is artificial and that the same result is achieved whichever of the two concepts is used. However, this is not the case. There are inherent shortcomings in the use of the equal treatment standard, and in many ways it is a standard which is inappropriate in the area of gender-based discrimination.

In the first place, equal treatment presupposes for women the existence of a male comparator who enjoys certain rights women are deprived of in a given situation. This shortcoming is clearly reflected in *Macarthys* and *Murphy*. Another good example is the absence of occupational schemes in undertakings employing mainly women mentioned in Chapter 7. If there is no relevant male comparator, the equal treatment standard will bring no relief to the situation of a disadvantaged group.

Second, the equal treatment standard does not guarantee an overall raising of standards for men and women. As has been amply demonstrated, Member States have interpreted the equal treatment standard as an opportunity to 'level down'. In the area of social security, for example, the preferred solution, based on the supposed high cost of levelling up, has sometimes led to a diminution of the treatment of men and no improvement for women. It really must be questioned, particularly for those individuals dependent on social security for their livelihoods, whether the aim of equality is worth the cost. A cynical observer might argue that, given that States appear to be able to get away with level-down solutions, they may become enthusiastic supporters of the equality principle whereas before they were more laggardly.

In the third place, there are, too, many aspects of life which cannot be solved by adopting an equal treatment principle. Men and women may need special and different rights in certain circumstances. There may be special protection required for pregnant women or to protect men against hazards which are known to be injurious to them. These special circumstances are permissible under existing Community provisions but they may lead to abuse.

Finally, a straightforward application of the equal treatment standard means to treat men and women as if their positions were the same and it ignores the very real differences which still do exist nowadays in the respective role of men and women. This is not to argue that there are inherent disabilities in women, nor that they are in any respect inferior, but it is to argue that their culturally defined position in society places them at an obvious disadvantage when they seek to exercise the rights which Community law opens to them. Where the base-line is so different for men and women to start with, the equal treatment standard, unless accompanied by additional measures, is ineffective and may even cause more harm than a discriminatory measure itself.

The participation of women in the labour market is limited due, primarily, to child bearing and child rearing, and to other home responsibilities which are closely related to and following upon the former. Consequently, the conditions under which men and women supply their labour to the labour market are unequal. Women are less likely to be employed or, at least, to be employed in jobs that fully utilize their abilities, skills and training and they are therefore not fully integrated into the public world of the workplace. The unequal distribution of family responsibilities also affects adversely women's participation in other areas of public life, for instance, in politics and in trade union activities. It can hardly be denied that to date men, more often than women, hold positions of power and influence, that they are economically better off than most women and have access to more economic, social and other opportunities to develop themselves in accordance with their own wishes. However, the unequal starting position and thus unequal distribution of opportunities is neither inherent nor inevitable. For the most part it is socially determined and can therefore be changed.

It is apparent that the equal treatment standard is not going to advance women very far. The existing norms that govern not only the workplace but also other aspects of our life nowadays are geared to the traditional situation of a male breadwinner supported by a wife who stays at home, at least for a period of a few years, and takes care of children. Under such circumstances the application of existing standards to women will only result in a double burden for the women concerned, if the latter succeed in combining their occupational activities and home responsibilities at all. It is at this stage that the right to be treated as an equal is a more useful way of improving the position of women. This right implies a differentiation necessary to guarantee real equality while taking into account biological and societal differences. This differentiation however, requires a very subtle balancing since focusing on what is deemed, sometimes mistakenly, to be a special female need may in fact reinforce the gender stereotypes that, on the contrary, should be broken down. The *Hofmann* case, for instance, is a good illustration of the dilemma. Furthermore, comprehensive policies are necessary to enable women and, in particular women with children, to participate in the labour market and to do so without disadvantage. Introduction of parental leave schemes, involvement of fathers in parenting and strong extension of diverse forms of child care facilities are essential conditions. Already in 1974, in its Social Action Programme, the European Community called for action to ensure that the family responsibilities of all concerned may be reconciled with their job aspirations. The quite recent 'Childcare and Equality of Opportunity Report'[3] teaches us, however, that the development in this field is minimal and the situation is highly unsatisfactory, especially in certain Member States. In this respect even a more far-reaching point should be made. It seems inevitable to question the existing life patterns and values, especially those of the workplace. As long as it is assumed that competitiveness and focus on work to the exclusion of the employees' family responsibilities (implying commitment to sometimes long or irregular working hours to suit the needs of the employer, employee's mobility and continuity of employment) is necessary to the productive functioning of the workplace, women will be unable to compete equally with men and for the latter it will be impossible to get involved in the care of children. The implicit or explicit assumption should be discussed, that it would cost too much, in terms of money and productivity, for an employer to make it possible for workers of both sexes to better integrate family responsibilities with job commitments. After all, the workplace accommodates other basic human needs, like holidays, and it is apparent that several social measures introduced through the years to humanize the values and structures of the workplace equally implied costs for the employer when considered from a strictly economic point of view. It may even be argued that in the long term both the employees and the employers and society as a whole may benefit from working conditions which take into account the employee's home commitments.

Given all these considerations, what are the achievements of the Community equality legislation? In the first place it has enabled us to eradicate and to continue to eradicate many blatant examples of discrimination. It equally contributed to the consciousness-raising process concerning sex discrimination in general and the specific problems women face in particular. Further, it proved to be able to deal with more subtle forms of discrimination, such as indirect ones. The concept of indirect discrimination as such is illustrative of a more substantive approach to equality as it takes into consideration social realities. The next step on this road to real equality is indeed additional legislation that balances the starting position of men and women and that meets the shortcomings of the principle of equal treatment.

Finally, although the Community legislation should rightly be considered as a source of social change, it must be stated that the law itself is a limited and unsophisticated means of ensuring even the formal equality laid down in its provisions, let alone of eradicating deep-rooted and insidious discriminatory ideas, practices and prejudices. The few successful cases may have some immediate impact but they do not get to the heart of the problem nor do they necessarily affect the lives of the majority of the Community's citizens. They are important symbols of a commitment to an ideal and, as such, serve some form of ideological purpose yet the very insistence on legal argumentation and the maintenance of the letter of the law also serves to demonstrate the difficulties in society coming to terms with the idea of the equality of the sexes. In this respect Community law is no different from national law and it is not likely to be any more successful than national law in eradicating gender-based discrimination.

Notes

1   From 1988, an important impetus came from the meetings of the European Council in Hanover and Rhodes in June and December 1988 respectively.
2   Dworkin (1977).
3   Consolidated Report to the European Commission, June 1988, V/746/88.

Text of Legislation

Article 119 EEC

Each Member State shall during the first stage ensure and subsequently maintain the application of the principle that men and women should receive equal pay for equal work.

For the purpose of this Article, 'pay' means the ordinary basic or minimum wage or salary and any other consideration, whether in cash or in kind, which the worker receives, directly or indirectly, in respect of his employment from his employer.

Equal pay without discrimination based on sex means:

(a)   that pay for the same work at piece rates shall be calculated on the basis of the same unit of measurement;

(b)   that pay for work at time rates shall be the same for the same job.

Council Directives*

Council Directive of 10 February 1975

on the approximation of the laws of the Member States relating to the application of the principle of equal pay for men and women (75/117/EEC)

THE COUNCIL OF THE EUROPEAN COMMUNITIES,

Having regard to the Treaty establishing the European Economic Community, and in particular Article 100 thereof;

Having regard to the proposal from the Commission;

Having regard to the Opinion of the European Parliament;[1]

Having regard to the Opinion of the Economic and Social Committee;[2]

Whereas implementation of the principle that men and women should receive equal pay contained in Article 119 of the Treaty is an integral part of the establishment and functioning of the common market;

Whereas it is primarily the responsibility of the Member States to ensure the application of this principle by means of appropriate laws, regulations and administrative provisions;

Whereas the Council resolution of 21 January 1974[3] concerning a social action programme, aimed at making it possible to harmonize living and working conditions while the improvement is being maintained and at achieving a balanced social and economic development of the Community, recognized that priority should be given to action taken on behalf of women as regards access to employment and vocational training and advancement, and as regards working conditions, including pay;

Whereas it is desirable to reinforce the basic laws by standards aimed at facilitating the practical application of the principle of equality in such a way that all employees in the Community can be protected in these matters;

Whereas differences continue to exist in the various Member States

*The text of these Council Directives is taken from the *Official Journal of the European Communities*, issues dated 19 February 1975, 14 February 1976 and 10 January 1979.

despite the efforts made to apply the resolution of the conference of the Member States of 30 December 1961 on equal pay for men and women and whereas, therefore, the national provisions should be approximated as regards application of the principle of equal pay,

HAS ADOPTED THIS DIRECTIVE:

Article 1

The principle of equal pay for men and women outlined in Article 119 of the Treaty, hereinafter called 'principle of equal pay', means, for the same work or for work to which equal value is attributed, the elimination of all discrimination on grounds of sex with regard to all aspects and conditions of remuneration.

In particular, where a job classification system is used for determining pay, it must be based on the same criteria for both men and women and so drawn up as to exclude any discrimination on grounds of sex.

Article 2

Member States shall introduce into their national legal systems such measures as are necessary to enable all employees who consider themselves wronged by failure to apply the principle of equal pay to pursue their claims by judicial process after possible recourse to other competent authorities.

Article 3

Member States shall abolish all discrimination between men and women arising from laws, regulations or administrative provisions which is contrary to the principles of equal pay.

Article 4

Member States shall take the necessary measures to ensure that provisions appearing in collective agreements, wage scales, wage agreements or individual contracts of employment which are contrary to the principle of equal pay shall be, or may be declared, null and void or may be amended.

Article 5

Member States shall take the necessary measures to protect employees against dismissal by the employer as a reaction to a complaint within the undertaking or to any legal proceedings aimed at enforcing compliance with the principle of equal pay.

Article 6

Member States shall, in accordance with their national circumstances and legal systems, take the measures necessary to ensure that the principle of equal pay is applied. They shall see that effective means are available to take care that this principle is observed.

Article 7

Member States shall take care that the provisions adopted pursuant to this Directive, together with the relevant provisions already in force, are brought to the attention of employees by all appropriate means, for example at their place of employment.

Article 8

1. Member States shall put into force the laws, regulations and administrative provisions necessary in order to comply with the Directive within one year of its notification and shall immediately inform the Commission thereof.

2. Member States shall communicate to the Commission the texts of the laws, regulations and administrative provisions which they adopt in the field covered by this Directive.

Article 9

Within two years of the expiry of the one-year period referred to in Article 8, Member States shall forward all necessary information to the Commission to enable it to draw up a report on the application of this Directive for submission to the Council.

Article 10

This Directive is addressed to the Member State.

Done at Brussels, 10 February 1975.

For the Council
The President
G. FITZGERALD

Notes

1   O.J. no. C 55, 13 May 1974, p. 43.
2   O.J. no. C 88, 26 July 1974, p. 7
3   O.J. no. C 13, 12 February 1974, p. 1.

Council Directive of 9 February 1976

on the implementation of the principle of equal treatment for men and women as regards access to employment, vocational training and promotion, and working conditions (76/207/EEC)

THE COUNCIL OF THE EUROPEAN COMMUNITIES,

Having regard to the Treaty establishing the European Economic Community, and in particular Article 235 thereof,

Having regard to the proposal from the Commission,

Having regard to the opinion of the European Parliament[1]

Having regard to the opinion of the Economic and Social Committee,[2]

Whereas the Council, in its resolution of 21 January 1974 concerning a social action programme,[3] included among the priorities action for the purpose of achieving equality between men and women as regards access to employment and vocational training and promotion and as regards working conditions, including pay;

Whereas, with regard to pay, the Council adopted on 10 February 1975 Directive 75/117/EEC on the approximation of the laws of the Member States relating to the application of the principle of equal pay for men and women;[4]

Whereas Community action to achieve the principle of equal treatment for men and women in respect of access to employment and vocational training and promotion and in respect of other working conditions also appears to be necessary; whereas, equal treatment for male and female workers constitutes one of the objectives of the Community, in so far as the harmonization of living and working conditions while maintaining their improvement are *inter alia* to be furthered; whereas the Treaty does not confer the necessary specific powers for this purpose;

Whereas the definition and progressive implementation of the principle of equal treatment in matters of social security should be ensured by means of subsequent instruments,

HAS ADOPTED THIS DIRECTIVE:

Article 1

1. The purpose of this Directive is to put into effect in the Member States the principle of equal treatment for men and women as regards

access to employment, including promotion, and to vocational training and as regards working conditions and, on the conditions referred to in paragraph 2, social security. This principle is hereinafter referred to as 'the principle of equal treatment'.

2. With a view to ensuring the progressive implementation of the principle of equal treatment in matters of social security, the Council, acting on a proposal from the Commission, will adopt provisions defining its substance, its scope and the arrangements for its application.

Article 2

1. For the purposes of the following provisions, the principle of equal treatment shall mean that there shall be no discrimination whatsoever on grounds of sex either directly or indirectly by reference in particular to marital or family status.

2. This Directive shall be without prejudice to the right of Member States to exclude from its field of application those occupational activities and, where appropriate, the training leading thereto, for which, by reason of their nature or the context in which they are carried out, the sex of the worker constitutes a determining factor.

3. This Directive shall be without prejudice to provisions concerning the protection of women, particularly as regards pregnancy and maternity.

4. This Directive shall be without prejudice to measures to promote equal opportunity for men and women, in particular by removing existing inequalities which affect women's opportunities in the areas referred to in Article 1(1).

Article 3

1. Application of the principle of equal treatment means that there shall be no discrimination whatsoever on grounds of sex in the conditions, including selection criteria, for access to all jobs or posts, whatever the sector or branch of activity, and to all levels of the occupational hierarchy.

2. To this end, Member States shall take the measures necessary to ensure that:

(a) any laws, regulations and administrative provisions contrary to the principle of equal treatment shall be abolished;

(b) any provisions contrary to the principle of equal treatment which are included in collective agreements, individual contracts of employment, internal rules of undertakings or in rules governing the independent occupations and professions shall be, or may be declared, null and void or may be amended;

(c) those laws, regulations and administrative provisions contrary to the principle of equal treatment when the concern for protection which originally inspired them is no longer well founded shall be revised; and that where similar provisions are included in collective agreements labour and management shall be requested to undertake the desired revision.

Article 4

Application of the principle of equal treatment with regard to access to all types and to all levels, of vocational guidance, vocational training, advanced vocational training and retraining, means that Member States shall take all necessary measures to ensure that:

(a) any laws, regulations and administrative provisions contrary to the principle of equal treatment shall be abolished;

(b) any provisions contrary to the principle of equal treatment which are included in collective agreements, individual contracts of employment, internal rules of undertakings or in rules governing the independent occupations and professions shall be, or may be declared, null and void or may be amended;

(c) without prejudice to the freedom granted in certain Member States to certain private training establishments, vocational guidance, vocational training, advanced vocational training and retraining shall be accessible on the basis of the same criteria and at the same levels without any discrimination on grounds of sex.

Article 5

1. Application of the principle of equal treatment with regard to working conditions, including the conditions governing dismissal, means that men and women shall be guaranteed the same conditions without discrimination on grounds of sex.

2. To this end, Member States shall take the measures necessary to ensure that:

(a) any laws, regulations and administrative provisions contrary to the principle of equal treatment shall be abolished;

(b)   any provisions contrary to the principle of equal treatment which are included in collective agreements, individual contracts of employment, internal rules of undertakings or in rules governing the independent occupations and professions shall be, or may be declared, null and void or may be amended;

(c)   those laws, regulations and administrative provisions contrary to the principle of equal treatment when the concern for protection which originally inspired them is no longer well founded shall be revised; and that where similar provisions are included in collective agreements labour and management shall be requested to undertake the desired revision.

Article 6

Member States shall introduce into their national legal systems such measures as are necessary to enable all persons who consider themselves wronged by failure to apply to them the principle of equal treatment within the meaning of Articles 3, 4 and 5 to pursue their claims by judicial process after possible recourse to other competent authorities.

Article 7

Member States shall take the necessary measures to protect employees against dismissal by the employer as a reaction to a complaint within the undertaking or to any legal proceedings aimed at enforcing compliance with the principle of equal treatment.

Article 8

Member States shall take care that the provisions adopted pursuant to this Directive, together with the relevant provisions already in force, are brought to the attention of employees by all appropriate means, for example at their place of employment.

Article 9

1. Member States shall put into force the laws, regulations and administrative provisions necessary in order to comply with this Directive within 30 months of its notification and shall immediately inform the Commission thereof.

However, as regards the first part of Article 3(2)(c) and the first part of Article 5(2)(c), Member States shall carry out a first examination and if necessary a first revision of the laws, regulations and administrative provisions referred to therein within four years of notification of this Directive.

2. Member States shall periodically assess the occupational activities referred to in Article 2(2) in order to decide, in the light of social developments, whether there is justification for maintaining the exclusions concerned. They shall notify the Commission of the results of this assessment.

3. Member States shall also communicate to the Commission the texts of laws, regulations and administrative provisions which they adopt in the field covered by this Directive.

Article 10

Within two years following expiry of the 30-month period laid down in the first subparagraph of Article 9(1), Member States shall forward all necessary information to the Commission to enable it to draw up a report on the application of this Directive for submission to the Council.

Article 11

This Directive is addressed to the Member States.

Done at Brussels, 9 February 1976.

For the Council
The President
G. THORN

Notes

1   O.J. no. C 111, 20 May 1975, p. 14.
2   O.J. no. C 286, 15 December 1975, p. 8.
3   O.J. no. C 13, 12 February 1974, p. 1.
4   O.J. no. L 45, 19 February 1975, p. 19.

Council Directive of 19 December 1978

on the progressive implementation of the principle of equal treatment for men and women in matters of social security (79/7/EEC)

THE COUNCIL OF THE EUROPEAN COMMUNITIES,

Having regard to the Treaty establishing the European Economic Community, and in particular Article 235 thereof,

Having regard to the proposal from the Commission,[1]

Having regard to the opinion of the European Parliament,[2]

Having regard to the opinion of the Economic and Social Committee,[3]

Whereas Article 1 (2) of Council Directive 76/207/EEC of 9 February 1976 on the implementation of the principle of equal treatment for men and women as regards access to employment, vocational training and promotion, and working conditions[4] provides that, with a view to ensuring the progressive implementation of the principle of equal treatment in matters of social security, the Council, acting on a proposal from the Commission, will adopt provisions defining its substance, its scope and the arrangement for its application; whereas the Treaty does not confer the specific powers required for this purpose;

Whereas the principle of equal treatment in matters of social security should be implemented in the first place in the statutory schemes which provide protection against the risks of sickness, invalidity, old age, accidents at work, occupational diseases and unemployment, and in social assistance in so far as it is intended to supplement or replace the abovementioned schemes;

Whereas the implementation of the principle of equal treatment in matters of social security does not prejudice the provisions relating to the protection of women on the ground of maternity; whereas, in this respect, Member States may adopt specific provisions for women to remove existing instances of unequal treatment,

HAS ADOPTED THIS DIRECTIVE:

Article 1

The purpose of this Directive is the progressive implementation, in the field of social security and other elements of social protection provided for in Article 3, of the principle of equal treatment for men and women in matters of social security, hereinafter referred to as 'the principle of equal treatment'.

Article 2

This Directive shall apply to the working population – including self-employed persons, workers and self-employed persons whose activity is interrupted by illness, accident or involuntary unemployment and persons seeking employment – and to retired or invalided workers and self-employed persons.

Article 3

1.   This Directive shall apply to:

(a)   statutory schemes which provide protection against the following risks:

– sickness,
– invalidity,
– old age,
– accidents at work and occupational diseases,
– unemployment;

(b)   social assistance, in so far as it is intended to supplement or replace the schemes referred to in (a).

2.   This Directive shall not apply to the provisions concerning survivors' benefits nor to those concerning family benefits, except in the case of family benefits granted by way of increases of benefits due in respect of the risks referred to in paragraph 1 (a).

3.   With a view to ensuring implementation of the principle of equal treatment in occupational schemes, the Council, acting on a proposal from the Commission, will adopt provisions defining its substance, its scope and the arrangements for its application.

Article 4

1.   The principle of equal treatment means that there shall be no discrimination whatsoever on ground of sex either directly, or indirectly by reference in particular to marital or family status, in particular as concerns:

–   the scope of the schemes and the conditions of access thereto,
–   the obligation to contribute and the calculation of contributions,
–   the calculation of benefits including increases due in respect of
      a spouse and for dependants and the conditions governing the
      duration and retention of entitlement to benefits.

2.   The principle of equal treatment shall be without prejudice to the
provisions relating to the protection of women on the grounds of
maternity.

Article 5

Member States shall take the measures necessary to ensure that any
laws, regulations and administrative provisions contrary to the principle
of equal treatment are abolished.

Article 6

Member States shall introduce into their national legal systems such
measures as are necessary to enable all persons who consider themselves
wronged by failure to apply the principle of equal treatment to pursue
their claims by judicial process, possibly after recourse to other competent
authorities.

Article 7

1.   This Directive shall be without prejudice to the right of Member States
to exclude from its scope:

(a)   the determination of pensionable age for the purposes of granting
      old-age and retirement pensions and the possible consequences
      thereof for other benefits;
(b)   advantages in respect of old-age pension schemes granted to persons
      who have brought up children; the acquisition of benefit entitlements
      following periods of interruption of employment due to the bringing
      up of children;
(c)   the granting of old-age or invalidity benefit entitlements by virtue of
      the derived entitlements of a wife;
(d)   the granting of increases of long-term invalidity, old-age, accidents at
      work and occupational disease benefits for a dependent wife;
(e)   the consequences of the exercise, before the adoption of this Directive,
      of a right of option not to acquire rights or incur obligations under a
      statutory scheme.

2.   Member States shall periodically examine matters excluded under

paragraph 1 in order to ascertain, in the light of social developments in the matter concerned, whether there is justification for maintaining the exclusions concerned.

Article 8

1. Member States shall bring into force the laws, regulations and administrative provisions necessary to comply with this Directive within six years of its notification. They shall immediately inform the Commission thereof.

2. Member States shall communicate to the Commission the text of laws, regulations and administrative provisions which they adopt in the field covered by this Directive, including measures adopted pursuant to Article 7 (2).

They shall inform the Commission of their reasons for maintaining any existing provisions on the matters referred to in Article 7 (1) and of the possibilities for reviewing them at a later date.

Article 9

Within seven years of notification of this Directive, Member States shall forward all information necessary to the Commission to enable it to draw up a report on the application of this Directive for submission to the Council and to propose such further measures as may be required for the implementation of the principle of equal treatment.

Article 10

This Directive is addressed to the Member States.

Done at Brussels, 19 December 1978.

For the Council
The President
H.-D. GENSCHER

Notes

1   O.J. no. C 34, 11 February 1977, p. 3.
2   O.J. no. C 299, 12 December 1977, p. 13.
3   O.J. no. C 180, 28 July 1977, p. 36.
4   O.J. no. L 39, 14 February 1976, p. 40.

List of
Relevant cases

Cases relating to gender discrimination before the European Court of Justice

Abbreviations

AB	Nederlandse jurisprudentie – administratiefrechtelijke beslissingen
A.J.C.L.	The American Journal of Comparative Law
All. E.R.	All England Law Reports
B.B.	Der Betriebs-Berater
C.M.L.R.	Common Market Law Reports
C.M.L. Rev.	Common Market Law Review
D.B.	Der Betrieb
D.U.L.J.	Dublin University Law Journal
E.C.R.	European Court Reports
EuR	Europarecht
E.I.R.R.	European Industrial Relations Review
E.L.R.	European Law Review
I.C.R.	Industrial Court Reports
I.L.J.	The Industrial Law Journal
I.L.R.	International Labour Review
I.R.L.R.	Industrial Relations Law Review
J.S.W.L	Journal of Social Welfare Law
J.T.T.	Journal des Tribunaux du Travail
M.L.R.	Modern Law Review
N.I.L.Q.	Northern Ireland Legal Quarterly
N.J.	Nederlandse Jurisprudentie – uitspraken in burgerlikje – enstrafzaken
N.J.B.	Nederlands Juristenblad
O.J.	Official Journal (of the European Communities)
P.S.	Periodiek voor sociale verzekering, sociale voorzieningen en arbeidsrecht
RdA	Recht der Arbeit
R.D.S.	Revue de Droit Social
R.I.T.	Revue Internationale du Travail
R.M.C.	Revue de Marché Commun
R.S.V.	Rechtspraak Sociale Verzekering
R.T.D.E.	Revue Trimestrielle de Droit Européen
S.L.T.	Scots Law Times

S.M.A.	Sociaal Maandblad Arbeid
S.R.	Sociaal Recht
T.A.R.	Tijdschrift voor Ambtenarenrecht
U.N.T.S.	United Nations Treaty Series

Bibliography

Andringa, L., 'De niet-betaalde premies AOW/AWW nog steeds een heet hangijzer,' *Nemesis*, 1987, pp. 203–208.

Atkins, S. and Hoggett, B., *Women and the Law*, Basil Blackwell, Oxford, 1984.

Bates, J., 'Gender, Social Security and Pensions', in McLean, S. and Burrows, N., *The Legal Relevance of Gender*, Macmillan Press Ltd, Basingstoke, 1988.

Bebr, G., *Development of Judicial Control of the European Communities*, Nijhoff, The Hague, 1981.

Bertelsmann, K.and Pfarr, H.M., 'Diskriminierung von Frauen bei der Einstellung und Beforderung', DB, 1984, pp. 1297–1301.

Bleckmann, A., 'Gleichbehandlung von Männern und Frauen hinsichtlich des Zugangs zur Beschäftigung', DB, 1984, pp. 1574–1577.

Bout, A., 'Een herhaling van onrechtmatige zetten', NJB, 1988, pp. 1640-1644.

Brownlie, I. (ed.), *Basic Documents in International Law*, 3rd ed., Clarendon Press, Oxford, 1983.

Byre, A., *Indirect Discrimination*, Equal Opportunities Commission, London, 1987.

Colneric, N., 'Gleichberechtigung von Mann und Frau im Europäischen Gemeinschaften', BB, 1988, pp. 968–976.

Conaghan, J., 'Gender-specific Protective Legislation: Second-class Status?', in McLaughlin, S. (ed.), *Women and the Law*, Bentham House, London, 1987.

Cornelissen, R.C., 'Gelijke behandeling van mannen en vrouwen en inkomensafhankelijke uitkeringen', in Franssen, W.L.G. *et al.* (eds), *Inkomenstoets in de sociale zekerheid*, VUGA, The Hague, 1987.

Curtin, D., 'Occupational Pension Schemes and Article 119: Beyond the Fringe?', CMLRev., 1987, pp. 215–257 (I).

Curtin, D., 'Labour Law - Equal Pay - Equality's Riddle', DULJ, 1987, pp. 132–136 (II).

Docksey, C., 'The European Community and the Promotion of Equality', in McCrudden, Ch. (ed), *Women, Employment and European Equality Law*, Eclipse Publications, London, 1987.

Dworkin, R., *Taking Rights Seriously*, Duckworth, London, 1977.

Easson, A., 'Can Directiveness Impose Obligations on Individuals?', E.L.R. 1979, pp. 67–79.

Fase, W.J.P.M. (ed), *Gelijke behandeling van vrouw en man in de sociale zekerheid*, Kluwer, Denventer, 1986.

Fitzpatrick, B., 'The Sex Discrimination Act', 50 MLR, 1986, pp. 934–951.

Foster, N., '*Duke* v. *G.E.C. Reliance Systems Ltd* 1988' CML Rev. pp. 629–639.

Franssen, W.L.G. *et al.* (eds), *Inkomenstoets in de sociale zekerheid*, VUGA, The Hague, 1987.

Fredman, S., Anotations to the Sex Discrimination Act in Scottish Current Law Statutes 1986, C59.

Frenkel, B.S. and Betten, L., 'Gelijke behandeling en bijstand', in Fase, W.J.P.M. (ed.), *Gelijke behandeling van man en vrouw in de sociale zekerheid*, Kluwer, Deventer, 1986.

Gamillscheg, F. et al. (eds), *In memoriam Sir Otto Kan-Freund*, C.H. Beck, München, 1980.

Hanau, P., 'Der gleiche Zugang zur Beschäftigung in der Privatwirtschaft nach deutschem Recht', in Gamillscheg, F. *et al.* (eds), *In memoriam Sir Otto Kahn-Freund*, C.H. Beck, München, 1980.

Hartley, T.C., *The Foundations of European Community Law*, 2nd ed., Clarendon Press, Oxford, 1988.

Imbrechts, L., 'L.égalité de rémuneration entre hommes et femmes', RTDE, 1986, pp. 231–242.

Kapteyn, P.J.G. and VerLoren van Themaat, P., *Introduction to the Law of the European Communities*, 2nd. ed., Kluwer, Deventer, Graham and Trotman, Deventer, 1989.

Kapteyn, P.J.G. and VerLoren van Themaat, P., *Inleiding tot het recht van de Europese Gemeenschappen*, 4th ed., Kluwer, Deventer, 1987.

Knopper, E.V., 'De ontwerp-richtlijn beroepsregelingen', in Fase, W.J.P.M. (ed.), *Gelijke behandeling van man en vrouw in de sociale zekerheid*, Kluwer, Deventer, 1986.

Laurent, A., 'European Community Law and Equal Treatment for Men and Women in Social Security', ILR, 1982, pp. 373–385.

Laurent, A., 'Les CE éliminent des discriminations fondées sur le sexe dan les régimes professionnels de sécurité sociale', RIT, 1986, pp. 753–762.

Laurent, A., 'Community Law and National Laws of the Member States Relating to the Principle of Equal Treatment in Matters of Social Security', in Verwilghen, M. (ed.), *Equality in Law between Men and Women in the European Community*, Vol. I, Presses Universitaires de Louvain, Louvain-La-Neuve, 1986.

Leenen, A.Th.S., 'De derde richtlijn nader beschouwd', in Fase, W.J.P.M. (ed.), *Gelijke behandeling van man en vrouw in de sociale zekerheid*, Kluwer, Deventer, 1986.

Levelt-Overmars, W.M., 'De uitspraken van de CRvB d.d. 15-1-1988 over artikel 26 BuPo-Verdrag', NJB, 1988, pp. 589–599 (I).

Levelt-Overmars, W.M., 'Gelijke behandeling en de AOW', *Tijdschrift voor pensioenvraagstukken*, 1988, pp. 2–4 (II).

Levelt-Overmars, W.M., 'Reparatiewetgeving AAW', SMA, 1988, pp. 640–649 (III).

Luckhaus, L., 'Test Case Strategy and the Drake Case: A Feminist View', in McLaughlin, S. (ed.), *Women and the Law*, Bentham House, London, 1987.

Luckhaus, L., 'Severe Disablement Allowance: The Old Dressed up as New', J.S.W.L., 1986, pp. 153–169.

Madlener, B., *Gelijke behandeling mannen en vrouwen in het pensioenstelsel*, Samson, Alphen aan den Rijn, 1984.

McCrudden, Ch., 'Rethinking Positive Action', ILJ, 1986, pp. 219–243.

McCrudden, Ch., (ed.), *Women, Employment and European Equality Law*, Eclipse Publications, London, 1987.

McLaughlin, S., (ed.), *Women and the Law*, Bentham House, London, 1987.

Nicolaysen G., 'Richtlinienwirkung und Gleichbehandlung von Männern und Frauen beim Zugang zum Beruf', EuR, 1984, pp. 380–392.

Paisley, S., 'Arms and the Man? Johnston v Chief Constable of the RUC', NILQ, 1987, pp. 352–366.

Pescatore, P., 'Les principes généraux du droit en tant que source de droit communautaire,' FIDE, 12e Congres, Paris 1986.

Plender, R., 'Equal Pay for Men and Women: Two Recent Decisions of the European Court', AJCL, 1982, pp. 627–653.

Prechal, S. and Heukels, T., 'General Legal Principles in Dutch Law and Community Law; Comparison and Interaction' FIDE, 12e Congres, Paris 1986.

Prechal, S., 'Een rechterlijk misverstand', NJCM-Bulletin, 1987, pp. 155–161.

Quintin, O., 'L'égalité entre hommes et femmes: une realisation spécifique de la politique sociale communautaire', RMC, 1985, pp. 309–318.

Quintin, O. et al., 'Ten Years of Community Policy on Equal Opportunities for Men and Women', Social Europe, supplement 2/86, 1986.

Raetsen, M-Y., 'Positive Measures', in Quintin, O. et al., Ten Years of Community Policy on Equal Opportunities for Men and Women, Social Europe, supplement 2/86, 1986.

Schermers, H.G. and Waelbroeck, D., Judicial Protection in the European Communities, 4th ed., Kluwer, Deventer, 1987.

Schleicher, H., 'Mutterschutz und Grundgesetz', BB, 1985, pp. 340–344.

Sjerps, C.M., 'Voldoet de adviesaanvrage stelselherziening aan de derde EG-richtlijn inzake gelijke behandeling in de sociale zekerheid?', SMA, 1984, pp. 81–89.

Sloot, B.P., Positieve discriminatie, Tjeenk Willink, Zwolle, 1986.

Sousi-Roubi, B., 'L'égalité professionnelle entre les hommes et les femmes', Gazette du Palais, 1981, pp. 167–175.

Szyszczak, E., 'Pay Inequalities and Equal Value Claims', MLR, 1985, pp. 139–157.

Timmermans, C., 'Directives: Their Effects within the National Legal Systems', CML Rev. 1979, pp. 533–555.

Treu, T., 'Case Law at Community and National Level Relating to Equal Treatment', in Verwilghen, M. (ed.), Equality in Law between Men and Women in the European Community, Vol. I, Presses Universitaires de Louvain, Louvain-La-Neuve, 1986.

Van der Weele, J.J., Wet gelijke behandeling van mannen en vrouwen, Kluwer, Deventer, 1983.

Verwilghen, M. (ed.), Equality in Law between Men and Women in the European Community, Vol. I, Presses Universitaires de Louvain, Louvain-La-Neuve, 1986.

Vogel-Polsky, E., 'Positive action programmes for women', ILR, 1985, pp. 253–265 and pp. 385–399.

Wyatt, D., 'The Direct Effect of Community Social Law', ELR., 1983, pp. 241–248.

Zorbas, G., 'Some Examples of Commission Intervention on Equality', in Quintin, O. et al., Ten Years of Community Policy on Equal Opportunities for Men and Women, Social Europe, supplement 2/86, 1986.

Zuleeg, M., 'Gleicher Zugang von Männern und Frauen zu beruflicher Tatigkeit', RdA, 1984, pp. 325–332.

Index